Advance Prai
At The Intersection: Understanding and Su

"In this edited volume, Robert Longwell-Grice and Hope Longwell-Grice, alongside the contributing authors, have extended to us an invitation and a challenge to honor the whole identities and lived truths of first-generation students. This book is a necessary read for educators, policymakers and administrators looking to support first-generation students. Through research that highlights the complexities of the first-generation student population, features identity-based support programs, and calls attention to how we can center the dignity of our first-generation students, I am moved to be a more loving and informed educator. This is a significant justice issue of our time."—*Mamta Motwani Accapadi, Vice Provost for University Life, University of Pennsylvania*

"Robert and Hope Longwell-Grice are among a very select group of scholars who can be considered respected authorities on the demographics and issues of first-generation college students. They have presented and published on this topic for the past 20 years. In this volume, they complement their own considerable knowledge by gathering an impressive assemblage of other renowned scholars to explore carefully a wide array of identities and nuanced topics within the first-gen community. The result is one of the most comprehensive and thorough examinations of first-generation college students ever produced."—*Michael J. Cuyjet, Professor Emeritus, University of Louisville*

"FINALLY . . . A BOOK THAT 'GETS IT!' *At the Intersection* is an aptly titled new work from the team of Rob and Hope Longwell-Grice which offers tremendous insight on the complicated journey taken by first-generation students to and through college. What is different about this book is that as the collective authors note, the first-generation students of today hail from a diverse array of demographic, cultural, and socioeconomic backgrounds that are not some sort of inconvenient challenges to be transcended—as some prior 'experts' seem to have suggested—but rather as strengths and characteristics to be understood and appreciated as these students stand at the complex intersection of their respective personal worlds and the institutions of higher education they attend. As a university graduate school faculty member whose students are preparing to work as higher education administrators, I consider *At the Intersection* to be a critical resource, offering the sort of essential guidance these future professionals are going to need to support, and learn from, the first-generation students with whom they will be working. Kudos to Rob and Hope Longwell-Grice for not only the content but also the long overdue tone and message of the book!"—*Thomas Grace, College of Education and Human Services, Montclair State University*

"The phrase, first-generation student, has become such a ubiquitous moniker in higher education that the diversity of experiences and needs of the first-in-family enrolled college students it denotes has been obscured and reduced to a hollow catchphrase. In their edited text, *At the Intersection: Understanding and Supporting First-Generation Students,* Robert and Hope Longwell-Grice—along with an assemblage of expert scholar-practitioners—recapture the value and substance of the designation by providing readers with an accessible primer and guidebook. *At the Intersection* offers readers an instrumental resource for understanding and effectively responding to these students' divergent, shared, and intersectional identities in service of their access, retention, learning, well-being, and success."—*Jason A. Laker, Professor of Higher Education, Student Affairs, and Community Development, San José State University*

"I loved *At the Intersection.* As a first-generation college student myself who ended up a dean at a major university, the content of this book tells a lot of my story, both the challenges I had to work through and the supports I needed to make it. The section on identity makes this an imperative read for understanding *today's* first-gen population. The section on recommended programs, policies, and practices, makes it essential reading for faculty and students in student affairs, student success, counseling, and higher education. It's also a quick and lively read!"—*Ellen McIntyre, Dean, College of Education, Health, and Human Sciences, University of Tennessee*

"If you care deeply about the dynamic, lived experiences of first-generation college students then this book is a must-read. This book has garnered critical conversations and insightful contributions to embolden our deep understanding of the kaleidoscope of identities first-generation college students possess. This is the book I longed to see when I first started researching first-generation college students! This book is surely seminal and paves a path forward for all of us to recognize the untold stories of first-generation college students."—*Lindsay Romasanta, Director of Student Success Programs, UC San Diego, and Coeditor, NASPA* Journal on First-generation Student Success

"This exciting new text is a welcomed addition to the higher education landscape and offers a critical and deeply important examination of the intersectional nature of the first-generation college student identity. As we attempt to rid the first-generation space of misconceptions and deficit-based approaches, this book thoughtfully considers the importance of understanding how multiple identities shape the college-going experience. Moreover, how the intersectional nature of the first-generation identity must be central in scholarship and service-provision as we welcome a shifting demographic into higher education. The premise that we must consider and reconsider all that we know and do not know about first-generation students is a consequential and necessary reminder for us all." —*Sarah E. Whitley, Assistant Vice President, Center for First-Generation Student Success, NASPA*

AT THE INTERSECTION

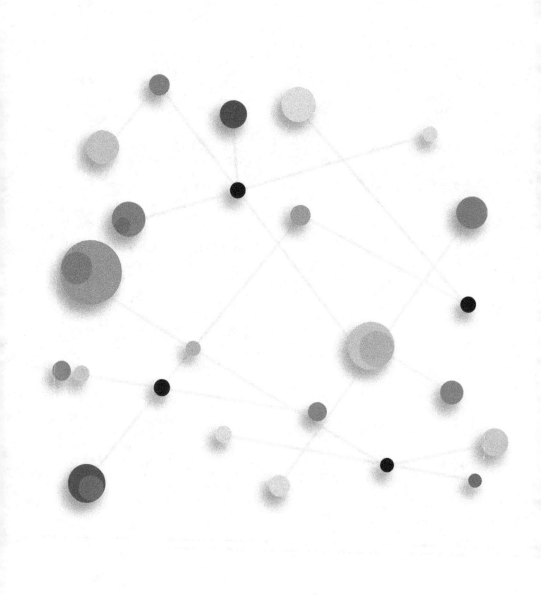

AT THE INTERSECTION

Understanding and Supporting
First-Generation Students

Edited by Robert Longwell-Grice and
Hope Longwell-Grice

1996-2021 **25**TH ANNIVERSARY

Sty/us PUBLISHING, LLC.

STERLING, VIRGINIA

Published by Stylus Publishing, LLC.
22883 Quicksilver Drive
Sterling, Virginia 20166-2019

Library of Congress Cataloging-in-Publication Data
Names: Longwell-Grice, Robert M., 1955- editor. | Longwell-Grice, Hope (Hope Robann), 1956- editor.
Title: At the intersection : understanding and supporting first-generation students / edited by Robert Longwell-Grice and Hope Longwell-Grice.
Description: First edition. | Sterling, Virginia : Stylus Publishing, LLC., 2021. | Includes bibliographical references and index. | Summary: "The experiences of first-generation college students are not monolithic. The nexus of identities matter, and this book is intended to challenge the reader to explore what it means to be a first-generation college student in higher education. Designed for use in classrooms and for use by the higher education practitioner on a college campus today, At the Intersections will be of value to the reader throughout their professional career"-- Provided by publisher.
Identifiers: LCCN 2021009200 (print) | LCCN 2021009201 (ebook) | ISBN 9781642670608 (hardback) | ISBN 9781642670615 (paperback) | ISBN 9781642670622 (adobe pdf) | ISBN 9781642670639 (epub)
Subjects: LCSH: First-generation college students--United States.
Classification: LCC LC4069.6 .A82 2021 (print) | LCC LC4069.6 (ebook) | DDC 378.1/982--dc23
LC record available at https://lccn.loc.gov/2021009200
LC ebook record available at https://lccn.loc.gov/2021009201

13-digit ISBN: 978-1-64267-060-8 (cloth)
13-digit ISBN: 978-1-64267-061-5 (paperback)
13-digit ISBN: 978-1-64267-062-2 (library networkable e-edition)
13-digit ISBN: 978-1-64267-063-9 (consumer e-edition)

Printed in the United States of America

All first editions printed on acid-free paper
that meets the American National Standards Institute
Z39-48 Standard.

Bulk Purchases
Quantity discounts are available for use in workshops and for staff development.
Call 1-800-232-0223

First Edition, 2021

To Emily and Baer,
You are the reasons.
With our love always.

CONTENTS

PART TWO: THE INTERSECTIONS OF IDENTITY

PART THREE: PROGRAMS AND PRACTICES

I was introduced to the notion of first-generation college student identity and the intersection with other identities on a car ride between Louisville, Kentucky, and Cincinnati, Ohio, in the fall of 2000 as my partner and coeditor was conceptualizing his dissertation. *First-generation* was not new to me in either a theoretical sense or as a part of my life experience.

While I came from a continuing-generation family back multiple generations, my partner of then 24 years did not. I went to college with full financial and emotional support from family and, even more, with the expectation that I would go to college and graduate.

I knew that Rob's and my experience about coming to higher education was significantly different. Rob came from a family of seven boys and one girl. His father was a partner in a small, second-generation family construction business. While some of his older brothers did go to college, the support— both emotional and financial—did not come from home. What I learned in that conversation was that his gender and social class mattered in ways that even further complicated his college-going experience.

That complexity of a first-generation college student's identities is the essence of this book. The experiences of first-generation college students are not monolithic. The nexus of identities matter. It is our hope that the research and thought pieces in *At the Intersection* will challenge the reader to understand and to continue to explore what it means to be a first-generation college student in higher education.

Our book shares the work of both new and established scholars and practitioners in the field. It offers both research and theory. There are chapters for individuals to engage with on their own and thought pieces to inspire conversation in groups. Designed for use in classrooms and for use by the higher education practitioner on a college campus today, *At the Intersections* will be of value to the reader throughout their professional career.

We have divided the book into four parts, with chapters of research and theory interspersed with thought pieces to complement contributors' arguments and provide personalized stories to integrate the research and theory into lived experience. Instructors can use the thought pieces in a variety of ways. Each thought piece ends with questions to inspire readers to wrestle with the theses of the chapters. Thought pieces may be used to follow up the research and theory chapters as they provide questions to help students build new knowledge about the profession. The thought pieces may also be used to spark interest in the research and theory chapters. In this instance, the questions act as conversation starters to help readers unearth some of their preconceptions of the field.

Part One: Who Is a First-Generation College Student? provides the reader an entrée into the field with up-to-date data on both 4-year and 2-year college-going first-generation students. The first three chapters set the table for the chapters that follow in the book. Each contributor brings fundamental information to develop a deep understanding of the field. The first Critical Conversation of the book challenges the reader to consider theoretical and ethical next steps in their own practice and the lives of the students with whom they work. The next two chapters begin to explore some of the issues that first-generation students face. These chapters share insights into the forces—personal and social—that impact first-generation decision-making. Part One ends with a Critical Conversation that asks the reader to pull together some of the big ideas before moving on to look more closely at students' identities.

It may be too obvious even to write here that no one is only one identity. Yet, for too long higher education professionals have written, thought about, developed policies for, and practiced as if first-generation students are all one and only one identity. Part Two: The Intersections of Identity offers chapters that explore what it means to be a first-generation college student *and*. . . Chapters and Critical Conversations in Part Two of the book share the research, experience, and thoughts of contributors in relation to the individual and overlapping identities of LGBT, low-income, White, African American, Latinx, Native American, undocumented, female, male, and first-generation college students.

Part Three: Programs and Practices is an introduction to practices, policies, and programs across the country. Each chapter and Critical Conversation offers promise and direction for future work as institutions try to find a considered and complimentary array of approaches to make the campus an inclusive place for the diverse population that is first-generation college students. We trust that at this point of the book, those looking for only one answer to support first-generation college students have learned that there is no one answer. The population is too diverse.

Finally, in our epilogue, we close out the book with a rich analysis of the *first-generation* label. This chapter brings us back to two of the underlying themes of the book. First, professionals must consider and reconsider all that we know and do not know about first-generation students. Second, to make a difference we must learn better what the identities mean for our practice, policies, and college communities.

In closing, the editors would like to thank the contributors included in this book for sharing their work with us and the reader. Your thoughtfulness and written work describing your efforts in the field will have an impact on the success of first-generation students for years to come. We would also like to thank our publisher, Stylus Publishing, for recognizing that the diversity of the first-generation experience matters enough to share the work of these scholars and professionals. We single out David Brightman for his unfailing assistance as we edited this volume. Finally, during the time of editing this volume we were lucky enough to become grandparents for the first time. Baer will not experience what it means to be first-generation when he attends college. He will be a continuing-generation student. We hope that his first-generation peers will be entering a new space that has benefited from the understanding and practices you will bring to the future of higher education.

Hope Longwell-Grice

INTRODUCTION

Robert Longwell-Grice and Hope Longwell-Grice

To date, the literature on first-generation (first-gen) college students tends to portray first-gens as a monolithic whole. This leads to serious issues as colleges try to understand the problems facing first-gens pursuing their degrees and try to develop programs. If first-gens are seen as a monolithic whole, then surely there must be a singular way to solve the "problem." If all first-gens are the same, then surely somewhere is *the* answer to the myriad issues first-gens face. If true, then someone would have already come up with the magic elixir needed. Since this magic elixir has yet to emerge, there must be something else going on. This edited volume is written to address the false idea that all first-gens think, act, and experience things in the same way. The chapters in this volume offer readers opportunities to learn about the intersectionality of first-generation identity and identities of race, class, gender, and sexual orientation.

Although there have been a multitude of initiatives in recent years designed to help first-gens succeed, the gaps between first-gens and continuing-generation (continuing-gen) students persist. For example, educational achievement gaps between first-gen and continuing-gen students continue. Additionally, first-gen college students continue to lack a sense of belonging to the campus and continue to feel a lack of support on the campus (Choy, 2001). This much we know.

The review of the literature completed for this edited volume found numerous studies, dissertations, and musings on the topic of intersecting identities related to first-gen students. The review found new scholars who were publishing on this topic and numerous articles from practitioners describing their experiences working with first-gen students. Not surprisingly, many of the contributors to this book are first-gen college students themselves, and they have been asked to share their thoughts based on lived experience or personal research in the Critical Conversation chapters that are located throughout the book.

So what is the solution to the problem of treating all first-gen college students alike? How does this book deal with the issue? And how does looking at first-gen college students through a lens of intersectionality help colleges?

1

While this edited volume is many things, it is not the magic elixir campuses are seeking. This is because there *is no one single answer!* What the book does is explore and explain the intricacies of being a first-gen college student based on intersections of identities. The chapters reveal what it means to be a first-gen college student *and. . . .*

This book is written for academic advisers, for faculty, for aspiring student affairs educators, and for anyone who seeks to understand the experiences of first-gen college students. After reading this book readers will have a richer and more nuanced understanding of the diverse lives of first-gen college students. Throughout the book there are examples of current efforts, demonstrating how practitioners are making their campuses work for first-gen students. These examples will be invaluable for practitioners.

In addition to traditional chapters, readers can engage with the issues through guided reflections called Critical Conversations. These pieces give insight into the first-gen experience. These reflections and the questions that accompany them provide stimulations for class discussion.

In the preface, Hope provided an overview of the sections. These sections are thematic in nature and Part One: Who Is a First-Generation College Student? provides the reader an entrée into the field.

In chapter 1, "A Review of the Data," Robert Longwell-Grice sets the tone for the book by compiling the most recent data related to first-gen college students. According to the U.S. Department of Education, 58% of students attending postsecondary institutions in the United States are first-gen college students (Redford & Hoyer, 2017), depending on the definition one uses. In this chapter, Longwell-Grice discusses the first-gen definition. He also presents us with current data on enrollment patterns, race/ethnicity; income/social class; types of institutions attended; timing of college attendance; and educational attainment levels of first-gen college students. The data in this chapter suggest that attending college presents significant challenges for a first-gen student. Institutions of higher education who accept first-gens onto their campus must accept the responsibility to successfully integrate first-gens into the campus culture and create real pathways through to graduation. Campuses must endeavor to learn the answer to the question, why? Why does being a first-gen college student make it difficult to attain a college degree?

In chapter 2, "Unpacking First-Gen Discourse: A Sociological Perspective," Steven P. Dandaneau asks readers to consider what the pursuit of the "American Dream" has to do with higher education. Dandaneau argues that success in academic pursuits is among the most celebrated of all forms of upward mobility: Work hard in school, go to college, and leave farm and factory for white collars and white picket fences. Along with this education is a large price tag, however. Dandaneau explores concepts already used in the literature regarding first-gen students, adding to their nuance and complexity. Because *un*-learning may be necessary to fully grasp first-gen discourse, he challenges typically unexamined assumptions and biases and introduces critical insights.

Chapter 3, "Setting the Foundation: Understanding the Impact of College on First-Generation Students," reviews the research on first-generation students and their transition from the college-choice process through to degree completion. According to Ryan Padgett, a simple scholarly article search yielded more mentions of "first-generation students" in the past decade from 2008–2018 than in the entire prior century from 1907–2007. Padgett argues that the proliferation of recent articles may be attributed to a number of factors. His article sets the foundation for our current under-standing of the impact of college on first-generation students by introducing a conceptual framework around first-generation status that is supplemented by historical and emerging research.

Sherry Lee Linkon presents us with Critical Conversation One. In her piece, "First-Gen or Working Class? The Politics of Terminology," she expresses her dilemma about the term *first-gen*. Because she wants students to take advantage of the support that universities can provide, she recog-nizes the value of identifying these efforts as aimed at first-gen students. At the same time, however, she expresses her concern that we are losing yet another opportunity to talk about class. More important, Linkon main-tains, first-gen erases the systemic and collective elements of class. The neutrality of first-gen draws students in, she says, but it does not encourage us to understand and take action against the injustices that shaped first-gen students' lives.

"Background Characteristics of First-Generation Students and Their Reasons for Pursuing Higher Education," chapter 4 by Khanh Bui, reviews the findings of a research study examining (a) the background characteristics of first-gen students, (b) their reasons for pursuing higher education, and (c) their first-year experiences. Such analyses can identify challenges that are more particular to first-generation college students and inform student sup-port service professionals of the kinds of help that these students need to succeed at a 4-year institution. This study contributes greatly to our under-standing of the first-generation experience.

Michael J. Smith presents us with a qualitative research study of three African American single parents in chapter 5, "Message Received: Parental Encouragement and Its Effect on the College-Choice Process." The experi-ences of the three African American, single mothers in this study suggest outreach that would be most effective in converting educational aspirations from high school diplomas to college degrees. Smith asks us to consider, in this era of expanding economic inequality, what approaches will effectively encourage and convince low-income families that college is worth it.

The first part of the book ends with Critical Conversation Two, this one from David Hernández. In "Inheriting Inequality: Hidden Challenges of First-Gen Students," Hernández asks us to consider all the peculiarities of the first-gen experience from our own personal experiences. What is often unrecognized, Hernández maintains, is that for first-gen students, attending college is a break from family history. It's not a rite of passage drawing first-gens closer to their college-educated parents and siblings, but often a suspicious activity, drawing them away from family and making them different. Campuses can provide a welcoming, hostile, or indifferent reception to first-gen students.

Part Two: The Intersections of Identity offers chapters that explore what it means to be a first-generation college student *and* . . . . Chapters and Critical Conversation pieces in Part Two of the book share the research, experience, and thoughts of contributors in relation to the individual and overlapping identities of LGBTQ, low-income, White, African American, Latinx, Native American, undocumented, female, male, and first-gen college students.

Sonja Ardoin starts this second part off with chapter 6, "The Nuances of First-Generation College Students' Social Class Identity." Ardoin shows us that the social class identity of first-generation college students is nuanced and complex, much like the first-generation college student status itself. She argues that higher education institutions and the individuals who work at them need to engage in education and training around first-generation status and develop a holistic understanding of social class identity. "Remember, it is more than just money!" Ardoin says (p. 98, this volume). Further, Ardoin maintains, an emphasis on the heterogeneity of this population might influence creation of programs and services that reflect the collection of identities that first-generation college students bring with them, including being from poor, working-class, middle-class, and affluent backgrounds. If, at the very least, administrators, faculty members, campuses, systems, and scholars can stop using *first-generation* as a proxy for *poor* and *working class*, that will be progress, she concludes.

Chapter 7 by Roxanne Moschetti, "I Don't Need Any Help: Working with First-Generation, Low-Income, White Males" is a research study that attempts to disentangle some of the influences of race, class, and gender on first-generation college students' transitions and adjustment to college life. Her study examines how low socioeconomic status (SES), first-generation White males in community college orient themselves in their new, unfamiliar campus environment. Existing literature suggests that access to beneficial social capital can be vital in aiding underserved students with the transition into college. The results of the study support existing research conducted with first-generation ethnic minority students while also presenting new information regarding the value of social capital for low SES, first-generation White male students who like to "handle things on their own" (p. 110, this volume).

"Reflections on Being a First-Generation, African American Male College Student," Critical Conversation Three, is the first in Part Two. Here, Nate Deans Jr. shares his personal journey from unfocused high school student to honors student and certified teacher. When Deans tells his story, most people see it as a success story, and, indeed he has been recognized for his success. However, his story is not that simple. The reader will be challenged to consider it through the context of a systemic racist educational experience. If society really cared enough to change the disparities that exist, Deans says, then we would seriously look at changing educational systems that don't allow first-generation college students to succeed.

The intersection of first-generation college students' and LGBTQ students' identities is the focus of chapter 8 by Pheng Xiong, "Dual Invisibilities: The Intersection of First-Generation and LGBT Identities." According to Xiong, the LGBTQ community represents a segment of society that has historically been marginalized and stigmatized. In higher education, LGBTQ student needs are at times overlooked or go unaddressed, which further reinforces their marginalization. Xiong's study on how first-generation college students experience and make meaning from their LGBTQ identity is the focal point of this chapter. The meaning-making process ultimately impacts how students see themselves and perceive the world around them and sheds light on the first-generation, LGBTQ student experience. Xiong's positing the use of intersectionality research offers readers, researchers, and professionals in the field new opportunities for richer understanding of lived experiences of students.

In chapter 9, "First-Generation Latinx Students Seeking Information at College," Vasti Torres, Lucy LePeau, and Yvonne Garcia illustrate how the intersection of Latinx and first-generation college student identities influences the campus experiences of students. Latinx students are a growing population within higher education and are likely to be first-generation in college, making this an important topic for practitioners to consider. The chapter provides a synthesis of current research noting the effects of familial expectations and of trying to navigate the college environment and the importance of creating personal relationships. The contributors apply lenses of cultural and social assets contributing to our understanding of how Latinx first-generation students interpret and navigate the campus environment.

"First-Generation and Undocumented" is the title of Critical Conversation Four, authored by Ana Karina Soltero López. The contributor discusses the unique intersection of being both an undocumented and a first-generation college student from her personal and professional point of view. For many first-generation college students, being the first in their family to attend college means facing a wave of unknowns. What happens when the experience is compounded with an added characteristic of being undocumented?

Recently the media has paid attention to first-gen college students in highly selective private institutions due to a variety of scandals. However, little formal research has been done on women's academic experiences within private institutions. Nicole Zervas Adsitt's chapter 10, "It's All About the Journey: Exploring the College Experience of First-Generation Women," describes findings from her study that researched how first-generation female college students experience their educational journey in a private 4-year institution of higher education. This chapter addresses gaps in the literature by looking at how women who are first-generation college students describe their path to college and feel about their experience at private 4-year institutions. The chapter's goal is to help readers gain a better understanding of first-generation women's perspectives about their educational journey and potential paths to promote their successes.

Les Riding-In and Scott Amundsen assert in chapter 11, "Crossing Bridges: First-Generation Native American Students at College," that Native American students attending colleges and universities for the first time are more than simply first-generation students. In addition to overcoming the obstacles that are continually placed in the path of all first-generation college students, Native American college students are also attempting to bridge their own identity with Western learning methodologies in order to find success. Exploring the nexus of the two identities, the contributors provide the reader new insights into the lived experiences of this underserved student group.

Part Two ends with Critical Conversation Five, titled "Project MALES: Serving and Engaging First-Generation Students Through Mentoring and Service-Learning." The contributors, Victor B. Sáenz, Emmet Campos, Mike Gutierrez, and Rodrigo Aguayo, introduce us to the Mentoring to Achieve Latino Educational Success program—Project MALES. With approximately 20% of the University of Texas at Austin's (UT-Austin) overall student populations being first-generation students, faculty at UT-Austin and Texas A&M University work collaboratively to support the success of male students of color. While this chapter explores another intersection of identities in the first-generation student population, it is also a transition into the third part of this book, which shares inspiring "Programs and Practices."

Part Three has a focus on programs and practices that are currently being implemented on campuses across the country. The purpose of this part is to provide readers with ideas on what programs are possible on their campus.

Analyzing existing research on the impact of six different types of services offered within student affairs in chapter 12, "And the Research Says . . .: Program Supports Across the Spectrum," Robert Longwell-Grice and Mackenzie Hoffman discuss best practices and make suggestions for improvements in student affairs program offerings for first-gen students. Each of the six services reviewed—financial aid, living learning communities, tutoring, counseling, student involvement, and career development—had significant gaps in addressing the needs of first-gen student affairs. This chapter identifies the need for more specialized programming catering to the known academic and social barriers faced by first-gen students to help the students succeed. Institutions have a responsibility for assessing what works and bringing what works to all students.

Chapter 13, "College Preparation Through College Access and Support Programs," by Staci Weber is a research study that looks at the effects of college access, support, and preparation programs on the development of students and developing a college-going mindset. The data in Weber's study demonstrate the tangible support services offered by these programs (e.g., SAT preparation, application fee waivers, assistance in writing college essays) appear to help students gain access to college. As college access programs build students' college-going mindset, the programs also seem to equip first-gen college students with the tools, experiences, and resources needed for their successful transition to college.

University, college, school, major, minor, prerequisites (pre-reqs), credit hours, liberal arts: This small sampling of the terms we assume people know can create in-groups and out-groups among students, families, administrators, and faculty. In Critical Conversation Six, "It's All a Bunch of B.S.: How Institutional Jargon Creates In-Groups and Out-Groups in Higher Education," Sonja Ardoin asks the reader to consider how the linguistic shortcuts used to describe programs and practices common in higher education might exacerbate the outsider feeling many first-generation students have when they arrive on campus. The question for the reader to consider becomes: For whom are we using our higher education jargon?

Today, community colleges are the entry point for nearly 40% of the approximately 17.1 million undergraduate students in higher education. Although research shows that more than 80% of students enroll in community colleges with the intent to earn a bachelor's degree, only about 25% transfer within 5 years, and fewer successfully complete a bachelor's degree. In "Supporting Transfer for First-Generation Community College Students," chapter 14, Gloria Crisp, Rebecca Robertson, and Elizabeth Cox Brand examine transfer data of first-generation students who enroll at a community college. The contributors provide implications for institutional practice and policy related to promoting transfer.

Pablo Muirhead offers his thoughts in Critical Conversation Seven: "Moving on in Milwaukee: Easing the College Transition Process for 2-Year College Students." Muirhead, who works at Milwaukee Area Technical College (MATC), a 2-year school in Milwaukee, feels that first-generation college students offer much to the educational institutions they inhabit. Their life experiences, perspectives, and motivations enhance the learning experience for their peers as well as their instructors. In this reflection, Muirhead shares the work he does in supporting students seeking to earn a teaching license by starting at MATC before transferring to a 4-year partner institution.

Paul Gallagher discusses the first-generation residence hall experience in chapter 15, "Learning Where They Live: First-Generation College Students in the Residence Halls." According to Gallagher, peer support is crucial to first-generation students who come to college from an intersection of identities, both conspicuous and less obvious, namely, social class. With luck and/or conscious effort, first-generation students may acquire valuable cultural capital through their residential experience. However, first-generation students need more than a network of informal peer support. Residence life professionals will be interested in learning what Gallagher reveals about the potential they hold.

"Advice for Advisers" is the title of Critical Conversation Eight, written by Hadyn Swecker and Matthew Fifolt. Academic advising has long been considered one of the leading resources for retaining first-generation students in higher education, but in its current format, is it doing enough? Swecker and Fifolt ask the reader to reconsider the adviser role and how it might be modified to truly meet the diverse student bodies at most colleges and universities.

In chapter 16, "Career Development Needs of First-Generation College Students," Heather Maietta focuses on a relatively neglected campus asset available that, if utilized, has a remarkable impact on retention rates. According to Maietta, there are numerous barriers that impact the career development and postgraduate trajectory of first-generation college students: social capital and residential status, cultural capital and the academy, employment and finances, and challenges forming career goals. After analyzing the obstacles, Maietta examines other supports that can be provided to first-generation college students and assist them in making a successful college-to-career transition.

Retention of first-generation college students is an issue for all professionals in higher education. Katherine Moffat argues that campuses can (and should) commit to the success of first-generation college students through intentional mentoring programs. The extra effort and willingness to provide advice, perspective, and reassurance can be instrumental for a student who is on the fence about returning. According to Moffat a mentoring program that partners first-generation college students with faculty and staff may be the best path forward. In Critical Conversation Nine, "They're Here. Now, What Can We Do to Keep Them?" Moffat explores ways in which faculty and staff across campuses can identify and target first-generation students to establish and sustain mentoring initiatives.

Chapter 17 by Hyacinth Mason, Jeffrey Winseman, and Erin Ayala discusses findings from a national wellness study of U.S. medical students that investigated whether stress, self-care, and quality of life differed by generation status (i.e., first-generation versus continuing generation). In "Admissions Isn't Access: First-Generation College Graduates in Medical School," Mason, Winseman, and Ayala hypothesize that differences exist such that first-generation medical students report higher stress, lower self-care, and lower quality of life scores. The findings inform practical suggestions for retaining, supporting, and maximizing positive academic and wellness outcomes for first-generation students.

New research studies are beginning to showcase the ways in which first-gen graduate student identity is distinct from the first-gen undergraduate experience. In Critical Conversation Ten, "Becoming the Architect: First-Gen Graduate Students Claiming the Label," Adj Marshall explores how being a first-gen graduate student impacts the college experience for students. She notes more first-gens are standing proudly to be counted amongst the ranks of those who have succeeded despite odds being stacked against them. The chapter poses questions for the reader to consider how first-gen status informs the graduate student experience.

Successful workplaces including institutes of higher education are diverse. There are too few underrepresented students, including first-gens, enrolling in doctoral programs to truly create diverse workplaces. "When First-Generation College Students Become Doctoral Candidates," chapter 18, tackles an often-overlooked topic: doctoral student attrition in higher education. Heather Maietta asks the reader to consider why the topic of first-generation doctoral student success is a hidden crisis. If we in the academy truly value and are committed to equal workplace representation, this hidden crisis needs to be discussed, researched, and addressed.

We end with Critical Conversation Eleven, "How a College Rebuilt Itself by Centering First-Generation College Students," written by Staci Weber. Pine Manor College was founded in 1911 to serve traditionally underserved students and women. About 100 years later, like many colleges facing decreasing enrollments, Pine Manor College went through a major revisioning. Weber shares the process and leads the reader to ponder the potential of revisioning with an eye on first-gens.

"What's in a Name? Narratives and Counternarratives of the First-Generation Moniker" serves as the epilogue to the book. Rashné Jehangir writes that despite the complexity of the term *first-generation* and the way in which institutions use it, there has also been empowerment and agency connected with the way this word has recently gained positive visibility in higher education. First-generation allies, advocates, and scholars have a part in supporting students in claiming their first-generation identities by actively reflecting on their linguistic, navigational, and familial capital. This is a way to capitalize on the strengths of their intersectional identities and to demonstrate that the skills they have already cultivated are significant— we must name them and claim them as such. Speaking multiple languages, code-switching, navigating government offices and rental agreements, translating for their parents, and working two jobs have prepared them to succeed in college. And yes, there are things they are unprepared for too; like many newcomers they must learn new protocols—without being forced to give up all they came with, but rather to translate these skills into new settings.

People are complex. Everyone's identity has multiple dimensions. It is imperative that higher education professionals acknowledge the complexities of first-gen status as they develop policies and practices that affect first-generation students. We hope this book will inspire the reader to look more closely and listen more carefully to the students in our colleges and universities. Inspired to acknowledge and understand the differences of our diverse first-gen student populations, professionals can create new practices and policies and inclusive and supportive environments. As institutions of higher education face declines in traditional college-age population and as they must reconsider who will be in their classes, the time is now.

References

Choy, S. (2001). *The condition of education, 2001.* National Center for Education Statistics (Publication No. 2001072). https://nces.ed.gov/pubs2001/2001126.pdf

Redford, J., & Hoyer, K. (2017). *First-generation college students: A comparison of school and post-secondary experiences.* National Center for Education Statistics: Institute of Education Science. https://nces.ed.gov/pubs2018/2018009.pdf

PART ONE

WHO IS A FIRST-GENERATION COLLEGE STUDENT?

I

A REVIEW OF THE DATA

Robert Longwell-Grice

In high school, I didn't really have to study 'cause it was pretty simple stuff. In high school you just go in there and take the information and the teachers did a lot better in going over it and reviewing it. These teachers here at college, when they are through talking about it, it is like, "Ok, see you all." That is something I am trying to adjust to. It is not exactly all the one on one that you had in high school.

(Longwell-Grice & Longwell-Grice, 2008, p. 415)

This quote from Bryant, a first-generation college student, exemplifies the culture shock first-generation (first-gen) students experience upon entering college. First-gen students experience great changes in their lives as they attempt to integrate into the culture of academia. First-gen students confront all the anxieties, dislocations, and difficulties of any other college student, and their experiences often involve cultural as well as social and academic transitions (Pascarella et al., 2004). Compared with their peers, first-gens receive less assistance in preparing for college; feel less supported for attending college; and lack a sense of belonging to the college they attend (Choy, 2001). All of these risk factors play a role in the recruitment and retention of students from working-class backgrounds. The transition to college for first-gens is particularly challenging because of these numerous at-risk factors (Lohfink & Paulsen, 2005).

According to the U.S. Department of Education, 58% of students attending postsecondary institutions in the United States are *first-gen college students* (Redford & Hoyer, 2017), depending on the definition one uses. These levels have varied slightly over time, but overall the numbers of first-gens in college are trending higher as a college degree becomes necessary for more entry-level jobs (McCarron & Inkelas, 2006; Strayhorn, 2006). Because first-gens have different characteristics and experiences than the student's higher education has traditionally served, they are a group at risk and

13

are clearly in need of greater research and administrative attention if they are to survive and succeed in college.

Defining First-Gen College Students

Definitions of *first-gen* college students are contested. One definition commonly found in the literature states: "First-generation college students are students whose parents do not have a college degree" (Cataldi et al., 2018, p. 2). The second, more restrictive definition, and the one that the National Center for Education Statistics (NCES) uses, is: "First-generation college students are students who are the first in their family to pursue education beyond high school" (Cataldi et al., 2018, p. 2). This second definition would disqualify students who had a parent attempt college, regardless of how short the attendance was, and regardless of whether the attendance resulted in some sort of graduation or certification.

Ward et al. (2012) argue while the distinction (definition) used is not necessarily right or wrong, there can be administrative implications for choosing one definition over another. Some would argue that there can be a difference between students whose parents have some college and/or attempted college and those students whose parents have never attended college. This is more of a theoretical argument than a proven point, however. As if to muddy the waters further, some are now arguing that the offspring of parents who receive their degree from an online college should be considered first-gens since their parents never actually lived in a residence hall, participated in traditional campus activities, and so on. This would seem to stretch the limits of the definition, but it does point out how fluid the definition is and how complex it may be to respond to the needs of future generations of college students.

Data on First-Gen College Students

To use a snapshot of how higher education is changing in light of the increasing numbers of first-gen college students, I share here information from NCES. Data based on the 2002 high school sophomores who subsequently enrolled in college showed that 24% were first-gen college students, using the NCES definition (Redford & Hoyer, 2017) (see Figure 1.1). Using a broader definition, 58% of first-gen students enrolled in college upon high school graduation. This compares with 42% of *continuing-gen* students, defined as students who had at least one parent with a college degree.

Figure 1.1. Percentage distribution of spring 2002 high school sophomores with subsequent postsecondary enrollment, by college generation status: 2012.

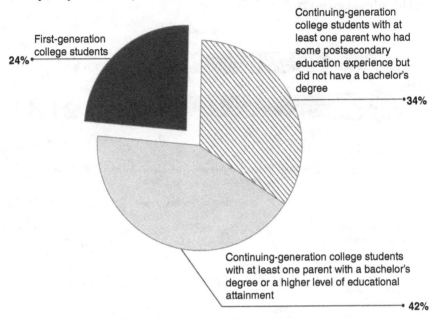

First-generation college students 24%

Continuing-generation college students with at least one parent who had some postsecondary education experience but did not have a bachelor's degree 34%

Continuing-generation college students with at least one parent with a bachelor's degree or a higher level of educational attainment 42%

Note: First-gen college students are students whose parents do not have any postsecondary education experience.

Source: National Center for Education Statistics, (n.d.). *Education Longitudinal Study of 2002* (ELS:2002), Third Follow-up, 2012. Restricted-Use Data File.

In terms of race/ethnicity, 49% of first-gen college students were White, 14% were Black, and 27% were Hispanic. An additional 5% of first-gen college students were Asian, and 5% were classified as "Other" (Figure 1.2). This means that 51% of first-gen college students were from minority populations in the United States. This number becomes even more significant when it is compared to the demographics of continuing-education students. Of the continuing-education student group, 70% identified as White, and 90% were native English speakers. First-gen students, in contrast, had a non-native–English speaking level of 21%.

One of the largest gaps between first-gen and continuing-gen students is in household income, one measure of social class. As Figure 1.2 shows, 77% of first-gens come from households where the annual family income was $50,000 or less. This compares to 29% for households of continuing-gen students. Conversely, 48% of continuing-gen students come from households

Figure 1.2. College generation status of spring 2002 high school sophomores with subsequent postsecondary enrollment, by race/ethnicity, native language, and household income: 2012.

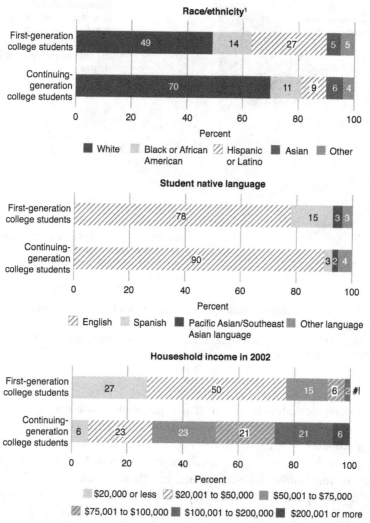

Rounds to zero.

! Interpret data with caution. The coefficient of variation (CV) for this estimate is 30 percent or greater.

[1] All race categories exclude Hispanic or Latino origin, unless specified. "Other" includes American Indian/Alaska Native, Native Hawaiian/Pacific Islander, and students of Two or more races.

Note: First-generation college students are students whose parents do not have any postsecondary education experience. Continuing-generation college students are students who have at least one parent who had some postsecondary education experience. Continuing-generation students whose parents had some postsecondary education but did not have a bachelor's degree are excluded from this figure.

Source: U.S. Department of Education, National Center for Education Statistics, Education Longitudinal Study of 2002 (ELS:2002), Third Follow-up, 2012. Restricted-Use Data File.

where the family income was $75,000 or higher, compared to 23% for first-gens. Additionally, looking at the top wage earners, 27% of continuing-gen students come from families where the family income is $100,000 or more. By comparison, only 3% of first-gen college students come from families where the family income is above $100,000.

Figure 1.3 provides a picture of the type of institution first-gen college students (and continuing-gen college students) first attended upon graduating from high school. While the number of students attending public institutions is comparable between the two groups (76% for first-gen college students; 72% for continuing-gen students), there are fairly large differences in the two other sectors: private, nonprofit colleges and private, for-profit colleges.

The number of students attending private, nonprofit schools is 9% for first-gens and 23% for continuing-gen college students. One of the most likely reasons for this discrepancy is cost. Private colleges tend to charge more for tuition. Even though many private colleges engage in so-called tuition discounting, the price tag to attend most private colleges would seem unaffordable to first-gen students and their families. Most first-gen college student families have little to no experience navigating the financial aid maze, so they would be unlikely to attempt to negotiate the tuition of a private school.

Perhaps not surprisingly, given recent headlines, the number of first-gen college students attending private, for-profit colleges is much higher for first-gens than it is for continuing-gens: 16% for first-gens, and 5% for continuing-gens. Despite the fact that these schools usually charge higher tuition than their public school counterparts, their offices put together financial aid packages that make the tuition seem acceptable. These schools also are usually attractive to first-gens (especially returning adult first-gens) with their online offerings, night courses, flexibility, and promises of accelerated programs. As headlines have shown, however, many of the for-profit colleges have gone bankrupt in recent years, leaving first-gen students with nothing to show for their efforts.

Related to the statistics on type of institution attended is the selectivity and level of colleges first attended by students (Figure 1.3).

Fifty-two percent of first-gen college students enroll in a 2-year institution initially. This compares to 28% of continuing-gen college students. Conversely, a full 55% of continuing-gen students initially attend a moderately or highly selective 4-year college. Only 22% of first-gen college students initially enroll in a moderately or highly selective college. The effects of this initial enrollment can be quite devastating. As Crisp et al. and Moschetti write in chapters 14 and 7 respectively, the successful transfer rate for students who

Figure 1.3. College generation status of spring 2002 high school sophomores with subsequent postsecondary enrollment, by type of institution first attended and selectivity and level of first-attended postsecondary institution: 2012.

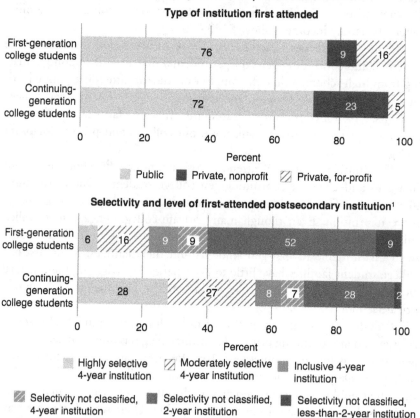

¹ Selectivity categories are based on 2010 Carnegie classifications. "Highly selective" 4-year institutions refer to those whose first-year students' postsecondary entrance test scores place them in roughly the top fifth of baccalaureate institutions; "moderately selective" 4-year institutions refer to those whose first-year students' postsecondary entrance test scores place them in roughly the middle two-fifths of baccalaureate institutions; and "inclusive" 4-year institutions either did not report postsecondary entrance test score data, or their scores indicate that they extend educational opportunity to a wide range of students with respect to academic preparation and achievement; "selectivity not classified" 4-year institutions refer to those with unknown Carnegie selectivity. Selectivity ratings only apply to 4-year institutions.

Note: First-generation college students are students whose parents do not have any postsecondary education experience. Continuing-generation college students are students who have at least one parent who had some postsecondary education experience. Continuing-generation students whose parents had some postsecondary education but did not have a bachelor's degree are excluded from this figure. Detail may not sum to totals because of rounding.

Source: U.S. Department of Education, National Center for Education Statistics, Education Longitudinal Study of 2002 (ELS:2002), Third Follow-up, 2012. Restricted-Use Data File.

begin their college career at a 2-year college is extremely low. Thus, students who start their career at a 2-year college run the risk of obtaining debt and completing an associate degree, while not securing the benefits that come with completing a 4-year degree.

Many of the chapters in this text discuss the issues confronting first-gen college students as they attempt to complete their 4-year degree. Figure 1.4 lists the main reasons first-gens gave for not completing college. Although the percentages do not appear to be significantly higher in some categories, it is worth noting that there is a higher percentage of first-gen students responding in five of the nine categories.

Regarding the category demands at home, Longwell-Grice and Longwell-Grice (2008) postulated that first-gen college students often find conflicts at home as they experience and explore education as part of one's social class. Students may gain social capital formerly unavailable to them. This conflict frequently forces students to make decisions about whether the degree they are earning is worth the effort.

Figure 1.5 provides other significant information about first-gen college students. Regarding the timing of attendance, 79% of continuing-gen students begin college within 3 months of completing high school. This compares to 58% of first-gen students, a 21% difference. The consequences of waiting to enroll in college can be devastating, so it is also disconcerting that 27% of first-gens do not enroll in college for 13 months or more. When students wait to enroll, there is a greater likelihood that they will attend part time (adding time and cost to degree) and have additional responsibilities that will conflict with their goal of earning a college degree.

Figure 1.5 also shows the level of educational attainment. As of 2012, only 23% of the first-gen students in this study had completed at least a bachelor's degree. This compares to 55% of the continuing-gen students. A full 47% of the first-gen students left college before completing any type of degree or certificate, compared to 30% of the continuing-gen students. Regarding graduate degrees, 3% of the first-gen students continued for their graduate degree, as compared to 13% of continuing-gen students. While it is encouraging that some first-gen students managed to pursue a graduate degree, as several chapters in this text show, the issues for first-gen college students do not end with graduate school enrollment.

These data present a compelling picture of the differences between first-gen college students and their continuing-gen peers. These data also demonstrate the need for those of us working in education to work harder to help first-gen college students succeed. Beside the data presented in this chapter, a considerable body of research also indicates that students whose parents have

Figure 1.4. College generation status of spring 2002 high school sophomores with subsequent postsecondary enrollment who left school without obtaining a postsecondary credential, by reasons for leaving: 2012.

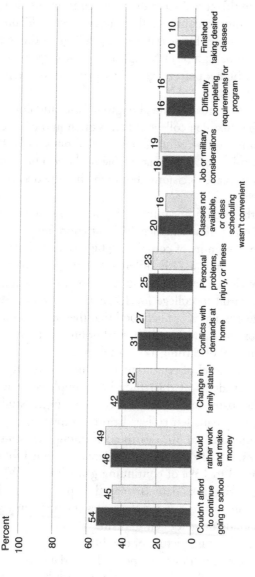

Reasons for leaving without obtaining a postsecondary credential

■ First-gen college students   □ Continuing-gen college students

[1] Examples of changes in family status include a marriage, baby, or death in the family.

Note: First-generation college students are students whose parents do not have any postsecondary education experience. Continuing-generation college students are students who have at least one parent who had some postsecondary education experience. Continuing-generation students whose parents had some postsecondary education but did not have a bachelor's degree are excluded from this figure. Respondents were able to answer "Yes" for more than one reason for leaving without obtaining a postsecondary credential.

Source: U.S. Department of Education, National Center for Education Statistics, Education Longitudinal Study of 2002 (ELS:2002), Third Follow-up, 2012. Restricted-Use Data File.

Figure 1.5. College generation status of spring 2002 high school sophomores with subsequent postsecondary enrollment, by timing of first postsecondary enrollment and educational attainment as of 2012.

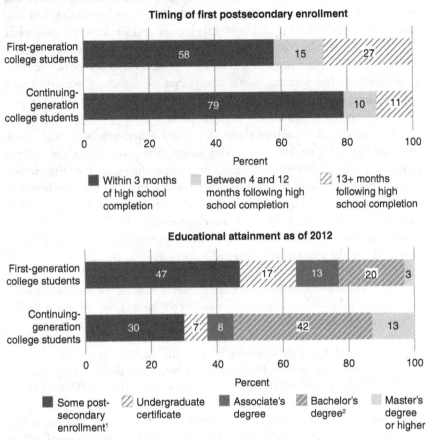

¹ Some postsecondary enrollment, but no postsecondary credential.

² Includes those whose highest level of education is a postbaccalaureate certificate.

Note: First-generation college students are students whose parents do not have any postsecondary education experience. Continuing-generation college students are students who have at least one parent who had some postsecondary education experience. Continuing-generation students whose parents had some postsecondary education but did not have a bachelor's degree are excluded from this figure. Detail may not sum to totals because of rounding.

Source: U.S. Department of Education, National Center for Education Statistics, Education Longitudinal Study of 2002 (ELS:2002), Third Follow-up, 2012. Restricted-Use Data File.

not attended college face significant challenges in accessing postsecondary education. Once enrolled, they face significant hurdles in succeeding academically, and graduating (Choy, 2001; Ishitani, 2006; Stephens et al., 2012; Woosley & Shepler, 2011).

First-gen college students do not have the same opportunity to learn from their parents because the concept of college can be foreign to someone who has never attended. First-gen students are at greater risk of dropping out due to the many challenges they face. These challenges include being less prepared academically; having children of their own; and working full-time while attending college (Chen & Carroll, 2005; Mangan, 2015; Nunez & Cuccaro-Alamin, 1998). In addition, first-gens often possess other demographic characteristics (e.g., low socioeconomic status) that are associated with dropping out. All these factors and interactions increase first-gens' risk of failing to persist, as compared to their continuing-gen peers.

The data in this chapter show that being a first-gen is a tough road. Institutions of higher education who accept first-gens onto their campus must accept the challenge to successfully integrate first-gens into the campus culture and guide them through to graduation. Campuses must endeavor to learn the answer to the question, why? Why does being a first-gen college student make it difficult to attain a college degree? During my interviews, Patrick helped me understand why, when he answered the question, "What do you think the purpose of college is?"

> The purpose of college is to weed out the weak. To weed out the ones that don't have the work ethic to survive or who couldn't do good. Of course, to get an education, that's a given. I think what it does is take people, pretenders, the ones who say "Well, I'm gonna do this" but they don't have what it takes. And, really, the ones who graduate are the ones cut out for these jobs. It makes the quality of life better. So it benefits us all that college does that. That's the purpose. (Longwell-Grice & Longwell-Grice, 2008, p. 414)

On many college campuses, new students are left to make their own way through the maze upon their arrival. Students must learn the ropes of college life largely on their own (Tinto, 1988). Because social interactions are the primary vehicle through which students become integrated (and establish that crucial sense of belonging), students must establish contact with other members of the college, especially faculty and other students. Failure to do so, Tinto says, may lead to the absence of integration and a sense of isolation. And if, as Patrick feels, colleges truly are serving to "weed out the weak," first-gen students without the necessary assistance may quickly come to feel that they are the ones not cut out for the job of a college education.

Tinto (1999) notes that the ability of an institution to retain students lies less in the formal program they devise and more in their underlying orientation toward students. Many colleges, Tinto maintains, allocate the commitment to students to a small number of program staff, most typically student affairs, whose responsibility centers on student life. Retention efforts are successful, Tinto argues, when the commitment to serve students spreads beyond student affairs to encompass faculty and other staff such as academic advisers.

This chapter provides data on first-gen college students to put their situation into a broader context. Taken together, these data combine to show that, indeed, first-gen college students are a group at risk and deserving of attention.

References

Cataldi, E., Bennett, C., & Xianglei, C. (2018). *First-generation students: College access, persistence, and postbachelor's outcomes.* National Center for Educational Statistics: Institute of Education Sciences. https://nces.ed.gov/pubsearch/pubsinfo.asp?pubid=2018421

Chen, X., & Carroll, C. D. (2005). *First-generation students in postsecondary education: A look at their college transcripts* (NCES 2005-171). National Center for Education Statistics. https://nces.ed.gov/pubs2005/2005171.pdf

Choy, S. (2001). *The condition of education, 2001.* National Center for Education Statistics (Publication 2001072). https://doi.org/10.1002/ir.10704\

Ishitani, T. T. (2006). Studying attrition and degree completion behavior among first-generation college students in the United States. *The Journal of Higher Education, 77*(5), 861–885. https://doi.org/10.1080/00221546.2006.11778947

Lohfink, M., & Paulsen, M. (2005). Comparing the determinants of persistence for first-generation and continuing-generation students. *Journal of College Student Development, 46*(4), 409–428. http://www.csun.edu/afye/documents/Lohfink-and-Paulsen-2005-determinants-of-persistence.pdf

Longwell-Grice, R., & Longwell-Grice, H. (2008). Testing Tinto: How do retention theories work for first-generation, working-class students? *Journal of College Student Retention: Research, Theory & Practice, 9*(4), 407–420. http://doi.org/10.2190/cs.9.4.a

Mangan, K. (2015, May 18). The challenge of the first-generation college student. *The Chronicle of Higher Education.* https://www.chronicle.com/article/the-challenge-of-the-first-generation-student/

McCarron, G. P., & Inkelas, K. K. (2006). The gap between aspirations and attainment for first-generation college students and the role of parental involvement. *Journal of College Student Development, 47*(5), 534–549. https://doi.org/10.1353/csd.2006.0059

National Center for Education Statistics. (n.d.). *Educational Longitudinal Study of 2002.* https://nces.ed.gov/surveys/els2002/

Nunez, A.-M., & Cuccaro-Alamin, S. (1998, June). *First generation students: Undergraduates whose parents have never enrolled in postsecondary education* (NCES 98-082). National Center for Education Statistics. https://nces.ed.gov/pubs98/98082.pdf

Pascarella, E. T., Pierson, C. T., Wolniak, G. C., & Terenzini, P. T. (2004). First-generation college students: Additional evidence on college experiences and outcomes. *The Journal of Higher Education, 75*(3), 249–284. https://doi.org/10.1353/jhe.2004.0016

Redford, J., & Hoyer, K. (2017, September). *First-generation college students: A comparison of school and post-secondary experiences* (NCES 2018–009). National Center for Education Statistics: Institute of Education Science. https://nces.ed.gov/pubs2018/2018009.pdf

Stephens, N. M., Fryberg, S. A., Markus, H. R., Johnson, C. S., & Covarrubias, R. (2012). Unseen disadvantage: How American universities' focus on independence undermines the academic performance of first-generation college students. *Journal of Personality and Social Psychology, 102*(6), 1178–1197. https://web.stanford.edu/~hazelm/publications/2012%20Stephens%20Fryberg%20Markus%20Johnson,%20&%20Covarrubias%20Unseen%20disadvantage.pdf

Strayhorn, T. L. (2006). Factors influencing the academic achievement of first-generation college students. *NASPA Journal*, 82–111. https://www.tandfonline.com/doi/abs/10.2202/1949-6605.1724

Tinto, V. (1988). Stages of student departure: Reflections on the longitudinal character of student living. *The Journal of Higher Education, 59*(4), 438–455. https://doi.org/10.1080/00221546.1988.11780199

Tinto, V. (1999). Taking retention seriously: Rethinking the first year of college. *NACADA Journal, 19*, 5–9. https://doi.org/10.12930/0271-9517-19.2.5

Ward, L., Siegal, M. J., & Davenport, Z. (2012). *First-generation college students: Understanding and improving the experience from recruitment to commencement.* Jossy-Bass. https://www.wiley.com/en-us/First+Generation+College+Students%3A+Understanding+and+Improving+the+Experience+from+Recruitment+to+Commencement-p-9780470474440

Woosley, S., & Shepler, D. K. (2011). Understanding the early integration experiences of first-generation college students. *College Student Journal, 45*, 700–714.

2

UNPACKING FIRST-GEN DISCOURSE

A Sociological Perspective

Steven P. Dandaneau

The most general definition of *first-generation (first-gen) college students* is people striving to be the first in their family to earn a bachelor's degree. But why create policies and programs around this familial characteristic? What explains and, indeed, what justifies, attention to the prior educational attainment of students' parents?

The significance of the *first-gen* term is that it locates students in a discourse of upward social mobility, intergenerational upward social mobility particularly. That is, the concept of first-gen students derives from the broader theory of social class. The storyline is familiar: Through hard work and pluck, people from economically modest family backgrounds can (and should try to?) move up the rungs of an otherwise hierarchal society. Born and raised in rural poverty? You could end up a billionaire or president of the United States. The child of a single-parent head of household whose mother toils in multiple low-paid pink-collar service, clerical, or sales jobs? Excel in school, go to college, and become the CEO of a multinational corporation, the subsidiary of which employs Mom. Ours is not a *caste system*, it is thought, in which moving up (or down) in the hierarchy is made extraordinarily difficult or largely prevented (at least in this life). Modern class societies are supposed to be fluid meritocracies that boast ubiquitous opportunities to improve one's lot. The legitimacy of such societies, the United States included, depends largely on their often and regularly making good on the promise of upward social mobility.

But what does pursuit of the "American Dream" have to do with higher education? (Mettler, 2014). Ask most students why they plan to attend postsecondary institutions of higher learning, or, among current students, why they chose their major, and one doesn't usually wait long before discovering that the primary motivation for both is to secure and, ideally, improve upon the economic standing of them and their families (Higher Education Research Institute, n.d.). Success in academic pursuits is among the most celebrated of all forms of upward mobility. I repeat: Work hard "in school," go "to college," and leave farm and factory for white collars, white picket fences, and even more expensive college education for one's children and grandchildren (Aisch et al., 2017; Chetty et al., 2017).

In this chapter, I expand on concepts already used, adding to their nuance and complexity and pointing to key sources for further study. Because *un*-learning may be necessary to fully grasp first-gen discourse—that is, because we probably need to challenge typically unexamined assumptions and biases—I introduce critical insights into what is otherwise straightforward explication. Because this volume serves those who work with and on behalf of first-gen college students, I also offer practical ideas, discuss a notable real-world example, and conclude with a few words of advice. The goal is to reveal what lies behind first-gen discourse and then to apply that deeper understanding to germane institutional and programmatic issues in contemporary higher education.

Before going any further, though, let me disclose that it has been 30-odd years since I was the first in my family to earn a bachelor's degree and that I continue to identify as first-gen. Moreover, what I experienced as a student and what I have learned since as a faculty member and university administrator leads me to think that those of us who work in higher education, despite many encouraging efforts and recent developments, continue to scratch the surface of what it means to be first-gen. I am probably guilty of this too. Consequently, I believe that there are abundant opportunities to deepen and advance our work in this increasingly critical area for higher education. As the stakes grow higher, it is not difficult to envision that a democratic future for U.S. society may hang in the balance (Califano, 2018; Newfield, 2016). It is thought that there is perhaps no greater engine of democracy than accessible transformative higher education, and no greater system of higher education than that which has been created in the United States (Cole, 2009; Thorp & Goldstein, 2018). First-gen discourse is thus more than a parlor game. First-gen signals social class, and social class contains a world of meaning. I invite you to hear what is being said.

Social Class 101

Sociology is a social science. We sociologists like data for the stories data can tell about otherwise difficult to precisely gauge contexts. Consider data on the distribution of wealth. *Wealth* generally refers to privately held assets like commercial real estate; stocks; bonds; or the accumulation of cash and valuable materials like gold, silver, oil, and gas. *Wealth* is a form of property that is not meant for consumption; *wealth* is capital, that which is used to create that which is consumed. Defined as such, wealth is difficult to measure. Assets fluctuate in value, may be traded rapidly, or are hidden by the multifaceted social power that accrues to those who amass wealth. Despite such challenges, we know that the distribution of wealth is a key determinate of living standards and life chances. The ownership and control of wealth creates an economically stratified society where some people are rich and fabulously rich, some are hungry and destitute, and many live modestly if not paycheck to paycheck.

In the United States in 2017, the wealthiest 1% owned approximately 35.5% of all wealth, while the wealthiest 10% owned 75% of total wealth (Statista, 2018). Think about this for a moment: 90% of people made do with 25% of total wealth. But even these facts obscure. The least wealthy 20% of the population had *negative wealth* (more liabilities than assets), while the lowest 40% held approximately 0% of wealth. Maintaining this approach, consider that the least-wealthy 50% owned an estimated 1.1% of total wealth, the least-wealthy 60% owned 3.2% of total wealth, and the least-wealthy 70% owned just 6.9% of total wealth. In other words, the top 20% of households owned fully 87% of total U.S. wealth (Statista, 2018). This is what is meant when it is said that wealth is *concentrated*. And when people who are not wealthy *do* own something of transferable value, it is usually a house in which they and their families live, not factories, commercial farms, or a diversified stock portfolio managed on Wall Street. Remove basic housing and shelter from the analysis and what emerges is a society in which a very small proportion of its population owns the vast proportion of its total wealth (Krugman, 2019; Van Dam, 2018).

How does this relate to higher education? Very few who hail from the top 1%, 10%, or even 20% of the wealth distribution send their children to community colleges or regional universities (Aisch et al., 2017). Likewise, very few who occupy the highest strata attended such institutions themselves (Loundenback & Gould, 2017). If you have never heard of, much less met anyone who attended Exeter, Choate, or Miss Porter's School, then you are not probably a scion of wealth. Even elite institutions like these have elite groups within them. One might attend Harvard University, Yale University, or Williams College, but as member of which club, sorority, or fraternity? Much the same occurs throughout higher education, from the size of university endowments and the luxuriousness of one or another school's groomed campus and stately and/or architecturally renowned facilities to the role played by exclusive clubs and groups even at public and ostensibly democratic institutions (Camera, 2017; Flanagan, 2014).

From the other angle, relatively few in the bottom half of the class system, as defined by wealth ownership, can afford the cost of attendance at even relatively reasonably priced 4-year public universities, where the average annual cost of tuition and fees (excluding room and board, books, and other expenses) was approximately $12,000 in 2017 (and nearly four times that for private 4-year universities in that same year) (Statista, 2020). What's more, Michigan State; the University of California, Los Angeles (UCLA); and Virginia Tech can feel as culturally elite as Harvard, Princeton, and Yale, although it is probably more significant to observe that Michigan State, the University of California (UC) Davis, and Virginia Tech are, for those in the bottom half of class society, similarly foreign. It is as much of a struggle for first-gens to successfully navigate large land-grant universities as it is their public flagship or private cousins; that is, from the perspective of the bottom half, the differences between Washington University in St. Louis; the University of Washington, Seattle; and Washington State University, Pullman, are subtle in the extreme. They all seem out of reach.

If we consider income—what one earns as salary and wages rather than what one owns—the inequality, though not as stark, remains very significant. Consider that at Kansas State University (KSU), located in "The Little Apple" of Manhattan, Kansas, the median family income of students is $101,800 and that 45% of students hail from the top 20% of the distribution of family income (Aisch et al., 2017). KSU is not unusual. In the same study, students at Penn State also reported $101,800 in average family income. Looked at from another angle, only 1.6% of KSU Wildcats hail from the top 1% of family incomes, that is, families whose annual earnings in 2015 dollars was $630,000 or more. Like all major 4-year research universities, most KSU students are far from poor, but few are truly wealthy either. KSU and those like it are predominantly upper–middle class institutions of higher learning, with small differences between them shaping the look and feel of their campus culture (Aisch et al., 2017).

Lawrence, Kansas, lies 81 miles from Manhattan, but students at the University of Kansas (KU)—Jayhawks—hail from families that on average earn $125,500, not $101,800, annually. What's more, 59% of KU students, as opposed to KSU's 45%, are in the top 20% of family incomes (Aisch et al., 2017). Again, few students from the wealthiest 1% attend either public institution, but income-based differences shape campus life as well as, importantly, educational outcomes. It might be said that KU is upper upper–middle class in character and that KSU is middle upper–middle class. Where true divergence lies is between two national research universities in Kansas and, say, Dartmouth College and Sarah Lawrence College in one direction, and Hutchinson Community College or Fort Hays State University in the other. Higher education is highly stratified by wealth and income, including the wealth and income of students. This is so obvious and taken for granted that it may seem odd to note it or describe it in detail.

Of course, social class is not only about students experiencing hunger versus students comparing the size and opulence of their parents' houses, boats, and vacation homes, nor is it solely about how freely students can swipe for this and that purchase or occasion ATMs. Social class is also, well, social. In one social class, leisure may include bountiful quantities of bowling and professional wrestling. In another, it may involve Wednesday mornings dedicated to tennis and golf. One social class might enjoy hunting with rifles and shotguns, another hunting so-called exotic animals in remote locations, strictly with bow and arrow. Social class is expressed through tastes as well as activities: one food (iceberg lettuce) versus another (arugula); one vacation spot (Vegas) versus another (Macau), one lawn ornament (pink flamingo) versus another (pink flamingo dripping in irony).

Sociologists refer to varying types of, and unequal access to, *cultural capital* (Bourdieu, 1986). Those at the apex of the class system usually have the power to define what is most valued, how best to speak, what is chic (Bourdieu, 1984). Middle-brow reflects high-brow, only as knock-off. Those at the bottom, for their part, are invited to worship one or another royal family (Windsors, Kennedys, etc.), wrap themselves in flags (nations, football teams, etc.), travel the world and dine, albeit vicariously via television programs and video games, all while their earnings are reduced by mandatory income tax withholdings, Social Security taxes, and the disproportionate cost of staples: food, housing, clothing, cell phone data plans, health care, and so forth (Desmond, 2016; Reeves, 2017; Taylor, 2018; Woskie, 2018).

Social class is also about what sociology terms *networks*. Who do you know? In which organizations are you, by familial and neighborhood affiliation, a member? What kind of socially useful knowledge have you gleaned from these associations (how to act in X or Y situation? What it is like to "be a doctor" or "be a lawyer" or serve as a "member of Congress?" etc.). On whom are you able to rely for trusted advice and mentoring? These questions point to what sociologists call *social capital* (Bourdieu, 1986; Putnam, 2000). Does it matter in a college admissions interview if a candidate knows what a provost does, is able to shake hands in a professional manner, and is able to utter the word *résumé* with the correct pronunciation or write it with the correct diacritics? Sure. But does it also help if the candidate's mother knows the prospective employer's mother via their volunteer work in the community? Does it also matter that a friend's dad facilitated the interview in the first place? I have witnessed a well-qualified candidate for an academic position have his pronunciation of "orien-tate-ed" used to sink his chances. I have also witnessed candidates identified through colleagueship networks, their rough edges overlooked in favor of their being known quantities and therefore, presumably, more trustworthy, reliable, and a better "fit." Social and cultural capital may weigh more heavily in academic life than in other institutional spheres and settings (Gaskell & Lingwood, 2017; Jensen & Jetten, 2015).

Social Class and Social Change

If society is stratified by social class—as defined and determined by the unequal distributions of wealth, income, and social and cultural capital—then how is it that social mobility of any kind happens at all? It is important to underscore that people do not choose the unequal world of their birth any more than they chose their own parents and immediate caregivers. From the point of view of the individual, these are givens, and these givens shape us profoundly from before we are even birthed and throughout our years. This noted, it is also true that humans are possessed of agency, the power to act toward that which seems given and unchangeable, and to change it. Usually lasting change requires widespread alignment of individual agency, say, in the form of social movements or mass voting, but individuals can and do act in ways that shape their individual lives. This includes our journeys in the class system, aided by institutions designed, at least in part, to facilitate mobility (Giddens, 1984; Melucci, 1989; Willis, 1977).

As noted, educational attainment is typically viewed as one of the most legitimate and encouraged means to secure upward social mobility. Entrepreneurship and public service, such as military service, are others. (Organized crime, not so much.) Some people are born in the working class, perform well in school, borrow money from family members, attend a college or university, succeed in their studies, and translate their learning—the skills won, the knowledge obtained, the connections made, the cultivation of their tastes and outlook—into upward rise in the class system. They achieve solidly middle-class status or perhaps even upper middle-class status as a doctor, business executive, or fashion designer. Some might stick around as a member of one or another faculty and teach others about the class system.

If social conditions are ripe, this scenario can play itself out across a wide cross section of society, as it did after WWII when the GI Bill gave returning veterans and their families a boost into an already growing economy. The Morrill Act of 1862 was a similar impetus to societal-wide class mobility. Recall the low-cost UC system in the 1950s and 1960s, the Wisconsin

Idea, and so forth. Upward social mobility is and has been a lived experience for millions, and higher education has played a leading role. Downward mobility is also a reality. A complex society of over 300 million, the United States fosters considerable class *im*mobility and stagnation as well. Mobility chances are limited, a double-edged sword, and unevenly distributed (Apple, 2011, 2013; Bowles & Gintis, 1976). Inequalities are rife.

Educators who support first-gen college students, and who are animated by the promise of democratic society, seek to maximize students' chances of navigating the educational system, the known vagaries of the class system notwithstanding. We do this by recognizing the strengths that first-gen students bring to higher education. We do this by heightening our own awareness of the obstacles that discourage learning and sharing this awareness with others through professional development and contributions to the public sphere. We do this by working to change not the students (who are so often unjustly blamed as individuals for the class system and its consequences), but institutional policies and practices that, often unthinkingly and unintentionally, discriminate against first-gen students. From unnecessary academic jargon to financial aid policy to healthy, available, and affordable food options, democratically minded college and university educators ask: *Are we first-gen student ready?* (Ardoin, 2017; Goldrick-Rab, 2016; Soares & Mazzeo, 2008; White, 2016).

We aim for first-gen student-ready institutions because we take responsibility for maximizing upward social mobility over and against the workings of the class system. We seek access for deserving students and the highest quality of educational experience even if, given social and economic inequalities, this education needs to be delivered at a discounted price and in an intentional, class-conscious manner (Soria, 2015). Democratic values—equality, community, every human as deserving of and in fact requiring the beneficent influence of education—undergird this thinking and approach, even while they are largely at odds with the values—the liberal values of individualism, competition, and spoils to the victors—that undergird the class system. It is as though John Dewey (1916) and Milton Friedman (1962), University of Chicago dons both, were debating one another across different eras.

But it is important to stress that even those who lean toward Friedman's way of looking at the world can and do get behind first-gen students, for there is an element in each students' very presence in higher education—usually a large element—of individual effort, self-determination, striving and grit, to satisfy those for whom these qualities are essential ingredients for the making of a good and fair society (Duckworth, 2016; Vance, 2016). Indeed, one great appeal of first-gen discourse lies in this ideological common ground. First-gen discourse appeals to every, or nearly every, political stripe.

It is also, notably, a marker without race/ethnic distinction, even though one half of first-gen college students also face prejudice and discrimination based on race/ethnicity and immigrant status. Given the substance as well as the tone and tenor of famous recent U.S. Supreme Court affirmative action in higher education cases such as *Grutter* and *Fisher*, many see first-gen policies and programs as aligning with the new law of the land by providing acceptable means to address institutional priorities for diverse, inclusive, and just scholarly communities, that is, the type of academic communities where, educators generally agree, learning is best promoted and most fully realized in practice (Bohon, 2016).

First Scholars

An example of how these ideas and values are applied in practice in U.S. higher education is First Scholars (2018), a program of the Suder Foundation. First Scholars is an innovative first-gen student success program that has been piloted since 2008 at a diverse group of institutions—the University of Kentucky, University of Memphis, Washington State University, Northern Arizona University, and KSU among others. The Suder Foundation has also funded central offices on campuses designed to scale the benefits of the First Scholars program for thousands rather than hundreds of students, and they have partnered with NASPA: Student Affairs Administrators in Higher Education, the largest student affairs professional society, to create a national Center for First-Gen Student Success (Suder Foundation, 2018).

First Scholars are selected because they present themselves, not as extraordinary, but as perfectly ordinary would-be college students who seek to be the first in their immediate families to earn a bachelor's degree. Only those with middle-range standardized academic and noncognitive skills test scores are eligible. Once selected, First Scholars are supported in two principal ways: They receive a need-based scholarship, and, as part of a small cohort (usually of 20 per year), they participate in a 4-year integrated and developmentally construed support program led by a dedicated First Scholars coordinator. This approach has proven effective everywhere it has been tried. Typically, First Scholars persist and graduate at rates that exceed institution averages. Since national average first-gen graduation rates are probably no better than 50% (estimates vary and rigorous study is hampered by competing definitions of first-gen status as well as reliance on student self-reporting), the First Scholars Program's 70%-plus graduation rates are as notable as they are encouraging (Suder Foundation, 2017).

We can see how First Scholars—and other first-gen programs—address different facets of social class and couch their efforts, usually implicitly, within the discourse of upward social mobility. First Scholars' need-based scholarship is fundamental because it permits students without great familial wealth and income to afford the cost of attendance at 4-year institutions. This basic economic accessibility trumps all competing considerations because it facilitates matriculation. From there, the cohort design, which entails participation in a required living/learning community and exclusive 1 credit hour course, addresses the need for investments in social capital by nurturing bonds among peers who share similar backgrounds and with a coordinator who serves as a source of guidance and wraparound support. The required curriculum and cocurricular activities bolster cultural capital as well, by providing college-specific information through intentional instruction and peer learning, imparting types of knowledge that upper middle-class students often (no criticism implied) simply take for granted.

First Scholars receive advising, coaching, mentoring, and counseling, all with a clear focus on their strengths (which diminishes the ill-effects of stereotype threat), the developmental challenges before them (which keeps them engaged as they experience the transformative quality of residential higher education during a formative period of learning and personal growth), and the common challenges they face as first-gen college students (which builds solidarity). When I worked with First Scholars at a land-grant university, I would tell them that the university was *their* university; that Justin Morrill and Abraham Lincoln meant it *for them* but that it was nice of them to share it with others. This last statement, although meant to call out a smile, was neither cheerleading nor empty rhetoric. It is historically accurate to stress the role that intergenerational upward social mobility has played in the development of the United States as a democratic society, that is, a society in which "all men [*sic*] are created equal." There is no condescension in viewing first-gen college students in this light. Lincoln did not require university education, but those who hail from today's log cabins should not, and shall not, be denied the opportunity for an intellectually liberating, life-changing educational experience.

Conclusion

First named in the 1980 Higher Education Amendments and long served principally by federally funded TRIO Programs (Groutt, 2003), first-gen college students have received increasing attention of late, especially since the

Great Recession of 2008. When the post-2008 rise in inequality combined with the precipitous decline in public support for higher education that began in the 1980s, the very viability of higher education as a functioning mechanism of upward social mobility came into question. Could the bottom one half of society afford quality higher education? Could even the bottom three quarters? And, if students *could* gain access (usually through increasing student loan borrowing), was a 60% chance of graduation (only 50% for first-gen students) worth the investment?

That's a lot to ask of a prospective first-gen family: Send your student to us, the proprietors of this strange and alien institution and, by the way, include more money than you can afford to spend. In return, we will, about half of the time, provide your student with empowering and potentially life-changing higher education and, for the other half, alienation, failure, and potentially life-altering debt. Take it or leave it. And, remember: People sans bachelor's degrees are likely to struggle to retire debt.

It is not hard to imagine how the social psychology of this situation could lead many who face it to then deride college and universities as worth neither their time nor money, nor even of being fair or democratic. It's not hard to imagine their seeing colleges and universities as elitist, bastions of the upper middle classes enjoying arugula and study abroad. Those fighting class polarization know that they need to make higher education accessible and welcoming for students who are not from the upper reaches of the class system. Increasingly, colleges and universities (public and private) have a vested interest in this direction (more students means more revenue). But many also have an ideological interest, in that they want to stabilize the class system and bolster society, the legitimacy of which, as noted, is based on myriad effective pathways for upward mobility. Enter into this world "first-gen college students," embraced from Cornell University to Colorado State University, students who are the majority on a number of campuses in California's public university systems (California State University, n.d.; UC, n.d.).

I promised advice. I advise that we educate ourselves about social class and that we begin by appreciating what were once called the "hidden injuries of class" (Sennett & Cobb, 1972). We should take note of the lives and characteristic perspectives of the truly wealthy (Giridharadas, 2018) as well as the lives and characteristic perspectives of those who have been dubbed "the truly disadvantaged" (Wilson, 1987). It is impossible to understand and deeply appreciate the multifaceted strengths that poor, working-, and middle-class students bring to our college or university communities without first understanding what social class, as such, is all about (hooks, 2000). Understanding first-gen college students is a prerequisite for supporting them, and support them we shall and must (Ward et al., 2012).

I recommend as second and third lines of inquiry the discriminatory nature of standardized testing (Hubler, 2020; Lemann, 1999; Soares, 2009), which sorts by class more than it identifies merit and is therefore powerful institutional discrimination against would-be first-gen students, and study of literatures that invite an intersectional understanding of class with race and gender and other determinates of identity, inequality, and injustice (Ardoin & Martinez, 2019; Collins & Bilge, 2016), because we must not permit the discourse around first-gen students to distract us from our students' complex, cross-cutting identities or from the oppression that is perpetuated by racism, sexism, heterosexism, ableism, and so on.

One can imagine a U.S. society in which, as John Dewey hoped, education was understood as essential to human flourishing, and where, therefore, opportunities to engage in higher education were equally robust for all who sought them. Those who tend the first-gen vineyard work implicitly in this larger garden, where we cannot evade our larger responsibilities. As we cultivate sociological self-understanding, let us not forget to attend to every individual, each a microcosm of universal aspirations as well as a singular and irreducible being. Let us pursue social justice via every setting, situation, and person, with a mind toward history-making. Only then shall we fulfill our professional responsibilities.

References

Aisch, G., Buchanan, L., Cox, A., & Qualy, K. (2017, January 18). Some colleges have more students from the top 1 percent than the bottom 60. *New York Times*. https://www.nytimes.com/interactive/2017/01/18/upshot/some-colleges-have-more-students-from-the-top-1-percent-than-the-bottom-60.html

Apple, M. (2011). *Education and power* (3rd ed.). Routledge.

Apple, M. (2013). *Can education change society?* Routledge.

Ardoin, S. (2017). *College aspirations and access in working-class rural communities*. Lexington.

Ardoin, S., & Martinez, B. (2019). *Straddling class in the academy: 26 stories of students, administrators, and faculty from poor and working-class backgrounds and their compelling lessons for higher education policy and practice*. Stylus.

Bohon, S. A. (2016). On the value of diversity in higher education. *Footnotes: A Publication of the American Sociological Association, 44*(7). https://www.asanet.org/news-events/footnotes/nov-2016/features/value-diversity-higher-education

Bourdieu, P. (1984). *Distinction: A social critique of the judgement of taste*. Routledge.

Bourdieu, P. (1986). The forms of capital. In J. Richardson (Ed.), *Handbook of theory and research for the sociology of education* (pp. 241–258). Greenwood.

Bowles, S., & Gintis, H. (1976). *Schooling in capitalist America: Educational reform and the contradictions of economic life*. Haymarket.

Califano, J. A., with Semple, R. (2018). *Our damaged democracy: We the people must act*. Touchstone.

California State University. (n.d.). *Basic needs initiative*. https://www2.calstate.edu/impact-of-the-csu/student-success/basic-needs-initiative

Camera, L. (2017, December 4). Is Greek life worth saving? *U.S. News & World Report*. https://www.usnews.com/news/education-news/articles/2017-12-04/is-greek-life-worth-saving

Chetty, R., Friedman, J. N., Saez, E., Turner, N., & Yalgan, D. (2017, July). *Mobility report cards: The role of colleges in intergenerational mobility*. http://www.equality-of-opportunity.org/papers/coll_mrc_paper.pdf

Cole, J. (2009). *The great American university: Its rise to preeminence, its indispensable national role, why it must be protected*. PublicAffairs.

Collins, P. H., & Bilge, S. (2016). *Intersectionality*. Polity.

Desmond, M. (2016). *Evicted: Poverty and profit in the American city*. Crown.

Dewey, J. (1916). *Democracy and education: An introduction to the philosophy of education*. Macmillan.

Duckworth, A. (2016). *Grit: The power of passion and perseverance*. Scribner.

Flanagan, C. (2014, March). The dark power of fraternities. *The Atlantic*. https://www.theatlantic.com/magazine/archive/2014/03/the-dark-power-of-fraternities/357580/

Friedman, M. (1962). *Capitalism and freedom*. University of Chicago Press.

Gaskell, S., & Lingwood, R. (2017, October 2). Social capital: The new frontier in widening participation at universities. *The Guardian*. https://www.theguardian.com/higher-education-network/2017/oct/02/social-capital-new-frontier-widening-participation-university-higher-education

Giddens, A. (1984). *The constitution of society: Outline of the theory of structuration*. University of California Press.

Giridharadas, A. (2018). *Winners take all: The elite charade of changing the world*. Knopf.

Goldrick-Rab, S. (2016). *Paying the price: College costs, financial aid, and the betrayal of the american dream*. University of Chicago Press.

Groutt, J. (2003, September). *Milestones of TRIO history, part II*. http://www.pellinstitute.org/downloads/trio_clearinghouse-Groutt_September_2003.pdf

Higher Education Research Institute. (n.d.). https://heri.ucla.edu/

hooks, b. (2000). *Where we stand: Class matters*. Routledge.

Hubler, S. (2020, May 21). University of California will end use of SAT and ACT in admissions. *New York Times*. https://www.nytimes.com/2020/05/21/us/university-california-sat-act.html

Jensen, D. H., & Jetten, J. (2015, February 13). Bridging and bonding interactions in higher education: Social capital and students' academic and professional identity. *Frontiers in Psychology*. https://www.frontiersin.org/articles/10.3389/fpsyg.2015.00126/full

Krugman, P. (2019, June 22). Notes on excessive wealth disorder. *New York Times*. https://www.nytimes.com/2019/06/22/opinion/notes-on-excessive-wealth-disorder.html

Lemann, N. (1999). *The big test: The secret history of the American meritocracy.* Farrar, Straus, and Giroux.

Loudenback, T., & Gould, S. (2017, May 29). One chart shows how many millionaires and billionaires graduated from Harvard, Stanford, MIT, and 17 other top colleges. *Business Insider.* https://www.businessinsider.com/chart-where-the-wealthiest-people-went-to-college-2017-5

Melucci, A. (1989). *Nomads of the present: Social movements and individual needs in contemporary society.* Temple University Press.

Mettler, S. (2014). *Degrees of inequality: How the politics of higher education sabotaged the American dream.* Basic Books.

Newfield, C. (2016). *The great mistake: How we wrecked public universities and how we can fix them.* Johns Hopkins University Press.

Putnam, R. D. (2000). *Bowling alone: The collapse and revival of American community.* Simon & Schuster.

Reeves, R. (2017). *Dream hoarders: How the American upper middle class is leaving everyone else in the dust, why that is a problem, and what to do about it.* Brookings Institution.

Sennett, R., & Cobb, J. (1972). *The hidden injuries of class.* Norton.

Soares, J., & Mazzeo, C. (2008). College-ready students, student-ready colleges. *Center for American Progress.* https://www.americanprogress.org/issues/education-postsecondary/reports/2008/08/12/4845/college-ready-students-student-ready-colleges/

Soares, J. A. (Ed.). (2009). *SAT wars: The case for test-optional college admissions.* Teachers College Press.

Soria, K. (2015). *Welcoming blue-collar scholars into the ivory tower: Developing class-conscious strategies for student success.* National Resource Center for the First-Year Experience and Students in Transition.

Statista. (2018, October). *Wealth distribution in the United States in 2016.* https://www.statista.com/statistics/203961/wealth-distribution-for-the-us/

Statista. (2020). *Average annual cost to attend university in the United States, by institution type, 2013–2021.* https://www.statista.com/statistics/235651/us-university-attendance-cost/

The Suder Foundation. (2017). *First Scholars impact report, 2010–2016.* http://firstscholars.org/wp-content/uploads/2017/04/First-scholars-report-2017-04-13-FINAL.pdf

The Suder Foundation. (2018). *Center for First-Generation Student Success, an initiative of NASPA and the Suder Foundation.* https://firstgen.naspa.org/

Taylor, K. (2018, April 11). America's "permanent underclass" isn't going anywhere—and that's great news for stores like Dollar General and Dollar Tree. *Business Insider.* https://www.businessinsider.com/dollar-stores-thrive-thanks-to-americas-permanent-underclass-2018-4

Thorp, H., & Goldstein, B. (2018). *Our higher calling: Rebuilding the partnership between America and its colleges and universities.* University of North Carolina Press.

University of California. (n.d.). *Student opportunity: First-gen.* https://www
.universityofcalifornia.edu/initiative/student-opportunity/first-generation-
students

Van Dam, A. (2018, October 30). Owning your own home doesn't make you rich.
Owning somebody else's does. *Washington Post.* https://www.washingtonpost
.com/business/2018/10/30/owning-your-own-home-doesnt-make-you-rich-
owning-somebody-elses-does/

Vance, J. D. (2016). *Hillbilly elegy: A memoir of a family and culture in crisis.* Harper.

Ward, L., Segel, M. J., & Davenport, Z. (2012). *First-generation college students:
Understanding and improving the experience from recruitment to commencement.*
Jossey-Bass.

White, B. (2016, March 21). The myth of the college-ready student. *Inside Higher
Ed.* https://www.insidehighered.com/views/2016/03/21/instead-focusing-col-
lege-ready-students-institutions-should-become-more-student

Willis, P. (1977). *Learning to labour: How working class kids get working class jobs.*
Saxon House.

Wilson, W. J. (1987). *The truly disadvantaged: The inner city, the underclass, and
public policy.* University of Chicago Press.

Woskie, L. (2018, March). What's behind high U.S. health care costs. *The
Harvard Gazette.* https://news.harvard.edu/gazette/story/2018/03/u-s-pays-
more-for-health-care-with-worse-population-health-outcomes/

3

SETTING THE FOUNDATION

Understanding the Impact of College on First-Generation Students

Ryan D. Padgett

R esearch on first-generation students and their transition from the college-choice process through to degree completion has exploded over the last decade. A simple scholarly article search yielded more mentions of *first-generation students* in the past decade from 2008–2018 than in the entire prior century from 1907–2007. The proliferation of recent articles may be attributed to a number of factors, including but not limited to (a) the number of first-generation students entering postsecondary education; (b) national and institutional data suggesting that first-generation students do not perform equally as non-first-generation students across a series of key performance indicators; (c) state-performance funding models that allocate additional resources to institutions that are able to demonstrate increases in degree attainment for low-income and underrepresented minorities (URM), which are subgroups that proportionally have higher percentages of first-generation students; and (d) the continued growth of educational research around conditional and interactional effects.

This chapter will set the foundation around our current understanding of the impact of college on first-generation students by introducing a conceptual framework around first-generation status that is supplemented by historical and emerging research. To set this foundation, I have drawn from components of my doctoral dissertation, "The Effects of the First Year of College on Undergraduates' Development of Altruistic and Socially Responsible Behavior" (Padgett, 2011). This literature review is not intended to be extensive, but rather a broad overview of conceptual frameworks that help shape the current research examining methodologically appropriate subsamples of first-generation students.

Sociological and Economic Concepts as a Broad Framework

Higher education serves and benefits both the individual and society, and as such, college graduates are expected to develop outcomes that generate both private or internal benefits (e.g., personal satisfaction) and public or external benefits (e.g., altruism and an educated society). The sociological and economic concepts of human, social, and cultural capital serve as useful elements when exploring the impact of postsecondary education on first-generation students.

Human Capital

Within the study of economics, an individual is viewed as both a consumer and producer of services. The term *human capital* was created to define the quantitative measure of an individual's productivity (Thurow, 1970). *Human capital* is defined as an individual's productive capacities such as knowledge, skills, talents, competences, and attributes (Becker, 1975; Paulsen, 2001; Riordan, 1997; Schuller, 2001; Schultz, 1971; Thurow, 1970). Human capital is quantifiable, and as such can be measured by the value of services produced by an individual (Thurow, 1970). Individuals invest in their human capital to optimize their productivity and yield greater earnings over their lifetime (Gunaratne, 1985). One way in which an individual can strengthen their knowledge and skill set is by enrolling in formal education and training supplements (Gunaratne, 1985; Paulsen, 2001; Schuller, 2001; Toutkoushian, 2006). Schultz (1971) refers to acquired education—elementary school, high school, and higher education—as a form of human capital. In the broadest application, possessing a college degree allows an individual to be more productive. The educational setting provides students the opportunity to engage in a number of experiences and social engagements that contribute to the acquisition of human capital, including civic, political, and charitable experiences. However, attending a postsecondary institution requires a substantial monetary investment so that individuals compare the expected benefits of higher education with the underlying costs and loss of foregone earnings (see McMahon, 2009; Paulsen, 2001; Paulsen & Toutkoushian, 2007, 2008).

When students decide to financially invest in college, they primarily consider the internal benefits—better pay, job security—that accrue to them personally (Paulsen & Toutkoushian, 2007). But individuals who engage in altruistic behaviors are more likely to generate public or external benefits. Empirical evidence indicates that external benefits can also accrue to society as a result of individuals increasing their human capital through public investments in college (see Baum & Payea, 2004; Leslie & Brinkman, 1988; Paulsen & Toutkoushian, 2007). Few would argue the public or external benefits generated from subsidizing elementary and secondary education (see Baum, 2004). Literacy is necessary for a democratic society and a functioning workforce that supports said society (Baum, 2004). Yet, the perceived public or external benefits associated with higher education—especially those generated from the altruism or altruistic behaviors of college students or graduates that are nonmarket public benefits—tend to be more subtle. This is clearly portrayed by how the academic community within postsecondary education equips and provides students with opportunities to assume roles in public service. In general, the academic community promotes concerns with social issues and problems, presents students with the opportunity to engage in the study of these issues and problems, and intentionally provides students with forums for discussion and debate (Bowen, 1977). Because these experiences, curriculum, and opportunities are engrained within the college milieu, the extent to which a student actively participates in college increases their investment in human capital.

Social Capital

College-educated individuals as members of society directly influence the values, attitudes, and behavior of other members of society simply through social interactions (Bowen, 1977). These interactions provide noncollege graduates in society with new and diverse outlooks on life, views on race relations, environmental issues, and public policy (Bowen, 1977). Though these interactions and associations are most common among family and friends, such influences certainly extend into the community. The presence of significant others—family, peers, colleagues—is also an integral part of social capital theory (Coleman, 1988). Social capital refers to the norms, networks, relationships, and other social connections that serve as a reciprocal resource for individuals to draw upon (Attewell & Lavin, 2007; Coleman, 1988; Field, 2008; Glaeser, 2001; Putnam, 2001; Riordan, 1997). The primary function of social capital is to allow the individual access to human and cultural capital through social networks (see Perna & Titus, 2005). From a civic and political scientist perspective, "social capital is conceptualized as a societal resource that links citizens to each other and enables them to pursue their common objectives more effectively" (Stolle, 2003, p. 19). Sociologists prefer to frame social capital within egocentric traits and networks (Dekker, 2004). From the sociologists' perspective, what differentiates social capital from human and cultural capital is the individual possession of charisma, social contacts, linguistic skills, and social trust (Glaeser, 2001). As such, Osbourne et al. (2007) identify three categories of connections and ties related to social capital: (a) bonding connections, comprising family and close friends; (b) bridging ties, comprising people with similar background and shared interests (e.g., hobbies, job, neighbors); and (c) linking ties, which comprise people from dissimilar backgrounds. These categories illustrate that investment in social capital can be gained in a number of settings. In other words, the more people you know and with whom you share common interests, the greater one's social capital will be (Field, 2008). However, social capital can come in various forms that are influential in different ways, including moral enlightenment (e.g., volunteering, civic engagement, and other forms of altruism) or moral repugnance (e.g., terrorists' organizations, hate organizations, gangs). The social network with which individuals surround themselves shapes their perceptions on values and norms.

College campuses are a haven for social networks and social interactions. Extensive empirical evidence examining both formal interactions on campus—for example, cocurricular involvement, in-class faculty–student interactions, receiving feedback from faculty—and informal interactions—for example, out-of-class peer interactions, extracurricular activities, out-of-class faculty interactions—have yielded overwhelmingly positive effects on a range of valued outcomes (see Astin, 1993; Chickering & Gamson, 1987, 1991; Pascarella & Terenzini, 1991, 2005). As college students continually invest in their social capital through formal and informal interaction in college, they directly increase their social network and social resources. Students who participate in curricular, cocurricular, or extracurricular experiences related to civic, political, and charitable involvement are instantaneously surrounded by individuals who value altruistic behaviors. These experiences are prominent in college impact research (see Astin, 1993, Pascarella & Terenzini, 2005) and support the empirical evidence that the college experience is both a cause and outcome of social capital.

Relationships and friendships forged between family members and personal friends are often labeled *strong social ties* (Fernandez Kelly, 2002). These social ties provide the individual with a sense of belonging, trust, and identity. A student, for example, whose parents are highly educated has an additive advantage of engaging in a social structure that is likely to be composed of other highly educated individuals compared to a peer whose parents are not highly educated. The student inherently becomes a member of an educated social structure that supports their values and beliefs. Furthermore, the degree of parental involvement in the child's academic activities is likely to increase with level of parental education (Wong, 2002). Research suggests that highly educated parents are more likely to mobilize additional resources to increase their child's social network and educational opportunities (Wong, 2002). This research further suggests that less educated parents are less able to provide their children with additional benefits and resources because of their limited capital. In other words, individuals from less educated families are less likely to have a social network that values or has the resources to support a student's transition through college. Conversely, *weak social ties* comprise interactions with individuals outside one's personal relationships, but the interactions are with more knowledgeable and powerful individuals (Fernandez Kelly, 2002). A student's interaction with a faculty member is an example of a weak social tie, in which the relationship between student and faculty is informal but the student interacts with a knowledgeable agent in an institutional setting.

These concepts of social capital indirectly imply that the level of social networks varies across different racial and socioeconomic groups. Attewell and Lavin (2007) hypothesize that lower socioeconomic status (SES) minority families have fewer social networks compared to middle and upper SES Whites, and the reduced social capital of low SES individuals produces less opportunities for employment and education. Using data from the second and third follow-ups to the National Education Longitudinal Study (NELS) to examine parental involvement as a form of social capital on college enrollment, Perna and Titus (2005) conclude:

> On average, African Americans and Hispanics are disadvantaged in the college enrollment process not only because of their own low levels of the types of economic, human, and cultural capital that are valued in the college enrollment process but also because of the low levels of resources that are available to promote college enrollment through the social networks at the schools they attend. . . . Research demonstrates that parental involvement as a form of social capital is positively related to college enrollment regardless of the level of individual and school resources. (p. 511)

Additional empirical analyses using data from the 1988 NELS confirm Perna and Titus, suggesting that educational aspirations of African American, Hispanic, and Asian American children significantly increase from having involved, optimistic parents (Kao, 2002). These results suggest that high levels of parental involvement can supplement lower levels of social capital for students of color and low SES.

Cultural Capital

Whereas *human capital* refers to the productive capacities an individual desires to optimize, and *social capital* refers to the social network and social connections individuals can draw upon, the sociological concept of *cultural capital* tends to be defined within the familial and social framework (see Perna & Titus, 2005). *Cultural capital* is broadly defined as the cultural resources and knowledge transmitted by individuals of high and middle SES to their children as a means to supplement wealth and maintain class status (Bourdieu, 1977; McDonough, 1997; Paulsen, 2001; Riordan, 1997). In other words, cultural capital typically defines the family's lifestyle and tastes (Attewell & Lavin, 2007).

Parents with more disposable income are better able to provide their children with cultural experiences—visits to museums, attending a symphony performance, visits to a historical site, learning a second language, and frequent visits to the library, just to name a few—compared to low SES and less educated families. These cultural experiences can serve as an encouragement and introduction into societal benefits, such as higher education.

Cultural capital is not taught within the classroom; students possess it as they enter academia (Attewell & Lavin, 2007; Dumais, 2002). However, the academic success of high and middle SES students may be mistaken due to superior ability rather than being attributed to cultural capital. Attewell and Lavin (2007) suggest this phenomenon "disguises, legitimates, and reproduces class inequality in education by handicapping and excluding children of the working and lower classes" (p. 81). If students from lower SES are introduced to environments abundant with diverse cultural activities such as college campuses, they will be exposed to various cultural experiences that may expand their interests and values. To this end, higher education provides students with the opportunity to surround themselves with individuals who share similar cultural beliefs.

Cultural capital is rooted within educational attainment, often referring to the credentials and educational assets parents bestow to their children (Schuller, 2001). As such, cultural capital can be viewed as a mechanism through which high and middle SES families provide quality educational opportunities that enable their children to reproduce their class status. Furthermore, college-educated individuals are more likely to change the cultural landscape and patterns within society (Bowen, 1977), which could enable high and middle SES families to continue reinforcing their class status. Parents transmit cultural capital to their children by chronicling and reinforcing the value and wealth higher education can provide (McDonough, 1997). Conversely, cultural capital can also be used to explore how lower SES families use education to climb the class hierarchy (Schuller, 2001).

In summary, individuals seek to optimize their productivity and to increase their human capital through their knowledge, skills, talents, competences, and attributes. Because of the importance society places on the societal benefits provided by college graduates, higher education fosters growth in students through various curriculum and college experiences. The social networks, relationships, and interactions individuals maintain refer to their social capital. The social network individuals surround themselves with—including those on a college campus—influences their perceptions of important values and norms. Colleges provide students with the opportunity to continually invest in their social capital through formal and informal interactions. Upon reviewing and disseminating years of research, Astin (1993) labeled peers the "single most important environmental influence on student development" (p. xxii). Lastly, what makes cultural capital such an influential factor is the direct link between cultural experiences and college campuses. To this end, higher education—and the college experience across campuses—heavily promotes and fosters personal development.

Defining First-Generation Status

A consistent theme throughout the research in defining *first-generation status* is the inconsistency in the definitions. The ways in which researchers define first-generation status vary across studies; there is no universal definition of a *first-generation student* (see Davis, 2010). The definitions vary from being narrowly defined to broadly defined. The U.S. Department of Education (as recorded by the University of Washington [n.d.]) defines a *first-generation student* as

> an individual, neither of whose parents completed a baccalaureate degree; or an individual who, prior to the age of 18, regularly resided with and received support from only one parent and whose supporting parent did not complete a baccalaureate degree; or an individual who, prior to the age of 18, did not regularly reside with or receive support from a natural or adoptive parent.

In other words, if a student's parent(s) or guardian(s) did not obtain at least a bachelor's degree, they are considered by the federal government as first-generation. Students whose parent(s) earned an associate degree or completed 3-and-a-half-years of a bachelor's degree but did not graduate would still be considered first-generation. This is the definition utilized by federal TRIO programs (e.g., Student Support Services) and often adopted by state institutions.

Using data from the Education Longitudinal Study of 2002, Toutkoushian et al. (2018) found that the percentage of students who were identified as first-generation varied across a sample of eight alternative definitions of first-generation status. They concluded that who gets counted as a first-generation student can be greatly affected by the particulars of how one defines first-generation status. This result alone has important implications for postsecondary institutions and government agencies to consider as they design programs to help first-generation college students succeed in academia because the cost of implementing such programs will naturally vary with the size of the group. (pp. 24–25)

Within the research, these variations are prevalent. Level of parental education is typically coded as a dichotomous variable (first-generation versus non-first-generation). Other researchers have introduced level of parental education coded as a series of dichotomous variables while others select first-generation students as a population of interest as a unique subsample and compare them with their non-first-generation peers, where the effect of the college experiences included within each model is unique to each subsample on the outcome. Regardless, care must be taken when interpreting results and, more importantly, applying these studies to designing institutional programs and policies.

A Snapshot of Historical and Emerging Research

The college environment comprises a multitude of structural and programmatic characteristics that influence the growth, development, and experiences of undergraduate students. To fully examine the degree to which these structural and programmatic elements significantly impact the effects of selected in-college experiences on students' growth or development, it is necessary to account for potentially biasing background characteristics, precollege experiences, and college-level experiences and engagement using college-impact methodology. To this end, there has been an emergence of robust research on first-generation students as a conditional effect or subgroup of interest.

In 1971, first-generation students represented 38.5% of all first-time, full-time students at 4-year colleges and universities (Saenz et al., 2007). By 1991, the percent of first-generation students in 4-year colleges and universities dropped to 31% (Warburton et al., 2001). However, coupled with the surge of minority students into postsecondary education, the proportion of first-generation students was expected to increase (Strayhorn, 2006), though it has remained relatively steady at around 33% (Cataldi et al., 2018) depending on how one defines first-generation status (see Toutkoushian et al., 2018).

First-generation students enter college with substantially different levels of human, cultural, and social capital compared to their non-first-generation peers. These deficiencies in capital place first-generation students at a considerable disadvantage when arriving on college campuses. Complicating matters even further for first-generation students are the resources and policies currently in place within higher education. College experiences and the college milieu were designed and developed with traditional students in mind. Furthermore, the research supporting these experiences was often conducted on data sets primarily comprising traditional White students. The extent to which these experiences may be benefiting or hampering first-generation student development was both underresearched and unknown. Longitudinal evidence (see Padgett et al., 2010, 2012; Pascarella et al., 2004; Terenzini et al., 1996) suggests first-generation students are uniquely sensitive to a wide range of college experiences and their impact on college outcomes.

First-generation college students are more likely to be of minority status, come from lower socioeconomic households, speak English as their secondary language, be non- U.S. citizens, and female (Bui, 2002; Lee et al., 2004; Saenz et al., 2007; Warburton et al., 2001). Although first-generation students tend to be a dominant proportion of college enrollees, the range and scope of analyses examining first-generation students are limited to three areas of research: (a) college choice decisions and aspirations (e.g., Bui, 2005; Ceja, 2006; Gibbons & Shoffner, 2004), (b) academic achievement (e.g., Chen & Carroll, 2005; Dennis et al., 2005; Ting, 2003), and (c) persistence (e.g., Duggan, 2001; Harrell & Forney, 2003; Ishitani, 2006; Lohfink & Paulsen, 2005; Rendon, 1995; Somers et al., 2004; Thomas & Quinn, 2007; Warburton et al., 2001). Only recently have researchers begun to investigate the extent to which college experiences significantly affect first-generation students across cognitive and psychosocial development (see Padgett et al., 2010, 2012; Pascarella et al., 2004).

From a historical perspective on the impact of college on first-generation students, three scholarly works provide an in-depth review of the prior literature: (a) Lohfink and Paulsen's (2005) *Comparing the Determinants of Persistence for First-Generation and Continuing-Generation Students*; (b) Davis's (2010) *The First-Generation Student Experiences: Implications for Campus Practice, and Strategies for Improving Persistence and Success*; and (c) Mayhew et al.'s (2016) *How College Affects Students: 21st Century Evidence that Higher Education Works* (Vol. 3). These three works illustrate the differences that exist between first-generation and non-first-generation students across a number of performance-based indicators (e.g., grade point average, persistence, graduation, etc.), student development measures (e.g., cognitive and psychosocial outcomes), and student engagement and involvement.

While emerging research still falls within the topical areas of college choice decisions and aspirations (e.g., Bui & Rush, 2016; Redford & Hoyer, 2017), academic achievement (e.g., Wibrowski et al., 2017), and persistence (e.g., Ishitani, 2016; Pratt et al., 2017), the scope and breadth has branched into other forms of academic, cocurricular, and personal engagement and involvement. These studies include career development (Kantamneni et al., 2018; Tate et al., 2015), engagement in STEM fields (Carver et al., 2017), personal well-being and stress (Becker et al., 2017; Stephens et al., 2015), institutional support (Phillips et al., 2020), parental support (Palbusa & Gauvain, 2017), and social support (Schwartz et al., 2018), just to highlight a few.

Like most published research (see Mayhew et al., 2016; Pascarella & Terenzini, 1991, 2005), the evidence continues to show how the college experience—from college selection to earning a degree—is often significantly different between first-generation and non-first-generation students. This is not to state that all the research on first-generation students paints a bleak picture. Rather, there still exist incremental differences in how first-generation students' experience college and transition through to a degree. The social and cultural capital that a first-generation student brings into their college experience shapes how they interact within the college milieu. Because of these varying experiences for first-generation students, many colleges and universities are introducing strategic programming and interventions—particularly during the transition into the first year—to help students' academic achievement, development, and persistence. As these programs and services continue to be vetted, future research will likely highlight the impact of these interventions.

More than 2 decades ago, Chickering and Gamson (1987) evaluated prior research on college impact and identified seven broad categories of good practices within higher education, now widely recognized as the seven principles for good practice in undergraduate education (also see Chickering & Gamson, 1991). These practices include encouraging cooperation among students, encouraging active learning, communicating high expectations, encouraging contact between students and faculty, giving prompt feedback, respecting diverse talents and ways of learning, and emphasizing time on task. The incorporation of the good practices within higher education research has been extensive (see Cruce et al., 2006). A myriad of empirical evidence supports the predictive validity of these good practices and are positively linked to cognitive, psychosocial, and personal development in college (e.g., Astin, 1993; Cruce et al., 2006; Mayhew et al., 2016; Padgett et al., 2008, 2012; Pascarella & Terenzini, 1991, 2005; Sorcinelli, 1991). As many colleges and universities have embedded these practices within the college experience, college administrators have turned to predictive analytics to help identify at-risk students and intervene before the problem becomes too large to overcome. These data are becoming the new wave of research within higher education. With student characteristics—such as first-generation status—so readily available and being monitored, future research on first-generation students will likely dive deeper into these proactive interventions and strategies. Support for first-generation students appears to be growing, and the research around their experiences will only increase.

References

Astin, A.W. (1993). *What matters in college? Four critical years revisited.* Jossey-Bass.

Attewell, P., & Lavin, D. E. (2007). *Passing the torch: Does higher education for the disadvantaged pay off across the generations?* Russell Sage Foundation.

Baum, S. (2004). *A primer on economics for financial aid professionals.* College Board.

Baum, S., & Payea, K. (2004) *Education pays: The benefits of higher education for individuals and society.* College Board.

Becker, G. S. (1975). *Human capital: A theoretical and empirical analysis, with special reference to education* (2nd ed.). Columbia University Press.

Becker, M. A. S., Schelbe, L., Romano, K., & Spinelli, C. (2017). Promoting first-generation college students' mental well-being: Student perceptions of an academic enrichment program. *Journal of College Student Development, 58*(8), 1166–1183.

Bourdieu, P. (1977). Cultural reproduction and social reproduction. In J. Karabel & A. H. Halsey (Eds.), *Power and ideology in education* (pp. 487–511). Oxford University Press.

Bowen, H. R. (1977). *Investment in learning: The individual and social value of American higher education.* Jossey-Bass.

Bui, K. V. T. (2002). First-generation college students at a 4-year university: Background characteristics, reasons for pursuing higher education, and first-year experiences. *College Student Journal, 36*(1), 3–11.

Bui, K. V. T. (2005). Middle school variables that predict college attendance for first-generation students. *Education, 126*, 203–220.

Bui, K., & Rush, R. A. (2016). Parental involvement in middle school predicting college attendance for first-generation students. *Education, 136*(4), 473–489.

Carver, S., Van Sickle, J., Holcomb, J., Quinn, C., Jackson, D., Resnick, A., & Duffy, S. F., Sridhar, N., Marquard, A. (2017). Operation STEM: Increasing success and improving retention among first-generation and underrepresented minority students in STEM. *Journal of STEM Education, 18*(3), 20–29.

Cataldi, E. F., Bennett, C. T., & Chen, X. (2018, February). *First-generation students: College access, persistence, and postbachelor's outcomes* (NCES 2018-421). National Center for Education Statistics. https://nces.ed.gov/pubs2018/2018421.pdf

Ceja, M. (2006). Understanding the role of parents and siblings as information sources in the college choice process of Chicana students. *Journal of College Student Development, 47*, 87–104.

Chen, X., & Carroll, C. D. (2005). *First-generation students in postsecondary education: A look at their college transcripts* (NCES 2005-171). National Center for Education Statistics. https://nces.ed.gov/das/epubs/pdf/2005171_es.pdf

Chickering, A. W., & Gamson, Z. F. (1987). Seven principles for good practice in undergraduate education. *AAHE Bulletin, 39*(7), 3–7.

Chickering, A. W., & Gamson, Z. F. (Eds.). (1991). *Applying the seven principles for good practice in higher education* (New Directions for Teaching and Learning, no. 47, pp. 1–104). Jossey-Bass. https://onlinelibrary.wiley.com/toc/15360768/1991/1991/47

Coleman, J. S. (1988). Social capital in the creation of human capital. *The American Journal of Sociology, 94*, S95–S120.

Cruce, T. M., Wolniak, G. C., Seifert, T. A., & Pascarella, E. T. (2006). Impacts of good practices on cognitive development, learning orientations, and graduate degree plans during the first year of college. *Journal of College Student Development, 47*(4), 365–383.

Davis, J. (2010). *The first-generation student experience: Implications for campus practice, and strategies for improving persistence and success.* Stylus.

Dekker, P. (2004). Social capital of individuals: Relational asset or personal quality? In S. Prakash & P. Selle (Eds.), *Investigating social capital: Comparative perspectives on civil society, participation and governance* (pp. 88–110). SAGE.

Dennis, J. M., Phinney, J. S., & Ivey-Chuateco, L. (2005). The role of motivation, parental support, and peer support in the academic success of ethnic minority first-generation college students. *Journal of College Student Development, 46*, 223–236.

Duggan, M. (2001). *Factors influencing the first-year persistence of first-generation college students* [Paper presentation]. North East Association for Institutional Research Annual Meeting, Cambridge, MA.

Dumais, S. A. (2002). Cultural capital, gender, and school success: The role of habitus. *Sociology of Education, 75*(1), 44–68.

Fernandez Kelly, P. (2002). Commentary: Uses and misuses of social capital in studying school attainment. In B. Fuller & E. Hannum (Eds.), *Schooling and social capital in diverse cultures* (pp. 73–83). Elsevier Science.

Field. J. (2008). *Social capital* (2nd ed.). Routledge.

Gibbons, M. M., & Shoffner, M. F. (2004). Prospective first-generation college students: Meeting their needs through social cognitive career theory. *Professional School Counselors, 8*, 91–97.

Glaeser, E. L. (2001). The formation of social capital. In R. Putnam (Ed.), *The contribution of human and social capital to sustained economic growth and well-being: International Symposium Report* (pp. 381–393). Human Resources Development Canada.

Gunaratne, L. (1985). *Human capital and distribution of personal income: A theoretical analysis and an examination of some aspects of income distribution in Sri Lanka.* Central Bank Press.

Harrell, P. E., & Forney, W. S. (2003). Ready or not, here we come: Retaining Hispanic and first-generation students in postsecondary education. *Community College Journal of Research and Practice, 27*, 147–156.

Ishitani, T. T. (2006). Studying attrition and degree completion behavior among first-generation college students in the United States. *The Journal of Higher Education, 77*, 861–885.

Ishitani, T. T. (2016). First-generation students' persistence at four-year institutions. *College & University, 91*(3).

Kantamneni, N., McCain, M. R., Shada, N., Hellwege, M. A., & Tate, J. (2018). Contextual factors in the career development of prospective first-generation college students: An application of social cognitive career theory. *Journal of Career Assessment, 26*(1), 183–196.

Kao, G. (2002). Ethnic differences in parents' educational aspirations. In B. Fuller & E. Hannum (Eds.), *Schooling and social capital in diverse cultures* (pp. 85–103). Elsevier Science.

Lee, J. J., Sax, L. J., Kim, K. A., & Hagedorn (2004). Understanding students' parental education beyond first-generation status. *Community College Review, 32*(1), 1–20.

Leslie, L. L., & Brinkman, P. T. (1988). *The economic value of higher education.* Macmillan.

Lohfink, M., & Paulsen, M. B. (2005). Comparing the determinants of persistence for first-generation and continuing-generation students. *Journal of College Student Development, 46*, 409–428.

Mayhew, M. J., Rockenbach, A. N., Bowman, N. A., Seifert, T. A., Wolniak, G. C., Pascarella, E. T., & Terenzini, P. T. (2016). *How college affects students: 21st century evidence that higher education works* (Vol. 3). Wiley.

McDonough, P. M. (1997). *Choosing college: How social class and schools structure opportunity.* State University of New York Press.

McMahon. W. W. (2009). *Higher learning, greater good: The private and social benefits of higher education.* Johns Hopkins University Press.

Osborne, M., Sankey, K., & Wilson, B. (2007). Introduction. In M. Osborne, K. Sankey, & B. Wilson (Eds.), *Social capital, lifelong learning and the management of place* (pp. 1–14). Routledge.

Padgett, R. D. (2011). *The effects of the first year of college on undergraduates' development of altruistic and socially responsible behavior* [Doctoral dissertation, The University of Iowa]. Iowa Research Online. https://ir.uiowa.edu/cgi/viewcontent.cgi?article=2437&context=etd

Padgett, R. D., Goodman, K. M., Johnson, M. P., Saichaie, K., Umbach, P. D., & Pascarella, E. T. (2010). The impact of college student socialization, social class, and race on need for cognition. In S. Herzog (Ed.), *Diversity and educational benefits* (New Directions for Institutional Research, no. 145, pp. 99–111). Jossey-Bass. https://doi.org/10.1002/ir.324

Padgett, R. D., Johnson, M. P., & Pascarella, E. T. (2012). First-generation undergraduate students and the impacts of the first year of college: Additional evidence. *Journal of College Student Development, 53*(2), 243–266.

Palbusa, J. A., & Gauvain, M. (2017). Parent–student communication about college and freshman grades in first-generation and non-first-generation students. *Journal of College Student Development, 58*(1), 107–112.

Pascarella, E. T., Pierson, C. T., Wolniak, G. C., & Terenzini, P. T. (2004). First-generation college students: Additional evidence on college experiences and outcomes. *Journal of Higher Education, 75*, 249–284.

Pascarella, E. T., & Terenzini, P. T. (1991). *How college affects students.* Jossey-Bass.

Pascarella, E. T., & Terenzini, P. T. (2005). *How college affects students: A third decade of research* (Vol. 2). Jossey-Bass.

Paulsen, M. B. (2001). The economics of human capital and investment in higher education. In M. B. Paulsen & J. C. Smart (Eds.), *The finance of higher education: Theory, research, policy & practice* (pp. 55–94). Agathon.

Paulsen, M. B., & Toutkoushian, R. K. (2007). Overview of economic concepts, models, and methods for institutional research. In R. K. Toutkoushian & M. B. Paulsen (Eds.), *Applying economics to institutional research* (New Directions for Institutional Research, no. 132, pp. 5–24). Jossey-Bass. https://doi.org/10.1002/ir.193

Paulsen, M. B., & Toutkoushian, R. K. (2008). Economic models and policy analysis in higher education: A diagrammatic exposition. In J. C. Smart (Ed.), *Higher education: Handbook of theory and research* (Vol. 23) (pp. 1–48). Springer.

Perna, L. W., & Titus, M. A. (2005). The relationship between parental involvement as social capital and college enrollment: An examination of racial/ethnic group differences. *The Journal of Higher Education, 76*(5), 485–518.

Phillips, L. T., Stephens, N. M., Townsend, S. S., & Goudeau, S. (2020). Access is not enough: Cultural mismatch persists to limit first-generation students' opportunities for achievement throughout college. *Journal of Personality and Social Psychology, 119*(5), 1112–1131. https://doi.org/10.1037/pspi0000234

Pratt, I. S., Harwood, H. B., Cavazos, J. T., & Ditzfeld, C. P. (2017). Should I stay or should I go? Retention in first-generation college students. *Journal of College Student Retention: Research, Theory & Practice, 21*(1), 105–118. https://doi.org/10.1177/1521025117690868

Putnam, R. D. (2001). Social capital—Measurement and consequences. In J. F. Helliwell (Ed.), *The contribution of human and social capital to sustained economic growth and well-being: International symposium report* (pp. 117–135). Human Resources Development Canada.

Redford, J., & Hoyer, K. M. (2017). *First-generation and continuing-generation college students: A comparison of high school and postsecondary experiences* (NCES 2018-009). National Center for Education Statistics. https://nces.ed.gov/pubs2018/2018009.pdf

Rendon, L. I. (1995). *Facilitating retention and transfer for first-generation students in community colleges* [Paper presentation]. New Mexico Institute Rural Community College Initiative, Espanola, NM.

Riordan, C. (1997). *Equality and achievement: An introduction to the sociology of education.* Addison-Wesley.

Saenz, V. B., Hurtado, S., Barrera, D., Wolf, D., & Yeung, F. (2007). *First in my family: A profile of first-generation college students at four-year institutions since 1971.* Higher Education Research Institute, University of California, Los Angeles.

Schuller, T. (2001). The complementary roles of human and social capital. In J. F. Helliwell (Ed.), *The contribution of human and social capital to sustained economic growth and well-being: International Symposium Report* (pp. 89–105). Human Resources Development Canada.

Schultz, T. W. (1971). *Investment in human capital: The role of education and of research.* The Free Press.

Schwartz, S. E., Kanchewa, S. S., Rhodes, J. E., Gowdy, G., Stark, A. M., Horn, J. P., Harnes, N., & Spencer, R. (2018). "I'm having a little struggle with this, can you help me out?": Examining impacts and processes of a social capital intervention for first-generation college students. *American Journal of Community Psychology, 61*(1–2), 166–178.

Somers, P., Woodhouse, S., & Cofer, J. (2004). Pushing the boulder uphill: The persistence of first-generation college students. *NASPA Journal, 41,* 418–435.

Sorcinelli, M. D. (1991). Research findings on the seven principles. In A. W. Chickering & G. F. Gamson (Eds.), *Applying the seven principles of good practice in undergraduate education (New Directions for Teaching and Learning),* no. *47,* 13–23.

Stephens, N. M., Townsend, S. S., Hamedani, M. G., Destin, M., & Manzo, V. (2015). A difference-education intervention equips first-generation college students to thrive in the face of stressful college situations. *Psychological Science, 26*(10), 1556–1566.

Stolle, D. (2003). The sources of social capital. In M. Hooghe & D. Stolle (Eds.), *Generating social capital: Civil society and institutions in comparative perspective* (pp. 19–42). Palgrave MacMillan.

Strayhorn, T. L. (2006). Factors influencing the academic achievement of first-generation college students. *NASPA Journal, 43,* 82–111.

Tate, K. A., Caperton, W., Kaiser, D., Pruitt, N. T., White, H., & Hall, E. (2015). An exploration of first-generation college students' career development beliefs and experiences. *Journal of Career Development, 42*(4), 294–310.

Terenzini, P. T., Springer, L., Yaeger, P. M., Pascarella, E. T., & Nora, A. (1996). First-generation college students: Characteristics, experiences, and cognitive development. *Research in Higher Education, 37*(1), 1–22.

Thomas, L., & Quinn, J. (2007). *First-generation entry into higher education: An international study.* Open University Press.

Thurow, L. C. (1970). *Investment in human capital.* Wadsworth.

Ting, S. M. (2003). A longitudinal study of non-cognitive variables in predicting academic success of first-generation college students. *College and University, 78*(4), 27–31.

Toutkoushian, R. K. (2006). Economic contributions to institutional research on faculty. In R. K. Toutkoushiam & M. B. Paulsen (Eds.), *Applying economics to institutional research* (New Directions for Institutional Research, no. 132, pp. 75–93). Jossey-Bass. https://doi.org/10.1002/ir.197

Toutkoushian, R. K., Stollberg, R. S., & Slaton, K. A. (2018). Talking 'bout my generation. *Teachers College Record, 120*(4), 1–38.

University of Washington (n.d.). *U.S, Department of Education definitions of low-income and first-generation students.* https://www2.ed.gov/about/offices/list/ope/trio/triohea.pdf

Warburton, E. C., Bugarin, R., & Nunez, A. (2001). *Bridging the gap: Academic preparation and postsecondary success of first-generation students* (NCES 2001-153). National Center for Education Statistics.

Wibrowski, C. R., Matthews, W. K., & Kitsantas, A. (2017). The role of a skills learning support program on first-generation college students' self-regulation, motivation, and academic achievement: A longitudinal study. *Journal of College Student Retention: Research, Theory & Practice, 19*(3), 317–332.

Wong, R. S. K. (2002). Commentary: Cultural and social capital in educational research. In B. Fuller & E. Hannum (Eds.), *Schooling and social capital in diverse cultures* (pp. 161–169). Elsevier Science.

FIRST-GEN OR WORKING CLASS?

The Politics of Terminology

Sherry Lee Linkon

Working-class studies scholars often complain when researchers use a single aspect of people's lives—most often education—to determine their social class. Any time we define class in one way, we oversimplify it and miss important insights about how class works. Class is too complicated to be captured in one metric, and that is one of its strengths as a category of analysis. Class involves economic and social structures, cultural practices and attitudes, how people understand their place in the world, and how they interact with each other. The slipperiness and complexity of class also explains why it often gets sidelined or misrepresented. As the coordinator of a research center on race and gender once told me, explaining why she didn't highlight class in her project, "Class is just too difficult."

I've been especially troubled by an increasingly widespread version of that difficulty: the adoption of "first-generation (first-gen)" as the dominant way of identifying student services programs aimed at who I would call working-class students. As I have argued in various settings, institutions need to do more than recruit these students or try to make college affordable (something that Goldrick-Rab et al. [2016] argue institutions have not done very well). We also need to help students get the most out of higher education. I'm excited to see more and more schools establishing resource centers, mentoring projects, student groups, and other efforts to help working-class students, many of them students of color, thrive academically and socially. Yet I am troubled that so many of these projects describe their work as serving first-gen students.

To be fair, first-gen has some advantages over working class as a label. While I worry that it focuses on just one element of a student's experience, parents' education often predicts other factors—class, income, race, and immigration status. First-gen also points to two of the challenges working-class students face: feeling out of place and not knowing how to navigate the institution. Students whose parents went to college, and especially the significant number at elite institutions whose parents went to the same college they now attend, often feel a sense of ownership and belonging. They see themselves as having a right to be there, while first-gen students may feel like interlopers, displaced from home as they begin to construct their student lives in the privileged world of the university. Similarly, students whose parents went to college have in-house experts who can provide advice on where to get help and encourage students to feel entitled to ask for help. All of this highlights the significance of cultural capital, which might include familial attitudes about reading and knowledge, travel experiences, exposure to Culture with a capital C, and so on. In this sense, *first-gen* is an accurate and useful term.

First-gen may also be more inclusive and inviting than working-class. Despite evidence that more Americans than we might think identify themselves as working class (see the General Social Survey [n.d.] question on class identification, or a recent Gallup poll [Newport, 2015] suggesting that younger adults are becoming more likely to define themselves as working class), the term also carries negative connotations. In working-class studies courses at Youngstown State University, my mostly working-class students often shied away from using the term—not only to refer to themselves but also to even talk about the writers or subjects of the books we read. Nearly every semester, students explained that they saw working class as an insult. To call someone working class drew attention to their failure to succeed in our supposedly equal-opportunity society. That provided good "teachable moments" that helped us interrogate the meaning of class, but those discussions also taught me why announcing a project as aimed at working-class students often doesn't work. Students don't necessarily define themselves as working class, and some may actively reject that language. This may be especially true for students of color who, given political discourse these days, may reasonably—if inaccurately—hear "working class" as code for "White working class." Similarly, students from rural areas or whose families work in service jobs may assume that working class refers primarily to industrial workers, not to people like them.

First-gen, in contrast, is both clearer—it refers to a single, explicit fact—and relatively neutral. While some raise questions about whether a student counts as first-gen if their parents have some college or if only one of them went to college, for most, it's a straightforward definition, and because it's a fairly new term in higher education and public discourse, it carries almost no baggage. Indeed, for many students, being the first in their family to go to college is a source of pride, while coming from a working-class family is still too often a source of shame.

Nonetheless, first-gen hides some important issues about how class influences students' experiences. In a way, first-gen efforts may go too far in the direction that I and others have advocated, putting the focus on culture and self-efficacy, all in the name of helping working-class students succeed. But that can also mask the sometimes dramatic economic problems that Goldrick-Rab et al. (2016) have identified. I'm sure many first-gen programs acknowledge the economic inequities, and some address them directly, by actively helping students access basic needs like food, housing, winter coats, and so on. Still, I was struck by the words of Emily Loftis (2012), writing about the "anger of a first-generation student" on the Class Action blog a few years ago:

> No one told me about the anger I'd feel when 90% of my class raises their hand when the professor asks who has visited country x, y, and z when I've never left the country. Or how frustrating it feels to have to check my bank account before every purchase while my classmates receive money week after week from parents' seemingly bottomless bank accounts. The anger that springs up when I'm searching for a summer internship because they're all unpaid and I don't have enough experience for the paid ones because I spend my summers working. The anger from spending my holiday breaks cleaning houses while my classmates take trips around the world. (para. 2)

Clearly, Loftis's anger is primarily about money, not her parents' education, and that needs to be part of the campus, political, and public discussions of the challenges working-class students face. Indeed, it may well be money more than culture that accounts for the decline in college attendance among first-gen students, reported by the U.S. Department of Education (Cataldi et al., 2018).

More important, first-gen erases the systemic and collective elements of class. To identify as first-gen is to define oneself based on the specific conditions of one's own family, not of a large and varied group that shares many experiences and whose opportunities are systematically—not incidentally or situationally—constrained. This individualizes students' experiences, functioning perhaps inadvertently to push students into middle-class culture. It also emphasizes the pressure students feel to be the one to lift their families out of their economic marginalization. It defines the problem as individual and temporary, and it suggests that the answer to a family's struggles is individual success, based on education and employment rather than social changes that would enable those who do working-class jobs to have more stable, comfortable lives. To be fair, first-gen projects often work hard to foster a sense of community and shared experience among students, but that solidarity is not necessarily tied to broader social conditions or conflicts. The neutrality of first-gen draws students in, but it does not encourage them to understand and take action against the injustices that shaped their lives.

So I'm torn about first-gen. Because I want students to take advantage of the support that universities can provide, and because I want those programs to engage working-class students from a wide range of backgrounds, I recognize the value of identifying these efforts as aimed at first-gen students. At the same time, I don't want us to lose yet another opportunity to talk about class or to recognize how the commonalities (and differences) of working-class life influence not only students' experiences in college but the lives of their families and their own life paths after graduation.

As bell hooks (2000) wrote in reflecting on her own experience as a first-gen college student at Stanford, class matters. When we erase that, we undermine the possibility for organizing against the economic and political constraints faced by the working-class families first-gen students are leaving behind.

Discussion Questions

1. As instructors, student affairs staff, and researchers, how can we frame our work to make class a more visible part of first-gen efforts?
2. How might first-gen programs help students understand that their experiences reflect not only individual circumstances but also broad social and economic patterns of inequality?
3. How can we equip students to be proactive not only for their individual success but also to change the social conditions that perpetuate inequality? Is this an appropriate goal for first-gen programs?
4. Is it ethical to help a few individuals improve their circumstances without also challenging the political, economic, and social forces that shaped those circumstances?

References

Cataldi, E. F., Bennett, C. T., & Chen, X. (2018). *First-generation students: College access, persistence, and postbachelor's outcomes.* National Center for Education Statistics. https://nces.ed.gov/pubs2018/2018421.pdf

General Social Surveys. (n.d.). *Home page.* gssdataexplorer.norc.org

Goldrick-Rab, S., Anderson, D., & Kinsley, P. (2016). *Paying the price: College costs, financial aid, and the betrayal of the American dream.* University of Chicago Press.

hooks, b. (2000). *Where we stand: Class matters.* Routledge.

Loftis, E. (2012, January 30). *The anger of a first-generation student.* Class Action. https://classism.org/anger-firstgeneration-student/

Newport, F. (2015, April 28). *Fewer Americans identify as middle class in recent years.* Gallup. https://news.gallup.com/poll/182918/fewer-americans-identify-middle-class-recent-years.aspx

4

BACKGROUND CHARACTERISTICS OF FIRST-GENERATION STUDENTS AND THEIR REASONS FOR PURSUING HIGHER EDUCATION

Khanh Bui

First-generation college students are those whose parents have not attended college (Billson & Terry, 1982). Most of these students start college at a 2-year institution rather than a 4-year institution. For example, in a nationally representative sample of 2002 high school sophomores who had enrolled in postsecondary education by 2012, among first-generation college students, 52% of them first attended a 2-year institution (Redford & Hoyer, 2017, Figure 4). They tend to start at 2-year institutions for various reasons, including (a) their academic preparation is not competitive enough to gain admission to a 4-year institution, (b) they cannot afford the tuition costs at a 4-year institution, or (c) they need the flexibility of class schedules at a 2-year institution to meet their other responsibilities as workers, spouses, or parents (see Zwerling & London, 1992).

Research, however, has shown that first-generation students have a better chance of earning a bachelor's degree if they start postsecondary education at a 4-year college or university rather than a 2-year college. For example, statistics from the National Center for Education Statistics (Cataldi et al., 2018) show that, among first-generation college students who started higher education during the 2003–2004 academic year, 65% of them had attained a degree or were still enrolled in college if they had started at a 4-year college or university; in contrast, only 49% of them had attained a degree or were still enrolled in college if they had started at a public 2-year college.

Surprisingly, little research has been done on the background characteristics of first-generation college students at 4-year institutions. The few empirical studies that have been conducted on these students have mainly examined topics such as their risk of attrition (Billson & Terry, 1982; Pratt & Skaggs, 1989), their personality characteristics (McGregor et al., 1991), their relationships with their families (London, 1989), their academic preparation and first-year performance (Riehl, 1994), and their cognitive development (Terenzini et al., 1996; these researchers also included community college students among their participants).

The current study contributes to the literature on first-generation college students by focusing on those who start their higher education at a 4-year university. More specifically, this study examined (a) the background characteristics of these students, (b) their reasons for pursuing higher education, and (c) their first-year experiences. Their responses were compared to those of students whose parents had at least a bachelor's degree and to those of students whose parents had some college experience but no degrees. Such analyses can identify challenges that are particular to first-generation college students and inform offices of student support services of the kinds of assistance that these students need to succeed at a 4-year institution.

Methodology

Participants

First-generation college students (n = 64) were recruited from the Program Leading to Undergraduate Success at the University of California, Los Angeles (UCLA). This program serves first-generation college students by providing professional academic counseling, informal peer counseling, and academic tutoring. Students who volunteered for this study had their names put in a lottery drawing for gift certificates to the student store.

Participants from the comparison groups came from the UCLA introductory psychology participant pool. One comparison group consisted of students whose parents had at least a bachelor's degree (n = 68), and the other comparison group consisted of students whose parents had some college experience but no degrees (n = 75). Students in the comparison groups participated in this study for course credit.

All participants were in the third quarter of their first year at UCLA. See Table 4.1 for additional demographic information about the participants.

TABLE 4.1
Students' Background Characteristics by College Generation

Variable	College Generation			Test for differences among groups
	First generation (n = 64)	Parents have some college but no degree (n = 75)	Both parents have at least bachelor's degrees (n = 68)	
Gender				$\chi^2(2) = 1.34, p = .51$
Female	54.69 %	48.00 %	57.35 %	
Male	45.31 %	52.00 %	42.65 %	
Age				$F(2, 204) = .46, p = .63$
Mean	18.56	18.65	18.59	
Standard deviation	.61	.56	.58	
Ethnicity				$\chi^2(8) = 38.95, p < .001$
White	7.81 %	17.33 %	38.24 %	
Black	0.00 %	8.00 %	1.47 %	
Latino	31.25 %	20.00 %	2.94 %	
Asian	53.13 %	45.33 %	51.47 %	
Other	7.81 %	9.33 %	5.88 %	
Socioeconomic status				$\chi^2(10) = 76.32, p < .001$
Poor	14.06 %	6.67 %	0.00 %	
Working class	39.06 %	13.33 %	5.88 %	
Lower middle	20.31 %	20.00 %	11.76 %	
Middle middle	17.19 %	45.33 %	26.47 %	
Upper middle	9.38 %	13.33 %	47.06 %	
Upper	0.00 %	1.33 %	8.82 %	
Home language				$\chi^2(8) = 29.86, p < .001$
English only	7.81 %	30.67 %	36.76 %	
Mostly English	14.06 %	21.33 %	27.94 %	

(Continues)

TABLE 4.1 *(Continued)*

Variable	College Generation			Test for differences among groups
	First generation (n = 64)	*Parents have some college but no degree (n = 75)*	*Both parents have at least bachelor's degrees (n = 68)*	
Half English and half other	31.25 %	24.00 %	20.59 %	
Mostly other	35.94 %	20.00 %	10.29 %	
Other only	10.94 %	4.00 %	4.41 %	
SAT scores				
Verbal section				$F(2, 198) = 19.44, p < .001$
Mean	458.20	508.65	560.76	
Standard deviation	91.39	92.47	94.04	
Quantitative section				$F(2, 198) = 7.20, p < .005$
Mean	576.07	611.01	644.24	
Standard deviation	103.90	103.79	95.35	

Measures

A questionnaire was used for this study. The questionnaire assessed students' background information, their reasons for attending college, and their first-year experiences. The questionnaire also included other measures that are not relevant to this report.

Background Characteristics

In addition to answering standard demographic questions (gender, age, ethnic identity, and socioeconomic status), students reported the language spoken at home and their SAT scores.

Reasons for Pursuing Higher Education

Students indicated how important 16 reasons were to them in their decision to enroll in college. The reasons included familial expectations, financial goals, and career goals (see the first column of Table 4.2 for a complete list of the reasons). For each reason, students indicated their assessment of how

TABLE 4.2

Means (and Standard Deviations) for Reasons for Pursuing Higher Education by College Generation

Reason	College Generation			Univariate F-value
	First generation (n = 62)	Parents have some college but no degrees (n = 75)	Both parents have at least bachelor's degrees (n = 65)	
1. My friends were going to college.	2.55 (1.86)	2.37 (1.64)	2.72 (1.71)	.71
2. My siblings or other relatives were going (or went) to college.	2.53 (1.80)	2.56 (1.94)	3.52 (2.08)	5.56**,a
3. My parents wanted/expected me to go to college.	5.35 (1.79)	5.33 (1.70)	5.48 (1.80)	.13
4. My high school teachers/counselor persuaded me to go to college.	2.97 (1.83)	2.71 (1.80)	2.65 (1.77)	.58
5. I need a college degree to achieve my career goal(s).	6.81 (.57)	6.36 (1.27)	6.46 (1.37)	2.77
6. I wanted to earn a better income with a college degree.	6.65 (.99)	6.36 (1.11)	6.18 (1.33)	2.57
7. I want(ed) to gain respect/status by having a college degree.	6.21 (1.31)	5.56 (1.65)	5.60 (1.67)	3.54*,b
8. I want(ed) to bring honor to my family.	6.00 (1.40)	5.37 (1.75)	5.03 (1.91)	5.24**,b

9. I want(ed) to help my family out after I'm done with college.	6.27 (1.45)	5.88 (1.54)	4.49 (2.17)	18.60***,a
10. I like to learn/study.	5.32 (1.54)	5.09 (1.60)	5.31 (1.69)	.45
11. I want(ed) to provide a better life for my own children.	6.53 (1.00)	6.27 (1.21)	6.05 (1.43)	2.48
12. I wanted to gain my independence.	5.45 (1.65)	5.27 (1.88)	5.74 (1.41)	1.40
13. I wanted to move out of my parents' home.	2.98 (1.92)	3.68 (2.22)	4.35 (1.92)	7.17**,b
14. I want(ed) to acquire skills to function effectively in society.	5.89 (1.40)	5.56 (1.67)	5.40 (1.74)	1.49
15. I wanted to get out of my parents' neighborhood.	2.21 (1.64)	2.69 (1.93)	2.43 (1.79)	1.24
16. I did not want to work immediately after high school.	3.10 (2.12)	2.99 (2.23)	3.26 (1.81)	.31

Note. Students indicated how important each reason was in their decision to enroll in college on a 7-point rating scale ranging from 1(*not at all important*) to 7 (*extremely important*). For the univariate *F*-tests, $df_{bm} = 2$ and $df_{wm} = 199$.

$*p < .05, **p < .01, ***p < .001$

[a] The mean for first-generation college students is significantly different from the mean for students whose parents have at least a bachelor's.

[b] The mean for first-generation college students is significantly different from both the mean for students whose parents have at least a bachelor's and the mean for students whose parents have some college experience but no degrees.

important the reason was for them on a 7-point scale ranging from 1 (*not at all important*) to 7 (*extremely important*).

First-Year Experiences

Students indicated how true each of 10 experiences was for them. The experiences included fearing failure at their university, worrying about financial aid, and feeling accepted at their university (see the first column of Table 4.3 for a complete list of the experiences). For each experience, students indicated their assessment of how true the experience was for them on a 7-point scale ranging from 1 (*not at all true*) to 7 (*completely true*).

Procedure

Participants completed the questionnaire in groups of three to 12 students in either a conference room or a lab room.

Results

Background Characteristics

As shown in Table 4.1, first-generation college students were more likely to be ethnic minority students, to come from a lower socioeconomic background, to speak a language other than English at home, and to score lower on the SAT than were the other students.

Reasons for Pursuing Higher Education

A multivariate analysis of variance showed that the three groups differed overall in their reasons for attending college, $F(32, 370) = 2.52$, $p < .001$. Follow-up univariate tests showed that the differences arose for five reasons. As shown in Table 4.2, first-generation college students gave lower ratings of importance to the following reasons than did the students whose parents had at least a bachelor's degree: Their siblings or other relatives were going (or went) to college and they wanted to move out of their parents' home. In contrast, they gave higher ratings of importance for the reasons of gaining respect/status, bringing honor to their family, and helping their family out financially after they are done with college.

For the remaining 11 reasons, however, first-generation college students did not differ from the other two groups in their ratings of the importance of those reasons in their decision to attend college. In other words, the three groups gave similar ratings of importance for the following reasons: Their friends were going to college, their parents expected them to go to college, their high school teachers/counselor persuaded them to go, they wanted a college degree to achieve their career goals, they wanted a better income with a college degree, they liked to learn, they wanted to provide a better life for their own children, they wanted to gain their independence, they wanted to acquire skills to function effectively in society, they wanted to get out of their parents' neighborhood, and they did not want to work immediately after high school.

First-Year Experiences

A multivariate analysis of variance showed that the three groups differed overall in their first-year experiences, $F(20, 390) = 2.67, p < .001$. Follow-up univariate tests showed that the differences arose specifically in five areas. As shown in Table 4.3, first-generation college students felt less prepared for college and worried more about financial aid in comparison to the other students. They feared failing in college more than did the students whose parents had at least a bachelor's degree. They reported knowing less about the social environment at the university than did the other students (as did York-Anderson & Bowman, 1991). Finally, they felt that they had to put more time into studying than did the other students.

For the remaining five areas of experiences, however, first-generation college students did not differ from the other two groups in their ratings of how true the experiences were for them. More specifically, first-generation college students were not different from the other students in their reports of feeling comfortable making decisions related to college on their own, knowing about the academic programs at their university prior to enrollment, making friends at their university, enjoying being a student at their university, and feeling accepted at their university.

Discussion

More and more students whose parents have not attended college are pursuing higher education (Levine, 1989). Most of these first-generation college students attend 2-year institutions rather than 4-year institutions (Redford & Hoyer, 2017). However, first-generation college students who start at 4-year institutions are more likely to earn their bachelor's degree than are those who start at 2-year institutions (National Center for Education Statistics, 2000). Systematic knowledge about first-generation college students who start higher education at 4-year institutions would help these institutions to better facilitate these students' success.

The results of this study show that first-generation college students who have enrolled in a competitive 4-year university are demographically different

TABLE 4.3

First-Year Experiences by College Generation

Experience	College Generation			Univariate F-value
	First generation (n = 63)	Parents have some college but no degrees (n = 75)	Both parents have at least bachelor's degrees (n = 68)	
1. I am equally prepared for college as other students are.	4.03 (1.73)	4.63 (1.62)	4.69 (1.53)	3.23*,b
2. I am afraid of failing in college.	5.52 (1.79)	4.68 (2.04)	4.34 (2.04)	6.19**,b
3. I feel comfortable making most decisions related to college on my own.	4.84 (1.61)	4.89 (1.87)	4.97 (1.51)	.10
4. I worry a lot about financial aid and/or money for school.	4.90 (2.12)	4.71 (2.08)	3.60 (2.31)	7.03**,a
5. I knew a lot about the academic programs at UCLA before coming to this school.	2.90 (1.67)	2.77 (1.61)	2.75 (1.47)	.19
6. I knew a lot about the social environment at UCLA before coming to this school.	2.57 (1.48)	3.15 (1.66)	3.25 (1.63)	3.44*,b
7. It is easy for me to make friends at UCLA.	4.21 (1.75)	4.73 (1.66)	4.19 (1.75)	2.29
8. I like being a student at UCLA.	5.52 (1.35)	5.59 (1.43)	5.55 (1.48)	.03
9. I feel I have to put more time into studying than other students do because my high school did not prepare me well for college.	4.71 (1.91)	3.52 (2.05)	3.40 (2.05)	8.50***,b

(*Continues*)

TABLE 4.3 (*Continued*)

Experience	College Generation			Univariate F-value
	First generation (n = 63)	Parents have some college but no degrees (n = 75)	Both parents have at least bachelor's degrees (n = 68)	
10. Overall, I feel accepted at UCLA.	4.97 (1.31)	5.20 (1.46)	5.25 (1.39)	.77

Note. Students indicated to what extent each experience was true for them on a 7-point rating scale ranging from 1(*not at all true*) to 7 (*completely true*). For the univariate F-tests, df_{bn} = 2 and df_{wn} = 203.

*$p < .05$, ** $p < .01$, *** $p < .001$

[a] The mean for first-generation college students is significantly different from the mean for students whose parents have at least a bachelor's.

[b] The mean for first-generation college students is significantly different from both the mean for students whose parents have at least a bachelor's and the mean for students whose parents have some college experience but no degrees.

from students whose parents have had some college experience or whose parents have actually earned at least a bachelor's degree. More specifically, they are more likely to be ethnic minority students, to come from a lower socioeconomic background, and to speak a language other than English at home.

These demographic differences are reflected in several differences in their reasons for pursuing higher education. For example, pursuing higher education so that they can later help out their families is a more important reason for first-generation college students than it is for students whose parents have at least some college experience.

In addition, the demographic differences between the first-generation college students and the other students are reflected in several of their first-year experiences. For example, in comparison to the other students, first-generation college students express greater fear of failing in college, worry more about financial aid, and feel they have to put more time into studying.

Nonetheless, first-generation college students do not differ from the later-generation college students in some key areas. For example, they are similar in terms of feeling comfortable making decisions related to college on their own, knowing about the academic programs at their university prior to enrollment, and feeling accepted at their university.

It may be that the admission criteria at a competitive 4-year university are high enough that first-generation college students who gain admission and enroll are more similar to other students at such a university in their motivation for and knowledge about attending college. Nonetheless, first-generation college students are more concerned about certain issues, such as financial aid and helping their parents out after they are done with college.

Campus support programs for these students can foster their success by offering services that specifically address the concerns for these students. For example, financial aid counselors can help them (and their parents) with the daunting array of financial aid applications (Kane, 1999). In addition, professional and peer counselors can help them handle the social-emotional issues related to attending college. For example, some first-generation college students may feel guilty about pursuing higher education while their families are struggling financially to survive (Levine, 1989; Piorkowski, 1983). Given that the demands at a 4-year university are usually rigorous, first-generation college students can use all the assistance that their university can give them to persist and graduate. Society benefits from their graduating because there are no statistically significant differences in full-time employment rates or median annualized salaries 4 years after earning a bachelor's degree when comparing first-generation graduates to graduates whose parents have some college education or to graduates whose parents have at least a bachelor's degree (Cataldi et al., 2018).

References

Billson, J. M., & Terry, M. B. (1982). In search of the silken purse: Factors in attrition among first-generation students. *College and University, 58*(1), 57–75.

Cataldi, E. F., Bennett, C. T., & Chen, X.. (2018). First-generation students: College access, persistence, and postbachelor's outcomes. *Stats in Brief* (NCES 2018-421). National Center for Education Statistics. https://nces.ed.gov/pubs2018/2018421.pdf

Kane, T. J. (1999). *The price of admission: Rethinking how Americans pay for college.* Brookings Institution.

Levine, A. (1989). *Shaping higher education's future: Demographic realities and opportunities, 1990–2000.* Jossey-Bass.

London, H. B. (1989). Breaking away: A study of first-generation college students and their families. *American Journal of Education, 97*(2), 144–170. https://doi.org/10.1086/443919

McGregor, L. N., Mayleben, M. A., Buzzanga, V. L., Davis, S. F., & Becker, A. H. (1991). Selected personality characteristics of first-generation college students. *College Student Journal, 25*(2), 231–234.

National Center for Education Statistics. (2000). *Digest of education statistics 1999* (NCES 2000-031). https://nces.ed.gov/pubs2000/2000031.pdf

Piorkowski, G. K. (1983). Survivor guilt in the university setting. *The Personnel and Guidance Journal, 61*(10), 620–622. https://doi.org/10.1111/j.2164-4918.1983.tb00010.x

Pratt, P. A., & Skaggs, C. T. (1989). First generation college students: Are they at greater risk for attrition than their peers? *Research in Rural Education, 6*(2), 31–34. https://jrre.psu.edu/sites/default/files/2019-07/6-2_5.pdf

Redford, J., & Hoyer, K. M. (2017). *First-generation and continuing-generation college students: A comparison of high school and postsecondary experiences* (NCES 2018-009). National Center for Education Statistics. https://nces.ed.gov/pubs2018/2018009.pdf

Riehl, R. J. (1994). The academic preparation, aspirations, and first-year performance of first-generation students. *College and University, 70*(1), 14–19.

Terenzini, P. T., Springer, L, Yaeger, P. M., Pascarella, E. T., & Nora, A. (1996). First-generation college students: Characteristics, experiences, and cognitive development. *Research in Higher Education, 37*(1), 1–22.

York-Anderson, D. C., & Bowman, S. L. (1991). Assessing the college knowledge of first-generation and second-generation college students. *Journal of College Student Development, 32*, 116–122.

Zwerling, L. S., & London, H. B. (1992). *First-generation students: Confronting the cultural issues*. Jossey-Bass.

5

MESSAGE RECEIVED

Parental Encouragement and Its Effect on the College-Choice Process

Michael J. Smith

W hen it comes to education, it has always been the case that low-socioeconomic status (SES) youth have been marginalized, but today that marginalization is coupled with a climate that in many circles is decidedly anti-immigrant, anti-Latinx and anti-Black (Smith, 2001). With the election of Donald Trump in 2016 the national mood regarding higher education characterizes the entire enterprise as part of the "liberal elites" (Tomasky, 2017). Indeed, conservative politicians and pundits across the board have whipped up sentiments that link diversity to affirmative action and both to alleged reverse discrimination against White and in some cases Asian American college applicants (Levitz, 2018).

Given these recent developments and the pervasive "Make America Great Again" (MAGA) or the "America First" climate that is linked to anti-minority sentiments, it is even more important that researchers and practitioners alike find ways to more aggressively nurture and recruit talented, promising African American first-generation college students. It is even more important to find ways to support those students who were raised in the low-income, single-parent homes that are so frequently a part of today's African American communities.

In earlier work I advocated for encouraging parental involvement as a way to fight against the aforementioned marginalization (Smith, 2008, 2009). If the higher education community could find ways to support the parents of low-income African American high school students, it is quite possible to increase their children's participation in college and fight against today's toxic national anti–African American climate. Understanding the experiences of low SES

Black single female parents can inform the outreach approaches taken by colleges and universities to increase parental involvement in their children's college preparation and college-choice process. This paper describes the findings of a study that used a qualitative approach to explore how three Black single parents experienced involvement from their own parents during their K–12 years.

The study is guided by the following questions: "What were the messages that these low-SES Black women received about the value of education?" and "How were these women encouraged and to what end?"

Methodology

This study of three urban working-class Black single mothers emerged from a larger ethnographic study of how 12 urban Black mothers of college-bound teenaged daughters experienced the college-choice process. The three single mothers chosen for this study were themselves raised by low-SES, minimally educated parents who moved to California or encouraged their children to move to California as a way to escape a life of poverty in the South, Northeast, or Midwest. The three single mothers, all of whom have been assigned pseudonyms, may alternately be referred to as "the Three" for the remainder of this chapter when referring to the collective group.

Data Collection

The Three were asked to reflect back on their childhood to recount (a) their parent's level of education; (b) why they or their families migrated to California; (c) how their neighborhood and schools were chosen; (d) the messages they received from their parents about the core value and utility of education; (e) the frequency of their interaction with college degree holders; and (f) their opinions, doubts, and fears about college education and those who were college educated (the interview protocol is located in Appendix 5A). After the interviews were completed they were transcribed, analyzed using grounded theory, and verified by sharing with each the transcriptions of their interviews (Glaser & Strauss, 1999; Strauss & Corbin, 1998).

"The Three": Profiles of Three African American, Urban, Single Mothers

Lena, Kim, and Kathy are three African American single parents whose daughters were in their junior year of high school. What follows is a brief synopsis of my conversations with them during the data collection time of this study.

Lena

At the time of our interviews, Lena's daughter was a senior at Airport High School, a good 30 minutes east of where her mother worked as an administrative assistant in what is called the Mid-Wilshire area of Los Angeles. Lena attended high school in the late 1960s and in what was a predominantly Black area on the border of South-Central Los Angeles. She took some college classes at the local community college. Her father and mother migrated from Louisiana to Los Angeles in the 1950s, in order to pursue career opportunities for themselves and educational opportunities for their children in California. They chose the area they grew up in ostensibly because of their Black population; however, a closer examination of Los Angeles history in the 1950s would reveal that Blacks were channeled toward this area due to extreme housing segregation in other parts of the city. Lena came from a large family. She was one of seven children and one of five girls. We met on three occasions at a Starbucks close to her work, one of the many franchised by former professional basketball player Earvin "Magic" Johnson as part of an effort to accelerate economic development in the Black community.

Kim

Kim was a manager for a program providing services for Black women and Latinas in the same area that Lena grew up, a suburb on the border of South-Central Los Angeles. Like Lena, her 11th-grade daughter attended Airport High School and was college bound. For Kim, college was a goal dreamed of, but one she was unable to pursue. Her parents were separated, but both lived in the Los Angeles area after relocating from Mississippi in the 1960s. Kim's mother made the decision that, although they were separated, it was useful to have the children in the same city as their birth father. Being in the same city as her biological father made it possible to share childcare responsibilities while strengthening the bond between daughter and father. Kim went to high school in the 1970s when government programs like the Comprehensive Employment and Training Act (CETA) (which encouraged summer work for low-income youth) were the norm; she took full advantage of these programs; completed high school; and attempted, but did not finish, community college.

Kathy

Kathy's mother dropped out of high school in the 10th grade, and her father only completed the 5th grade. Accordingly, it is understandable that both of Kathy's parents spent their lives working in a Midwestern factory similar to General Motors (they worked in Indiana). When Kathy was 13 years old, her dad disappeared, effectively creating a single-parent family led by her mother. Kathy finished high school in Indiana; married a man enlisted in the U.S. Army; and, after a divorce, moved to Los Angeles to find economic opportunity and better schooling for her two daughters. Kathy worked as an administrative assistant in the counseling center for Airport High School, the school that her 11th-grade daughter attended. While never a college student herself, as a parent she was not a novice to the college-choice process. Her second daughter was an alumna of a historically Black college.

Invoking a Negative Educational Role Model: Parents Say "Don't Be Like Me!"

As noted by many scholars, the parents of African American and other racial and ethnic minorities who have no college experience believe that education can open doors for their children that were closed for them. As a result, they do everything they can to make this possible, up to and often including participation in their child's education (Chavkin, 1989; Chavkin & Williams, 1993; Freeman, 2005). This was the experience of the Three, who shared their stories about their parents' attitudes toward the value of education expressed to them while they were K–12 students. In working poor or poverty-stricken communities, the norms for educational aspirations are centered on earning a high school degree. As children, the Three were exposed to ideas about education that were consistent with the poverty-stricken, predominantly Black communities where they resided. That a high school diploma was seen as the best preparation for living-wage careers was explained by one of the three women, who said that such values were "just the generation I grew up in; I think all the neighborhoods felt the same way back then."

That single mother was Lena who is currently an administrative assistant in the field of business office maintenance after finishing high school and enrolling in college, even though she did not receive a degree. Prior to this work she was an administrative assistant in the insurance field. Lena's parents required that she and her siblings obtain the level of education sufficient to earn wages that would make it possible to maintain a living wage and raise a family. She cites her dad as being particularly supportive of his children's educational endeavors:

My dad's [educational expectation] was the highest. I mean he wanted you to go as far as you could and achieve as much as you could. And my mother too but it just I don't think the value that she put on education was as strong as my dad's. . . . But my dad always knew that education would take you anywhere in life you wanted to go and, uh, that was his, uh, he wanted that for all of his kids . . . all seven of us. . . . I remember when I came out of high school, business administration [i.e., secretarial work] is something women sought after. Well this is just the generation I grew up in; I think all the neighborhoods felt the same way back then.

Lena's father and to some extent her mother believed that education would adequately prepare her and her siblings for the challenges of the world and provide a lifetime of employment. Similar to what the students in Freeman's (2005) work had said about their parents, Lena's working-class parents wanted her and her siblings to exceed their own highest level of education attainment (see Table 5.1).

Kim's mother understood that with more education came more opportunity and a life with vocational options beyond the backbreaking jobs she held as a manual laborer in the cotton fields of Mississippi. Kim's mother was well aware that the life she led was a consequence of her 3rd-grade education and her family's dire economic condition, where every able-bodied person needed to work the cotton fields in order to keep a roof over their heads. Not wanting this future for her children, Kim's mother moved the family to California and enrolled them into the state's superior public K–12 system. All the while she insisted that Kim and her siblings earn high school

TABLE 5.1
Educational Attainment of the Three and Their Parents

Participant's Name	Participant's Childhood Family	Where Raised	Participant's Highest Level of Education	Participant's Parents' Level of Education
Kim	1 parent (mother)	Urban, CA	High school Diploma	Third grade (mom)
Lena	1 parent (mother) (father)	Urban, CA	High school Diploma	Fifth grade (mom); 12th grade (dad)
Kathy	1 parent (mother but dad still involved)	Rural, IN	High school Diploma	Tenth grade (mom); third grade (dad)

diplomas in order to escape the drudgery of farm labor, using her work life as the example of what not to be, invoking a negative educational role model to help her children. Her exhortation is similar in content but slightly different to what Freeman (2005) described as Black teenagers' tendency toward self-motivation for college by "avoidance of a negative role model" (p. 18). Whereas Freeman spoke of a low-SES, college-bound Black teenager having the agency to motivate themselves with examples of what minimal education does to a person's quality of life, these parents used their own life stories and narratives of hard times to inspire their children to do better. Kim's mother provides a powerful example of how this strategy was employed.

> Her main focus [for us] was graduating from high school. You know, so you just make sure that you get a high school diploma. She really, she really, she felt it was important. Because she wanted to go to school and couldn't because she had to work in the fields and different things like that so, so she wanted us to make sure that we took advantage of it.

In order for Kim's mother to use this well-thought-out and persistent strategy she had to be consistent and "on message." Rather than passively hoping her children would avoid her fate, she aggressively pushed education and empowered her children to believe that they could "do anything that [the children] want to do." Kim told me that "education as far as college, that wasn't a big thing in the house; just [the] high school diploma." Like Lena and her siblings, Kim and her siblings were taught that education was preparation for a higher quality of life through a more desirable vocation: work that paid more and taxed the body less. This level of education had visible, concrete financial and experiential pay-off, which is why the diploma became a goal that Kim's mother wholly supported.

Kathy heard similar things from her father and mother. Like Lena and Kim, Kathy's parents inspired her to be a high school graduate as she was implored to work hard in school so that she could earn the right to work under more desirable conditions than they did. Her mother and father worked grueling hours in a rural Indiana industrial factory and wanted nothing more than for her and her siblings to not do the same.

> Well, my father, he always told us to make sure we finish high school because he did not want us in a factory . . . like him. And that's what we did. Well, they just; they never really spoke about college. Again, they just always told us we would have to complete high school. We would have to get that diploma no matter what. That's all they talked about, finishing high school.

Her father and mother were strong advocates of education because they understood that their limited vocational opportunities at the factory were a result of their never having finished high school. As Kathy noted,

> My father quit his education as a 5th grader and my mother, she ended her education as a 10th grader in high school . . . that was really the main reason they were telling us to "complete your high school, complete your high school" because, you know, you're gonna end up in a factory [if you don't].

The foregoing comment is another example of one of the Three's parents aggressively promoting education by using harsh life experience to expose the dire consequences of not finishing high school. But like Kim, for Kathy's parents, college never entered the dialogue as it seemed a faraway dream. Kathy explained that to her parents "college was so expensive they knew they were not able to afford college so they just wanted to make sure we completed high school." This is very similar to what scholars have learned about Black student sensitivity to college costs and the distortion of college costs in their mind that come from a lack of college knowledge about scholarships and grants (McDonough & Calderone, 2006; St. John et al., 2005; Vargas, 2004).

For all of the women in this study, a high school diploma was the acceptable level of academic achievement and job preparation in the eyes of their parents. Additionally, education was promoted as a way to avoid a life of heavy labor and low wages. Since all of the women I interviewed are high school graduates who have gone on to full employment and single-parenthood, their parent's efforts could be considered a success given what they understood about education and work. What can we learn from their lives that can instruct us about how to help today's generation of low-income, working, poor parents target college as part of their children's education and postsecondary planning?

Discussion: College Choice Theory and the Involvement of a Past Generation of Low-SES Black Parents

The findings from this study seem to support what other college choice and education access and equity theorists state about the way families influence the college choice process. Each of the Three moved from childhood, through their teens, and into adulthood with solid support from their parents to exceed their level of education. Each of the women spoke of how their parents wanted them to earn a high school diploma since all but one parent (Lena's father) had failed in this regard. The findings also seem to support the ways in which poverty and race combine to discourage or conceal college aspirations from loving and well-meaning parents (Baum & Flores, 2011; Perez & McDonough, 2008). The parent's encouragement to not "be like [me]" has everything to do with the struggles they constantly faced as Americans with minimal education but also as Americans from a historically marginalized ethnic group. A similar point was made 26 years ago by Staples and Johnson's (1993) review of the literature around low-SES Black parents that found "a large proportion of Black lower income mothers and fathers not only hope that their children will attend college, but spend time discussing educational options with them" (pp. 175–176). It strongly supports college choice theorist Freeman's (2005) assertions that although Blacks value education as an important part of upward mobility, economic and sociocultural realities/barriers cause working, poor parents to send conflicting signals to their children about college aspirations. Overall, Freeman (2005) found that Black parents encourage their children to "go beyond their own level of schooling" (p. 17), which is an important signal sent during what college choice theorist Hossler calls the "predisposition stage" of college choice where the goals of college attendance are born (Hossler & Gallagher, 1987; Hossler et al., 1989, 1998).

As part of the effort to encourage their children to achieve academically, the Three recalled that their parents actively discouraged them from following their own failed educational journeys. Their encouragement varies slightly from what Freeman (2005) described as "avoidance of a negative role model" (p. 18). This study found that parents invoked the negative role model themselves by encouraging their children to make the kind of educational and career choices available with a high school education as opposed to dropping out of high school as they had done many years before. Findings from this study suggest that this process may be a positive example of parental involvement in the predisposition stage of college choice.

Finally, as suggested by Freeman (2005), this study shows that the parents of the Three did not have critical information about how to prepare for, apply to, and eventually enroll in college, nor information about how it could be funded. Kathy's parents, in particular, stated that "college was so expensive" and believed it was something "they [she and her parents] were not able to afford" even during a time of generous federal and state financial aid during the early 1970s. Simply stated, this information needs to reach all levels of the Black community, most particularly those members who comprise the lowest economic strata.

Conclusions and Implications for Practice

This qualitative inquiry of three African American single parents, combined with empirical research from higher education access/equity and college-choice theorists, helps us understand the educational experiences of urban, low-income, African American single mothers to help us build better intervention for the African American single mothers of today. This information could also be used to shed light on how low-income parents of other groups of low-SES, marginalized people appreciate the value of education in creating better life outcomes for their children. Most importantly the experiences of the three women of this study should inform the kind of outreach that would be most effective in converting educational aspirations from high school diplomas to college degrees, preferably a 4-year degree but inclusive of a 2-year associate degree. Essentially, the findings support the notion that these parents want their children to succeed but need assistance with making college a desirable postsecondary option for their children.

So how is this accomplished in an environment generally hostile to the condition of low-income African Americans? How can we prioritize college participation rates for impoverished or working, poor Black families when the top 1% of the wealthiest American citizens make 26.3 times as much income as a family in the bottom 99% (Sommeiller & Price, 2008)? In this era of expanding economic inequality where low-income Americans of all descriptions struggle to find living-wage opportunities, what approaches will effectively encourage hope for a better future for their children, but also convince our lowest income families that college is "worth it" in the face of a seemingly nationwide campaign to the contrary? How do we assert that we as a higher education community will be their allies against the "America First," "MAGA," "anti-immigration," and "anti-Black" national mood where affirmative action and other outreach tools are seen as an arm of "liberal elites" and evidence of "reverse discrimination" against Whites and some Asian Americans (Taylor, 2018)?

I have argued in the past that there are four steps that the academy can take to embrace a paradigm more inclusive to low-SES African American parents and their children (Smith, 2008). First, I still believe that through aggressive, unified, and consistent intervention efforts the higher education community can help first-generation, low-SES African American students and their parents be involved in the college choice process in ways that acknowledge the variety of barriers (structural, race, class, financial) that prevent them from full involvement/participation while making every effort to help them negotiate these barriers. Second, once created, all interventions must begin with the assumption that these parents want to support their children's educational attainment as a way to improve their quality of life regardless of the end goal (college or other postsecondary options). Third, a consistent effort should be made to convert this interest into college choice process participation by dispensing "college knowledge," especially in the arena of financial aid and understanding college costs. Fourth, the higher education community must embrace this population of parents and their children, performing outreach for the common good. When it concerns college choice, the fate of low-SES Black parents and their children depends on how badly we wish to reach out to, embrace, and become partners in the college choice process.

A study conducted by Gandara et al. (2005) not so long ago suggested that "skyrocketing tuition, shrinking capacity, and the demise of affirmative action in some states have all taken a toll on the hopes and dreams of many youth who are low income and minority" (p. 255). The higher education community needs to more effectively reach out to these families, and then embrace them as partners in the college choice process.

References

Baum, S., & Flores, S. M. (2011). Higher education and children in immigrant families. *The Future of Children, 21*(1), 171–193. https://doi.org/10.1353/foc.2011.0000

Chavkin, N. F. (1989). Debunking the myth about minority parents. *Educational Horizons, 67*(4), 119–123.

Chavkin, N. F., & Williams, D. L. (1993). Minority parents and the elementary school: Attitudes and practices. In N. F. Chavkin (Ed.), *Families and schools in a pluralistic society* (pp. 73–83). State University of New York Press.

Freeman, K. (2005). *African Americans and college choice: The influence of family and school.* State University of New York Press.

Gandara, P., Horn, C., & Orfield, G. (2005). The access crisis in higher education. *Educational Policy, 19*(2), 255–261. https://doi.org/10.1177/0895904804274060

Glaser, B. G., & Strauss A. L. (1999). *The discovery of grounded theory: Strategies for qualitative research.* Aldine De Gruyter.

Hossler, D., Braxton, J., & Coopersmith, G. (1989). Understanding student college choice. In J. C. Smart (Ed.), *Higher education: Handbook of theory and research* (Vol. 5) (pp. 231–288). Agathon.

Hossler, D., & Gallagher, K. S. (1987). Studying student college choice: A three-phase model and the implications for policymakers. *College and University, 62*(3), 207–221.

Hossler, D., Schmit, J., & Vesper, N. (1998). *Going to college: How social economic, and educational factors influence the decisions students make.* Johns Hopkins University Press.

Levitz, E. (2018, July 3). Trump administration calls on colleges to end affirmative action. *New York Magazine Intelligencer*. http://nymag.com/intelligencer/2018/07/trump-administration-calls-for-end-to-affirmative-action.html

McDonough, P. M., & Calderone, S. (2006). The meaning of money: Perceptual differences between college counselors and low-income families about college costs and financial aid. *American Behavioral Scientist, 49*(12), 1–16. https://doi.org/10.1177/0002764206289140

Perez, P. A., & McDonough, P. M. (2008). Understanding Latina and Latino college choice: A social capital and chain migration analysis. *Journal of Hispanic Higher Education, 7*(3), 249–265. https://doi.org/10.1177/1538192708317620

St. John, E. P., Paulsen, M. B., & Carter, D. F. (2005). Diversity, college costs, and postsecondary opportunity: An examination of the financial nexus between college choice and persistence for African Americans and Whites. *Journal of Higher Education, 76*(5), 545–569. https://doi.org/10.1080/00221546.2005.11772298

Smith, M. J. (2001). Low SES Black college choice: Playing on an unlevel playing field. *Journal of College Admission, 171*, 16–21.

Smith, M. J. (2008). College choice process of first-generation Black female students: Encouraged to what end? *The Negro Educational Review, 59*(3–4), 147–162.

Smith, M. J. (2009). Right directions, wrong maps: Understanding the involvement of low SES African American parents to enlist them as partners in college choice. *Education & Urban Society, 41*(2), 171–196. https://doi.org/10.1177/0013124508324028

Sommeiller, E., & Price, M. (2018, July 18). *The new gilded age: Income inequality in the U.S. by state, metropolitan area, and county*. Economic Policy Institute. https://www.epi.org/publication/the-new-gilded-age-income-inequality-in-the-u-s-by-state-metropolitan-area-and-county/

Staples, R., & Johnson, L. B. (1993). *Black families at the crossroads: Challenges and prospects*. Jossey-Bass.

Strauss, A. L., & Corbin, J. (1998). *Basics of qualitative research: Techniques and procedures for developing grounded theory* (2nd ed.). SAGE.

Taylor, K. Y. (2018). The White power presidency: Race and class in the Trump era. *New Political Science, 40*(1), 103–112. https://doi.org/10.1080/07393148.2018.1420555

Tomasky, M. (2017) The great democratic divide. *New Republic, 248*(6), 14–15.

Vargas, J. H. (2004). *College knowledge: Addressing information barriers to college*. College Access Services, The Education Resources Institute (TERI).

APPENDIX 5A

Protocol for Educational Interactions With Subject's Parents

1. Why did your "people" come out to California, or how did you get to California? *[Probe: Black migratory patterns in LA]*
2. What did your mother and father tell you about education? What are some of the core values you learned from your parents about education or the value of education? *[Probe: Level of your parent's education]*
3. Is education the only way to achieve success in America? *[Probe: Value of college degree versus other degrees or types of certification]*
4. What are other acceptable ways of achieving success in America? *[Probe: Value of college degree versus other degrees or types of certification]*
5. How did your parents feel about academic African Americans in general; did their feelings differ for boys and girls? *[Probe: Childhood exposure and interactions with African Americans or anyone with college degrees]*
6. What did your parents teach you about the difference between common or wit sense and book-learned knowledge?
7. What college experiences did they deem the most important?
8. Did they ever talk about how much education is enough? What are some concrete examples they gave you to support their points? *[Probe: Fears and attitudes about education as well as conceptualizations of the "educated"]*
9. Do you think that these values were flawed in any way, and if so how have you amended them for your children?
10. Regarding your parents, which of their attitudes and values about education were learned from their neighborhood, friends, family, church, media or popular press, or through spouses and significant others?

INHERITING INEQUALITY

Hidden Challenges of First-Generation Students

David Hernández

I am a professor at a liberal arts college. I was a first-generation undergraduate, graduate student, and now tenured professor. Recently, I related a story to a set of prospective students and their parents who were touring the area's colleges and universities—something I hope to do one day with my daughter, but I never experienced myself.

In high school, when I was ready to visit a university campus—the one I ended up attending—a friend and I ditched class midweek and took his mother's station wagon about 100 miles north to check out the school. We did this on our own initiative, without permission or any special programs or parents to guide us.

We were both first-generation college students. My buddy was from a White working-class family and I hailed from a Mexican American single-parent family on public assistance. We had plenty in common economically but less so racially. Buried within our identities were hidden qualities and inequalities. More importantly, we were friends with similar goals, but we lacked any guidance as we maneuvered into higher education.

There are many identities intersecting with first-generation status related to race, class, gender, and sexuality. There is also citizenship status, urban or rural background, and visible or unseen disabilities. First-generation college students might be veterans, parents, foster children, and more. The key factor to first-generation status, most often unrecognized, is that being first-generation is not an accident of birth, but a marker of multigenerational, hereditary inequalities flowing from parents to children. *First-generation* is by definition a family status.

Amid all the peculiarities of the first-generation experience discussed in this volume is the weight of family history. You are a first-generation student because your parents did not attend the university, or anyone before them. Now, why is this so? Answering this question will shed light on the personal, accidental, and perhaps unlucky facets of family history. It might help explain the kind of schools you attended prior to college. More so, such queries shed light on the entrenched structural factors (laws, policies, race, and class experiences, etc.) that might have served as barriers to university life. Answering this question will also help you understand your family, their struggles, and future challenges.

You see, what is often unrecognized is that for first-generation students, attending college is for better or worse a break from that family history. It's not a rite of passage drawing you closer to your college-educated parents and siblings, but often a suspicious activity, drawing you away from family and making you different. We become uncanny—strange at college, but also at home, simultaneously. This requires extra work in maintaining bonds and trust with family, and continuously proving your worth to the mainstream.

Campuses can provide a welcome, hostile, or indifferent reception to first-generation students. The latter seems to be the most common. There are lots of cracks to fall through, or in my case, a kind of quicksand. As a first-generation student, I never really got my motors running. College came and went. I had fun, made friends, studied. But I didn't take advantage of what was in front of me. These seemingly secret opportunities were hidden in plain sight. If I could do it all over again, I would engage more deeply with college life.

Like others, my parents never visited. I had to fend for myself financially in my college town during summers. I never found the campus computer lab or gym. Education abroad or unpaid internships too seemed like impossibilities. Financial aid was a literal lifeline, and as a result, staying in school was like staying employed.

When I neared graduation, I scarcely knew about the career development office—and to be honest, I was afraid to ask—where interviews would take place for persons in my major or for other entry-level white-collar work. The career development office was, for me, what it always had been: the want ads. I searched the local newspaper postgraduation, and as a result, I did the same kind of work after college that I did during and before my undergraduate education—working at copy shops and hotels, delivering pizzas.

The first-generation experience, you'll soon learn, continues long after graduation. It might go away as one's skills peak, and then rear its head when trying something new, perhaps a job or graduate school. The path to where I am now as a faculty member was, and to some extent is, riddled still with twists, turns, and blind spots.

I often tell my students that going to college can be a lot like migration to a foreign country. There are often first-time travel anxieties, new languages, challenges to or impossible family visitation. There is longing for home or sometimes a feeling of refuge. But there is also a work ethic and bravery that comes with operating without a safety net, with being "self-made." First-generation students often have the ability, likely activated since youth, to teach themselves things. Contrary to popular beliefs, they aren't operating from a deficit or as remedial students. First-generation students can be rough around the edges, but they cover far more ground in their achievements, having had to struggle just to get to the starting line.

These are the skills that should be recognized. Tenacity, responsibility, pressures of work can be translatable to education too. These are forms of cultural knowledge that first-generation students bring with them to our campuses. We need to find ways to identify and build on these skills.

So, one thing a college or university could do is to recognize that some of our students are making it on their own. At commencement ceremonies each spring, it's almost cliché to thank all the supporters of students—families, mentors, best friends. But it's also crucial to acknowledge the students who are succeeding without a support system and without a road map. They truly carved their own pathways forward. I urge them as they advance beyond graduation, not to do so in silence or in isolation—a classic behavior for a first-gen—but to openly seek guidance and share their experiences.

Discussion Questions

1. What is your family's history in higher education?
2. What was and how did you experience your introduction to college as a new student on campus?
3. What services on campus did you take advantage of?
4. What techniques did you develop during your college years to compensate for the 'knowledge" you didn't have about college?
5. Given your responses to these questions, what services and/or policies should campuses embrace to assist first-generation college students?

PART TWO

THE INTERSECTIONS OF IDENTITY

6

THE NUANCES OF FIRST-GENERATION COLLEGE STUDENTS' SOCIAL CLASS IDENTITY

Sonja Ardoin

As a first-generation college graduate from a working-class background, I care deeply about first-generation college student and poor and working-class student populations. This is why I choose to research and write about students, administrators, and faculty who identify with either or both of these identities and why I champion programs and services that seek to advance educational equity. I also have the advantage of being a first-generation college graduate from a working-class background with the majority identities of being White; a cisgender straight woman; currently able; someone who attended college at 18; and, now, someone who holds a PhD. So, I know that my experience as a first-generation college student does not represent individuals who are people of color and first-generation college students, students with disabilities who are first-generation college students, caregivers who are first-generation college students, veterans who are first-generation college students, or people from middle or affluent classes who are first-generation college students.

First-generation college students "have complex identities, making them hard to pigeonhole" (Jehangir, 2010, p. 2), yet the population of first-generation college students is often conflated with the population of poor and working-class students. This is rooted in how first-generation college students are grouped on campuses and researched by scholars (e.g., Ardoin, 2018; Jehangir, 2010; Martin, 2015; Oldfield, 2009). Often the conversation and campus services are focused on first-generation college students from poor or working-class backgrounds, when, in actuality, the social class identity of first-generation college students is often more nuanced and complex than that. This chapter will explore the intricacies of first-generation college students' various social class identities and consider how first-generation college status may be experienced differently based on social class identity.

Defining the Terms

In order to engage in a fruitful discussion, it is helpful to ensure all parties are on the same figurative page. Therefore, for this chapter on the nuances of first-generation college students and social class identity, it is key to offer how I am conceptualizing the terms *first-generation college student* and *social class*. These are complex terms with unclear definitions, and as such, I want to offer multiple resources for defining, questioning, and broadening the collective understanding of these terms as they are used in higher education.

First-Generation College Students

Although some people in the field of higher education believe there is some clarity around the term *first-generation college student*, there is not one set definition (Davis, 2010; Jehangir, 2010; Toutkoushian et al., 2019; Ward et al., 2012). Additionally, when definitions are closely examined, they start to become more ambiguous and less inclusive. Toutkoushian et al.'s (2019) study highlights how, depending on the definition used to assess their sample, the percentage of students identified as first-generation "could range from as low as 22% to a high of 76%" (p. 15). This definition confusion even occurs on the federal level. The National Center for Education Statistics (NCES) has offered multiple definitions for first-generation college students over the years with similar tenets, including "first members of their families to attend college" (Chen, 2005 p. iii), and "students who had enrolled in college whose parents did not participate in any postsecondary education" (Cataldi et al., 2018 p. 5). The U.S. Department of Education's (DOE) Office of Postsecondary Education offers TRIO programs for students when "neither parent has earned a four-year college degree" (U.S. DOE, 2016, para. 19).

While seemingly similar, these federal definitions have significant distinctions. Take education level, for example. The NCES definitions offer a smaller scope by stating first-generation college students are individuals whose parents/family have not sought education beyond high school (e.g., postsecondary education). This means that if students' parents/family have enrolled in any kind of postsecondary education (e.g., trade school, cosmetology, community college, or 4-year university) they would not be considered first-generation college students under the NCES definition. The U.S. DOE's TRIO programs offer a broader range definition, stating that if a students' parents have not earned a 4-year college degree, then they would be considered first-generation college students and could be served by TRIO's programs. This conflict between two federal education bodies' first-generation college student definitions underscores the complexity of distinguishing this population of students and providing services and programs to advance educational equity. If our supposedly guiding organizations on the federal level cannot agree who first-generation college students are, how can we expect the approximately 4,300 colleges and universities in the United States to collectively understand and define this population?

In addition to definition confusion, there are also numerous ways these definitions exclude students who could and should be served by first-generation college student programs and services. Even the term *first-generation college student* itself can create misperceptions because of the word *first*. Some students believe if their sibling attended higher education then, naturally, their sibling was first in their family and, therefore, they cannot be. Or, what if a parent or family member attends at the same time as the student? The use of the term *parent* adds intricacy as well. There are students who were not raised by their parents, whose parents are deceased, or who are independent from their parents. So, definitions that use *parent* may be omitting students who consider grandparents, aunts, uncles, family friends, siblings, or themselves as their primary caregivers. A final piece of complexity is that many definitions are assumed to cover only the U.S. context. Therefore, if a student's caregivers received a degree in another country, they would not be considered first-generation college students. This is challenging because the systems of higher education vary widely between countries, and even if a caregiver earned an international degree, they may not be familiar with how the U.S. higher education system works or be able to assist their student through the myriad of processes that exist in U.S. colleges and universities.

Taking all of these complexities into account, a definition I believe offers a comprehensive understanding of *first-generation college students* is: students whose caregivers have not earned a 4-year college degree in the United States. While I am sure some would dispute this definition and others could fittingly poke holes in it, I propose it as one way to begin considering how the field can create a more inclusive and holistic representation of first-generation college students. I also know and own that a challenge in broadening such a definition is that institutions and federal organizations would then be required, or at least encouraged, to serve more students, and that would necessitate resources that are likely not realistic. However, I still believe that if educational equity is the goal, then higher education administrators and faculty members should not create (more) barriers for first-generation college students—no matter which definition is used.

Social Class Identity

It is natural to associate social class and money or wealth (Ardoin, 2019). That is the most common characterization of social class identity and, while money and wealth is certainly an instrumental aspect of social class, it does not fully capture the essence of this dimension of identity (Stich & Freie, 2016). Rather, it is important to understand social class identity in a holistic capacity and how it layers with first-generation college student status. Higher education faculty and staff should take on responsibility to learn more about social class, to consider how social class influences their work and students' experiences, and to examine programs and services for classism.

In order to grasp the wholeness of social class identity, Liu et al.'s (2004) social class worldview model provides insight into the multiplicity of elements that inform someone's social class perspective. The model features three primary forms of capital: (a) social, (b) human, and (c) cultural and five interrelated domains: (a) consciousness, attitudes, and salience; (b) property relationships; (c) lifestyle; (d) behaviors; and (e) referent groups (Liu et al., 2004). The domains highlight how individuals may have different levels of awareness of their social-class identity, and, as such, their thoughts and feelings about their social class will vary. Typically, the more aware someone is of their social class, the more they will think about it and emotionally react to it. Liu et al.'s (2004) domains of property relationships, lifestyle, and behaviors describe how social class is performed: individuals' beliefs about material possessions and presentation of social class, how they spend their time (e.g., number of jobs, if they have "free time" and what they do with it), and how their social class manifests in their way of being. Finally, the model illustrates referent groups—those to whom individuals compare themselves—around social class, including groups of origin, peers, and aspiration. In short, Liu et al.'s (2004) social class worldview model offers a holistic picture of how social class manifests internally for an individual and how that may influence their external interactions with others. It also gives educators insight into why tension may exist between students from different social classes, such as roommates, group project members, or students within a first-generation program.

It is also key to recognize that social class is a fluid identity, meaning it can shift and change over time, and is "constantly being created and recreated" (Ardoin & martinez, 2018, p. 97; see also Bourdieu, 1986). A person's social class background—called their *class of origin*—has the potential to be different from their current social class as well as from the social class others assume about them (Barratt, 2011). Thus, each person has three components of their social class identity: (a) class of origin; (b) current, felt class; and (c) attributed class (Barratt, 2011). When these components align, the person may not have a high level of consciousness or salience around their social class (Liu et al., 2004) because how they define themselves and experience the world matches what others assume about them. However, one's social class identity may become more noticeable when they are in contexts or among communities that are dominated by individuals from different social classes. This is why poor and working-class students are often highly aware of their social class in higher education institutions: because colleges and universities continue to focus on the privileged, including those from upper class and affluent social classes (Ardoin, 2019; Hurst, 2012).

Despite all of these, and many other, useful tools to broaden our understanding of social class identity, there remains no agreement on clear definitions for the various social classes (Martin, 2015). This reaffirms the importance of engaging in self and group learning to train higher education administrators and faculty members to consider not only money and wealth but also cultural experiences, connections, information to navigate processes, language and dialect, and access to educational opportunities as part of social class identity (Ardoin & martinez, 2018).

Conflation of Terms

Knowing that first-generation college student status and social class identity are different things, it is curious that educational institutions and nonprofit organizations often conflate, or combine, the two into one. This leads to assumptions that all first-generation college students come from poor or working classes of origin and creates challenges for the first-generation college students from middle-class or affluent families who may not be served by exiting programs or services that conflate the terms. Faculty and staff working within the context of higher education need to contemplate if, when, how, and why they might be assuming first-generation college students' social classes through coded language and programs that serve multiple student populations.

Coded Language on Campus

Higher education is becoming increasingly comfortable with discussing and serving first-generation college students. With national resource centers like NASPA and the Suder Foundation's Center for First-Generation Student Success, system-wide programs such as the one at the University of California, and campus-specific initiatives at places like Northern Arizona University, University of Cincinnati, Arkansas Tech University, and the University of North Carolina at Chapel Hill, more students, administrators, and faculty members know about *first-generation college student* status and are finding pride in the term. However, discussing social class identity is often still new, awkward, and believed to be taboo (Ardoin, 2019; Ardoin & martinez, 2018; Martin & Elkins, 2019). This hints at why coded language may be used on campus, particularly around social class identity: The field is uncomfortable naming social class. As such, terms such as *low-income*, *Pell-eligible*, and *need-based aid* are favored over actual social class identity terms (e.g., *low-income, working-class, middle-class, affluent*).

One of many challenges with these coded terms is that they frame social class identity in only one way—money or wealth (Ardoin, 2019). As mentioned earlier in this chapter, this is a problem because social class is more than finances. In addition, these terms do not accurately capture all poor and working-class students because, for example, some may not apply or qualify for the Pell Grant because of citizenship status or shifting financial dynamics (sometimes called being on *the bubble*). If these are the terms a college or university leans on because they are easier to grasp and offer quantifiable data, then higher education administrators are reducing social class to only one of its multiple components and, thus, are limiting understanding of the identity and how students from different social classes are served. For example, these coded terms may lead someone to think that a student on full scholarship (tuition, fees, room and board, and books) will have few, if any, hiccups related to their social class and their student experience. However, even if the financial concerns of higher education were eliminated, differences in life experience, opportunity, beliefs, values, language, and ways of being rooted in social class would remain (Ardoin, 2019). Reducing financial barriers is certainly helpful; however, that tactic does not create social class equity in higher education.

Rather than using coded and limiting language, administrators and faculty should utilize terminology that captures the wholeness of social class (e.g., poor, working-class, middle-class, affluent) and engage in conversations about social class that go beyond money or wealth to portray the complete picture of how social class influences students' experiences in higher education.

Programs That Serve Multiple Identities

In addition to coded language that creates some limitation and conflation of first-generation college student status and social class identity, some of our federal and campus-based programs also contribute to the stereotype that first-generation college students must be from poor or working-class backgrounds. The Office of Postsecondary Education within the U.S. DOE offers grant funding for federal TRIO programs which are "outreach and student services programs designed to identify and provide services for individuals from disadvantaged backgrounds" (U.S. DOE, 2019, para. 2). The eight programs (e.g., Talent Search, Upward Bound, Student Support Services, etc.) under the TRIO umbrella are designed to serve "poor individuals, first-generation college students, and individuals with disabilities" (U.S. DOE, 2019, para. 2). While these programs are critical to college access and success for many students, how they are framed can create assumptions about all poor (or poor and working-class, to use more holistic social class terms) individuals being first-generation college students and vice versa when that is not factually the situation. The framing may also mean that some students are being left out of the programs because they identify with one of these identity dimensions but not the others.

Similar conflation also occurs in campus-based programs and services. A primary example is Brown University. In 2016 Brown opened the first center in the country to focus on poor (again—poor and working-class, to use more holistic social class terms) students, but also in an effort to have space and staff to assist first-generation college students, Brown originally named the new center the First-Generation College and Poor Student Center. Later, the name and office were expanded to include another minoritized student population: The Undocumented, First-Generation College, and Poor Student Center, nicknamed the U-FLi Center (Brown University, n.d.). There is no doubt that all of these student populations deserve attention at Brown, but the naming of the center may generate some stereotypes about all three populations and conflate these different identities. Because of this, students who may only identify with one or two identities may not seek support or services from the center. Additionally, the use of *low-income* (a coded term, as explained previously) may steer away students whose financial situation may be in flux but who still might benefit from assistance around cultural, social, linguistic, or academic forms of capital. As Ward et al. (2012) note, "there is no one-size-fits-all approach" (p. 79) to assisting first-generation college students, so higher education administrators need to consider how framing influences engagement and reevaluate if or how they are using first-generation status and social class as proxies.

First-Generation College Student Status Is Not a Proxy for Social Class

While higher education is a new contextual environment for all first-generation college students, how they experience that environment varies based on the combination of all dimensions of their identity, including but not limited to race, ethnicity, gender, age, sexuality, ability, religion, and social class. Further, students who have roles as caregivers or veterans have added layers of complexity to their first-generation college student status. This means that first-generation college students are a heterogenous population, even when they may be erroneously treated as homogenous. As such, higher education administrators and faculty members should not assume what a student's experience is like. Rather, it is important to broaden one's understanding of (and disaggregate data on) this student population to better comprehend their unique experiences of being first-generation. In the following sections, I will make an argument for why first-generation college student status should not be used as a proxy for poor or working-class social class identity.

Income or Socioeconomic Status

It is true that many first-generation college students come from poor or working classes of origin (Ardoin, 2018; Martin, 2015; Ward et al., 2012). It is also true that some first-generation college students have caregivers with varying income levels (or socioeconomic statuses), giving them access to different opportunities because finances may not be as much of a constraint. In short, not all first-generation college students are poor (Davis, 2010). For example, first-generation college students whose caregivers own their own businesses, manage successful farms, work in high-pay manual labor roles, or hit the lottery may fall into this category of first-generation but not poor. These students might have attended private high schools, engaged in high-cost extracurricular activities or travel, enjoyed zero concern about college tuition and fees, and arrived on campus with all the latest amenities for their residence hall room. In cases like this, suggesting a need-based scholarship to all first-generation students or families, while well intended, would be flawed (and could insult some people) because not every first-generation college student qualifies for such aid. This is the error in using first-generation as a proxy for social class—there are cases where the assumed combination does not, in fact, apply. However, this does not mean these particular first-generation college students are on equitable footing with their continuing-generation peers. Rather, it merely means these first-generation college students may not face the same financial barriers as some other students in this population.

Other Forms of Capital

Knowing that social class is about more than money, though, it is important to understand that, while a student may have access to more financial
resources, they still may possess other forms of capital that are not valued by
or useful in the academy. Yosso's (2005) community cultural wealth model
provides a framework for understanding forms of capital beyond finances
including aspirational capital, cultural capital, familial capital, linguistic cap-
ital, navigational capital, social capital, and resistant capital. While everyone
possesses each of these forms of capital, the kind of capital someone—a first-
generation college student in this case—possesses may not transfer to a new
environment, such as higher education. I will offer two examples.

First, *navigational capital* describes someone's ability to move through
processes (Yosso, 2005). Higher education involves numerous complex processes including but not limited to admissions, financial aid and scholarships, course registration, faculty communication, fraternity and sorority
life, and study abroad. Continuing-generation students have people in their
lives who can explain higher education processes, and, in some instances,
help manage those processes. Having someone to serve as a guide provides
continuing-generation students with an advantage, while first-generation
college students, from any social class background, may be learning these
processes through trial and error. It is not that first-generation students do
not have navigational capital; they absolutely do. It just may be that their
forms of navigational capital do not convert to their new college context.

Second, social capital is someone's connections and network—it is who
they know and who knows them (Barratt, 2011; Bourdieu, 1986; Yosso,
2005). While first-generation college students certainly know people from
their hometowns, high schools, and families, those connections may not
translate into people who can help them get an internship in their academic field of study, offer a location for the student organization fundraiser
or retreat, or facilitate a meeting with a high-level community member to
make a conduct violation disappear. This variance in connections can generate educational inequities because opportunities are not necessarily based on
aspiration, work ethic, or merit; instead, opportunities are frequently rooted
in who students and their families know—or don't.

These two examples of differences in forms of capital highlight how, even
if first-generation college students have middle to high levels of income, their
other forms of capital still need to be weighed as higher education administrators and faculty members consider social class identity and how it layers
with first-generation college student status. It is problematic to assume that
first-generation college students come from a particular social class or use the

term *first-generation* as a proxy for poor or working-class identity (or other elements of identity like race/ethnicity or geography). First-generation college students are a heterogenous population, and the academy, rather than pigeonholing them (Jehangir, 2010), should recognize and celebrate these students' rich assortment of identities and experiences.

Conclusion

The social class identity of first-generation college students is nuanced and complex, much like the first-generation college student status itself. Higher education institutions and the individuals who work at them need to engage in education and training around first-generation status and develop a holistic understanding of social class identity. Remember: It is more than just money! Emphasis on the heterogeneity of this population might influence creation of programs and services that reflect the collection of identities that first-generation college students bring with them, including being from poor, working-class, middle-class, and affluent backgrounds. If, at the very least, administrators, faculty members, campuses, systems, and scholars can stop using *first-generation* as a proxy for the poor and working classes, that will be progress.

References

Ardoin, S. (2018). *College aspirations and access in working-class, rural communities: The mixed signals, challenges, and new language first-generation students encounter.* Lexington.

Ardoin, S. (2019). Social class influences on student learning. In P. Magolda, M. B. Baxter Magolda, & R. Carducci (Eds.), *Contested issues in troubled times: Student affairs dialogues about equity, civility, and safety* (pp. 203–214). Stylus.

Ardoin, S. & martinez, b. (2018). No, I can't meet you for an $8 coffee: How class shows up in workspaces. In B. Reece, V. Tran, E. DeVore, & G. Porcaro (Eds.), *Debunking the myth of job fit in student affairs* (pp. 97–117). Stylus.

Barratt, W. (2011). *Social class on campus: Theories and manifestations.* Stylus.

Bourdieu, P. (1986). The forms of capital. In J. G. Richardson (Ed.), *Handbook of theory and research for the sociology of education* (pp. 241–258). Greenwood.

Brown University. (n.d.). *Undocumented, first-generation college and low-income student center.* https://www.brown.edu/campus-life/support/first-generation-students/

Cataldi, E. F., Bennett, C. T., & Chen, X. (2018). *First-generation students: College access, persistence, and postbachelor's outcomes* (NCES 2018-421). National Center for Educational Statistics. https://nces.ed.gov/pubs2018/2018421.pdf

Chen, X. (2005). *First-generation students in postsecondary education: A look at their college transcripts* (NCES 2005-171). National Center for Education Statistics. https://nces.ed.gov/pubs2005/2005171.pdf

Davis, J. (2010). *The first-generation student experience: Implications for campus practice, and strategies for improving persistence and success.* Stylus.

Hurst, A. L. (2012). *College and the working class: What it takes to make it.* Sense.

Jehangir, R. R. (2010). *Higher education and first-generation students: Cultivating community, voice, and place for the new majority.* Palgrave MacMillan.

Liu, W. M., Soleck, G., Hopps, J., Dunston, K., & Pickett Jr., T. (2004). A new framework to understand social class in counseling: The social class worldview model and modern classism theory. *Journal of Multicultural Counseling and Development, 32*(2), 95–122. https://doi.org/10.1002/j.2161-1912.2004.tb00364.x

Martin, G. L. (2015). "Tightly wound rubber bands": Exploring the college experiences of low-income, first-generation White students. *Journal of Student Affairs Research and Practice, 52*(3), 275–286. https://doi.org/10.1080/19496591.2015.1035384

Martin, G. L. & Elkins, B. (2019). Editors notes. In G. L. Martin & B. Elkins (Eds.), *Social class identity in student affairs* (New Directions for Student Services, no. 162, pp. 5–8). Jossey-Bass.

National Center for Education Statistics. (2007). *Digest of educational statistics 2006.* U.S. Department of Education.

Oldfield, K. (2009). Humble and hopeful: Welcoming first-generation poor and working class students to college. In T. H. Housel & V. L. Harvey (Eds.), *The invisibility factor: Administrators and faculty reach out to first-generation college students.* BrownWalker.

Stich, A. E., & Freie, C. (2016). The working classes and higher education: An introduction to a complicated relationship. In A. E. Stich & C. Freire (Eds.), *The working classes and higher education* (pp. 1–9). Routledge.

Toutkoushian, R. K., May-Trifiletti, J. A., & Clayton, A. B. (2019). From "first in the family" to "first to finish": Does college graduation vary by how first-generation college status is defined? *Educational Policy,* 1–41. https://doi.org/10.1177/0895904818823753

U.S. Department of Education. (2016). *OPE Program Guide.* https://www2.ed.gov/about/offices/list/ope/opeprogramguide.html.

U.S. Department of Education. (2019). *Federal TRIO programs home page.* https://www2.ed.gov/about/offices/list/ope/trio/index.html

Ward, L., Seigel, M. J., & Davenport, Z. (2012). *First-generation college students: Understanding and improving the experience from recruitment to commencement.* Jossey-Bass.

Yosso, T. (2005). Whose culture has capital? A critical race theory discussion of community cultural wealth. *Race, Ethnicity, and Education, 8*(1), 69–91. https://doi.org/10.1080/1361332052000341006

I DON'T NEED ANY HELP

Working With First-Generation, Low-Income, White Males

Roxanne Moschetti

Emerging adults transitioning into college often face simultaneous social, emotional, academic, and cultural adjustments. Starting a path into higher education can be particularly challenging for individuals who are the first in their family to go to college and who come from economically disadvantaged backgrounds (Pascarella & Terenzini, 2005). In 2011–2012, first-generation college students comprised approximately one third of students enrolled in U.S. postsecondary institutions (Skomsvold, 2015). First-generation students often have lower family income, lower graduation rates, and lower levels of academic preparation report less support and encouragement from family to attend college; and often need to be employed to pay for educational costs (Engle & Tinto, 2008; Padgett et al., 2012). Students who are both first-generation and from lower socioeconomic status (SES) backgrounds arrive on campus lacking basic knowledge about higher education, including degree expectations and planning, expenses and funding, and career preparation (Moschetti & Hudley 2014; Pascarella et al., 2004), which often places them at risk of lack of adjustment and poor persistence (Chen & Carroll, 2005). Low-SES students tend to spend fewer hours engaged in activities on campus and more hours working when compared to their high-SES peers (Jury et al., 2017; Walpole, 2003). Additionally, low-SES students were found to spend less time studying and had lower overall grade point averages (GPAs) than students from high-SES backgrounds (Chen & Carroll, 2005). Instead, low-SES students spend most of their time and energy working off campus, resulting in them having little time to devote to college experiences or activities (Walpole, 2003). Consequently, these students often report lower levels of a sense of belonging and connectedness on campus, which directly influences their overall well-being (Stebleton et al., 2014).

Low-SES, first-generation college students are at greater risk for dropping out of both high school and college when compared to their high-SES peers whose parents have completed a college degree (Pascarella et al., 2004; Stanton-Salazar, 2011). Once in college, research suggests that first-generation status in combination with social class are often strong determinants of educational and economic attainment (Engle & Tinto, 2008). Students with parents who possess college experience often have an advantage over first-generation college students due to the fact that their parents are able to offer guidance and support on managing college life (i.e., applying to college and for financial aid, selecting courses). Conversely, parents of first-generation students are often unable to offer help or advice on understanding the higher education system (Pascarella et al., 2004).

Value of Relationships

Pascarella and Terenzini (2005) posit that differences in the quality and quantity of social networks that first-generation students access influences their overall academic engagement and persistence in college. Supporting literature illustrates that interactions with institutional agents and involvement on campus has been found to positively impact first-generation students' success and intent to persist (Tovar, 2015). These findings highlight the importance of relationships for first-generation college student success (i.e., participation in activities on campus, faculty-student interactions, peer relationships, and family influence). *Social capital,* which is defined as resources that reside within networks of mutual relationships (Bourdieu, 1986), is a useful theoretical construct for understanding this link between school engagement and relationships.

According to Stanton-Salazar (2011), social capital refers to the resources acquired through relationships that help students navigate new territory by providing them with valuable guidance, information, and support. To date, a large amount of research has focused on investigating how social capital impacts low-SES and first-generation college students' experiences (e.g., Crisp & Nora, 2010; Fisher, 2007; Saunders & Serna, 2004). While this literature has provided vital evidence to support the value of social capital, much of the data has been limited to investigating the experiences of ethnic minority student populations.

Social Capital and the Transition Into College

Existing social capital literature highlights the importance of meaningful relationships for increasing university integration and connection, student retention, motivation, and overall achievement (Moschetti et al., 2017; Perna & Titus, 2005; Saunders & Serna, 2004). Individuals who come from high-SES backgrounds often possess social networks that directly provide them with emotional, social, and tangible resources and support (Stanton-Salazar, 2011). Students with college-educated parents are often provided with support in understanding the culture of higher education as well as its role in future life chances (Pascarella et al., 2004; Stuber, 2011; Wilkins, 2014). In contrast, first-generation college students often derive their support and understanding of the college culture from involvement in activities on campus and interactions with faculty and non-first-generation peers. In fact, interactions with faculty and peers have been shown to significantly enhance personal growth, motivation, and degree plans (Pascarella & Terenzini, 2005). Moreover, meeting with faculty outside of class and engaging in research with a professor was found to increase low-SES students' chances of graduating and attending graduate school (Jury et al., 2017; Walpole, 2003). These findings reinforce that the college experience itself can provide access to social capital that is especially helpful for low-SES, first-generation college students (Rios-Aguilar & Deil-Amen, 2012; Stanton-Salazar, 2011). While we know these students benefit greatly from these interactions, Engle and Tinto (2008) point out that low-SES and first-generation students are often less likely to be engaged in both academic and social experiences on campus.

While first-generation college students may manage to conquer barriers and enroll in college, once there, they often struggle to access beneficial social capital on campus (Pascarella et al., 2004; Saunders & Serna, 2004). By attending college, low-SES, first-generation students are starting down a path that no one in their family has traveled before. While their families may encourage upward mobility for their first-generation children, many of these students have difficulty adjusting to and succeeding in their new environment (Lippincott & German, 2007), which can be partially attributed to a lack of critical social capital to aid them with the transition (Saunders & Serna, 2004). College culture is unique, and low-SES first-generation students may endure a form of culture shock when they enter this new environment. First-generation students may feel out of place and less accepted and often do not have the same types of support from their families as their non-first-generation peers (Terenzini et al., 1996). These students now find themselves immersed in a culture that requires a specific set of resources that is not present within their existing social capital. Many first-generation college students struggle to navigate the culture of higher education and fail to take advantage of campus resources (Ostrove & Long, 2007). Detailed interviews revealed that first-generation students often felt conflicted between choosing to preserve or discard their home networks to pursue their academic goals (Terenzini et al., 1994). Facing these unfamiliar experiences while trying to balance two different cultures can lead to feelings of isolation and a sense that they do not belong (Lippincott & German, 2007; Ostrove & Long, 2007).

Additionally, SES and first-generation status continue to influence students' experiences (e.g., navigating campus life, accessing financial resources, and parental involvement) once in college. Low-SES college students reported familial and work obligations as continuous barriers to their academic success significantly more than their middle- and upper-class peers (Stebleton et al., 2014). At the same time, first-generation students tend to focus more on the needs of others over their own and often prioritize interdependence with close others, such as family and friends back home (Stephens et al., 2012). As a result, low-SES, first-generation students' existing social networks of family and friends may actually drag them away from the college campus, especially when these students live at home. Ultimately, attaining social capital has been found to have a positive impact on first-generation students' educational aspirations, academic performance, and persistence to graduation (Pascarella et al., 2004). The more networks students develop on campus and the more they are connected to campus life, the less likely they will be to disconnect. Yet, low-SES first-generation students typically live off campus while simultaneously balancing family, work, and school demands, often resulting in them having less time for academic engagement (Aries, 2013; Stuber, 2011).

Community Colleges

Many low-SES, first-generation college students begin their educational journey at community colleges (Juszkiewicz, 2015). In fact, community colleges enroll more students from the lowest socioeconomic quintile than all other types of higher education institutions. According to the Community College Survey of Student Engagement, in spring 2013, 43% of community college students reported that their mothers did not attend any college and 48% reported that their fathers did not attend any college (Smith-Morest, 2013). These 2-year institutions are especially attractive due to the fact that they use less stringent admissions policies and charge lower tuition than 4-year colleges, providing access for students who otherwise might not be able to attend college (Carnevale & Strohl, 2010). Low-SES first-generation students' motives to attend community college include cost, proximity to home, remedial classes that prepare them for college-level work, training for entry-level vocational and job skills, and classes that transfer to 4-year colleges (Moschetti & Hudley, 2014).

While first-generation, low-income students may be enrolling at 2-year institutions, research illustrates that attendance is not necessarily associated with completion. Community college 3-year graduation rates average around 20%, with many community colleges graduating fewer than this average (Juszkiewicz, 2015). Low-SES first-generation students frequently enter community college with lower social and academic skills, have lower degree progression and attainment, and are at greater risk for dropping out when compared to students with college-educated parents (Tovar, 2015). Further, the Community College Survey of Student Engagement (CCCSE, 2014) reported that 57% of students enrolled in community college were enrolled part-time (in six credits or less) and 75% of community college students worked outside of the home, with over half working between 11 and 35 hours per week. These findings complement the work of Prospero and Vohra-Gupta (2007), who documented that first-generation students work more hours when compared with their non-first-generation peers and were more likely to drop out of college by the second year. As a result, these students often indicate that they rarely interacted with community college faculty, personnel, or peers (Prospero & Vohra-Gupta, 2007). Gibson and Slate (2010) found that over a 1-year period "non first-generation first-year students were found to have significantly higher levels of engagement in educationally purposeful activities than first-generation first-year students" (p. 382). Collectively, this lack of engagement can make it challenging for low-SES first-generation community college students to obtain vital information about social and academic opportunities and to acquire advantageous social capital.

Nevertheless, it is well documented that creating positive connections on campus with peers, faculty, and staff is an important component of easing a students' transition into community college (Gibson & Slate, 2010) especially for first-generation students, who tend to experience more difficulty transitioning than their non-first-generation peers. First-generation students' involvement with their community college networks and institutional agents has been found to have strong positive effects on aspirations, intrinsic motivation, critical thinking, educational degree plans, and overall success (Crisp, 2010; Dowd et al., 2013). Dowd et al. (2013) noted that support and care from institutional agents significantly impacted community college students' transition, adjustment, and development. Ultimately, low-SES first-generation college students can glean valuable social capital from college experiences. Yet, these students may find themselves in a particularly stark conundrum, being unable to fully participate in the college experience and, thus, less likely to access benefits that may be uniquely advantageous for this population.

Race and Gender

While income and first-generation status clearly influence student outcomes, additional factors such as race and gender also play an important role. Data reveal that women's college enrollment has outpaced men's over the past 2 decades. According to the Pew Research Center (2014), in 1994, 63% of female high school graduates and 61% of male high school graduates registered for college directly after graduation. By 2012, female enrollment in college directly following high school increased to 71% but male enrollment remained the same at 61% (Pew Research Center, 2014). Not only are more women enrolling in college, but once in college, female students tend to engage in better study skills, participate in more activities, and are more likely than their male counterparts to seek out academic and institutional support, a conduit of social capital (Fisher, 2007). Women are also more likely to graduate from college and pursue graduate education (Sax, 2008).

Overall, less than two thirds (60%) of male students but almost all female students (93%) believe that social support is important to their academic success. Moreover, mentoring has been found to impact academic and social integration as well as both goal and institutional commitment among community college students, with female students being the primary beneficiaries of multiple types of mentoring (e.g., emotional, psychological, academic, career and degree support) (Crisp, 2010). Conversely, male students were found to relate help-seeking behaviors with personal feelings of inferiority and inadequacy (Winograd & Rust, 2014) and tended to conform to more traditionally masculine gender norms, including self-reliance, which has been found to be correlated with hesitance in seeking help (Wimer & Levant, 2011). Together, these data suggest that female students, when compared to their male counterparts, are more likely to access social and institutional support and, therefore are more likely to accumulate advantageous social capital.

Perhaps most interestingly, the Center for Community College Student Engagement (CCSE, 2014) reported that over half of the community college student population were White, non-Hispanic (58%), and 30% traditionally underrepresented minority students (Black, Hispanic, and Native American). Recall that a majority of community college students are low-SES, first-generation students. Being White (Frankenberg, 1993) is often connected with unearned privilege, based on historical and social hegemony (McIntosh, 2003). While being White may come with unearned privileges, an analysis of race relations and status competition among poor and working-class residents of Detroit (Hartigan, 1999) revealed that very low SES Whites were often labeled *White trash* and endured harsh stigma and marginalization from both Whites and Blacks due to their lack of power usually associated with Whiteness. Regardless of whether participants are aware of experiencing White privilege, subjects in this study experienced their Whiteness as a liability. These data lead one to wonder about low-SES, White college students' experiences. Above all, these students may experience class-based disadvantages due to their lack of valuable economic and social capital. At the same time, their Whiteness may cause others to presume a level of advantage and capital consistent with their racial identity. Limited research has attempted to disentangle how race and ethnicity, parents' educational level, and social class distinctly impact students' adjustment to college (e.g., Longwell-Grice & Longwell-Grice, 2008; Webb, 2014). Thus, there is sparse evidence that details the experiences of these students who are often invisible in higher education due to the fact that they are simultaneously part of the racial majority and socioeconomic minority.

Existing research on low-SES, first-generation White college students reveals that a significant proportion of students experienced social and academic isolation and disengagement on campus due to experiences similar to those documented for underrepresented students (Stuber, 2011). Low-SES, first-generation White students were likely to live at home and work considerable hours offcampus, which likely contributed to their disengagement. However, these students do not seem to believe that their alienation is linked to their social class or first-generation status. Stuber (2011) concluded that "these students struggled in isolation without a frame for understanding their experiences" (p. 128) because their racial backgrounds clouded their understanding of their current situation as marginalized.

Another study, conducted by Webb (2014), investigated how social class related to college students' academic and psychological outcomes as a function of race. Results indicated that students often carry negative feelings including shame and embarrassment about their social class background, impacting their desire and ability to seek help for fear of humiliation and a desire to maintain dignity (Stebleton et al., 2014; Webb, 2014). Social class shame was found to be negatively associated with multiple scales of psychological well-being for both White and Black participants. Perhaps most interesting, for White students only, shame was associated with less positive relations with others. These findings suggest that low-SES White students may potentially be less likely to develop relevant coping and help-seeking skills due to their devalued identity. Moreover, Hopkins (2014) highlighted the complicated class differences that affect low-income White students' sense of belonging and ability to engage in social networks. Low-SES White students often face personal and cultural obstacles that limit their ability to connect with valuable support services on campus. Additionally, these students frequently failed to recognize the value in befriending peers on campus (Aries, 2013; Hopkins, 2014), leaving them less likely to develop beneficial social networks. Further, low-SES White students noted feeling that the support structure within their college was inadequate and ineffective in helping them navigate college life (Hopkins, 2014). Most recently, Martin (2015) found that low-SES White students faced numerous social and economic barriers and felt overwhelmed and overextended due to academic demands combined with the necessity of having to work outside of school.

While limited, the previously discussed findings suggest that low-SES White students often experienced complicated class differences that impacted their sense of belonging, family and peer relationships, as well as their networking and career opportunities. Recall that first-generation, low-SES males are less engaged than their female peers, suggesting that low-SES, first-generation White males may particularly be at risk in regard to successfully making beneficial connections on campus. Yet, the experience of low-SES, first-generation White males is a particularly understudied phenomenon.

The scant literature available on this population reveals that low-SES, first-generation White males perceive the university to be foreign, uncomfortable, unfamiliar, and difficult to navigate (Longwell-Grice, 2003; Moschetti & Hudley, 2008). These students are at a great disadvantage regarding knowledge about the college culture and were intimidated to engage with faculty or ask for support, resulting in a lack of support from beneficial institutional agents on campus (Longwell-Grice & Longwell-Grice, 2008). Low-SES, first-generation White males expressed that while their parents were supportive, they were not proactive about their education (Wilkins, 2014). Their emotional preoccupation with a challenging home life and family issues frequently interfered with their academic performance, leaving these students struggling to negotiate expectations from two entirely separate worlds with little support (Aries, 2013; Longwell-Grice & Longwell-Grice, 2008).

In sum, low-SES, first-generation White students appear to carry a belief that getting a college education means a chance at upward mobility from socioeconomic hardship and the possibility for a better life. Paradoxically, for many of these individuals, "getting out" of their economically disadvantaged backgrounds comes with a great cost of often missing out on the full college experience (Martin, 2015). Further research is needed on low-SES, first-generation, White, male students, as these young men are often underrepresented in college, disengaged, and seem to face barriers accessing supportive services (Moschetti & Hudley, 2014). Research has continued to acknowledge the importance of underrepresented student groups identified by social identity labels (e.g., class, gender, ethnicity) gaining access to valuable institutional networks through various programs and services on campus (e.g., Educational Opportunity Program [EOP], women's studies, ethnic studies, and sexual minority centers). Less is known about the impact of these programs on the experiences of low-SES, first-generation White males. The limited evidence that does exist indicates that these students tend to access fewer services and undervalue the importance of what these services can offer. Consequently, low-SES White males often wind up trying to navigate new unfamiliar college territory on their own (Moschetti & Hudley, 2008). Since many of these students begin their journey into higher education at community colleges, these institutions may serve as ideal environments to continue investigating these students' experiences.

Low-SES White Men in Community College

Our previous work examined the effects of first-generation and SES on social capital, as measured by the amount and quality of low-SES, first-generation, White male students' ties to institutional agents on campus (Moschetti & Hudley, 2008). We operationalize institutional agents as individuals within the institution who have the ability to transmit or facilitate the transmission of opportunities and resources available at the institution (e.g., financial assistance, counseling, mentoring, tutoring) (Dowd et al., 2013). Our findings include responses from low-SES, White male community college students who are either first-generation students or students who indicated either one or both parents attended college. Students rated the frequency of communication with institutional agents as well as the variety of on-campus resources that they sought for assistance (e.g., professors, teaching assistants, classmates, peers, counselors, tutors), their aspirations for the future, and their current GPA. Our data revealed that first-generation students communicated with institutional agents marginally less frequently than their non-first-generation counterparts (13.0 versus 15.3 respectively, on a scale of 6 to 24; $p < .10$). Correlations also revealed that communication with institutional agents and institutional help with coursework were related to GPA for all male students, with relationships for first-generation students being stronger than their non-first-generation peers (.63 versus .49 respectively for communication, and .72 versus .66 respectively for help with coursework).

Last, expectations for the future were correlated with both communication and coursework assistance (.62 versus .07 respectively for communication, and .72 versus .31 respectively for coursework assistance) for first-generation students only.

Perhaps low-SES, first-generation, White male community college students who arrive with high aspirations for the future were more likely to access institutional agents on campus, or the reverse; perhaps developing connections with institutional agents positively influenced these students' aspirations. Irrespective of the direction of effects, our results suggest that first-generation low-SES male students' lack of communication is problematic for their engagement and achievement. The results of our correlational analyses are similar to past findings that out-of-class contacts with professors, peers, and various resources on campus had positive influences on students' views of their environment and degree plans (Crisp, 2010; Pascarella et al., 2004). These findings seem especially significant as they suggest that accessing social capital on campus may be particularly valuable for low-SES, first-generation White males (Moschetti & Hudley, 2014). Although our data were drawn from a smaller sample size, this specific group of students represents an understudied and underrepresented college student population.

Literature on students possessing multiple identities from historically oppressed groups (e.g., being both Latino/a and from a low-SES background, identifying as both Black and a first-generation college student) suggests students from underrepresented ethnic populations may have different experiences from low-SES White students (Reynolds & Pope, 1991). Additional research on this particular group of students may help provide guidance for the development of specific programs aimed at targeting and serving this population. At a minimum, our findings suggest that colleges should consider putting forth outreach efforts and services that specifically target and support the needs of this underrepresented student population during their college transition.

Conclusion

Low-SES, first-generation male community college students may be more at risk for academic failure than students who possess only one of these risk factors (Stanton-Salazar, 2011). Existing literature suggests that access to beneficial social capital can be vital in aiding underserved students with the transition into college. To date, research on social capital has predominantly focused on low-SES, first-generation ethnic minority students. Our work investigated social capital among low-SES, first-generation, White male community college students.

We were interested in disentangling some of the influences of race, class, and gender on first-generation college students' transitions and adjustment to college life. Consequently, we examined how low-SES, first-generation community college White males orient themselves in their new, unfamiliar campus environment. Results supported existing research conducted with first-generation ethnic minority students while also presenting new information regarding the value of social capital for low-SES, first-generation, White, male students. It seems that entering college as a first-generation low-SES student may impact the amount of social capital students both bring with them and accumulate, regardless of race or ethnicity. Our finding that social capital was positively correlated with aspirations for the future for first-generation students only is particularly important when compared with Stanton-Salazar's (2011) work. Comparably, they found that adolescents' expectations for the future influenced their willingness to seek out help. Therefore, these students' help-seeking behaviors may originate well before their transition into higher education. These findings may provide useful insight for institutions working to improve the engagement and success of low-SES and first-generation college students, irrespective of race and ethnicity (Moschetti & Hudley, 2008). While it may be challenging to identify and engage with low-SES, first-generation, White males, who seem to prefer to "handle things on their own," nevertheless, it is important to continue creating effective strategies that will hopefully change the institutional culture to be more responsive and supportive to this invisible population.

References

Aries, E. (2013). *Speaking of race and class: The student experience at an elite college.* Temple University Press.

Bourdieu, P. (1986). The forms of capital. In J. Richardson (Ed.), *Handbook of theory and research for the sociology of education* (pp. 241–258). Greenwood.

Carnevale, A. P., & Strohl, J. (2010). How increasing college access is increasing inequality, and what to do about it. In R. D. Kahlenberg (Ed.), *Rewarding the strivers: Helping low-income students succeed in college* (pp. 71–90). Century Foundation.

Center for Community College Student Engagement (2014). *CCSSE national student characteristics.* http://www.ccsse.org/survey/national2.cfm

Chen, X., & Carroll, C.D. (2005). *First-generation students in postsecondary education: A look at their college transcripts.* (NCES 2005-171). National Center for Education Statistics. https://nces.ed.gov/pubs2005/2005171.pdf

Crisp, G. (2010). The impact of mentoring on the success of community college students. *The Review of Higher Education, 34*, 39–60. https://doi.org/10.1353/rhe.2010.0003

Crisp, G., & Nora, A. (2010). Hispanic student success: Factors influencing the persistence and transfer decisions of Latino community college students enrolled in developmental education. *Research in Higher Education, 51*, 175–194. https://doi.org/10.1007/s11162-009-9151-x

Dowd, A. C., Pak, J. H., & Bensimon, E. M. (2013). The role of institutional agents in promoting transfer access. *Education Policy Analysis Archives, 21*(15), 1–39. https://doi.org/10.14507/epaa.v21n15.2013

Engle, J., & Tinto, V. (2008). *Moving beyond access: College for low-income, first-generation students*. The Pell Institute.

Fisher, M. J. (2007). Settling into campus life: Differences by race/ethnicity in college involvement and outcomes. *Journal of Higher Education, 78*, 125–161. https://doi.org/10.1353/jhe.2007.0009

Frankenberg, R. (1993). *White women, race matters: The social construction of Whiteness*. University of Minnesota Press.

Gibson, A. M., & Slate, J. R. (2010). Student engagement at two-year institutions: Age and generational status differences. *Community College Journal of Research and Practice, 34*(5), 371–385. https://doi.org/10.1080/10668920802466384

Hartigan, J. (1999). *Racial situations: Class predicaments of Whiteness in Detroit*. Princeton University Press.

Hopkins, L. (2014). Beyond the pearly gates: White, low-income student experiences at elite colleges [Doctoral dissertation, University of Massachussets, Amherst]. ScholarWorks. https://scholarworks.umass.edu/dissertations_2/96

Jury, M., Smeding, A., Stephens, N. M., Nelson, J. E., Aelenei, C., & Darnon, C. (2017). The experience of low-SES students in higher education: Psychological barriers to success and interventions to reduce social-class inequality. *Journal of Social Issues, 73*(1), 23–41. https://doi.org/10.1111/josi.12202

Juszkiewicz, J. (2015). *Trends in community college enrollment and completion data, 2015*. American Association of Community Colleges.

Lippincott, J. A., & German, N. (2007). From blue collar to ivory tower: Counseling first-generation, working-class students. In J. A. Lippincott & R. B. Lippincott (Eds.), *Special populations in college counseling: A handbook for mental health professionals* (pp. 89–98). American Counseling Association.

Longwell-Grice, R. (2003). Get a job: Working-class students discuss the purpose of college. *College Student Affairs Journal, 23*, 40–53.

Longwell-Grice, R., & Longwell-Grice, H. (2008). Testing Tinto: How do retention theories work for first-generation, working-class students? *Journal of College Student Retention: Research, Theory and Practice, 9*, 407–420. https://doi.org/10.2190/cs.9.4.a

Martin, G. L. (2015). "Tightly wound rubber bands": Exploring the college experiences of low-income, first-generation White students. *Journal of Student Affairs*

Research and Practice, 52(3), 275–286. https://doi.org/10.1080/19496591.2015 .1035384

McIntosh, P. (2003). White privilege: Unpacking the invisible knapsack. In S. Plous (Ed.), *Understanding prejudice and discrimination* (pp. 191–196). McGraw-Hill.

Moschetti, R., & Hudley, C. (2008). Measuring social capital among first-generation and non-first-generation, working-class, White males. *Journal of College Admission, 198*, 25–30.

Moschetti, R. V., & Hudley, C. (2014). Social capital and academic motivation among first-generation community college students. *Community College Journal of Research and Practice, 39*, 235–251. https://doi.org/10.1080/10668926.2013 .819304

Moschetti, R. V., Plunkett, S. W., Efrat, R., & Yomtov, D. (2017). Peer mentoring as social capital for Latina/o college students at a Hispanic-serving institution. *Journal of Hispanic Higher Education, 17*(4), 375–392. https://doi.org/ 10.1177/1538192717702949

Ostrove, J. M., & Long, S. M. (2007). Social class and belonging: Implications for college adjustment. *Review of Higher Education, 30*, 363–389. https://doi .org/10.1353/rhe.2007.0028

Padgett, R. D., Johnson, M. P., & Pascarella, E. T. (2012). First-generation undergraduate students and the impacts of the first year of college: Additional evidence. *Journal of College Student Development, 53*(2), 243–266. https://doi.org/10.1353/ csd.2012.0032

Pascarella, E., Pierson, C., Wolniak, G., & Terenzini, P. (2004). First-generation students: Additional evidence on college experiences and outcomes. *The Journal of Higher Education, 75*, 249–284. https://doi.org/10.1353/jhe.2004.0016

Pascarella, E., & Terenzini, P. (2005). *How college affects students: A third decade of research* (Vol. 2). Jossey-Bass.

Perna, L. W., & Titus, M. A. (2005). The relationship between parental involvement as social capital and college enrollment: An examination of racial/ethnic group differences. *Journal of Higher Education, 76*(5), 485–518. https://doi.org/ 10.1353/jhe.2005.0036

Pew Research Center. (2014). *Women's college enrollment gains leave men behind.* https://www.pewresearch.org/fact-tank/2014/03/06/womens-college-enrollment-gains-leave-men-behind/

Prospero, M., & Vohra-Gupta, S. (2007). First-generation college students: Motivation, integration, and academic achievement. *Community College Journal of Research and Practice, 31*, 963–975. https://doi.org/10.1080/ 10668920600902051

Reynolds, A. L., & Pope, R. L. (1991). The complexities of diversity: Exploring multiple oppressions. *Journal of Counseling & Development, 70*(1), 174–180. https:// doi.org/10.1002/j.1556-6676.1991.tb01580.x

Rios-Aguilar, C., & Deil-Amen, R. (2012). Beyond getting in and fitting in: An examination of social networks and professionally relevant social capital among Latina/o university students. *Journal of Hispanic Higher Education, 11*(2), 179–196. https://doi.org/10.1177/1538192711435555

Saunders, M., & Serna, I. (2004). Making college happen: The college experiences of first-generation Latino students. *Journal of Hispanic Higher Education, 3*(2), 146–163. https://doi.org/10.1177/1538192703262515

Sax, L. (2008). *The gender gap in college: Maximizing the developmental potential of women and men.* Jossey-Bass.

Skomsvold, P. (2015). *Web tables—Profile of undergraduate students: 2011–12* (NCES 2015-167). National Center for Education Statistics. https://nces.ed.gov/pubsearch/pubsinfo.asp?pubid=2015167

Smith-Morest, V. (2013). From access to opportunity: The evolving social roles of community colleges. *American Sociologist, 44*(4), 319–1328. https://doi.org/10.1007/s12108-013-9194-5

Stanton-Salazar, R. D. (2011). A social capital framework for the study of institutional agents and their role in the empowerment of low-status students and youth. *Youth and Society, 43*(3), 1066–1109. https://doi.org/10.1177/0044118x10382877

Stebleton, M. J., Soria, K. M., & Huesman, R. L. (2014). First-generation students' sense of belonging, mental health, and use of counseling services at public research universities. *Journal of College Counseling, 17*(1), 6–20. https://doi.org/10.1002/j.2161-1882.2014.00044.x

Stephens, N. M., Fryberg, S., Markus, H., Johnson, C., & Covarrubias, R. (2012). Unseen disadvantage: How American universities' focus on independence undermines the academic performance of first-generation college students. *Journal of Personality and Social Psychology, 102,* 1178–1197. https://doi.org/10.1037/a0027143

Stuber, J. (2011). Integrated, marginal and resilient: Race, class and the diverse experience of White first-generation college students. *International Journal of Qualitative Studies in Education, 24*(1), 117–136. https://doi.org/10.1080/09518391003641916

Terenzini, P. T., Rendon, L., Upcraft, M. L., Millar, S. B., Allion, K. W., Gregg, P. L., & Jalomo, R. (1994). The transition to college: Diverse student, diverse stories. *Research in Higher Education, 35*(1), 57–73. https://doi.org/10.1007/bf02496662

Terenzini, P. T., Springer, L., Yaeger, P., Pascarella, E. T., & Nora, A. (1996). First-generation college students: Characteristics, experiences, and cognitive development. *Research in Higher Education, 37*(1), 1–22. https://doi.org/10.1007/bf01680039

Tovar, E. (2015). The role of faculty, counselors, and support programs on Latino/a community college students' success and intent to persist. *Community College Review, 43*(1), 46–71. https://doi.org/10.1177/0091552114553788

Walpole, M. (2003) Socioeconomic status and college: How SES affects college experiences and outcomes. *The Review of Higher Education, 27*(1), 45–73. https://doi.org/10.1353/rhe.2003.0044

Webb, F. R. (2014). The role of social class identity: Implications for African American and White College students' psychological and academic outcomes [Unpublished doctoral dissertation]. University of Michigan, Ann Arbor, MI.

Wilkins, A. C. (2014). Race, age, and identity transformations in the transition from high school to college for Black and first-generation White men. *Sociology of Education 87*(3), 171–187. https://doi.org/10.1177/0038040714537901

Wimer, D. J., & Levant, R. F. (2011). The relation of masculinity and help-seeking style with the academic help-seeking behavior of college men. *Journal of Men's Studies, 19*(3), 256–274. https://doi.org/10.3149/jms.1903.256

Winograd, G., & Rust, J. (2014). Stigma, awareness of support services, and academic help-seeking among historically underrepresented first-year college students. *The Learning Assistance Review, 19*(2), 17–41.

REFLECTIONS ON BEING A FIRST-GENERATION, AFRICAN AMERICAN MALE COLLEGE STUDENT

Nate Deans Jr.

The end of my senior year of high school was an internal struggle. I was a confused teen being told that real life would begin as sure as high school would end. All I could tell myself was that if these last 4 years of my life were going to reflect what the rest of my life would be, I was in trouble. Being "the best student" was something that I never thought about because intelligent kids weren't accepted by my peers. I learned that in middle school when I got jumped by some fellow students, while riding on the bus, after we had attended an extracurricular activity. It was clear from the comments they made while pounding on me that I had a choice: Be one of the mean boys who never studies (and be safe), or be one of the smart kids and be forced to watch my back. I chose safety. Before this event and its aftermath, my family believed I could go to college to become whatever I wanted to be. They believed that I *would* go to college. My mom pleaded with me to get good grades in high school and go on to college, but she could only show me the result of not having a college degree. She had her own internal struggles when it came to school, and she never gained the confidence to go to college. I remember thinking in my senior year that I had messed up too much to be able to go to college and get a college degree. Given my behavior and my grades, there certainly were not any teachers at my high school who had faith that I could pursue a college degree. And who could really blame them? I was certainly not showing any potential. For the last year or so, I would go into a classroom and the first thing I would do is tell the teacher what I wasn't going to do. During my free time I would play spades and blackjack "for a buck," instead of doing my homework, or joining any student organization. At the end of the day I would grab a club sandwich from Cousins Subs and head home on the bus. My main motivation to stay in school was so that I could attend the open gym on Saturdays with my friends. For that you had to be a student at the school, so I made sure I was eligible for that at least.

With some of the things that I did, I was surprised I got to see my senior year. This was especially true because at times I felt that certain teachers wanted to get rid of me. By the time my senior year came along, I was a little scared and a little depressed and a little lost. I certainly lacked direction, and the future seemed bleak. As bleak as it seemed, though, I still looked forward to making my mother proud by graduating high school. Then came the moment that changed everything, a pivotal moment of my life that came during my last exam of my senior year.

I had just finished my final exam for Creative Writing, and I was waiting to get my yearbook signed by a girl that I liked. She also happened to work as a student assistant in the high school guidance office. I gave her my yearbook to sign while I was taking my final exam. She told me to stop by the office after my exam, so we could talk and she would return my yearbook to me then. I have no idea how I did on the test that day, but I do remember that I marched into the guidance office with the biggest grin imaginable on my face. I was looking forward to getting my yearbook, and I was looking forward to seeing my friend. As soon as I entered the guidance office, however, my grin disappeared. Instead of a warm greeting I was expecting from my friend, I heard a loud voice from the inner office say "Nathaniel Darnell Deans Jr.!" I at once knew the voice of my guidance counselor. And, having heard it more than once during my 4 years in high school, I knew that tone as well. I was in trouble. I just didn't know why.

"Yes?" I answered, hesitantly.

"My office now!" she said. Thinking on it now, I doubt she yelled, but at the time it felt like she yelled loudly enough for the entire school to hear. When I approached her, the smile my guidance counselor usually wore on her face was replaced with eyes that glared into my soul and pierced every bit of confidence I had.

In rapid-fire she said: "Why have you not filled out any college applications yet?" "You *are* going to school." And then, "What schools are we filling out applications for?" I had missed all of the deadlines for financial aid, and I had failed to complete any college applications. I didn't think I was going to go to college, so I didn't bother. In my mind, there was no reason to do any of those things. The counselor had already known this, and she had a plan for me before I even had a plan for myself!

After all, I didn't call her my second mom for nothing. She was the reason I went to open gyms on Saturdays. She was there, volunteering her time to open the gym for me and my friends. She had taken us to Circle City Classics in Indiana: a weekend historically Black colleges and universities (HBCUs) event full of football games, a Battle of the Bands, and a display of Black excellence through education and athletics. And even though we disappointed her on this trip by sneaking out and going to parties the night before we came back home, she never gave up on us. It was probably then that she knew I was going to college. We would talk about the things that I was learning, or how I could do the work I was given but just chose not to, or how others in the building treated me because they didn't understand how hard it was for my mom to raise two boys while trying to work, or that I had taken a job junior year to support my family and bail my friend out of jail when he got in trouble with the law. And then she handed me the application to a local technical college.

"Fill this out. After I turn this in, you will be getting a letter in the mail telling you to take the placement test. I will also help you fill out the FAFSA. You *will* follow up with me. Understand?" she said with a stern voice. It took everything for me not to say no, because I didn't want to go to college. I didn't want to be disappointed by failing in college. I didn't have anyone that had received a college degree so I didn't know what success would look like. Why would I want to go into debt for something that I was never going to complete?

In my mind, most people go to college and don't finish with a degree. I "knew" this because I had seen my friends fail and I felt that I would do no better than they had. But here I was, a scared 18-year-old facing a woman who was, in her mind, fighting for my life. Even though I had no idea of the significance of what I was about to do, I nodded and filled out the application. Looking back now, I fully realize the significance of that event in changing my life's trajectory.

While this is my story, there are traits that I believe those that grew up with similar life experiences may share when it comes to navigating the treacherous rapids leading to attending college as a first-generation student. As a first-generation college student there are those in one's family who are going to say that going to college is the way out of poverty. While that sounds great, because they haven't had the experience themselves it made me doubt what they were saying. It takes a person who has been there; someone who can guide you through, to make you believe. Someone who can help you gain the confidence to not just submit the college application and complete the dreaded FAFSA, but someone who believes that you have the ability to attend college and graduate. Fear is a first-generation college student's greatest enemy. The fear of failure. The fear of embarrassment. The fear of financial strain. The fear of lacking perseverance because no one in your family helps you understand the intricacies of study habits. As a Black man, the fear only intensified as I attended a predominantly White school for my degree. The fears of racism were ever present. So, too, were the fears of intimidation, stress from White privilege bearing down on you mentally and physically. The fear of believing that most people on campus don't think you can succeed. The fear of the professor pointing you out to answer "the race question" and hoping you have the courage to speak.

If we want to research how to destroy barriers for first-generation college students, I think this story gives us insight on where to focus our work. First-generation college students need mentorship from those who have been through college and succeeded, and preferably from someone who looks like them and can share life experiences. This mentorship needs to start early and needs to be more than words. While we must speak college success into existence, it must also come with guidance about how to make first-generation college students successful. Our systems must change to give first-generation college students priority when it comes to services, classes, financial aid, and other barriers that create the disparities in graduation rates for first-generation students. We must discover what equity at the collegiate level would be for first-generation college students who have suffered from inequities throughout their academic experiences.

When I tell my story, most people see it as a success story, but as I think of it from a systematic point of view, it really is a tragedy. It is a tragedy because while there are a few like me who have gained success, statistics show there are more people who have been failed by the education system as first-generation college students. If we really cared enough to change the disparities that exist, then we would seriously look at breaking down systems across the board that don't allow first-generation college students to succeed.

Discussion Questions

1. What are your responses to the strategy employed by the counselor in this story? Would you ever use this strategy and when might you use it?
2. How does the contributor see issues of race complicating his first-generation college student experience?
3. How do you feel about the contributor's statement that his story is more tragedy than triumph?

8

DUAL INVISIBILITIES

The Intersection of First-Generation and LGBTQ Identities

Pheng Xiong

While there are growing bodies of research about first-generation college students and about lesbian, gay, bisexual, trans*, and queer (LGBTQ) students, very few studies exist on the intersectionality between these two groups of students. *First-generation college students*, defined as those students whose parents have not attended or attended but did not graduate from college, are a growing presence on college campuses and make up at least 24% of the college student population (Engle & Tinto, 2008; Pascarella et al., 2004). They also have different challenges than their continuing education peers, such as with retention and persistence. First-generation college students are more likely to come from low-income and working-class families (Gibbons & Woodside, 2014; Jenkins et al., 2013) and sometimes identify as members of the LGBTQ community.

The LGBTQ community represents a segment of society that has historically been marginalized and stigmatized. In higher education, LGBTQ student needs are at times overlooked or go unaddressed, which further reinforces their marginalization (Brown et al., 2004; Rankin, 2006). Marginalization prevents LGBTQ individuals from fully exploring and accepting their sexual and gender identities.

Studies about LGBTQ student intersectionalities have grown in recent years, but research is still lacking (Stevens, 2004). How first-generation college students experience and make meaning from their LGBTQ identity as an aspect of the multiple dimensions of their identity is the focal point of this chapter. The meaning-making process ultimately impacts how students see themselves and perceive the world around them. This chapter explores the concept of intersectionality and how it can shed light on first-generation LGBTQ students' experiences and meaning-making.

Intersectionality: A Model of Multiple Dimensions of Identity

McCall (2005) defines *intersectionality* as "the relationship among multiple dimensions and modalities of social relations and subject formations" (p. 1771). Historically, intersectionality has come out of studies focusing on feminism, specifically studies that sought to explain and understand female experiences from social phenomena (Abes et al., 2007; Strayhorn, 2017).

Intersectionality has influenced research studies seeking to understand the social experiences of marginalized populations because it challenges traditional notions of race, gender, class, and sexuality. Intersectionality seeks to illuminate systems of oppression and privilege by explaining how these systems influence individuals' lived experiences. Specifically, intersectionality is an analytical framework through which investigating development of multiple identities can help bring into focus the effects inequalities have on a person's social identity formation (Abes & Jones, 2004; Abes et al., 2007; Strayhorn, 2017; Torres et al., 2009). Intersectionality has given rise to concepts that seek to understand how an individual's multiple dimensions of identities interact with one another and how these identities influence an individual's sense of self. Intersectionality is presented as a useful tool for conducting and shaping student affairs research (Strayhorn, 2017).

Jones and McEwen's (2000) model of multiple dimensions of identity posits that contextual influences, such as race, gender, and social background, have a significant impact on an individual's sense of self. The sense of self, defined by personal attributes, identities, and characteristics, is considered the core of one's identity. Circulating around the core are an individual's intersecting identity dimensions within the context of family background, sociocultural conditions, current experiences, career decisions, and life planning. The salience of each identity dimension is fluid and dynamic. Jones and McEwen (2000) highlighted how "identity can be understood and experienced differently at different points in time, particularly in relation to one's personal identity and in terms of relative resilience within each dimension" (pp. 411–412).

Intersectionality can help reveal how individuals negotiate differences in meaning-making. In 2007, Abes et al. built on Jones and McEwen's model of multiple dimensions of identity by drawing attention to the complexities of a student's meaning-making capacity and social identity development. The reconceptualized model of multiple dimensions of identity uses an individual's meaning-making capacity as a filter where contextual influences move through different degrees. The more complex an individual's meaning-making capacity, the more they were able to determine the relationship between contextual influences and multiple dimensions of their identity. Intersectionality at its core focuses on the lived experiences and struggles of marginalized groups, such as students of color who also identify as lesbian, gay, bisexual, transgender, or queer.

To illustrate this, Abes's (2016) research on intersectional interpretations of lesbian college students identified the ways in which sexual identity is one of many identities that contributes to how a person makes sense of their social self. Abes (2016) described how a White, working-class, first-generation college student who also identified as a lesbian negotiated the power structures of classism and heterosexism to make sense of her social identities. The student's social class and sexual identity intersect one another, with sexual identity becoming more salient as the result of the passing of her father. However, as she made sense of her social identities, she became more aware of how her White privilege provided some advantages that may not be for people of color. The sense of self and personal life experiences, (i.e., family and socioeconomic status) highlight how these factors influenced her experience.

First-Generation College Students

There are varying definitions of what it means to be a first-generation college student, but for the purposes of this literature review, *first-generation college students* are described as students whose parents have not attended college or earned a college degree. Although they comprise almost half of all college students and their numbers on campus are growing (Lightweis, 2014; Lundberg et al., 2007; Padgett et al., 2012; Petty, 2014), first-generation college students face greater challenges than students whose parents are college educated.

Existing research documents that first-generation college students face unique challenges when compared to students whose parents have already earned a degree. For example, they are more likely to leave college, be less engaged in the classroom, be academically underprepared, come from families with lower socioeconomic status, and receive little social and family support in making decisions about college (Ishitani, 2006, 2016; Lundberg et al., 2007; Pascarella et al., 2004). A study by Lohfink and Paulsen (2005) comparing first-generation college students with continuing-generation students found that in addition to their unique challenges, they also experience other modes of oppression, based on race, gender, and class. The findings of these studies indicate that challenges first-generation college students face make it difficult for them to integrate into the academic and social settings of college.

Social Capital

Social capital has been defined as "privileged knowledge, resources, and information attained through social networks . . . used to make beneficial decisions related to choosing colleges and what kinds of academic and social choices to make while enrolled in college" (Soria & Stebleton, 2012, p. 675). One of the unique challenges that first-generation college students face that their counterparts do not is having little to no social capital when it comes to making decisions about college. Compared to parents of traditional students, parents of first-generation college students lack the experience and knowledge of going to college and, therefore, cannot share that knowledge with their child. While traditional college students have knowledge of the college-choice process through their parents, first-generation college students are often left to create their own expectations as they do not have access to information, such as the importance of making positive academic and social choices (Coffman, 2011; Mardsen, 2014; Pascarella et al., 2004; Soria & Stebleton, 2012). Not having readily available access to such social capital means that first-generation college students may benefit less from their collegiate experience.

First-generation college students are asked to negotiate two separate cultures—that of higher education and of their home. As researchers have indicated, first-generation students are more likely to be from low-income families and as such may have to divide their classroom time with other responsibilities. For instance, first-generation college students are more likely to hold jobs outside of the classroom to support their families. This also means that they will spend less time studying or getting involved with campus activities, which in turn can impact their persistence, making them less likely to graduate. A study by Ishitani (2016) investigating college persistence of first-generation students found that first-generation college students were 80% more likely to drop out of college after their second year compared to students whose parents had a college degree. Those who did not graduate before their fourth year were twice as likely to dropout.

For college students who are the first in their families to go on to college, researchers have noted that they often felt guilty of surpassing their family members in this area of achievement. A study conducted by Covarrubias and Fryberg (2015) to determine the experiences of students who experienced guilt revealed that first-generation Latino students reported feelings of guilt more than other ethnicities. Overall, however, first-generation and minority students reported feeling more family achievement guilt than their counterparts whose parents had a college degree. Feelings of achievement guilt impacts students' adjustment to college and the likelihood that they will be retained.

Research studies have indicated that social capital is linked to a student's awareness of resources available, ability to seek academic support, and information that can provide success. Soria and Stebleton (2012), in their study about the differences between first-generation and continuing-generation college students, found that when first-generation students are unaware or unwilling to be engaged, they can become frustrated with and isolated from their college experience. In contrast, a study exploring the college-choice process of first-generation Latina female students indicated that in cases where parents were limited in information about the college application process but an older sibling had knowledge, that sibling acted as the parental figure when discussing the college-choice process (Ceja, 2006).

Academic Integration

There is a connection between social capital and academic integration. The first year is the most critical for a first-year college student and more so for first-generation college students. During this year, the student is attempting to determine whether they made the right decision to attend college. They are also attempting to integrate themselves into the fabric of the institution. However, social integration is harder for first-generation college students because their lower social capital often results in decreased academic engagement. Academic engagement is linked to persistence and a sense of belonging (Lundberg et al., 2007; Soria & Stebleton, 2012). Ishitani (2016), in her study about first-generation college student persistence, found that there was a positive effect on student persistence the more socially integrated the student was at college. Specifically, first-generation college students who were more socially integrated were 19% less likely to drop out during their second year and 22% less likely in their third year.

Tinto (1999) noted that active involvement is key to whether a student continues their studies. He wrote, "Students who are actively involved in learning activities and spend more time on task, especially with others, are more likely to learn and, in turn, more likely to stay" (p. 6). The first year is the most critical for the college student experience. During the year, students are learning about college norms and are still developing skills that would promote their learning and development.

LGBTQ College Students

LGBTQ students are often referred to as the "invisible minority" and their issues are nothing new to colleges and universities around the United States. Stewart and Howard-Hamilton (2015) wrote that LGBTQ students "represent an aspect of diversity that has been subject to oppression and marginalization in society at large, as well as in higher education" (p. 121). It is only in recent years that higher education and student affairs professionals started to recognize that this population of students has different needs and therefore may require different tools and resources to help them succeed in their higher education pursuits. Like first-generation college students, LGBTQ students experience the same challenges as it pertains to their academic success. There are, however, additional unique challenges such as facing discrimination, establishing same-sex relationships, and coming out to friends and families (Sanlo, 2005). These unique challenges are compounded when a student is also a first-generation college student.

A multiple-identities approach to intersectionality allows researchers to consider how social identities such as class, race, and gender, for example, influence sexual identity and simultaneously influence a student's academic persistence. Intersectionality can provide additional insight into how intertwined social identities are. It is impossible to understand a student's sexual identity development without also understanding how racial, economic, and social identities also influence their struggles and desires (Abes, 2016; Strayhorn, 2017). In other words, intersectionality, when applied to studies of multiple identities, highlights how social inequalities influence the sense of self.

Racial and Socioeconomic Status

Much like first-generation status, race and socioeconomic status both play an important role in LGBTQ student attrition. Mancini (2011) and Rankin (2005) point out that while attrition rates are higher for students of color who also identify as a member of the LGBTQ community because of their interactions with racism in addition to anti-gay bias, the issues become more complex when there is a lack of acceptance from either culture. This means that minority students, who also tend to be first-generation college students, are more likely to conceal their sexual and gender identity out of fear of harassment (Rankin, 2005). This in turns increases the students' feelings of isolation and their chances of dropping out.

Academic Integration

As mentioned previously, theorists like Tinto emphasized the importance of academic integration as a model to explain why students depart. Tinto's research indicates that the more academically and socially involved students are (e.g., interacting with classmates, faculty, and staff) the more likely they are to persist. The more positive those interactions and how integrated they are into the institution can also make the difference. Integration within the college environment can include their involvement in student organizations, the residence halls, and even in the classrooms (Renn & Reason, 2013; Tinto, 1998).

Sanlo (2005) examined the lived experiences of LGBTQ students in hopes of providing "an understanding of the students' language, behaviors, and stressors, and how those areas affected student's academic achievement and success in college" (p. 97). He pointed out that research has been slow on issues pertaining to LGBTQ student persistence in higher education and, like first-generation college students, there are challenges that LGBTQ students must overcome to persist and become academically integrated. This integration starts in the classroom.

While there is little research on the classroom experiences for LGBTQ students, based on other research studies conducted on student persistence (Garvey et al., 2014; Stevens, 2004; Tinto, 1998), we can conclude that the classroom experience plays a key role in the academic integration of LGBTQ college students. Stevens (2004), in his study about the development of gay male identity within the college environment and how incidents influenced other dimensions of their identities, discussed how classroom instructors had an impact on whether the homophobic classroom behavior was confronted to ensure that LGBTQ students felt safe. The study found that experiences of heterosexism and homophobia were critical to how gay-identified students experienced their identities. Classrooms were described as a place where students felt they did not have control of situations. Faculty who support gay students enable students to feel more comfortable and proud of their gay identity. Students who felt empowered were also able to dispel issues of heterosexism and homophobia. Having and finding support were important for students to navigate the environment.

Discussion

First-generation and LGBTQ students face challenges that include the maintenance of multiple aspects of their intersecting identities. LGBTQ students attempt to define who they are while seeking acceptance from friends, family, and peers. However, they need to feel safe and supported in doing so. The fear of invisibility and rejection negatively affects the experience of LGBTQ students. At the same time, first-generation college students are often navigating the college environment with little to no social capital. The lack of social capital has an impact on how integrated first-generation students are and therefore their persistence.

The use of intersectionality in future research offers a framework with which to understand the experiences of LGBTQ first-generation college students through exploring the many dimensions of their multiple identities. There is research that has explored the first-generation student experience from racial and cultural intersections, but few (if any) studies have been done exploring the LGBTQ-first-generation college experience. I argue that the theory of intersectionality should be used to analyze the complexity of first-generation LGBTQ college student experiences at the point where their identities meet. The reconceptualized model of multiple dimensions of identity (Abes et al., 2007) can be used as the lens from which scholars can understand how a first-generation college student's LGBTQ identity is constructed with their many other identities.

The theory of intersectionality calls for inclusion of the experiences of first-generation students who also identify as LGBTQ. This inclusion is needed because intersectionality at its core challenges systems of oppression and traditional concepts of race, gender, and sexuality (Strayhorn, 2017). By ignoring this subset of first-generation college students and their lived experiences, it makes meeting the needs of these students more difficult. Higher education and student affairs professionals play a key role in identifying ways that can encourage and empower students to persist in their college experiences.

References

Abes, E. S. (2016). Constructivist and intersectional interpretations of a lesbian college student's multiple social identities. *The Journal of Higher Education, 83*(2), 186–216. https://doi.org/10.1080/00221546.2012.11777239

Abes, E. S., & Jones, S. R. (2004). Meaning-making capacity and the dynamics of lesbian college students' multiple dimensions of identity. *Journal of College Student Development, 45*(6), 612–632. https://doi.org/10.1353/csd.2004.0065

Abes, E. S., Jones, S. R., & McEwen, M. K. (2007). Reconceptualizing the model of multiple dimensions of identity: The role of meaning-making capacity in the construction of multiple identities. *Journal of College Student Development, 48*(1), 1–22. https://doi.org/10.1353/csd.2007.0000

Brown, R. D., Clarke, B., Gortmaker, V., & Robinson-Keilg, R. (2004). Assessing the campus climate for gay, lesbian, bisexual, and transgender (GLBT) students using a multiple perspectives approach. *Journal of College Student Development, 45*(1), 8–26. https://muse.jhu.edu/article/52878

Ceja, M. (2006). Understanding the role of parents and siblings as information sources in the college choice process of Chicana students. *Journal of College Student Development, 47*(1), 87–104. https://doi.org/10.1353/csd.2006.0003

Coffman, S. (2011). A social constructionist view of issues confronting first-generation college students. In J. Wiggins (Ed.), *Faculty and first-generation college students: Bridging the classroom gap together* (New Directions for Teaching and Learning, no. 127, pp. 81–90). Jossey-Bass. https://doi.org/10.1002/tl.459

Covarrubias, R., & Fryberg, S. A. (2015). Movin' on up (to college): First-generation college students' experiences with family achievement guilt. *Cultural Diversity and Ethnic Minority Psychology, 21*(3), 420–429. https://doi.org/10.1037/a0037844

Engle, J., & Tinto, V. (2008). *Moving beyond access: College success for low income, first-generation students.* The Pell Institute. https://files.eric.ed.gov/fulltext/ED504448.pdf

Garvey, J. C., Taylor, J. L., & Rankin, S. (2014). An examination of campus climate for LGBTQ community college students. *Community College Journal of Research and Practice, 39*(6), 527–541. https://doi.org/10.1080/10668926.2013.861374

Gibbons, M. M., & Woodside, M. (2014). Addressing the needs of first-generation college students: Lessons learned from adults from low-education families. *Journal of College Counseling, 17*(1), 21–36. https://doi.org/10.1002/j.2161-1882.2014.00045.x

Ishitani, T. T. (2006). Studying attrition and degree completion behavior among first-generation college students in the United States. *Journal of Higher Education, 77*(5), 861-885. https://doi.org/10.1080/00221546.2006.11778947

Ishitani, T. T. (2016). First-generation students' persistence at four-year institutions. *College and University, 91*(3), 22–32.

Jenkins, S. R., Belanger, A., Connally, M. L., Boals, A., & Durón, K. M. (2013). First-generation undergraduate students' social support, depression, and life satisfaction. *Journal of College Counseling, 16*(2), 129–142. https://doi.org/10.1002/j.2161-1882.2013.00032.x

Jones, S. R., & McEwen, M. K. (2000). A conceptual model of multiple dimensions of identity. *Journal of College Student Development, 41*(4), 405–414.

Lightweis, S. (2014). The challenges, persistence, and success of White, working-class, first-generation college students. *College Student Journal, 48*(3), 461–467.

Lohfink, M. M., & Paulsen, M. B. (2005). Comparing the determinants of persistence for first-generation and continuing-generation students. *Journal of College Student Development, 46*(4), 409–428. https://doi.org/10.1353/csd.2005.0040

Lundberg, C. A., Schreiner, L. A., Hovaguimian, K., & Slavin Miller, S. (2007). First-generation status and student race/ethnicity as distinct predictors of student involvement and learning. *Journal of Student Affairs Research and Practice, 44*(1), 57–83. https://doi.org/10.2202/1949-6605.1755

Mancini, O. (2011). Attrition risk and resilience among sexual minority college students. *Columbia Social Work Review, 2*, 2–22. https://journals.library.columbia.edu/index.php/cswr/article/view/1961/919

Mardsen, L. M. (2014). The transition to college of first-generation freshmen. *Insight: Rivier Academic Journal, 10*(2), 1–7.

McCall, L. (2005). The complexity of intersectionality. *Signs: Journal of Women in Culture & Society, 30*(3), 1771–1800. https://doi.org/10.1086/426800

Padgett, R. D., Johnson, M. P., & Pascarella, E. T. (2012). First-generation undergraduate students and the impacts of the first year of college: Additional evidence. *Journal of College Student Development, 53*(2), 243–266. https://doi.org/10.1353/csd.2012.0032

Pascarella, E. T., Pierson, C. T., Wolniak, G. C., & Terenzini, P. T. (2004). First-generation college students—Additional evidence on college experiences and outcomes. *Journal of Higher Education, 75*(3), 249–289. https://doi.org/10.1353/jhe.2004.0016

Petty, T. (2014). Motivating first-generation students to academic success and college completion. *College Student Journal, 48*(2), 257–264.

Rankin, S. R. (2005). Campus climates for sexual minorities. In R. L. Sanlo (Ed.), *Gender identity and sexual orientation: Research, policy, and personal* (New Directions for Student Services, no. 111, pp. 17–23). Jossey-Bass. https://doi.org/10.1002/ss.170

Rankin, S. R. (2006). LGBTQA students on campus: Is higher education making the grade? *Journal of Gay & Lesbian Issues in Education, 3*(2–3), 111–117. https://doi.org/10.1300/J367v03n02_11

Renn, K. A., & Reason, R. D. (2013). *College students in the United States: Characteristics, experiences, and outcomes.* Jossey-Bass.

Sanlo, R. (2005). Lesbian, gay, and bisexual college students: Risk, resiliency, and retention. *Journal of College Student Retention, 6*(1), 97–110. https://journals.sagepub.com/doi/abs/10.2190/FH61-VE7V-HHCX-0PUR

Soria, K. M., & Stebleton, M. J. (2012). First-generation students' academic engagement and retention. *Teaching in Higher Education, 17*(6), 673–685. https://doi.org/10.1080/13562517.2012.666735

Stevens, R. A. (2004). Understanding gay identity development within the college environment. *Journal of College Student Development, 45*(2), 185–206. https://doi.org/10.1353/csd.2004.0028

Stewart, D.-L., & Howard-Hamilton, M. F. (2015). Engaging lesbian, gay, and bisexual students on college campuses. In S. J. Quaye & J. R. Harper (Eds.), *Student engagement in higher education: Theoretical perspectives and practical approaches for diverse populations* (2nd ed.) (pp. 121–134). Routledge.

Strayhorn, T. L. (2017). Using intersectionality in student affairs research. In C. L. Wijeysinghe (Ed.), *Enacting intersectionality in student affairs* (New Directions for Student Services, no. 157, pp. 57–67). Jossey-Bass. https://doi.org/10.1002/ss.20209

Tinto, V. (1998). Colleges as communities: Taking research on student persistence seriously. *The Review of Higher Education, 21*(2), 167–177.

Tinto, V. (1999). Taking retention seriously: Rethinking the first year of college. *NACADA Journal, 19*(2), 5–9.

Torres, V., Jones, S. R., & Renn, K. A. (2009). Identity development theories in student affairs: Origins, current status, and new approaches. *Journal of College Student Development, 50*(6), 577–596. https://doi.org/10.1353/csd.0.0102

9

FIRST-GENERATION LATINX STUDENTS' INFORMATION SEEKING IN COLLEGE

Vasti Torres, Lucy LePeau, and Yvonne Garcia

In this chapter, we illustrate how the intersection of Latinx and first-generation college student identities influences the campus experiences of students. Latinx students are a growing population within higher education and are likely to be first-generation in college, making this an important topic for practitioners to consider (National Center for Education Statistics, n.d.). To demonstrate the strengths possessed by Latinx students, we use a cultural and social assets lens (Museus, 2014; Yosso, 2005) that contributes to how we understand students' interpretations and navigations of the campus environment. Specifically, first-generation Latinx students bring cultural knowledge, skills, and abilities or capital from their home communities (e.g., linguistic, communicating experiences in more than one language, aspirational, hopes for the pursuit of education in college) that influence this asset-based lens (Yosso, 2005). This perspective allows practitioners to be better equipped to nurture Latinx student assets and promote their collegiate success.

The first goal of this chapter is to provide a synthesis of current research pertaining to issues that influence the college experience of first-generation Latinx students. These topics include familial expectations, navigating the college environment, and importance of creating personal relationships. Based on Vasti Torres's longitudinal study of Latinx students across multiple institutions, these topics emerged as salient to first-generation Latinx college student experiences. As part of this study, a model was created that established the process used by first-generation Latinx college students in seeking information (Torres et al., 2006). This model illustrated that first-generation

Latinx students may distrust authority figures (i.e., administrators, staff, faculty) and consequently seek peers and family members for information regarding college processes. While this approach may be congruent with students employing their cultural assets (Yosso, 2005), it can create unique challenges to students because of their lack of institutional knowledge (Balcacer, 2018). As a result, first-generation Latinx students need support to be successful. The second goal of this chapter aims to provide guidance on how these challenges can be mitigated for first-generation Latinx students from a multilayered, asset-based approach.

Familial Expectations

First-generation Latinx students may uphold a strong sense of responsibility, respect, and loyalty for their families that influences the way they navigate collegiate environments (Suarez-Orozco & Suarez-Orozco, 1995; Torres, 2004). In many respects, first-generation Latinx students may perceive they are earning their degree for the collective success of their family (Markus and Kitayama, 1991; Museus, 2014; Phinney et al., 2006) rather than merely their own individual pursuit (Steidel & Contreras, 2003). Markus and Kitayama (1991) elaborated that students who often identify with collectivist cultures, such as first-generation Latinx students, may be motivated by the needs and demands of others rather than merely meeting one's own motivations and desires.

To elaborate, *familismo* is a value held by many Latinx communities. Steidel and Contreras (2003) defined this as the belief that (a) the collective family comes before the individual, (b) the individual needs to be interconnected emotionally and physically to the family, (c) familial reciprocity is essential in time of need, and (d) the individual needs to act in line with family honor. Calzada et al. (2013) observed this concept play out in Mexican and Dominican families from low-income backgrounds. This sense of familismo was central to the livelihood of these families, as resources were low and they relied on one another for financial support, childcare, and living. Given that many first-generation Latinx students are socialized with these values in mind, they seek communities similar to these in college as well as yearn to be interconnected with their home communities (Yosso et al., 2009).

As Torres (2004, 2006) and Torres and Hernández, 2007 indicated, Latinx students have additional developmental tasks around learning how to manage their familial expectations. In managing, students tend to understand how to incorporate new educational and cultural norms within their cultural and familial values. While the idea of cultural conflict may seem insurmountable for some students, research shows that this conflict is managed over time rather than removed (Torres et al., 2019). For many students, their parents may continue to have expectations that their children will abide by the values of their country of origin, yet students learn to better manage this parental expectation rather than creating familial separation or changes. One example that emerged in the longitudinal study is around traditional gender norms for Latinx students. These norms could create conflict between parents and young adults that are based on the cultural norms in their country of origin. Few students felt they changed their parents' expectations around gender-related norms, but the students did say that they were able to explain the choices they made that did not fit the norms to their family in a respectful manner. In this sense, it is important to acknowledge the strengths first-generation Latinx students bring to the campus environment due to the support they receive from their family members while also navigating expectations that may conflict with the majority norms in the United States. These conflicts can be invisible to those who are not aware of how students are navigating their bicultural environments.

Therefore, practitioners can play an integral role in supporting first-generation Latinx students by creating programs and services that encourage family in journeying alongside their student rather than cultivating students separating from their families. For instance, Kiyama and Harper (2018) challenged the pejorative term *helicopter parents* to focus on the benefits of family engagement for students of color from first-generation and collectivistic orientation backgrounds to increase persistence and graduation rates. Sarrubi et al. (2019) discussed how practitioners in orientation and new student programs could exhibit an ideology of support and visibility that integrates the cultural wealth of first-generation Latinx students and their families. In their case study of nine orientation programs, they noted that one program used slogans such as "their story is your story" to welcome families, and this slogan symbolizes the collectivist cultural orientation that we discussed previously. They also shared how another institution incorporated Spanish-language program components that may support first-generation Latinx students' families in valuing their linguistic capital (Sarrubi et al., 2019; Yosso, 2005). In sum, practitioners who create programming and educational opportunities that embed the value of familismo may create mechanisms to better reach first-generation Latinx students, manage their familial expectations (Torres et al., 2019), and value their cultural knowledge.

Navigating the College Environment

Nuñez (2014) pointed out that research on Latinx students should attend to "historical, economic, and social contexts" (p. 90). This attention should also apply to practitioners when working with Latinx students. One example was provided in the previous section—familial and social contexts are critical for first-generation Latinx students. While there are multiple ways to investigate how first-generation Latinx identities influence how students may navigate the environment and find support, we emphasize three potential factors: Latinx culture represented on campus, responding to racism, and understanding how to be a trusted adviser for a Latinx student.

Latinx Culture Represented on Campus

It is vital to recognize how Latinx students' identities influence the ways students may engage in the college environment (Torres & Hernández, 2007). Balcacer (2018) found that Latinx first-generation college students had high aspirations in terms of their careers and education but endured challenges because of their campus environments. Particularly, students in this study noted underrepresentation of faculty and peers, isolation, imposter syndrome, limited cultural connections, financial barriers, and limited familial understanding of college as major challenges. However, students combatted these challenges by finding allies, attaining mentors, building resilience, and learning how to learn.

When students can see their culture within the college environment, this sense builds their perspective that the environment centers their cultural identity (Torres, 2006). To create inclusive environments, Balcacer (2018) recommended weaving the home culture of students into the fabric of colleges and universities to help student identity formation particularly because of the rich ties students have to their culture. She suggested creating informal and formal counterspaces that enhance a student's sense of belonging while also showcasing their resilience. *Counterspaces* represent places and groups where deficit thinking can be challenged. She recommended increasing compositional diversity of colleges, including their student, faculty, and staff populations.

Regardless of the type of institution a Latinx student attends, it is important to recognize when students need assistance navigating the campus culture. In the academic year 2012–2013 Hispanic-serving institutions (HSIs) enrolled 59% of Latinx students in higher education (Núñez et al., 2015). Community colleges comprise around half of all HSIs (Núñez et al., 2015) and are more likely to have Latinx first-generation college-going students (Núñez et al., 2011). When considering environmental factors, it makes sense that more Latinx students choose HSIs. The growth of the Latinx population at HSIs is attributed to low tuition cost and proximity to home (Núñez et al., 2015). One of the approaches institutions can use to promote students seeing their cultural identity on campus and assist students in navigating campus processes is to create mentoring programs for students with both peers and faculty who share cultural familiarity (Museus, 2014). Rios-Ellis et al. (2015) found that a mentoring program that paired students who share cultural knowledge (e.g., high-achieving students) with students who were struggling academically (2.49 GPA or below) helped students with managing both their familial and academic roles. These suggestions can help students navigate the collegiate environment when seeing their cultures reflected in the spaces and when peers may be able to relate to each other through cultural knowledge.

Recognizing Racism

When Latinx students experience dissonance between their home environment and the college environment this creates different developmental tasks (Torres, 2009). In the longitudinal study of Latinx students, it was found that the first time that students encountered racism was in college (Torres, 2009). In addition, Torres and Hernández (2007) found that Latinx identity development included the recognition of racism as part of the development processes Latinx students experience during their college career. To help Latinx students with the recognition of racism, practitioners must provide space, time, and an open attitude to help students make meaning of racism. Most students did not want to call their experiences racist—it took time for them to speak of the incident and to ask others to help them make meaning of the experience. This reaction suggests that campus practitioners should consider creating meaning-making spaces for students to talk about the experiences they have both on and off campus. This meaning-making process includes the integration of new information about oneself as well as others. This process allows for negative messages to be transformed in order for students to avoid deficit thinking.

One example of how colleges can help students make meaning of their experiences is Latino student organizations (LSOs). In recent work with Latino males at highly selective White institutions, Pérez (2016) found that LSOs played a role in providing ease into social transitions and providing leadership opportunities for students. Pérez (2016) elaborated on how LSOs helped Latino males' navigational capital by enhancing their skills and learning about other resources as result of their involvement in LSOs. The skills and resources allowed for these students to better navigate the campus climate and traditions. These examples illustrate the need to create spaces where students feel they can trust those around them to make meaning of their experiences.

Being a Trusted Adviser

Torres et al. (2006) and Sáenz et al. (2018) found that first-generation Latinx students were not comfortable asking college personnel for information. Sáenz found that male community college students were uneasy about seeking out information from personnel within the university because of the belief that success was their own feat to accomplish as well as not knowing where to seek support as a primary reason for their apprehension. However, Sáenz found that familismo and other forms of cultural capital helped students navigate the community college settings.

The Torres et al. (2006) model examined how students viewed advisers and gained academic information from their institutions. In this model, first-generation Latinx students were more comfortable asking a trusted other for information rather than designated college administrators. The issue is that students would seek out trusted others like peers, family members, or past friends who may not have accurate information about the current curricular requirements. The students expressed unease with formal advisers because they may be judged as less intelligent, yet in some cases students felt like administrators gave them different answers and confused them (Torres et al., 2006).

We provided evidence on three factors: (a) familial influences, (b) psychosocial influences like recognizing racism, and (c) the role of advisers that may influence first-generation Latinx students' collegial experiences. Next, we elaborate on why first-generation Latinx students' having meaningful personal relationships inside and outside of the campus environment can support their success.

Importance of Having a Trusted Other or Personal Relationship to Facilitate Success

Latinx students who also identify as first-generation may employ strategies to facilitate their successes that are congruent with collectivist culture and sense of community (Clayton et al., 2017; Markus & Kitayama, 1991; Museus, 2014). We highlight the importance of Latinx students connecting with professionals who can relate to their experiences as well as the importance of peers in supporting student success (Museus, 2014; Pérez, 2017; Torres et al., 2006). While scholars often promote the importance of faculty-student interactions as an influence of supporting student success (Mayhew et al., 2016), the quality of these interactions and whether or not students connect with faculty and staff who can relate to and understand their cultural identities needs more attention (Museus, 2014). Traditional ways of connecting to faculty and staff may not work in the same manner for first-generation

Latinx students. Some studies identified that faculty-student interactions are not necessarily related to Latinx students thriving and finding sense of belonging (Pérez, 2017; Pérez & Taylor, 2016).

Museus (2014) presented the culturally engaging campus model (CECE; pronounced *see-see*) from decades of empirically based research about what works for students of color studying at predominantly White institutions (PWIs). The model is broken into two sets of culturally relevant and responsive indicators; relevance indicators relate to how students see themselves reflected within the campus environment, and responsiveness indicators relate to what educators can do to cultivate success for diverse student populations. One of the culturally responsive indicators is holistic support. This indicator relates to students knowing that they can identify a person (e.g., peer, faculty, staff, support service practitioner, etc.) in the environment that they know will give them the support that they need or refer them to someone who will (Museus, 2014).

If Latinx first-generation students do not form meaningful relationships with faculty or administrators to support their success, they often rely on peers to make these types of connections (Pérez, 2017; Rodriguez et al., 2003; Torres et al., 2006). Pérez (2017) studied the academic determination and use of cultural capital of 21 Latinx males at 4-year selective institutions. He found that Latinos in his study had an overreliance on peers to facilitate their success. Success for participants in the study was defined as being both academically and socially engaged at the universities. Participants in his study noted that they did not seek out faculty for fear of being perceived as "stupid." Similarly, Torres et al. (2006) noted that students were not likely to seek out academic advisers related to support but were more likely to turn to peers or trusted others for information, even if that information was incorrect. These studies punctuate the importance of Latinx students finding *trusted* others and personal relationships to support their success. Therefore, educators who do not share Latinx identities should focus on understanding how to reach students to build their trust and their cultural identities.

Discussion

To cultivate student success for Latinx students, it's imperative to create culturally responsive practices that honor the intersection of identities. To have an understanding, practitioners must understand how these influences serve as assets for these students and work with the students to recognize and incorporate cultural perspectives (Museus, 2014; Yosso, 2005) and validation (Rendón, 2009). Students can then find cultural validation and sense of belonging within their respective campus environment to bolster their success.

Throughout this chapter we made recommendations for practitioners. We would like to close the chapter by providing foci intended to direct conversation and planning to support Latinx, first-generation students who are on our campuses.

- Proactively provide information to first-generation Latinx students and their families (sources of support) about information related to academic advising and why it is useful during transition programs (Museus, 2014; Torres et al., 2006).
- Meaningfully involve students' families in orientation and transition programs (Kiyama & Harper, 2018; Sarubbi et al., 2019).
- Connect students with peer and mentoring programs where they see themselves and their identities reflected in the educational opportunities (Balcacer, 2018; Museus, 2014).
- Routinely ask students to reflect (e.g., course assignments, cocurricular engagement) about how they seek information about navigating the college environment.
- Educate yourself about how to understand and recognize when a Latinx student is experiencing cultural conflict.
- Create trusted relationships with Latinx students on your campus. Work on making sure all students have a person who supports them and can help them navigate the environment.

References

Balcacer, A. (2018). *How persevering Latina/o first-generation college students navigate their college experience: Keeping who they are while learning and persisting in the culture of college* [Doctoral dissertation, Portland State University]. PDX Scholar. https://doi.org/10.15760/etd.6312

Calzada, E. J., Tamis-LeMonda, C. S., & Yoshikawa, H. (2013). *Familismo* in Mexican and Dominican families from low-income, urban communities. *Journal of Family Issues, 34*(12), 1696–1724. https://doi.org/10.1177/0192513X12460218

Clayton, A. B., Medina, M. C., & Wiseman, A. M. (2017). Culture and community: Perspectives from first-year, first-generation-in-college Latino students. *ournal of Latinos and Education, 18*(2), 134–150. https://doi.org/10.1080/1534 8431.2017.1386101

Kiyama, J. M., & Harper, C. E. (2018). Beyond hovering: A conceptual argument for an inclusive model of family engagement in higher education. *The Review of Higher Education, 41*(3), 365–385. https://doi.org/10.1080/19496591.2018 .1490304

Markus, H. R., & Kitayama, S. (1991). Culture and the self: Implications for cognition, emotion, and motivation. *Psychological Review*, *98*, 224–253. https://doi.org/10.1177/1745691610375557

Mayhew, M. J., Rockenbach, A. N., Bowman, N. A., Seifert, T. A., & Wolniak, G. C. (2016). *How college affects students: 21st century evidence that higher education works* (Vol. 3). Jossey-Bass.

Museus, S. D. (2014). The culturally engaging campus environments (CECE) model: A new theory of success among racially diverse college student populations. In L. Perna (Ed.), *Higher education: Handbook of theory and research* (pp. 189–227). Springer.

National Center for Education Statistics. (n.d.). *Enrollment*. https://nces.ed.gov/fastfacts/display.asp?id=98

Núñez, A.-M. (2014). Employing multilevel intersectionality in educational research: Latino identities, contexts, and college access. *Educational Researcher*, *43*(2), 85–92. https://doi.org/10.3102/0013189X14522320

Núñez, A-M., Hurtado, S., & Galdeano, E. C. (2015). Why study Hispanic-serving institutions? In A-M. Núñez, S. Hurtado, & E. C. Galdeano (Eds.), *Hispanic-serving institutions advancing research and transformative practice* (pp. 1–22). Routledge.

Núñez, A.-M., Johnelle Sparks, P., & Hernández, E. A. (2011). Latino access to community colleges and Hispanic-serving institutions: A national study. *Journal of Hispanic Higher Education*, *10*(1), 18–40. https://doi.org/10.1177/1538192710391801

Pérez, D., II. (2016). Over the ivy wall: Latino male achievers nurturing cultural wealth at highly selective predominantly White institutions. In V. B. Sáenz, L. Ponjuán, & J. L. Figueroa (Eds.), *Ensuring the success of Latino males in higher education: A national imperative* (pp. 132–151). Stylus.

Pérez, D., II. (2017). In pursuit of success: Latino male college students exercising academic determination and community cultural wealth. *Journal of College Student Development*, *58*(2), 123–140. https://doi.org/10.1353/csd.2017.0011

Pérez, D., II, & Taylor, K. B. (2016). *Cultivando logradores*: Nurturing and sustaining Latino male success in higher education. *Journal of Diversity in Higher Education*, *9*(1), 1–19. https://doi.org/10.1037/a0039145

Phinney, J. S., Dennis, J., & Osorio, S. (2006). Reasons to attend college among ethnically diverse college students. *Cultural Diversity and Ethnic Minority Psychology*, *12*(2), 347. https://doi.org/10.1037/1099-9809.12.2.347

Rendón, L. I. (2009). *Sentipensante pedagogy*. Stylus.

Rios–Ellis, B., Rascón, M., Galvez, G., Inzunza-Franco, G., Bellamy, L., & Torres, A. (2015). Creating a model of Latino peer education: Weaving cultural capital into the fabric of academic services in an urban university setting. *Education and Urban Society*, *47*(1), 33–55. https://doi.org/10.1177/0013124512468006

Rodriguez, N., Mira, C. B., Myers, H. F., Morris, J. K., & Cardoza, D. (2003). Family or friends: Who plays a greater supportive role for Latino college students? *Cultural Diversity and Ethnic Minority Psychology*, *9*, 236–250. https://doi.org/10.1037/1099-9809.9.3.236

Sáenz, V. B., García-Louis, C., Drake, A. P., & Guida, T. (2018). Leveraging their family capital: How Latino males successfully navigate the community college. *Community College Review, 46*(1), 40–61. https://doi.org/10.1177/0091552117743567

Sarubbi, M., Kiyama, J. M., & Harper, C. E. (2019). Ideologies of invisibility and support for families of color during orientation initiatives. *Journal of Student Affairs Research and Practice, 56*(1), 49–62. https://doi.org/10.1080/19496591.2018.1490304

Steidel, A. G. L., & Contreras, J. M. (2003). A new familism scale for use with Latino populations. *Hispanic Journal of Behavioral Sciences, 25*(3), 312–330. https://doi.org/10.1177/0739986303256912

Suarez-Orozco, C., & Suarez-Orozco, M. (1995). *Immigration, family life, and achievement motivation among Latino adolescents.* Stanford University Press.

Torres, V. (2004) Familial influences on the identity development of Latino first-year students. *Journal of College Student Development, 45*(4), 457– 469. https://doi.org/10.1353/csd.2004.0054

Torres, V. (2006). A mixed method study testing data-model fit of a retention model for Latino students at urban universities. *Journal of College Student Development, 47*(3), 299–318. https://doi.org/10.1353/csd.2006.0037

Torres, V. (2009). The developmental dimensions of recognizing racism. *Journal of College Student Development, 50*(5), 504–520. https://doi.org/10.1353/csd.0.0088

Torres, V., & Hernández, E. (2007). The influence of ethnic identity on self-authorship: A longitudinal study of Latino/a college students. *Journal of College Student Development, 48*(5), 558–573. https://doi.org/10.1353/csd.2007.0057

Torres, V., Hernández, E. & Martinez, S. (2019). *Understanding the Latinx experience: Developmental and contextual influences.* Stylus.

Torres, V., Reiser, A., LePeau, L., Davis, L., & Ruder, J. (2006). A model of first-generation Latino/a college students' approach to seeking academic information. *NACADA Journal, 26*(2) 65–70. https://doi.org/10.12930/0271-9517-26.2.65

Yosso, T. J. (2005). Whose culture has capital? A critical race theory discussion of community cultural wealth. *Race Ethnicity and Education, 8*(1), 69–91. https://doi.org/10.1080/1361332052000341006

Yosso, T. J., Smith, W. A., Ceja, M., & Solórzano, D. G. (2009). Critical race theory, racial microaggressions, and campus racial climate for Latina/o undergraduates. *Harvard Educational Review, 79*(4), 659–690. https://doi.org/10.17763/haer.79.4.m6867014157m707l

FIRST-GENERATION AND UNDOCUMENTED

Ana K. Soltero López

The experiences of undocumented college students have garnered scholarly attention within the last decade because of the undocumented youth movement. Based on my personal, professional, and research experience, I share thoughts on the unique intersection of being both an undocumented and a first-generation college student.

For many students, being the first in their family to attend college means facing a lot of unknowns. Leaving home, meeting new peers of diverse backgrounds, acclimating to the campus culture, adjusting to academic rigor, encountering discrimination/racism, dealing with imposter syndrome, and learning to manage a budget are just a few examples of the struggles first-generation college students face. What happens, then, when you compound these experiences with an added characteristic—being undocumented?

My personal experiences as both an undocumented and a first-generation student of color shaped my education and career aspirations. I learned about my undocumented status as a result of California's 1994 Proposition 187, which sought to regulate social services for "illegal aliens." The threat toward immigrants from this proposition negatively impacted my relationships with my teachers and peers. I lived in fear while I was undocumented, and I have devoted my 18-year career to working with first-generation, underrepresented, and low-income students. Undocumented college students not only share the same challenges as first-generation students but also have additional hurdles that make their access, retention, and persistence in higher education noteworthy.

Through my work in education, I have come to two significant realizations. First, undocumented youth are dealing with many of the same anxieties I experienced when I was undocumented. Like me, undocumented youth today are fearful of the consequences for disclosing their status. I understand this firsthand. My positionality as a Latina and the strong rapport I established with my students and their families allowed us to open up to each other about the struggles of being undocumented in America. I was saddened by the fact that neither I nor my students felt we could trust disclosing our immigration status to our teachers or counselors and wondered how this would impact our academic journeys.

Second, undocumented youth are constantly concerned about securing funding for their education. The literature, my professional work with this student population, and my research identify the cost of higher education as one of the biggest concerns impacting undocumented students. Due to their immigration status, undocumented students cannot receive any form of federal student aid. A handful of states like California have legislation that grants undocumented students the opportunity to pay in-state tuition and receive state aid. However, it is clear this support is insufficient.

As an undergraduate student at the University of California, Santa Barbara (UCSB), I worked closely with immigrant families and K–12 students as a school and home tutor and mentor for the California Student Opportunity and Access program (Cal-SOAP) and the UCSB ENgaging LAtino Communities for Education (ENLACE) program. The youth I mentored often felt discouraged and hopeless about their academic futures. Their parents were staunch supporters of their education but were unable to assist them due to language barriers. Most of the youth I worked with were brought to the United States as infants. As first-generation, American-raised youth, they were the first in their families to attend U.S. schools and were the first in their families to pursue college. It was pivotal that they received proper guidance throughout their K–12 schooling. However, given the rampant overcrowding in schools, the limited counseling available, and the students' general distrust of educators, these students needed additional support to ensure they accomplished their goals. As mentors, we provided them with study techniques, strategies to navigate school, scholarship opportunities, and accurate legislation information relevant to undocumented students. As a result, many mentees were successful in getting into and completing college and securing alternative forms of financial support.

As a graduate mentor for the University of California, Los Angeles's (UCLA) Academic Advancement program (AAP), I committed 7 years to demystifying the graduate/professional school application process for hundreds of underrepresented, low-income, and first-generation students. Outreach and support services for undocumented students were crucial for their success. Helping them navigate the institution, identify campus allies, accomplish postbaccalaureate plans, and find financial support for college and graduate studies mattered in their trajectories through college. Their powerful stories underscored the unique challenges that differentiated them from the average first-generation college student. Their undocumented status wielded immense control over their lives. In most contexts, these students could not get a job, obtain a driver's license, travel, or receive federal financial aid, which limited their prospects for graduate studies. Fortunately, the state of California had passed legislation benefiting undocumented youth. In 2001, Assembly Bill 540 passed, granting eligible students in-state tuition privileges. In 2011, the California DREAM Act was passed, granting eligible students in-state financial aid. In 2013, California passed Assembly Bill 60, granting driver's licenses for undocumented motorists. Nationally, in 2012, President Obama signed an executive order known as the Deferred Action for Childhood Arrivals (DACA) program, providing work permits and protections from deportation. The accumulation of these legislative acts has afforded many undocumented students opportunities that make achieving their life goals reachable. As a result of the changes brought about through the passage of these laws, most of my students were able to persist through college graduation. Many of them continued on to graduate/professional school. However, practice and research continue to identify financial support as the number-one obstacle that burdens first-generation undocumented students.

With the continuous increase in tuition, higher education becomes harder to access and sustain for first-generation students, especially for undocumented students who are unable to access federal student aid. Presently, our nation is experiencing amplified xenophobia that has resulted in an upsurge of draconian laws targeting immigrant communities—for example, family separation and exclusion policies, the barring of undocumented students from higher education in some states, and the threat of the termination of DACA. I refer the reader to chapter 2 in this book by Steven P. Dandaneau for a more in-depth look at the sociological underpinnings of these issues that manifest themselves in the punishing of first-generation and undocumented students. These policies and practices explicitly interrupt the education of first-generation, undocumented students. Students whose parents were deported often have to step in as the head of household and be responsible for rent, bills, and the care of younger siblings. It is common for students in these circumstances to take a leave of absence, which prolongs the completion of their studies. As educators, it is our responsibility to protect, to advocate for, and to support students who find themselves in such situations.

I am devoted to informing, empowering, and assisting first-generation students. The roadblocks and challenges I experienced as a first-generation, low-income student of color is what inspired me to pursue a career in education. In my mission to help students avoid all the pitfalls I endured, I have had the privilege of working with remarkable and courageous youth who persist despite the odds stacked against them. Their resiliency must be recognized and celebrated and the role of all educators, teachers, professors, counselors, coaches, and administrators must be elevated. The success of first-generation undocumented college students is contingent on loving, respectful, and devoted educators throughout the PreK–20 pipeline who will take the time to know their students personally and who will commit to doing everything in their power to help them succeed. Immigrant children are destined to be not only first-generation college students but also first-generation Americans.

Discussion Questions

1. The chapter contributor saw her ability to connect with undocumented youth heightened because she lived a similar experience. As a professional how can you develop a sense of empathy and understanding for first-generation undocumented college students while being aware of your status?
2. What would be the benefit of requiring all faculty, staff, and administrators to do cultural sensitivity training? Would there be any costs to this requirement? If so, what might they be?
3. Why do you think few states have followed California's lead of providing state financial aid for eligible undocumented students?
4. The author argues that love, respect, and devotion direct the work of individuals in educational endeavors. Are these attributes necessary, reasonable, and/or worthwhile to expect? Are there other attributes that are better suited to working within educational settings?

IT'S ALL ABOUT THE JOURNEY

Exploring the College Experiences of First-Generation Women

Nicole Zervas Adsitt

This chapter focuses on a subset of findings from a qualitative study that explored how first-generation college students experienced their educational journey in a private 4-year institution of higher education (Adsitt, 2017). Much of the initial research on first-generation college students provides us with a quantitative analysis of these students' experiences in the academy (Choy, 2001; Ishitani, 2003, 2006; Nunez & Cuccaro-Alamin, 1998; Somers et al., 2004; Warburton et al., 2001). Conversely, most of the qualitative literature is practice-oriented (London, 1996; Riehl, 1994) or surveys of 2-year college students (Padron, 1992; Richardson & Skinner, 1992; Windham, 1996). There are even fewer studies that examine the experiences of first-generation college students at private 4-year colleges and universities. While the media has recently paid some attention to first-generation college students in highly selective private institutions (primarily Ivy League schools), little formal research has been done in this area (Pappano, 2015). In particular, women are a group within private institutions that have not been studied extensively.

This chapter addresses gaps in the literature by looking at how women who are first-generation college students talked about their path to college and their experiences at private 4-year institutions. I chose to utilize qualitative methods in order to better understand the lived experience of this population of students. I was interested in learning firsthand how first-generation college students made sense of their educational experiences. My goal was to gain a better understanding of their perspectives about their educational journey, including what they perceived to be challenges and opportunities in their path to college.

Literature Review

Currently, access to higher education appears to be growing. Between 1989 and 1995, the total fall enrollment of undergraduates in higher education increased from 11.7 to 12.2 million (Horn et al., 2004). Even more recently, from 2000 to 2010, total enrollments rose from 15.3 to 21 million (Snyder & Dillow, 2015). Yet, closer analysis shows that patterns of access and attainment are highly stratified (Tinto, 2005). Despite the fact that first-generation college students are part of a growing group of students in higher education, representing 24% of the undergraduate population, patterns of access to higher education are stratified for this group (Choy, 2001; Engle & Tinto, 2008; King, 1996). In fact, it appears that access has decreased over time for first-generation college students. Astin and Oseguera (2004) pointed out that in 1971 the number of first-generation students entering college was nearly equal to the number of students whose parents both went to college. Yet, from 1971 to 2007, the proportion of first-generation college students in the overall population of first-time, full-time students entering 4-year institutions progressively declined (Saenz et al., 2007). According to Choy (2001), among high school students from the 1992 graduating class, only 59% of first-generation students whose parents never attended college had enrolled in some form of postsecondary education by 1994, compared to 93% of those whose parents had at least a bachelor's degree. Even after controlling for several factors, including educational expectations and academic preparation, first-generation students still faced a disadvantage regarding enrollment in college (Choy, 2001).

While it is disconcerting that overall enrollment is lower for first-generation students, patterns of enrollment within this group are even more troubling. Those who are the first in their family to go to college are often underrepresented in highly selective private schools (especially when compared to their peers from higher socioeconomic brackets) and over-represented in the least selective institutions of higher education (Astin & Oseguera, 2004; Pascarella et al., 2004; Warburton et al., 2001). Many researchers argue that low socioeconomic status (SES) and first-generation status negatively impact the chances of enrollment in highly selective schools (Astin & Oseguera, 2004; Berkner & Chavez, 1997; Chen & Carroll, 2005; King; 1996; Nuñez & Cuccaro-Alamin, 1998).

Attendance at selective colleges can provide increased opportunities for graduates, including careers in prestigious fields, higher earning potential, and enrollment in selective graduate programs (Bowen & Bok, 1998; Carnevale & Rose, 2004; Mullen, 2010). On the other end of the spectrum, transfer and completion rates for students in community colleges are low (Horn et al., 2004). In fact, a longitudinal study showed that of students who graduated in 1992, only 37% of students who started at a community college transferred to a 4-year college (Adelman, 2005). Therefore, access and enrollment of diverse groups of students in selective colleges, including first-generation and low-income students, is an issue of educational equity (Astin & Oseguera, 2004; Bowen & Bok, 1998).

Access to higher education is only the first step. Many low-income and first-generation college students face tremendous barriers and obstacles as they pursue a path of upward mobility through education (DeParle, 2012). Women in this study demonstrated their resiliency in the ways they drew on often unrecognized forms of capital and their own strength in order to find their way through the educational system. Success or failure for first-generation, low-income, or other marginalized populations cannot be left to chance. Higher education researchers and practitioners owe it to students like the ones in this study, and to all students, to look at issues of equity in higher education and to do better.

Several significant theoretical influences helped inform my work and are important to note. Elements of Black feminist ideology, cultural and social capital, and the community cultural wealth model shaped my work (Bourdieu, 1977, 1986; Crenshaw, 1991; Yosso, 2005). These constructs recognize the complexities of my participants' identity beyond the category of *first-generation* and allowed me to center their stories of women with complex intersecting identities to add to our understanding of their lived experiences within private 4-year institutions.

The identity of first-generation college students is not static. Black feminist ideology, specifically the notion of intersectionality and the work of bell hooks (1994a, 1994b), framed my understanding of how race and class interacted in the lived realities of my informants. *Intersectionality* is a theoretical construct that avoids the oversimplification of identities within the context of societies and systems. Much of the quantitative literature focused on first-generation college students does not disaggregate the data for analysis with specific subsets of first-generation college students (Choy, 2001; Ishitani, 2003, 2006; Nunez & Cuccaro-Alamin, 1998; Somers et al., 2004; Warburton et al., 2001). First-generation college students are not a homogenous group, and it limits our understanding of their experience to treat them as such in research. Markers of identity work together at all times and, because of this, individual markers of identity cannot be parsed out and identified as the only salient piece of identity. Reductionism and essentialism are dangerous when used to simplify identity in ways that ignore and make invisible the complicated differences in and among members of the same social location or group. This concept was important to my work, as I made an intentional effort to avoid using reductionist strategies while investigating the lived reality of my informants.

Cultural and social capital also served to inform my work. Bourdieu (1977, 1986) defined *cultural capital* as different sets of skills and competencies, passed down through generations, that play a critical role in the transference of social status and power. He also theorized that since capital is transferred through generations, it plays a role in the reproduction of inequality, especially in locations like schools (*habitus*) where certain skills and characteristics are rewarded over others. The constructs of cultural, social, and other forms of capital have often been applied in ways that limit our understanding of the experiences of first-generation college students. Their stories and experiences are frequently omitted or interpreted in ways that only show part of the picture.

Yosso (2005) challenges how cultural capital has been interpreted and utilized in ways that reproduce inequality. Yosso's community cultural wealth model is informed by critical race theory (CRT) and centers the lived experiences of people of color by challenging structural and social inequalities (Yosso, 2005). CRT is a theoretical framework that emerged from a legal perspective and examines how power structures are maintained through racism (Delgado & Stefancic, 2012). CRT has essential components that recognize the ways that institutional racism is deeply engrained in American culture and society as well as the intersectional nature of oppression. The communities of cultural wealth model rejects the use of deficit frameworks, particularly as they are connected to cultural capital. My work expands the understanding of the lived experiences of first-generation college students by moving beyond the limitations of framing students as *at risk* or deficient (Yosso, 2005).

Methods

This work examines a subset of participants from my dissertation study about first-generation college students at private colleges and universities (Adsitt, 2017). The full study was a qualitative study involving 19 first-generation college students from three different institutions of higher education. Since I wanted to know about the schooling experiences of first-generation college students, many of whom are women and Black or Latina, I chose methods that centered their experience and recognized the value of their narratives (Choy, 2001; Inman & Mayes, 1999; Lee et al., 2004). I centered informants' perspectives to understand how they made meaning of their experiences within a given context (Blumer, 1969).

After careful listening and review of the initial themes from my pilot project, I decided to focus on students' experiences of "being first" at private 4-year institutions. My research questions were related to first-generation students and how they navigated the conditions that promote or hinder their ability to succeed:

- How do participants make sense of race, class, gender, and SES as it intersects with their first-generation status as part of their lived experience, especially within a private educational setting?
- How do first-generation students traverse the borders and margins (literally and figuratively) of different communities as they pursue higher education, and how does this negotiation inform their ideas about their identity?
- How do first-generation students describe different spaces on campus, and what kinds of cultural capital do first-generation students draw on to help them as they navigate the academic setting?

My work answers these questions in relation to how participants negotiated their path into college, their experiences at college, and their experiences within their family and communities.

I decided to keep two of my sites and add a third location after my pilot study concluded. The three sites were all private 4-year colleges or universities, with slightly different missions and student populations. They were all in the same geographic region, and each was a predominantly White institution (PWI). The three institutions differed from each other mostly in the size of the undergraduate populations. College A was a large research institution with a total undergraduate enrollment that is typically around 15,000 undergraduate students. College B was a medium-sized institution, with an undergraduate population of around 6,000. College C was a smaller, religiously affiliated liberal arts institution with an undergraduate population of around 3,000. All three institutions had low percentages of Pell-eligible students, ranging from 19% to 35% in 2015 (National Center for Education Statistics, n.d.).

I intentionally searched for a diverse group of participants that would reflect the national demographic profile of first-generation college students. Intersectionality influenced my decision to recruit a diverse set of participants, as I wanted to ensure that my work reflected the complex and intersectional identities of first-generation college students (Delgado & Stefanic, 2012). I used purposeful sampling to select these students by reaching out to a variety of groups on campus (Patton, 1990). Examples include the Collegiate Science and Technology Program (CSTEP), a multicultural living learning program, the admissions office, a student affairs office, and program or department administrators. In all of my recruitment efforts I explained to students that I wanted to learn more about the experiences of first-generation college students and how they made sense of their college-going experience. I used the federal government's definition of *first-generation college student*, which is a student whose parents (or parent who they primarily reside with) have not completed a baccalaureate degree (U.S. Department of Education, 1994).

Of my 19 participants, 15 identified as female. This chapter focuses on the women who were part of this larger study. The women in the study were a diverse group. There were White, East Asian, African American, Native American, and Latina women in the group. Eleven students were from College A, two from College B, and two from College C. Two students were transfer students to College A. Almost all of the women participants (11) went to a public high school. There were two first-year students, four sophomores, six juniors, and three seniors (including one recent graduate).

Findings

The women in my study talked about their college experience in a very holistic way, which included carving out their path to, through, and beyond college. I utilized the community cultural wealth model to analyze how women in this study experienced structural inequalities and utilized strategies and support structures not often included in traditional cultural capital models to mitigate the effects of inequalities in their experiences (Yosso, 2005). This model identified six forms of capital that are part of the community cultural wealth theory: aspirational, navigational, social, linguistic, familial, and resistant capital as previously unrecognized forms of capital that communities of color utilize to "survive and resist" oppression (Yosso, 2005, p. 77). Participants shared the ways they drew on these types of capital to navigate the educational pipeline in order to gain access to college, to manage their marginalization at college, and to negotiate their experiences with their community beyond college.

For the women in my study, the path to college was riddled with challenges. Participants talked about how community schools were underresourced and how the lack of resources limited learning and preparation for college. They utilized navigational capital to move through and around these structures (Yosso, 2005). In most cases, participants described the ways their community schools were severely underresourced. Justine said this about her high school in the New York City school system:

> It's a public high school. . . . When I left, we were extremely overcrowded . . . but that was due to a lot of changes that were going on in New York. . . . a lot of high schools were going under review . . . and then, of course, they decided to close down a lot of schools, which really didn't help. It ended up pushing a lot of students into schools that were already becoming overcrowded. (Adsitt, 2017, p. 100)

Kozol (1991) famously cited the disparities commonly seen in the New York City public school system in his book *Savage Inequalities*. He referenced the way that overcrowding increases class sizes and limits utilization of space for computer labs, library facilities, or even gymnasiums, since every space available must be used for teaching. Maria was not in New York City but described her high school this way, "They didn't have real walls; they had these dividers up" (p. 102). While she did not go into detail about the effects of the dividers, they may have been a result of not only limited funding but also limited space. As such, one might imagine that larger spaces have now been cut in half, decreasing space and increasing noise. Julie took this point a step further by sharing how structures impacted her experience, stating, "I think just the way the building was set up itself. It's kind of like you're locked in, like jail almost. (Adsitt, 2017, p. 102)." For Julie, who had moved from a middle-class neighborhood to a lower-income neighborhood, the experience felt foreign.

Aspirational capital in the form of high expectations and educational advocacy within participants' families or communities often countered these conditions. Several informants said that the expectation to go to college was unquestioned (Yosso, 2005). Jessica told me, "That was never argued. Like, education is just something always sought out. It was something always emphasized by the home" (Adsitt, 2017, p. 117). Education was valued by the families of the women in this study because it was seen as an opportunity that had the power to change their lives. The women in this study also drew on navigational, social, and resistant capital as they navigated into more selective high schools or specialized programs or schools (Yosso, 2005). High aspirations led families to draw on their social capital within the community to seek out what they perceived to be opportunities for their students. For example, Justine used a family member's address to attend a school that her family perceived to be able to provide better opportunities. Alejandra's parents also had specific expectations about where she should attend school, as they told her, "Well, if you go to public school, you can only get into . . . a specialized high school. If you don't, then we'll start looking at other options" (Adsitt, 2017, p. 122). In the end, her family sent her to private school despite the financial burden this created. Other families pursued special programs. Chandra's mother pursued a program called A Better Chance. Chandra said, "They take city kids and bring them in the suburbs for a better education. So I lived in a . . . rich suburban, area . . . throughout high school" (p. 124). Thus, Chandra had the kind of schooling that is usually available only to those who live in well-funded school districts.

Many students in this study had limited access to credible and reliable information about the college application process. Students who had families who expected them to go to college had a tremendous amount of family support, but that did not always mean they had all the information they needed. For example, Jessica's mother sat her down and tearfully told her that she couldn't afford college, and she didn't know what to do. Jessica said, "She was like, '*You* need to figure out something. I don't have the knowledge to figure out something for you. I work at Dunkin' Donuts; I can't think of anything'" (p. 113). For Jessica, this created stress as she tried to find resources to assist her in her process. Jessica and the women in this study found resources in their communities in the process. From encouragement to pursue college to having a mentor pay for a college application fee, students described the many ways they had access to forms of aspirational, navigational, and social capital that were critical to their ability to access higher education, specifically private 4-year schools (Yosso, 2005).

Once in college, the women in this study felt like outsiders in college, which influenced how they engaged with the campus. Participants cited examples of overt racism and classism and subtle microagressions that contributed to their perceptions of a campus climate that was not welcoming or inclusive (Solorzano et al., 2000; Yosso et al., 2009). The concept of *microaggressions* was helpful as a framework for understanding the ways students experienced the private school setting. Maria talked about college as a different world where all the rules were different and often connected to social class. Prominent parts of the academic culture at a private 4-year school can create a sense of cultural isolation for first-generation college students (Housel, 2011). Examples of the culture are intellectual arguments, valuing competition, and dinner parties at faculty members' homes. Often upper–middle class values are projected through almost every aspect of campus life. Icebreakers that ask about parents' jobs, class activities that require students to disclose information related to SES, and being indiscreet about provided support all draw often unwanted attention to first-generation and low-income students (Pappano, 2015).

For women in this study, interactions often took on an additional layer. As Maria described, the expectations around networking were complex,

> Even when you go to these career events and they have employers on hand, and, you know, you get an opportunity to talk to them. It's a great opportunity, but we were taught . . . especially as women not to . . . promote ourselves so much, so it's difficult for me. (Adsitt, 2017, p. 156)

When I asked where these messages about self-promotion came from, she explained:

> From my family and friends and neighborhood and everything. But I think the culture in general. I think even for rich women it probably doesn't come as naturally as it does for most men. They seem to have [an] easier way at it. But I think it gets easier the more important you and your family are. . . . Yeah, it's like, your smile, your clothes, whatever, it's more important. (Adsitt, 2017, p. 156)

Maria believed that all women struggle with self-promotion, but the extent to which they struggle has to do with the intersection of gender and class. Her observation that "even for rich women, it probably doesn't come as naturally for them" shows how she saw that class privilege cannot fully mitigate gendered norms. This is a good example of intersectionality and how multiple forms of oppression are hard to untangle.

Several women talked about their experiences in the classroom, where their middle-class peers did not understand their experiences and faculty members often singled out students of color to share their perspectives. Faculty relationships can prove challenging to many first-generation college students (Longwell-Grice & Longwell-Grice, 2008). In the following example, Kara shows how there may be added challenges for women who may be uncomfortable seeking out faculty support. Kara told me why she felt uncomfortable approaching faculty:

> It's always been hard for me to actually open up and speak to my professors in general and everything because I've always been instilled [with the message], "Don't be alone with your teacher, don't be alone," 'cause like coming from where I came from, the teachers just messed with the students and everything, so it's like, I've been instilled [with] that since [I was a] little girl. (Adsitt, 2017, p. 138)

In past schooling experiences, Kara was taught to keep herself safe with adults, particularly men and including teachers. The values instilled in Kara to protect her and keep her safe were not aligned with values in college, which rely on the belief that classrooms are safe spaces. This assumption is rooted in the experiences enjoyed by more privileged students (Solorzano et al., 2000; Tatum, 1992). When Andrea came to college, she was confronted by her hypervisibility within her major. She said,

> High school was . . . mostly African American . . . but I would say there was still a good amount of, you know, Caucasian, Asian, Native American. I just knew I had a group of everyone and it didn't, it's something that never fazed me. It was just . . . something that you didn't really think about. And then when I got here it was just like, "Oh, well, you're female and you're African American." . . . I was sort of intimidated. I sort of felt like, "Wow, there's not that many of me." So it's almost like a sense of pressure, a sense of, you need to finish, you need to do well. Having to prove to not only people, but to myself, that I was capable. (Adsitt, 2017, p. 137)

Her hypervisibility led to feelings of stress and intimidation in academic spaces. She also felt that it was her responsibility to make a smooth transition, even when she felt uncomfortable. This also led her to feel uncomfortable asking for help from her faculty.

Finally, participants shared the ways they straddled two worlds and the emotional toll it took on them. This included the emotion work required to negotiate upward social mobility and the potential distance it could create between themselves and their home communities (Hochschild, 1979). Julie shared her feelings about being the first person in her family to graduate from college, "It's kind of surreal, but it's, it's really cool. . . . I just really hope that I can do my family proud, I guess, and like graduate [with] some sort of honor" (Adsitt, 2017, pp. 195–196). She also wanted to pursue a doctoral degree and be able to support herself, rather than having to "rely on a man," as some of the women in her life needed to do to survive. Her education served the purpose of allowing her to "live a life of her own." Her identity as a woman provided an added layer in how she made sense of the role of her education.

For some participants, managing expectations was complicated by gendered expectations. For example, Jessica shared how a supervisor was harassing her at work and she had to quit. She described the conflict this caused her. She said, "I felt really bad because I was helping to put food on the table, and then I just took that away. I should just put up with it" (Adsitt, 2017, p. 179). Gender and class intertwined as Jessica was forced to make a decision about what was most important to her in this situation. She also expressed her desire to be finished with school, saying, "I wish I was financially stable or completely done with school and everything so that my mom can come [live with her]" (Adsitt, 2017, pp. 179–180). Jessica had to cope with the pressure she felt to contribute financially and to be successful in school. Hochschild (1979) described a cognitive technique as a form of emotion work where someone changes a thought associated with a feeling that makes them uncomfortable. By thinking about her desire to be finished, Jessica was using a cognitive technique in an attempt to mitigate the guilt, stress, and anxiety she felt about not being able to help her family financially.

Women in this study engaged in complex negotiations at home and school in order to experience success in their pursuit of their dreams. Students felt a sense of "homelessness" in their new identity, which was unsettling (hooks, 1994a, 1994b; Van Galen, 2007). For example, many students took on the emotional work associated with managing and negotiating perceptions they felt their families had about how education might change them or their value systems. They also managed the work of living up to the high expectations set out for them by their families, who often did not understand what those expectations required of their children. Participants then had to do the work of translating their experiences for their families, often for things that are commonly taken for granted, such as changing a major or needing to spend more time away from the family to get work done.

Discussion/Implications

As access to higher education continues to grow for first-generation college students, colleges and universities have a responsibility to do more to learn about their experiences and support their success, especially considering patterns of stratified access to higher education (Davis, 2010; Engstrom & Tinto, 2008). More research is critical, as intentional efforts to represent the diverse voices that make up the larger category of first-generation college students would allow for a richer and more complex understanding of their experiences in higher education. Much of the current research does not disaggregate the data, and so it does not portray an accurate picture of first-generation students or the fine-grained analysis that results from examining disaggregated data. First-generation students tend to have multiple and intersecting identities (Nuñez & Cuccaro-Alamin, 1998). As seen in this study, complicating the way that we think about first-generation students could result in much more nuanced and powerful research.

In order to see meaningful changes in the lived experiences of first-generation college students, practitioners will need to address the disparities of the public school system. CRT posits that the intersection of race and property rights is a powerful framework for making sense of inequalities in schooling. Public policy is an area that can have a tremendous impact on increased entry for students, especially those who face barriers to access. As Swail (2000) stated, "The long-term strategy involves the redefinition of our public school system. Without large-scale reform, we do not have much of a chance of changing the direction of mass numbers of lives" (p. 98). Increased resources for schools, such as lower counselor-to-student ratios, could benefit all students, but particularly first-generation college students (McDonough, 1994). More focused attention on issues of diversity and equity in graduate preparation programs and professional development for school counselors would equip them with the tools necessary to better support the varied and intersecting needs of all first-generation college students.

If we are to make a true commitment to increasing access to higher education, faculty, administrators, and policymakers must also talk about how to support students once they arrive (Tinto, 2005). This involves interrogating structures that privilege some students over others. In other words, access to higher education is only the first step. The goal has to also be how to increase student success. Currently, the 6-year graduation rate for low-income and first-generation college students is only 11% compared to 55% of non-low-income, non-first-generation college students (Engle & Tinto, 2008). Campuses have a responsibility to look critically at campus climate, including an evaluation of policies, practices, and general assumptions that undergird the campus culture. Other examples that can create barriers for students are transcript fees, activity fees for certain clubs, clothes, or costs to travel home. For example, in my work, Julie faced a situation where she was almost unable to return for her second year, but emergency funds were made available. Programs like Harvard's incidental fund can address these barriers (Housel, 2012).

As a 2012 *New York Times* article highlighted, the promise of education can be an empty one for many low-income and first-generation college students. Despite having the resilience to overcome many obstacles to get into higher education, it is often not enough. The article detailed the story of three students as they entered 4-year colleges and the barriers they faced there. As DeParle (2012) noted, "Four years later, their story seems less like a tribute to upward mobility than a study of obstacles in an age of soaring economic inequality" (p. 1). Success or failure for first-generation, low-income, or other marginalized populations cannot be left to chance. Higher education researchers and practitioners owe it to students like the women in this study, and to all students, to look at issues of equity in higher education and to do better.

References

Adelman, C. (2006). *The toolbox revisited: Paths to degree completion from high school through college*. U.S. Department of Education. https://www2.ed.gov/rschstat/research/pubs/toolboxrevisit/toolbox.pdf

Adsitt, Nicole Zervas. (2017). *Stretching the circle: First-generation college students navigate their educational journey* [Doctoral dissertation, Syracuse University]. https://surface.syr.edu/etd/756

Astin, A., & Oseguera, L. (2004). The declining "equity" of American higher education. *The Review of Higher Education, 27*(3), 321–341. https://doi.org/10.1353/rhe.2004.0001

Berkner, L., & Chavez, L. (1997, October). *Access to postsecondary education for the 1992 high school graduates* (NCES 98-105). National Center for Education Statistics. https://nces.ed.gov/pubs98/access/

Blumer, H. (1969). *Symbolic interactionism: Perspective and method*. Prentice Hall. https://doi.org/10.2307/2574696

Bowen, W. G., & Bok, D. (1998). *The shape of the river: Long-term consequences of considering race in college admissions*. Princeton University Press. https://doi.org/10.1515/9781400882793

Bourdieu, P. (1977). *Outline of a theory of practice*: Cambridge University Press. https://doi.org/10.1017/cbo9780511812507

Bourdieu, P. (1986). The forms of capital. In J. Richardson (Ed.), *Handbook of theory and research for the sociology of education* (pp. 241–258). Greenwood

Carnevale, A., & Rose, S. (2004). *Left behind: Unequal opportunity in higher education, reality check series*. The Century Foundation. https://immagic.com/eLibrary/ARCHIVES/GENERAL//TCF_US/C040319K.pdf

Chen, X., & Carroll, D. C. (2005). *First-generation students in postsecondary education: A look at their college transcripts* (NCES 2005–171). National Center for Education Statistics. https://nces.ed.gov/pubs2005/2005171.pdf

Choy, S. (2001). *Students whose parents did not go to college: Postsecondary access, persistence, and attainments* (NCES 2001-126). National Center for Education Statistics. https://nces.ed.gov/pubs2001/2001126.pdf

Crenshaw, K. (1991). Mapping the margins: Intersectionality, identity politics, and violence against women of color. *Stanford Law Review, 43*(6), 1241–1299. https://doi.org/10.2307/1229039

Davis, J. (2010). *The first-generation student experience: Implications for campus practice, and strategies for improving persistence and success*. Stylus. https://doi.org/10.1111/teth.12092

Delgado, R., & Stefancic, J. (2012). *Critical race theory: An introduction.* New York University Press. https://doi.org/10.2307/j.ctt1ggjjn3

DeParle, J. (2012, January 4). Harder for Americans to rise from the lower rungs. *New York Times,* p. A4. https://www.nytimes.com/2012/01/05/us/harder-for-americans-to-rise-from-lower-rungs.html

Engle, J., & Tinto, V. (2008). *Moving beyond access: College success for low-income, first-generation students.* The Pell Institute for the Study of Opportunity in Higher Education. http://www.pellinstitute.org/publications-Moving_Beyond_Access_2008 .shtml

Engstrom, C., & Tinto, V. (2008). Access without support is not opportunity. *Change: The Magazine of Higher Learning, 40*(1), 46–50. https://doi.org/10.3200/ chng.40.1.46-50

Hochschild, A. R. (1979). Emotion work, feeling rules, and social structure. *American Journal of Sociology, 85*(3), 551–575. https://doi.org/10.1086/227049

hooks, b. (1994a). Confronting class in the classroom. In *Teaching to Transgress* (pp. 177–199). Routledge. https://doi.org/10.4324/9780203700280

hooks, b. (1994b). Essentialism and experience. In *Teaching to Transgress* (pp. 77–92). Routledge. https://doi.org/10.4324/9780203700280

Horn, L., Berger, R., & Carroll, D. C. (2004). *College persistence on the rise? Changes in 5-year degree completion and postsecondary persistence rates between 1994 and 2000: Postsecondary education descriptive analysis reports* (NCES 2005-156). National Center for Education Statistics. https://nces.ed.gov/das/epubs/ pdf/2005156_es.pdf

Housel, T. H. (Ed.). (2011). *Faculty and first-generation college students: Bridging the classroom gap together* (New Directions for Teaching and Learning, no. 127). Jossey-Bass. https://doi.org/10.1002/tl.451

Housel, T. H. (2012). First-generation students need help in straddling their two cultures. *The Chronicle of Higher Education.* https://www.chronicle.com/article/ Helping-First-Generation/135312

Inman, W. E., & Mayes, L. (1999). The importance of being first: Unique characteristics of first-generation community college students. *Community College Review, 26*(4), 3–22. https://doi.org/10.1177/009155219902600402

Ishitani, T. T. (2003). A longitudinal approach to assessing attrition behavior among first-generation students: Time-varying effects of pre-college characteristics. *Research in Higher Education, 44*(4), 433–449. https://doi.org/10.1023/ A:1024284932709

Ishitani, T. T. (2006). Studying attrition and degree completion behavior among first-generation college students in the United States. *Journal of Higher Education, 77*(5), 861–885. https://doi.org/10.1080/00221546.2006.11778947

King, J. E. (1996). *The decision to go to college: Attitudes and experiences associated with college attendance among low-income students.* https://files.eric.ed.gov/ fulltext/ED398775.pdf

Kozol, J. (1991). *Savage inequalities: Children in America's schools.* Crown. https:// eric.ed.gov/?id=ED356035

Lee, J. J., Saz, L. J., Kim, K. A., & Hagedorn, L. S. (2004). Understanding students' parental education beyond first-generation status. *Community College Review, 32*(1), 1–20. https://doi.org/10.1177/009155210403200101

London, H. B. (1996). How college affects first-generation college students. *About Campus, 1*(5), 9–13. https://doi.org/10.1002/abc.6190010503

Longwell-Grice, H., & Longwell-Grice, R. (2008). Testing Tinto: How do retention theories work for first-generation, working-class students? *Journal of College Student Retention, 9*(4), 407–420. https://doi.org/10.2190/cs.9.4.a

McDonough, P. M. (1994). Buying and selling higher education: The social construction of the college applicant. *The Journal of Higher Education, 65*(4), 427–446. https://doi.org/10.1080/00221546.1993.11778509

Mullen, A. L. (2010). *Degrees of inequality. Culture, class, and gender in American higher education.* Johns Hopkins University Press. https://doi.org/10.1111/j.1467-9647.2012.00836.x

National Center for Education Statistics. (n.d.). *College navigator: Find the right college for you.* https://nces.ed.gov/collegenavigator/

Nuñez, A.-M., & Cuccaro-Alamin, S. (1998). *First-generation students: Undergraduates whose parents never enrolled in postsecondary education* (NCES 98-082). National Center for Education Statistics. https://nces.ed.gov/pubs98/98082.pdf

Padron, E. J. (1992). The challenge of first-generation college students: A Miami-Dade perspective. In L. S. Zwerling & H. B. London (Eds.), *First-generation college students: Confronting the cultural issues* (New Directions for Community Colleges, no 80, pp. 71–80). Jossey-Bass. https://doi.org/10.1002/cc.36819928009

Pappano, L. (2015, April 8). First-generation students unite. *New York Times.* https://www.nytimes.com/2015/04/12/education/edlife/first-generation-students-unite.html

Pascarella, E. T., Pierson, C. T., Wolniak, G. C., & Terenzini, P. T. (2004). First-generation college students: Additional evidence on college experiences and outcomes. *The Journal of Higher Education, 75*(3), 249–284. https://doi.org/10.1080/00221546.2004.11772256

Patton, M. Q. (1990). *Qualitative evaluation and research methods.* SAGE. https://doi.org/10.1002/nur.4770140111

Richardson, R. C., & Skinner, E. F. (1992). Helping first-generation minority students achieve degrees. In L. S. Zwerling & H. B. London (Eds.), *First-generation college students: Confronting the cultural issues* (New Directions for Community Colleges, no. 80, pp. 29–43.) Jossey-Bass. https://doi.org/10.1002/cc.36819928005

Riehl, R. (1994). The academic preparation, aspirations, and first-year performance of first-generation students. *College and University, 70,* 14–19. https://eric.ed.gov/?id=EJ499539

Saenz, V. B., Hurtado, S., Barrera, D., Wolf, D. S., & Yeung, F. (2007). *First in my family: A profile of first-generation college students at 4-year institutions since 1971.* Higher Education Research Institute. https://heri.ucla.edu/PDFs/resSummary051807-FirstGen.pdf

Snyder, T. D., & Dillow, S. A. (2015). *Digest of Education Statistics 2013* (NCES 2015-011). National Center for Education Statistics. https://nces.ed.gov/pubs2015/2015011.pdf

Solorzano, D., Ceja, M., & Yosso, T. (2000). Critical race theory, racial microaggressions, and campus racial climate: The experiences of African American college students. *Journal of Negro Education, 69*(1/2), 60–73. https://eric.ed.gov/?id=EJ636426

Somers, P., Woodhouse, S., & Cofer, J. (2004). Pushing the boulder uphill: The persistence of first-generation college students. *NASPA Journal, 41*(3), 418–435. https://doi.org/10.2202/0027-6014.1353

Swail, W. S. (2000). *Preparing America's disadvantaged for college: Programs that increase college opportunity* (New Directions for Institutional Research, no. 107, pp. 85–101). https://doi.org/10.1002/ir.10706

Tatum, B. D. (1992). Talking about race, learning about racism: The application of racial identity development theory in the classroom. *Harvard Educational Review, 62*(1), 1–25. https://doi.org/10.17763/haer.62.1.146k5v980r703023

Tinto, V. (2005). Moving from theory to action. In A. Seidman (Ed.), *College student retention: Formula for student success* (pp. 317–333). Praeger. https://eric.ed.gov/?id=ED491930

Van Galen, J. (2007). Late to class: Social class and schooling in the new economy. *Educational Horizons, 85*(3), 156–167. https://citeseerx.ist.psu.edu/viewdoc/download?doi=10.1.1.828.2113&rep=rep1&type=pdf

Warburton, E. C., Bugarin, R., & Nunez, A.-M. (2001). *Bridging the gap: Academic preparation and postsecondary success of first-generation students* (NCES 2001–153). National Center for Education Statistics. https://nces.ed.gov/pubs2001/2001153.pdf

Windham, P. A. (1996). *Demographics: diversity in more forms; student demographics now and later* [Paper presentation]. Annual Conference of Southern Association of Community College Research, Panama City, Florida. https://files.eric.ed.gov/fulltext/ED398951.pdf

Yosso, T. J. (2005). Whose culture has capital? A critical race theory discussion of community cultural wealth. *Race Ethnicity and Education, 8*(1), 69–91. https://doi.org/10.1080/1361332052000341006

Yosso, T. J., Smith, W. A., Ceja, M., & Solorzano, D. G. (2009). Critical race theory, racial microaggressions, and campus racial climate for Latina/o undergraduates. *Harvard Educational Review, 79*(4), 659–690. https://doi.org/10.17763/haer.79.4.m6867014157m707l

11

CROSSING BRIDGES

First-Generation Native American Students at College

Les Riding-In and Scott Amundsen

> *One day, I want to own a trailer, have a good job, and never leave home.*
>
> —Stephanie Vielle, Blackfeet Nation

L ike many Native Americans who grow up on a Native American reservation, Stephanie Vielle never thought of moving off the reservation to pursue a college degree. A member of the Blackfeet Nation, Stephanie grew up in Section 8 housing on the Flathead Indian Reservation, and her childhood dreams never left those boundaries. Her family and extended family only knew the Flathead Indian Reservation.

The Blackfeet have lived in the Rocky Mountain region for more than 10,000 years. Today the Blackfeet reservation stretches from northwestern Montana to the Canadian border and covers a half million acres. There are about 7,500 members of the Blackfeet tribe, according to the Census Bureau. The population is young—the median age is just 29—and poor. The median household income is around $30,000. More than one third of the families with children under the age of 18 live below the poverty line (Field, 2016).

In early 2001, Stephanie's life took a life-altering turn that would lay the groundwork of becoming an adult. Like generations of Native Americans before her, she answered the call to join the U.S. Armed Forces. Her dad was a Marine, so it made sense to her to follow in his footsteps and enlist for 5 years.

According to Kevin Gover (Pawnee), the director of the Smithsonian National Museum of the American Indian, Native Americans have served in the Armed Forces in greater numbers per capita than any other ethnic group, and they have served with distinction in every major conflict for over 200 years. Native Americans served in World War I even though they were not citizens of the United States. In fact, it was not until after World War II, with the 1965 passage of the Voting Rights Act, that all states were required to allow Native Americans to vote on the same basis as any other American. Despite decades of persecution and broken promises, despite being dispossessed of, and often forcibly removed from, their ancestral homelands, American Indians have served and continue to serve in our nation's Armed Forces in numbers that belie their small percentage of the American population. They step forward when they hear the call to duty (Gover, 2017).

It was only a couple of months after Stephanie enlisted that 9/11 happened. She did two tours in the Marines, one in Iraq and the second in Afghanistan. She met her future husband while serving in the Marines. Her husband was serving in the U.S. Navy. They had a child. Both Stephanie and her husband earned rank. A 5-year enlistment turned into 10 years, and then her husband got stationed at Carswell AFB in Fort Worth, Texas. Stephanie was able to get joint orders to go to Fort Worth as part of her second enlistment. She could never have imagined how dramatically her life would change because of this move to Texas.

When they arrived in Texas, Stephanie and her husband lived near the campus of the University of Texas at Arlington (UTA). One day while doing some errands, Stephanie happened upon the UTA campus and saw the phrase "Be a Maverick" on one of their billboards. The ad (and the sight of the campus) made Stephanie pause and consider her own story so far. Her life experiences beyond the reservation had contributed to her dreaming bigger than she had before. Now Stephanie had dreams of owning her own home and becoming a strong representative for the Blackfeet Nation. And now, she decided, it was time to take steps to make her dreams come true.

Because of the Indian Relocation Act of 1952, the Native American population in Texas had been growing. By 1970, over 20,000 Native people voluntarily moved from the reservation to Dallas with the hope they would find employment. Many ended up staying and starting families.

Of the population identified by the 600 recognized tribes in the United States, less than 1% is currently enrolled in an institution of higher education and only 15% has graduated with a bachelor's degree (Native American Students in Higher Education, 2019). While the admission rates of Native students have risen over the past 25 years, they are still considered the most underrepresented group in U.S. colleges and universities. Many institutions are simply unprepared to address the needs of first-generation Native students. Native American students have some of the lowest graduation rates in the country once they begin college. The only underrepresented groups less likely to graduate college at their initial institution than American Indian/ Alaskan Native males (at 39%) are Black males (at 35%).

The factors affecting Native Americans attempting college include but are not limited to being academically underprepared for college, financial problems, social isolation, lack of culturally competent health systems, and problems with family and self (Keith et al., 2017). Many of these factors mirror those faced by first-generation college students.

Stephanie's timing to apply to UTA could not have been better. By the time Stephanie arrived in Fort Worth, UTA was already able to meet her primary needs as a first-generation minority student. A recognized Hispanic-serving institution, UTA's undergraduate population was approaching over 30,000 students. Stephanie enrolled, joined the Native American student group on campus, and became very active in the Dallas–Fort Worth Native community. Stephanie soon became a regular fixture on the regional radio show *Beyond Bows and Arrows*. This program focused on Native American stories and developed a strong following among Native Americans living in North Texas. The Native American community in North Texas welcomed Stephanie, and her story was soon featured in news stories for UTA and the greater UTA community. Stephanie was becoming a celebrity in her own right, while also realizing her dream of becoming a strong representative for the Blackfeet Nation. Stephanie graduated in 2017 with her bachelor's degree in political science and returned to the Blackfeet reservation. She is now director of tourism for the reservation.

Everyone loves an underdog, and Stephanie's personal story certainly highlights her identity as a Native American woman who grew up on one of the poorest reservations in the United States. However, her identity as a first-generation college student is not clear. In fact, much of the literature regarding Native American student persistence concentrates heavily on the Native American identity, and not on the challenges faced by first-generation college students. Yet significant overlap appears to exist between the two.

An important question then emerges: Do Native American students have more success at universities that focus heavily on first-generation students? This is particularly difficult to answer because Native American students are not a critical mass at many large universities. However, we can focus on how some universities tie in Native American student needs with meeting the needs of first-generation students.

Engagement With the Campus

Living on campus can be a challenging adjustment for first-generation college-students (Barefoot, 2008). According to Ecklund and Terrance

(2013), the transition to residence hall living may be more complicated and difficult for Native American students. How connected or immersed students are in their Native American culture may have a significant impact on their transition to residence hall living. The place where a Native American college student lives is an essential component of their success at the institution.

Several institutions, such as Cornell University, Dartmouth College, the University of Arizona, and the University of Minnesota, have developed successful living units and cultural centers for Native American students. The creation of Native American residential units or living learning centers on college campuses appears to have led to success in addressing the unique needs of Native American college students (Ecklund & Terrance 2013).

Engagement With Parents and Families

According to the Higher Education Research Institute (HERI), first-generation college students tend to be more reliant on their families (Saenz et al., 2007). It is a cultural value and responsibility of Native relatives to be highly involved in their children's lives (Martin & Thunder, 2013).

> Culture, to me, is to live with compassion and love for one another, to share what we have, to help one another, to live a balanced life, and to be thankful for what the Creator has given us. There are rules, protocols, and procedures for almost everything, including how to conduct myself and how to express myself. I grew up knowing everything had a place and that, most important, I had a place—in my family, in my clan, in my tribe, and in the world. I learned from what my elders taught me, that I am important. I am needed, as we all are needed, to uphold my place and my responsibilities within each set of relationships. (Martin & Thunder, 2013, p. 40)

First-year programs are typically built with the assumption that families are knowledgeable about college life and the families have the ability to connect with their child's college through multiple outlets. Unfortunately, these same programs are not always effective in involving the families of first-generation college students or students of color. For many of these families, the college-going experience is new and unfamiliar, which can make it difficult for them to help their child make a successful transition to college life (Donovan & McKelfresh, 2008). Helping the families of first-generation college students build social capital and become engaged with campus in an identity-conscious manner will help first-generation students feel supported in all aspects of their life (Azruaga, 2016). Efforts to include Native American students and their families will help them to avoid feeling like tourists on campus: uncomfortable with their surroundings and eager to go home to find familiarity and comfort (Rodriguez, 2001).

Engagement for Learning

Learning in Native American communities was accomplished through community educational systems involving elders, kinfolk, and clans. Benham and Stein (2003) suggested that such learning would be passed down to the next generation through sharing and storytelling. European colonization changed this emphasis from community success to individual success. Today's colleges and universities retain this learning model, thus deemphasizing many core values of community learning such as harmony, sharing, and cooperation.

According to Martin and Thunder (2013), family and cultural programming is highly valued in the Native community. Student affairs units should strive to offer year-round activities, not just be limited to pow-wows and Native American Heritage Month. Native faculty and staff should be included in programming whenever possible, as these members of the campus community provide students with opportunities to develop cognitively, socially, and professionally. Often, Native American faculty and staff members may be the only one in their respective department, so the sense of community benefits them as well. Extended family is important to Native student success. When possible develop cultural programming that includes families and community.

Final Thoughts

It's time to return to Stephanie. Stephanie was a first-generation student. Today, she is director of tourism for her tribe. She now owns her own home on the reservation and envisions a wonderful future for her and the Blackfeet Nation. And what of Stephanie's college career? Statistically speaking, Stephanie is among the least likely female populations to complete a college degree. Yet Stephanie did it!

Research on Native American first-generation college students is limited. Our chapter provides a few first steps into the questions and implications for exploring the nexus of these two identities. A useful read for those interested in better understanding the complexity of Native American education is Jana Noel's 2002 article, "Education Toward Cultural Shame: A Century of Native American Education."

What is important to understand is that Native American students attending colleges and universities for the first time are students who have overcome great obstacles to even get to the point of submitting their first college application. As the first members of their families, they experience the obstacles, transitions, and negotiations faced by first-generation students across the country. All experience the necessity to adjust to the new environment of higher education, often building bridges alone without the support of the institution. In addition to overcoming obstacles like all first-generation students, Native American college students are also attempting to bridge their own identity with Western learning methodologies to find success. There remains a significant need to research the lived experiences of first-generation Native American students to foster success for all students.

References

Azruaga, A. (2016). Family engagement for first-generation families and families of color. In V. Pendakur (Ed.), *Closing the opportunity gap: Identity-conscious strategies for retention and student success* (pp. 10–24). Stylus.

Barefoot, B. O. (2008). *The first year and beyond: Rethinking the challenge of collegiate transition.* Jossey-Bass.

Benham, K. P. A., & Stein, W. J. (2003). *The renaissance of American Indian higher education: Capturing the dream.* Routledge.

Donovan, J. A., & McKelfresh, D. A. (2008). In community with student's parents and families. *NASPA Journal, 45*(3), 384–405.

Ecklund, T., & Terrance, D. (2013). Extending the rafters: Cultural context for Native American students. In S. J. Waterman, S. C. Lowe, & H. J. Shotton (Eds), *Beyond the asterisk: Understanding Native students in higher education* (pp. 53–66). Stylus.

Field, K. (2016, July 26). For Native students, education's promise has long been broken. *The Chronicle of Higher Education.* https://www.chronicle.com/article/-For-Native-Students/237210

Gover, K. (2017, May 22). American Indians serve in the U.S. military in greater numbers than any ethnic group and have since the Revolution. *Huffington Post.* https://www.huffingtonpost.com/national-museum-of-the-american-indian/american-indians-serve-in-the-us-military_b_7417854.html

Keith, J. F., Stastny, S. N., & Brunt, A. (2016). Barriers and strategies for success for American Indian college students: A review. *Journal of College Student Development, 57,* 698–714.

Martin, S., & Thunder, A. (2013). Incorporating culture into student affairs. In H. J. Shotton, S. C. Lowe, & S. J. Waterman (Eds.), *Beyond the asterisk: Understanding native students in higher education* (pp. 39–52). Stylus.

National Center for Education Statistics. (2016). *Table 306.30. Fall enrollment of U.S. residents in degree-granting postsecondary institutions, by race/ethnicity: Selected years, 1976 through 2026.* https://nces.ed.gov/programs/digest/d16/tables/dt16_306.30.asp

Noel, J. (2002). Education toward cultural shame: A century of Native American education. *Educational Foundations, 16*(1), 19–32.

Postsecondary National Policy Institute. (2019). *Fact sheets: Native American students.* https://pnpi.org/native-american-students

Rodriguez, S. (2001). *Giants among us: First-generation college graduates who lead activist lives.* Vanderbilt University Press.

Saenz, V. B., Hurtado, S., Barrera, D., Wolf, D., & Yeung, F. (2007). *First in my family: A profile of first-generation college students at four-year institutions since 1971.* Higher Education Research Institute. http://www.heri.ucla.edu/publications

PROJECT MALES

Serving and Engaging First-Generation Students Through Mentoring and Service-Learning

Victor B. Sáenz, Emmet Campos, Mike Gutierrez, and Rodrigo Aguayo

Increasingly, college campuses across the country are designing more programs to serve and meet the needs of their first-generation college student populations (Whitley et al., 2018). This growing focus on first-generation students can be seen at the University of Texas at Austin (UT Austin), which enrolls more than 9,000 first-generation students, representing 20% of the overall student population. One effort that stands out as distinct from these institutional efforts is a faculty- and student-led initiative called Project MALES (Mentoring to Achieve Latino Educational Success) with its cultural assets–based approach to working with first-generation college students.

Project MALES was launched in 2010 by a team of faculty, staff, and students from UT Austin and Texas A&M University (TAMU) to enhance the success of male students of color, many of whom are first-generation college students. First-generation college students have been the key focus of Project MALES since the program's inception. The university students in our one-credit service-learning course, Instructing Males Through Peer Advising Course Tracks, or IMPACT, serve as mentors for youth at the local communities and schools in the greater Austin region. This class introduces them to cutting-edge research on male students of color and to our mentoring practices and prepares our mentors to successfully engage with the middle and high school men we serve. Through this work, we have developed a set of mentoring and cocurricular strategies that seize on the aspirational and resilience capital (Yosso, 2005) that these first-generation students bring with them to college. This critical conversation will explain our Project MALES student mentoring program, including a discussion about how it was developed as an assets-based strategy, the frameworks used to design our curriculum and theory of change, and the intervention strategies that we use to engage first-generation students.

Project MALES Overview

Project MALES is led by a team of nationally recognized researchers from various institutions across the country. These researchers work at 2-year and 4-year predominantly White institutions (PWIs), Hispanic-serving institutions (HSIs), and historically Black colleges and universities (HBCUs), and the researchers utilize the cultural assets of boys and young men of color to address and overcome institutional and systemic barriers. Founded by Victor B. Saenz (UT Austin) and Luis Ponjuan (TAMU) in 2010, Project MALES addresses the research literature gap on Latinx males and since its inception a decade ago has grown this research agenda exponentially. Our research institute functions as the research arm of Project MALES and has grown to include two research teams—one based at UT Austin and the other based at TAMU. It also includes a network of almost 50 faculty and research affiliates spread across tier I research institutions in the United States. In the past 3 years, we have added a graduate scholars apprentice program that supports advanced-level doctoral students and pairs them with a faculty/research affiliate mentor. Additionally, Project MALES directs various initiatives, like our research institute, that focus on Latinx, first-generation students in the K–16 setting. Initiatives that Project MALES directs include the following:

- The Project MALES research institute, the goal of which is to build and expand the research agenda on Latinx males and other male students of color and raise the visibility of our affiliates' research on young males of color by amplifying their work to our growing national network of P–16 practitioners and administrators. Current faculty and research affiliates include emerging and established scholars whose research focuses on the educational experiences of males of color.
- The Project MALES leadership council, which is made up of national leaders from secondary and postsecondary institutions that are committed to advancing the success of male students of color across the educational spectrum.
- The Texas Education Consortium for Male Students of Color, a state-level group that convenes faculty, staff, administrators, and students from school districts, community colleges, and 4-year universities annually in professional development institutes and student leadership summits to focus on the successes and challenges of male students of color in six major urban areas in Texas.

Project MALES Student Mentoring Program

At the local/regional level is the Project MALES student mentoring program. This program recruits, trains, and supervises a network of UT Austin undergraduate students (most of whom are male, first-generation college students) to work with middle and high school male students of color in school districts across central Texas.

The Project MALES student mentoring program connects undergraduate students from UT Austin with Austin-area high school and middle school male students. Partnering with Central Texas school districts, Project MALES student mentors work to improve the educational attainment and college-going competencies of young men of color. The mentoring program is based on the frameworks of critical mentoring, social emotional learning, and restorative practices for youth engagement. The program utilizes the critical mentoring strategy developed from Weiston-Serdan's (2017) mentoring work with youth. This strategy stresses the interplay of race, ethnicity, class, and gender and how these play a factor in developing successful mentoring strategies. Weiston-Serdan's framework utilizes elements of social justice and a critical approach to discussions about power, race, and privilege. By utilizing a critical framework that contextualizes their experiences, the middle and high school students often engage in topics and subjects that college students often have on campus, both in and out of the classroom. The Austin Independent School District has made social emotional learning an important pillar of its work district wide in recent years to support student's personal development to build the social and emotional skills necessary for them to succeed academically. Elements of this social emotional learning program are implemented in our curriculum as a way to assist the middle and high school youth in developing fundamental social life skills. Social emotional learning is one avenue for young men of color to understand methods in discussing their emotions, self-regulate, and gain lifelong skills. Our mentoring sessions also employ restorative practices and circles, a pedagogical practice that centers students' experiences in a culturally responsive manner and allows for discussions about race, power, and privilege that they may not have encountered otherwise (Austin Independent School District, n.d.). Together, these frameworks provide a teaching and learning environment for students that is context specific and assets based and that empowers students in their educational journey.

Our mentoring approach is based on research that demonstrates the power of relationships and to that end we carefully recruit and match our undergraduate students of color, most of whom are from predominantly low socioeconomic status backgrounds and identify as first-generation students, with middle school and high school male students of color who come from similar backgrounds. These students, who will be the first in their families to attend college, range in academic standing. Project MALES student mentors are recruited through major university events and fairs held at the beginning of the semester. These fairs cater to underrepresented, first-generation students and attract students from a wide array of backgrounds, many of whom are interested in finding ways to "give back" to their community. Most of the mentors also belong to the University Leadership Network (ULN), a scholarship-based program with over 2,000 students from all across Texas, most of whom have several of the racial, ethnic, and class identity characteristics outlined (UT Austin, n.d.). Mentor matching occurs at the beginning of every academic semester, through a series of interviews in which middle school and high school youth interview undergraduate mentors with the objective of choosing a mentor they believe will be the best match for them. Although every attempt is made to recruit males of color to become Project MALES mentors, due to the high demand for quality mentors, many of our student mentors are female and excel and are leaders in this role.

Many of the challenges that male students of color face are economic factors that impact them outside the classroom. Often, their families face economic challenges and changes in their communities and neighborhoods by means of gentrification, economic segregation, and policies that impact the schools students enroll in. And Austin and our central Texas communities are no different in experiencing the negative impacts of these social economic polices and practices, which translate to additional challenges these young men and their families face. Our undergraduate mentors provide youth with the skills, tools, and access to a powerful network of current students, staff, faculty, and alumni to enable them to succeed despite these challenges. Through team-building activities, leadership development, and critical conversations, mentors establish meaningful connections with the young men of color to assist in their holistic development. Since the mentors share similar backgrounds with their student mentees, strong and meaningful relationships are quickly developed.

In 2016–2017 the mentor cohort consisted of 46 undergraduate mentors, who were 67% first generation, 71% low income, 91% Latinx, and 54% male. In 2017–2018 the mentor cohort increased to 60 students with 66% first generation, 80% low income, 86% Latinx, and 60% male. In 2018–2019 the mentor cohort was made up of 58 students with 84% first generation, 98% low income, 83% Latinx, and 68% male. As indicated before, the middle school and high school male students who are served by the mentoring program share the same profile as the undergraduate mentors. Across the 16 middle and high schools in the Austin Independent School

District and Del Valle Independent School District that are currently being served, approximately 70% to 80% of the students are Latino and 10% to 15% are African American.

The Project MALES mentoring program is led by a project coordinator and a team of graduate students, the majority of whom identify as first-generation students. Graduate students, recruited from the College of Education at UTA, serve as the liaison contact between Project MALES and the partnering local area high schools and middle schools in order to facilitate student mentoring efforts. Together with about 60-plus undergraduate student mentors, the student mentoring program uses the critical mentoring-based curricular and pedagogical approach, which we have described and we organize under five central themes: brotherhood, leadership, identity, health/wellness and college/career readiness (Project MALES, 2020). The undergraduate mentors can foster close connections with their mentees through the activities developed in the mentoring curriculum, attending sporting or musical events the middle/high school students belong to, and meeting families during back-to-school nights and other community events.

A key element of the Project MALES student mentoring program is the ongoing professional development provided to the mentors. In addition to our Project MALES mentor retreats, which kick off our fall and spring semesters, mentors also participate in a service-learning course (IMPACT), offered through the College of Liberal Arts at UT Austin and taught by faculty and graduate teaching assistants. The IMPACT class serves as a training space for undergraduate mentors and as a form of experiential learning linking theory to practice. In addition to introducing students to the literature on males of color, faculty and teaching assistants also use the class to reflect on weekly mentoring sessions and further strengthen mentoring skills. Course topics and readings range from examining the K–12 experience, the school-to-prison pipeline, zero-tolerance policies in schools and society, and understanding the postsecondary experiences for students of color. Our monthly Platica series, where we invite faculty and local community members to present on their research and community work, also serves as a rich training experience for our student mentors.

The Project MALES student mentoring program also tracks student outcomes to ensure that students are progressing in measurable ways. For example, we utilize pre- and posttest assessments with youth to gather feedback as the semester goes on. This information allows the staff to do two things: (a) advocate for students and amplify the student voice and (b) provide campus leadership with data on the progress of students in the program. Lessons learned from the robust expansion of the Project MALES mentoring program in the last 8 years include ways to increase student outreach, center student voices, and incorporate effective methods of mentoring by putting theory into practice. Because of the data collected and the lessons we have learned, we are better able to work with and pair youth of color with mentors in fields similar to their interests and shared characteristics. The success of our mentoring program has been recognized nationally by *Excelencia* in Education in 2019 for our work with our undergraduate students. We have also expanded our mentoring program model to other cities in Texas, first in El Paso, and soon in San Antonio, where we are working with our consortium partners to build this program and support middle and high school students there. As we work to realize the vision, mission, and core values that Project MALES represents, our mentoring program will continue to empower K–16 students with the tools and aptitudes to be successful academic and community leaders and respond proactively to the ever-changing social and educational landscape. Visit our website diversity.utexas.edu/projectmales for more information on Project MALES.

Discussion Questions

1. What mentoring programs exist on your campus for first-generation college students?
2. What mentoring programs exist on your campus for students of color?
3. If your campus offers services for these two groups of students, what are the possibilities for collaboration within your institution and across eductional sectors?
4. What would it take to create a program like Project MALES on your campus?

References

Austin Independent School District. (n.d.). *Overview.* https://www.austinisd.org/cpi/restorative-practices

Project MALES. (2020). *Advancing equitable educational outcomes for male students of color.* https://diversity.utexas.edu/projectmales

University of Texas at Austin. (n.d.). *Leadership network.* Student Success Initiatives. https://studentsuccess.utexas.edu/uln/faq

Weiston-Serdan, T. (2017). *Critical mentoring: A practical guide.* Stylus.

Whitley, S. E., Benson, G., & Wesaw, A. (2018). *First-generation student success: A landscape analysis of programs and services at four-year institutions.* NASPA—Student Affairs Administrators in Higher Education.

Yosso, T. J. (2005). Whose culture has capital? A critical race theory discussion of community cultural wealth. *Race Ethnicity and Education, 8*(1), 69–91.

PART THREE

PROGRAMS AND PRACTICES

12

AND THE RESEARCH SAYS . . .

Program Supports Across the Spectrum

Robert Longwell-Grice and Mackenzie Hoffman

C olleges and universities offer a wide range of services under the umbrella of student affairs. And while it might be the goal of these services to help students succeed, unfortunately, this is not always the outcome. For example, the amount and type of academic support needed among first-generation (first-gen) college students is often much more extensive than that of continuing-generation students. It is, therefore, inherently more difficult for student affairs professionals to offer worthwhile and beneficial support to first-gen college students. This chapter examines the needs of first-gen college students considering research related to six critical areas within student affairs: financial aid, living learning communities, tutoring, counseling services, campus involvement and career services. Suggestions for changes and improvements are made.

Support for First-Gen College Students

While most continuing-generation students enter their first year of college with a general understanding of the new expectations of the college culture, this is often not the case for first-gen students. As stated by a participant in a study of first-gen college, "My parents don't know anything about college . . . they didn't even graduate from high school" (Engle et al., 2006, p. 23). Unfortunately, navigating the college process alone is common among first-gen students and can leave first-gen students feeling overwhelmed and underprepared.

One of the most significant statistics on first-gen students is the fact that they are less likely to graduate than their continuing-generation peers who come from households with parents equipped to guide them through the complicated and difficult transition from high school. Specifically, while "54% of students complete a degree within six years . . . these rates are even lower among underrepresented students" (Bryant & Duke-Benfield, 2014, p. 1). Explanations for lower retention rates among first-gen students are explained in the research by Williams (2009), who lists factors such as lack of academic preparedness, limited financial support from family, and inability to feel connected to the college or university. With just 24% of first-gen students meeting the college readiness benchmark in reading (Bryant & Duke-Benfield, 2014), it should come as no surprise that first-gens often feel overwhelmed by the new rigors and expectations of college academics.

According to Williams (2009), 41% of entering community college students and 29% of entering university students were underprepared for the academic rigors of college life in at least one of the basic skills: math, reading, or writing. Additionally, Williams (2009) argues that a lack of awareness for college culture and enrolling in fewer courses are also causes for concern about first-gen college students.

Impact of Specific Services on First-Gen College Students

Although some universities are able to successfully implement student affairs–related services, others are not. In relation to this, different services offered on a campus tend to vary in ability to serve first-gen students. Through research on how the areas of financial aid, living learning communities (LLCs), tutoring and counseling, student involvement, and career development are used by first-gen students, some themes specific to each service arose. A further analysis regarding how these services either are or are not of benefit to first-gen students is provided in detail in the following sections.

Financial Aid

Many first-gen college students come from low-income families. Therefore, there is a high need for first-gens to have access to information regarding financial aid opportunities. First-gen college students regularly express feelings of disappointment with the level of financial support they receive from their college or university (Engle et al., 2006).

The primary reason for the dissatisfaction with financial aid stems from a simple lack of proactive practices on the part of financial aid offices. Specifically, Engle et al. (2006) discussed how many first-gen students are simply unaware of how to gain access to and/or apply for different opportunities for aid. One explanation for this relates to the idea that first-gen students are less likely to understand the college culture, and thus lack knowledge of the professionals and resources on campus that could be of assistance to them. In a study of financial aid policies, researchers Susan Dynarski and Judith Scott-Clayton (2013) identified the problems of "complexity, delay and lack of transparency in the aid process" (p. 15). Dynarski and Scott-Clayton (2013) also referenced a recent national survey on the topic, indicating that "fewer than three in ten individuals without a college degree had any idea what a FAFSA was" (p. 15). With many first-gen students lacking knowledge of how to access and/or fill out the Free Application for Federal Student Aid (FAFSA), it becomes nearly impossible for them to gain access to the financial assistance they need.

Many colleges and universities are extremely limited in the amount of aid they have available, which creates another issue for first-gen college students. As Engle et al. (2006) explained, "The amount of aid awarded to students is also insufficient because increases in grant aid are not keeping pace with increases in tuition and fees" (p. 34). So even in scenarios where first-gen students are aware of the steps to take when applying for aid, there is no guarantee they will receive the amount of aid needed.

Research has also shown that first-gen students tend to be led into less manageable alternatives for paying for school. First-gen students express feeling pressure to get a full-time job on top of working toward a degree as well (Engle et al., 2006). While it may be true that having an income during college can help alleviate some of the debt accrued during college, the commitment of a full-time job has the potential to take away students' ability to be successful academically. Due to the lack of information on applying for financial aid, insufficient funds being available for school, and misguided notions on paying for school, financial aid as an area of support for first-gen college students needs much improvement.

LLCs

LLCs have been shown to have a very meaningful impact on first-gen students. One of the biggest reasons for this is the extra support and connections students gain when they choose to join an LLC. The extra support from mentors, residence hall assistants, and instructors results in significant academic and social benefits. Researcher Linda DeAngelo (2014) contributed much of the benefits to the meaningful academic engagement that happens outside of the classroom. Specifically, she explained, "The more students are getting together outside of the classroom to discuss the content of their courses, the higher probability that they will persist to their second year" (p. 66). DeAngelo also maintained that first-gen students are especially susceptible to feeling disconnected from campus and as a result experience lower retention rates than their more integrated peers. However, when first-gens opt to join an LLC, they are more inclined to get involved, make friends, and have a smoother transition to their first year of college (DeAngelo, 2014).

According to DeAngelo, another beneficial aspect of LLCs includes the presence of knowledgeable peer mentors and residence hall assistants. These individuals serve an important role, as they typically are responsible for setting the tone of how that particular LLC will operate. For example, often these individuals will work together to come up with creative and fun ways to help their residents feel comfortable, involved, and well integrated into the campus. First-year and first-gen students alike report feeling more comfortable approaching a peer leader rather than a professor with course-related questions, as this individual appears more relatable to them.

There is an abundance of evidence indicating the benefits of LLCs. The amount of information regarding first-gen students involved in them is limited, however, making it unclear whether first-gen students are aware of, interested in, and/or utilizing the different learning communities available to them.

Tutorial Services

As previously mentioned, first-gen students are at higher risk than continuing-generation students of not graduating. This has been confirmed by Stebleton and Soria (2013) who found, "First-generation, low-income students were nearly four times more likely to leave higher education after the first year than non-first-gen students" (p. 8).

A primary reason this occurs is due to the significant number of obstacles first-gen college students face. As Stebleton and Soria (2013) explained, "First-gen students are more likely than their non-first-gen counterparts to have additional characteristics that may serve as a disadvantage as they purse their college degree" (p. 8). At the top of this list is the inadequate academic preparedness many first-gens have, which stems from weak English/math skills and poor studying strategies (Stebleton & Soria, 2013).

First-gen students welcome the extra help from tutors as they recognize the importance of such support. According to Stebleton and Soria (2013), "First-gen students often recognize and acknowledge that they will need assistance to address the outlined barriers to academic success" (p. 12). In relation to this, the more a student is able to combat previous negative learning experiences with positive ones, the more likely they are to find confidence, purpose, and enjoyment in what they are studying.

First-gen students are often juggling other commitments, such as families and work obligations. The lack of time first-gen students may have, combined with their general lack of awareness about tutoring services, limits their ability to access these services. Students may see tutoring as adding to their already hectic schedules. Stebleton and Soria (2013) identified the internal struggle of having to choose between financial stability and high academic performance as a major issue for first-gen college students. Because most campuses know the positive impact that tutoring can have, they are making efforts to increase first-gen students' and their parents' awareness of the tutoring services that are available to them. It is now a matter of getting from awareness to usage.

Counseling Services

According to Stebleton et al. (2014), first-gen college students face unique counseling needs. They argued that first-gen students must deal with issues related to academics, adjustment to college life, and family-of-origin issues that many of their peers do not face. In addition, although the need for counseling among first-gens is present, the action by which this population of students goes about seeking help is limited. First-gen college students have historically expressed a reluctance to seek out counseling services, as they have the mis-understanding that counseling services are only for people dealing with severe mental health–related issues, not for everyday anxieties. Stebleton et al. (2014) found a strong correlation between the lack of a sense of belonging to the campus first-gens often feel and depression, anxiety, and stress. Unfortunately, such needs do not appear to be being met, as they found "first-gen students reporting slightly higher responses of needing but not using services" than their continuing-generation peers (Stebleton et al., 2014, p. 14).

Student Involvement

Existing research on the integration of first-gen students to an institution indicate the importance of involvement opportunities. Of the different types of involvement opportunities, those determined to have the highest impact offer students the chance to establish an academic and social support net-work. In addition, involvement opportunities that students join within their first 6 weeks on campus increase retention rates among first-gen students (Finley, 2012). Research has not yet identified the most beneficial model or type of involvement opportunities for first-gen students to date. It is still clear, however, that becoming involved on the campus has definite potential benefits for first-gen college students.

Goral (2012) points to the positive impact of forming a *posse* or cohort group where first-year, first-gen students are connected through occasional meet-ups. The idea behind this type of involvement opportunity stems from existing research on the cultural disconnects experienced by first-gen students. The research of Woosley and Shelper shows that first-gen students are more likely to feel like outsiders to their institution due to this disconnect in cultural norms. As Woosley and Shepler (2011) explain, "First-gen students often feel overwhelmed and as if they are vacillating between two cultures" (p. 703). Similarly, Rendon (1994) found that first-gen college students who did not receive reinforcing messages early in their first semester about their ability to fit in on campus were unlikely to persist. By connecting first-gen students with peers who are likely feeling a similar sense of disconnect, an awareness that they are not alone in their stressors, concerns, obstacles, and so on, becomes more apparent. The perception of like struggles improves the overall social integration and sense of belonging for first-gens to the institution.

Another involvement opportunity seen to have significant impact to the integration of first-gen students are welcome programs. Welcome programs offer first-year students the opportunity to get connected and learn about topics relevant to their successful adjustment to the institution. Ishitani (2003) found the risk for departure by first-gen college students during the first year of study was 71% higher than for their continuing-generation peers. Given this, it is critical that first-gen college students get involved as soon as possible to get connected. Finley's (2012) research on welcome programs indicates that first-gen students who participate in such programs are more likely to persist to their second year: "These students tend to persist to their second college year at higher rates than those who do not participate and are highly involved student leaders" (p. 103). Factors influencing the effectiveness of welcome programming include length of program, the specific topics covered, the mentor or peer leaders involved, and the way that groups are assigned during the program. Finley (2012) found that this type of involvement opportunity can have a significant effect in increasing student's commitment and sense of pride to their university.

While the implementation of first-gen student cohort groups and workshops have proven effective, involvement opportunities that cater to first-gen students remain limited. Higher education professionals looking to develop or improve involvement opportunities for first-gens should consider

- establishing a support network of peers and staff for first-gens;
- organizing programming that educates first-gen students on academic and social adjustment to college; and
- developing opportunities for skill development and academic readiness.

Career and Professional Development

In reviewing recent research on the impact of career and professional development services, definite gaps exist in career services' ability to effectively serve first-gen students. One issue is unequal access and/or knowledge of how to utilize the career resources available at the institution. Access to career opportunities is limited by the social network of many first-gen students, as their network offers less upward mobility, thus leaving them to work that much harder both to educate themselves and to build up their network in order to create additional career opportunities. While career and professional development resources are available at institutions, first-gen students are less likely to be aware of their importance.

First-gen students are less likely to have parents or relatives readily discussing the importance of utilizing career resources at their institution. The familial situation of one first-gen student illustrates the discrepancy in receiving this valuable information: "She received little financial or social support from her family . . . nor did she receive any information or guidance regarding the importance of using collegiate resources to asset and achieve high career aspirations" (Parks-Yancy, 2012, p. 516).

Institutions should take a more proactive stance to ensure first-gen students receive early and frequent messaging on the benefit of available career services. This stance would most likely benefit all students, not just first-gen students. According to Parks-Yancy (2012), while career centers are important, additional mentorship provided by university professionals working in other offices on campus can prove just as beneficial: "First-gen students from low-income backgrounds need to be systematically encouraged by all orientation personnel, university administrators, and professors outside of class" (p. 521).

Conclusion

Through the analysis of existing research on the impact of six different types of services offered within student affairs, conclusions of best practices and suggestions for improvements are more easily identified. According to the research on student services provided to first-gen college students, each of the six services reviewed—financial aid, LLCs, tutoring, counseling, student involvement, and career services—has ways they can positively impact the first-gen college student experience. Conversely, the research identified ways in which these same offices can improve the experience for first-gen college students.

While some services such as LLCs, tutoring, and student involvement have significant benefits, others have "room to grow" before they can say that they are successfully supporting the needs of first-gen students. Overall, this literature review identified the need for more specialized programming catering to the known academic and social barriers faced by first-gen students in order to help first-gens succeed. Institutions have a responsibility for assessing what works and bringing what works to all students.

Further research should be conducted in the area of student services, in order to gain a deeper understanding of what works and does not work for first-gen students so the benefits can be effectively replicated. Programs designed to tell all students that they can be successful and that they can be proud of their achievement of enrolling in college are crucial for first-gen student success. Accordingly, programs that use a strengths-based, validating approach to working with all students, particularly first-gen college students, are equally critical.

References

Bryant, R. T. & Duke-Benfield, A. (2014). *Keeping college within reach: Sharing best practices for serving low-income and first-generation students (recommendations for Reauthorization of the Higher Education Act)*. BePress. https://works.bepress.com/rhonda_tsoiafattbryant/19/

DeAngelo, L. (2014). Programs and practices that retain students from the first to second Year: Results from a national study. In R. Padgett (Ed.), *Emerging research and practices on students* (New Directions for Institutional Research, no. 160, pp. 53–75). Jossey-Bass. https://doi.org/10.1002/ir.20061

Dynarski, S., & Scott-Clayton, J. (2013). *Financial aid policy: Lessons from research*. National Bureau of Economic Research. http://www.nber.org/papers/w18710

Engle, J., Bermeo, A., & O'Brien, C. (2006). *Straight from the source: What works for first-generation college students*. The Pell Institute for the Study in Higher Education.

Finley, J. (2012). *Early integration of first-generation students*. [Unpublished doctoral dissertation]. Northeastern University.

Goral, T. (2012). Toward first-generation success. *University Business, 15*(5), 8.

Ishitani, T. (2003, August). A longitudinal approach to assessing attrition behavior among first-generation students: Time-varying effects of pre-college characteristics. *Research in Higher Education, 44*(4), 433–449. https://www.jstor.org/stable/40197314?seq=1

Parks-Yancy, R. (2012). Interactions into opportunities: Career management for low-income, first-generation African-American college students. *Journal of College Student Development, 53*(4), 510–523.

Rendon, L. (1994). Validating culturally diverse students: Toward a new model of learning and student development. *Innovative Higher Education, 19*(1),33–51.

Stebleton, M., & Soria, K. (2013). Breaking down barriers: Academic obstacles of first-generation students at research universities. *The Learning Assistance Review*, *17*(2), 7–19.

Stebleton, M., Soria, K., & Huesman, R. (2014). First-generation students' sense of belonging, mental health, and use of counseling services at public research universities. *Journal of College Counseling*, *17*(1), 6–20. https://doi.org/10.1002/ j.2161-1882.2014.00044.x

Williams, G. B. (2009). *Comparison of retention factors between first-generation and second- and third-generation college students and development of the likelihood of success model* (Publication No. AAT 3447686) [Doctoral dissertation, Lamar University]. ProQuest Dissertations Publishing.

Woosley, S., & Shepler, D. (2011). Understanding the early integration experiences of first-generation college students. *College Student Journal*, *45*(4), 700–714.

13

COLLEGE PREPARATION THROUGH COLLEGE ACCESS AND SUPPORT PROGRAMS

Staci Weber

Nineteen percent of first-generation students graduated colleges and universities with their baccalaureate degree (Institute of Education Sciences, 2020), while upward of 94% (Minds Matter, 2016) and 90% (Posse Foundation, n.d.) of first-generation college students who used community-based, nonprofit college access and support programs graduated colleges and universities with their baccalaureate degree. Based on the National College Access Network (2011) and National Association for College Admission Counseling (n.d.), I define *college access programs* as nonprofit or government-funded programs or organizations that assist students with college readiness and/or access. Such programs often offer students SAT preparation classes, provide college application fee waivers, help students secure tutoring services, increase students' knowledge about college, give students stipends for summer internships, and/or offer workshops for parents about the college experience (Coles & Engstrom, 2012; Hagedorn & Fogel, 2002; Tuitt et al., 2011). This chapter reports on the findings that show how college access programs that teach students soft, life skills also aided in their transition to college and, ultimately, enhanced their college experience.

Methodology

This research is part of a larger study that took place at a selective, private, research I university. Forty-seven individuals who identified as first-generation college students and who had used nonprofit or government-funded college access programs participated in the study. I conducted interviews and focus groups with the participants to learn about their experiences in the precollege programs and how the programs helped prepare them for college. The project was supported by the NASPA Foundation and College Student Personnel Association of New York State, Inc.

Participants

Participants included 30 students who identified as female and 17 who identified as male. Forty-five students identified as students of color, one student identified as White, and one student did not report their race. The participants used over 40 college access programs, and many students referenced the same programs; 27 students used more than one college access program. The parental income from the students' Free Application for Federal Student Aid (FAFSA) averaged $35,117.32. Twelve students immigrated to the United States before college. Of the 35 students born in the United States, at least eight students' parents immigrated to the United States from another country. Nineteen students mentioned that they spoke two languages. None of the students in the study self-identified as undocumented or homeless at the time of the research; however, two students discussed being undocumented during high school. All the students in this study lived in college-owned housing or lived off campus with roommates; no students commuted from home. All the students in this study also matriculated into college directly after high school. While these enrollment and housing patterns represented the undergraduate population at the university where the research took place, the patterns did not reflect national trends on first-generation college students (Engle & Tinto, 2008).

College Access Programs and Life Skills

In interviews, students described how their college access programs provided personal and professional development opportunities to enhance students' leadership and communication skills, cultural competencies, and sense of responsibility. Further, students acknowledged how their college access programs fostered and contributed to their college-going journey. What follows are excerpts from the 47 interviews that highlight how students' participation set them up and provided skills for success in college.

Carlos received leadership opportunities through his college access organizations. He first described the leadership opportunities that ASPIRA and Youth Bridge offered him: "Through ASPIRA, I was community service chair and through Youth Bridge, I was diversity in the workplace chair" (Weber, 2016, p. 110). Through these roles, Carlos developed:

Email etiquette . . . phone etiquette, just even time management like in terms of figuring out deadlines for planning, . . . how to manage or how to work in groups with people your age. That was one of the main things that I actually got from it. . . . Set out agendas, create minutes, or just create a task for whoever's on my team and things like that. (Weber, 2016, p. 110)

Carlos then connected these leadership skills to his engagement in college campus life:

It became easy for me to just contact other organizations around the [university] area and just go out and do community service, because I had already done all those things [in high school]. I had already knowledge on how to plan those [events] and how to contact people. (Weber, 2016, p. 110)

Carlos felt at ease interacting with people, community organizations, and campus clubs, because of his experiences with ASPIRA and Youth Bridge. He learned about engagement, professionalism, time management, and facilitating meetings. Carlos continued:

[I learned through my role in ASPIRA] things that you're supposed to have, that you develop professionally. . . . So, I think that helped me a lot in becoming an involved leader on [my university] campus, it set me up for that. For being able to come on campus and just join organizations and be able to work with them effectively. (Weber, 2016, pp. 110–111)

The leadership skills Carlos received through his college access organization helped him become more engaged in college life. As researchers found, student engagement in college benefited students' sense of belonging on campus, decision-making skills, teamwork, and critical and analytical thinking (Kuh, 1995, 2012; Kuh et al., 2008; O'Keeffe, 2013). ASPIRA's and Youth Bridge's opportunities facilitated Carlos's collegiate success.

Julianna also believed her college access programs advanced her leadership skills, which helped in college. Julianna's involvement with the YMCA started at a young age and continued through her teenage years, when she participated in Global Teens, Career Connections, Team Club, and Leaders Club. Julianna continued:

The organizations allow me to time manage, so as I said before, I like to keep myself busy. Because with these organizations it really gives me time where I must allocate to homework, because I don't have a lot of time to just say, "Okay, I can hang out all day and then do my homework later," because I don't have later. . . . So, I must make sure I study, pace myself, and keep up-to-date with my work. (Weber, 2016, p. 111)

The YMCA taught Julianna time-management skills, which often contribute to college students' reduced stress levels and enhance their college experiences (Krumrei-Mancuso et al., 2013). Julianna also reflected on how good time-management skills and her cocurricular involvement during high school helped her make friends in college and would likely help her transition to a management career:

> I feel like it [the leadership opportunities] gives me, it's, a simulation for the real life. 'Cause I'm [a] management [major] and soon, I don't know exactly what type of management I want to go into, but I want to go into some type of management. And, taking on leadership positions and senior roles in any organization[s] allows me to know how to become more of a people person and work with people from different backgrounds. And, I feel like it allows me to gain friends. So, if you don't have a lot of friends when you first come in [to college], the organizations, you sometimes meet your best friends in these organizations. (Weber, 2016, p. 112)

Julianna saw how campus engagement helped her make friends, which contributed to her sense of belonging (Gummadam et al., 2016; O'Keeffe, 2013; Ostrove & Long, 2007; Soria & Stebleton, 2013; Stebleton et al., 2014). Julianna also spoke about the advantages that came from diverse social circles:

> I like organizations . . . because you meet people who are similar to you. 'Cause sometimes you meet friends in college or in high school and they don't really join organizations or maybe they are just your friends that you eat lunch with or just your friends that you party with. But, the people in the organizations, you meet people who are really passionate about community service; people who really have a lot going for themselves and may be the next future CEOs and stuff. And, you have a lot more in common. . . . I feel like in these organizations, I am able to meet a lot of productive friends who keep me going and who have the same interests as me. (Weber, 2016, pp. 112–113)

Julianna articulated the benefits of having diverse friend groups and how they fulfilled her academic, social, and career needs. Similarly, Hackett and Hogg (2014) found that people who surrounded themselves with a diverse peer group with mutual values, interests, or goals felt more connected to their communities, and Kuh (2012) found that diverse and global learning aids in college student persistence. Julianna's academic, social, and career networks created a mutual support system on a campus many hours from home. Julianna summarized her relationships and captured the familial capital that students learned through their college access programs and later applied in college: "They help me out, I help them out" (Weber, 2016, p. 113).

For Lucas, his mentor from the Fulfillment Fund taught him a success strategy to ease into a new situation by taking his hands out of his pockets and relaxing:

> I remember actually what the first college [visit] that we went to . . . it was my first time out of the house, first time ever being really away from my parents. When it was dinner time, one of my counselors [from the Fulfillment Fund] approached me, Grace, that's her name, and she told me that everybody was getting food and I was just there, just standing outside with my hands in my pockets. It was completely out of my comfort zone and I was trying to put myself in that shell and she just came up to me and was like, "You're nervous, aren't you?" and I'm like, "Yeah. What am I supposed to do here?" And, she's like, "Ok, first of all, take your hands out of your pockets. Relax." (Weber, 2016, p. 113)

Lucas lived with his aunt in El Salvador until he moved to California when he was 11 years old to live with his mother and stepfather. Lucas had not left California since he moved. He felt nervous on his college visit. His college access and success program's counselor, Grace, calmed him down:

> She just talked to me and we got food, I went and sit down with them, I got to know them better and I just hanged out. I felt in that comfort zone, out of my house, which was really weird. It was weird, but that was one of the life lessons that I vividly remember because it was really, it's something very small. (Weber, 2016, p. 113)

Grace built on Lucas's linguistic capital (Yosso, 2005) and taught him the value of nonverbal communication, physically opening to new experiences, and using talking as a tool for relaxation and connecting with people. While Lucas described Grace's advice as a "life lesson," he did not connect it to college (Weber, 2016, p. 114). Lucas did use Grace's advice, however, when he felt homesick his first month on campus:

> Just having someone to talk to, and like complain to. . . . Let it out . . . instead of drowning with all these things that you have. So, that's how we [Lucas and his hallmate] coped with it and we're still very good friends. He's one of my best friends now. (Weber, 2016, p. 114)

Lucas moved past feelings of homesickness through talking, as Grace suggested, reiterating the value of relationships and importance of belonging to students' college-going experience (Gummadam et al., 2016; O'Keeffe, 2013; Ostrove & Long, 2007; Soria & Stebleton, 2013; Stebleton et al., 2014).

Lilly also learned the importance of opening herself up to new experiences and developed her intercultural communication skills and cultural competencies when she traveled to Argentina. The high school, which was part of the Knowledge Is Power Program (KIPP), required students to participate in summer programs so students remained engaged throughout the summer and experienced learning outside the classroom. KIPP helped Lilly find the right opportunity and a scholarship to cover the costs of a service-learning trip to Argentina. Lilly described her experience:

> [The students] all were located at Rosario [in Santa Fe, Argentina,] and we all had different host families and we all did the same volunteer work. But, I felt like even within the group of the United States, I learned a lot about where they're coming from, their perspectives on life. And, just their interests. For example, my family, we don't, well, not my family, just reading in general, just read, just because it wasn't a big thing. And, then I went to the study abroad program this girl had brought a big book and she was just reading for fun. (Weber, 2016, p. 115)

The idea of "reading for fun" surprised Lilly; however, it aligned with researchers who found children in low-income homes had less exposure to vocabulary words and books than children from higher-income families (which contributed to their overall literacy development and academic readiness) (Coley, 2002; Gee, 1989; Weber, 2016). Lilly's communication skills expanded as she learned from her peers and everyone she met in Rosario.

> I just felt like that was really good and it motivated me to just, there's different people, and how they just think. It made me want to be more like that, more active, and just better myself. And, reading does help, so improving your skills and writing and just communicating with others, and that's an example, I just learned about different ways of living. And, as far as the Argentinean culture, history, [and] background. (Weber, 2016, pp. 115–116)

Through traveling and volunteering, Lilly gained an intercultural knowledge from watching, conversing, reading, and surrounding herself with people from different cultures and backgrounds. Lilly later shared that her trip to Argentina built her self-confidence to attend college out of state.

Jia's experience with YMCA's Global Teens in Thailand opened her up to new cultures and new ways of thinking. It greatly influenced her college major:

They send a group of 16 students with two chaperones over to the local YMCA in different countries, so I chose to go to Thailand. And, it was really nice there. They provided, we lived in a hotel, because in Thailand, it's really still developing. So, where they had the bathrooms they had to still squat and everything, but the hotel had real bathrooms, real showers. Because if we actually lived in a host family's house, we had to use a bucket of water to take a shower and everything. (Weber, 2016, pp. 116–117)

Jia's experience also exposed her to poverty in an underdeveloped country. While Jia's family lived in New York City just above the poverty line, what she experienced in Thailand made her question her own identity within a larger, global context. Jia reflected on what she learned through her experience:

Although it was just 2 weeks, it was just with a new group of people and seeing how somewhere else is. . . . And, there [are] so many poor people, because we worked at an orphanage, and we also worked at a school that served half orphans and 50% of the lowest income people. And, they're just so happy. They look, they come to school in uniforms that don't look as clean. We also worked with street children, and they literally lived on the streets. . . . And, it just made me appreciate what I had a lot more here. . . . I came back, and I felt so lost, because I wasn't doing something every day like going to visit the kids in the orphanage or something. (Weber, 2016, p. 117)

Jia's trip to Thailand showed the value in experiential learning as a persistence strategy, since it helped her make meaning of her travel and sense of purpose (Chickering & Reisser, 1993; Kuh, 2012).

Just after Jia returned from Thailand, she moved away to start college. Simultaneously, doctors in New York City diagnosed Jia's father with cancer. His illness, coupled with her recent travels to Thailand through the YMCA and her experiences with Edgies and Henry Street Settlement (two other college access programs), influenced Jia's college-going journey and her "desire to help" as she did in Thailand:

Seeing all the problems in my community [a neighborhood in New York], and seeing people suffer, and you just don't want that to happen. I remember seeing an old lady just pushing carts of cans, because they collect a lot of those canned sodas and they bring them down [to a recycling drop-off center where the state pays up to $.08 per can or bottle recycled], and there's a desire to help them; probably because we are helped. All of these college access programs are free programs to help you. To help the community that needs to be helped. (Weber, 2016, p. 118)

Jia saw how the "desire to help" went full circle and benefited her—"to help the community that needs to be helped" (Weber, 2016, p. 118). Jia's travel with her college access program furthered her aspirational capital and built on her familial, collective identity (Yosso, 2005). Once in college, Jia decided to pursue a career in public health, so she could better educate and serve her community.

Janey's experience with Project Reach taught her about other cultures, open-mindedness, and communication when they promoted and hosted conversations on race, socioeconomic status, and sexual orientation with a diverse group of high school students. Janey explained:

> There was one summer where [Project Reach] had us go out to other organizations and tell other organizations what we're about. . . . A lot of what I had to do was just facilitate workshops. We had workshops on racism, classism, homophobia, so it's helped me just not be afraid to talk to people. . . . I grew up in Chinatown and it was just only Asian people. I, for me, I like working with Asian people, but also working with White people, Latino people, Black people, people of all different races, color, personality. . . . I'm proud that I know people of all different types of backgrounds and because I enjoy working with people and I am passionate about working with people that's what I'm really proud of throughout my whole lifetime. (Weber, 2016, pp. 118–119)

Janey's appreciation for working with people and facilitating workshops on social justice led her to her major. Janey continued, "I'm a sociology major; I'm really interested in education policies. So, I try to get involved with, in the education field as much as possible, 'cause I like working with students" (Weber, 2016, p. 119).

Janey continued to share the different ways she incorporated this into her work-study jobs and volunteer positions during college, such as working with refugees on Saturdays and participating in Literacy Corp. Janey said:

> I'm part of the live blog and we're actually facilitating a workshop at [a local high school] . . . April 20th. And, basically we're gonna go in and talk to the students about our process: getting into college and what college is about, giving them an idea of options after high school. (Weber, 2016, p. 119)

Janey used her facilitation and communication skills and her appreciation for diversity that she learned through Project Reach in college. Janey's experiences with Project Reach and college engagements reflected community-based learning and global/diversity learning, two high-impact practices Kuh (2012) found that helped increase college students' persistence.

Along with students developing leadership and communication skills and intercultural knowledge, college access and support programs cultivated students' independence and sense of responsibility. Tom's college access and success program, Liberty LEADS, connected him with summer opportunities that fostered his independence:

> I was told [by Liberty LEADS] that we had to do something during the summer, and they were like, there's an opportunity to study abroad. So, I was like, "Okay," and I really wanted to study in Spain. And, they covered about all of it, except for $300 for both the airfare and the studying. And then, I went to school and I asked them for money, so it was basically all covered, and, well, the program did not only that, they also had leadership programs and so, every summer, I would do something affiliated through them, or they would help me find something to do during the summer. And, that got me into becoming more independent of myself and growing and seeing what I want to do. (Weber, 2016, pp. 119–120)

Tom believed that traveling to Spain and participating in leadership programs during high school through Liberty LEADS helped him gain his independence and sense of responsibility.

Like Tom, Yong also thought his college access program, Educational Alliance, contributed to and furthered his independence:

> I changed as a person. I feel [Educational Alliance] definitely made me more resourceful, more independent. And, I mean, I was always the one, I mean, personally, the main reason I decided to look for a job was so I could buy more food for myself because I felt bad for taking my parents' money to buy food. 'Cause I never got an allowance, so when I needed money I would just ask them for it. And, I felt bad about that because I loved eating, so I would just buy a bunch of food. I didn't want to waste my parents' money, so I was, if I wanted something I would afford it myself. (Weber, 2016, p. 120)

Yong described how Educational Alliance further cultivated his independence:

> The program itself never really changed my mind set, but it more reinforced the idea of, if I want something I should just get it done myself. If I had resources to help me take advantage of it, be grateful to them for it, but ultimately, I'm always going to be independent. I would just always do my own thing, be resourceful. I guess, the program just helped me reinforce that character. (Weber, 2016, p. 121)

Yong's reflection on Educational Alliance showed how they validated his drive to be autonomous and resourceful to take initiative (Rendón Linares &

Muñoz, 2011). The organization did not try to make Yong something he was not, but rather fostered his agency as an individual.

Students' college access programs helped them develop their leadership, communication, and intercultural skills and strengthen their independence to become more college ready. I call this *developing a college-going mindset.* While some students clearly articulated how these personal growths contributed to their college transition and success, other students demonstrated it through stories that utilized their newly acquired skill set or their stories were supported by research connections (e.g., better time management contributes to college success).

Conclusion

My research explored how students described the impact of college access programs on their development. As other researchers (Coles & Engstrom, 2012; Hagedorn & Fogel, 2002; Tuitt et al., 2011) have shown and the data in my study echo, the tangible support services offered by these programs (e.g., SAT preparation, application fee waivers, assistance in writing college essays) appear to help students gain access to college. The students in my research study also suggested that their experiences with similar programs offered them much more. Many researchers and programs appear to ignore or decline to name the development of personal and leadership attributes that they may foster. College access programs appeared to instill a college-going mindset in students to help them realize their potential of getting a postsecondary degree. Tom succinctly said, "With Liberty LEADS . . . I found that college is the choice for me" (Weber, 2016, p. 105). As college access programs build students' college-going mindset, the programs are also equipping first-generation college students with the tools, experiences, and resources needed for their successful transition to college.

References

Chickering, A. W., & Reisser, L. (1993). *Education and identity* (2nd ed.). Jossey-Bass.

Coles, A. S., & Engstrom, C. M. (2012). *Changing Syracuse degree by degree: How On Point for College is transforming the lives of underserved young adults.* Texas Guaranteed Student Loan Corporation.

Coley, R. J. (2002). *An uneven start: Indicators of inequality in school readiness.* Educational Testing Service.

Engle, J., & Tinto, V. (2008). *Moving beyond access: College success for low-income, first-generation students.* The Pell Institute for the Study of Opportunity in Higher Education.

Gee, J. P. (1989). What is literacy? *Journal of Education, 171*(1), 18–25. https://doi .org/10.1177/002205748917100102

Gummadam, P., Pittman, L. D., & Ioffe, M. (2016). School belonging, ethnic identity, and psychological adjustment among ethnic minority college students. *The Journal of Experimental Education, 84*(2), 289–306. https://doi.org/10.1080/00 220973.2015.1048844

Hackett, J. D., & Hogg, M. A. (2014). The diversity paradox: When people who value diversity surround themselves with like-minded others. *Journal of Applied Social Psychology, 44*(6), 415–422. https://doi.org/10.1111/jasp.12233

Hagedorn, L. S., & Fogel, S. (2002). Making school to college programs work: Academics, goals, and aspirations. In W. G. Tierney & L. S. Hagedorn (Eds.), *Increasing access to college: Extending possibilities for all students* (pp. 169–193). State University of New York Press.

Institute of Education Sciences. (2020, August). *A 2017 follow-up: Six-year persistence and attainment at any institution for 2011-12 first-time postsecondary students.* National Center for Education Statistics. https://nces.ed.gov/pubs2020/2020238 .pdf

Krumrei-Mancuso, E. J., Newton, F. B., Kim, E., & Wilcox, D. (2013). Psychosocial factors predicting first-year college student success. *Journal of College Student Development, 54*(3), 247–266. https://doi.org/10.1353/csd.2013.0034

Kuh, G. (1995). The other curriculum: Out-of-class experiences associated with student learning and personal development. *Journal of Higher Education, 66*(2), 125–155. http://dx.doi.org/10.2307/2943909

Kuh, G. (2012). *High-impact educational practices: What they are, who has access to them, and why they matter.* American Association of Colleges & Universities.

Kuh, G., Cruce, T. M., Shoup, R., Kinzie, J., & Gonyea, R. M. (2008). Unmasking the effects of student engagement on first-year college grades and persistence. *Journal of Higher Education, 79*(5), 540–563. http://dx.doi.org/10.1080/00221 546.2008.11772116

Minds Matter. (2016). *About Minds Matter.* https://www.mindsmatter.org/about/

National Association for College Admission Counseling. (n.d.). *NACAC directory of college access & success programs.* http://casp.nacacnet.org/

National College Access Network. (2011). *About us.* https://www.ncan.org/page/ Publications

O'Keeffe, P. (2013). A sense of belonging: Improving student retention. *College Student Journal, 47*(4), 605–613. https://researchrepository.rmit.edu.au/ discovery/delivery?vid=61RMIT_INST:ResearchRepository&repId= 12247864990001341#13248365430001341

Ostrove, J. M., & Long, S. M. (2007). Social class and belonging: Implications for college adjustment. *The Review of Higher Education, 30*(4), 363–389. https://doi .org/10.1353/rhe.2007.0028

Posse Foundation. (n.d.). *The Posse Foundation, Inc.* https://www.possefoundation .org/posse-facts

Rendón Linares, L., & Muñoz, S. (2011, Summer). Revisiting validation theory: Theoretical foundations, applications, and extensions. *Enrollment Management Journal: Student Access, Finance, and Success in Higher Education, 5*(2), 12–33. https://www.researchgate.net/publication/282294812_Revisiting_validation_theory_Theoretical_foundations_applications_and_extensions

Soria, K. M., & Stebleton, M. J. (2013). Social capital, academic engagement, and sense of belonging among working-class college students. *College Student Affairs Journal, 31*(2), 139–151.

Stebleton, M. J., Soria, K. M., & Huesman, R. L. (2014). First-generation students' sense of belonging, mental health, and use of counseling services at public research universities. *Journal of College Counseling, 17*(1), 6–20. https://doi.org/10.1002/j.2161-1882.2014.00044.x

Tuitt, F. A., Van Horn, B. N., & Sulick, D. F. (2011, Spring). Transmitting the right signals: The continued significance of promoting college entry to students of color. *Enrollment Management Journal, 10*, 31. https://doi.org/10.1002/j.2161-1882.2014.00044.x

Weber, S. (2016). *"My training wheels are off": How first generation college students made meaning of the influence of their college access and support programs* [Doctoral dissertation, Syracuse University]. https://surface.syr.edu/etd/600/

Yosso, T. J. (2005). Whose culture has capital? A critical race theory discussion of community cultural wealth. *Race, Ethnicity and Education, 8*(1), 69–91. http://dx.doi.org/10.1080/1361332052000341006

IT'S ALL A BUNCH OF B.S.

How Institutional Jargon Creates In-Groups and Out-Groups in Higher Education

Sonja Ardoin

U niversity. College. School. AP. IB. Major. Minor. Credit hours. Prerequisite. Liberal arts. Office hours. FAFSA. Work study. Subsidized loans. These are just a small sampling of the terms that are used in higher education, terms that we assume people know and terms that create in-groups and out-groups among students, families, administrators, and faculty. While an individual may have heard of B.S., their understanding of what the acronym stands for may be different because, at least where I come from, B.S. means "bullshit" more often than it means "bachelor of science." The question becomes: Must we use jargon in our higher education practice and, if so, how might we ensure explanations for widespread understanding?

The College Knowledge Challenge

College knowledge is the information and resources students need to navigate through the higher education system and is found to be one of the four most significant predictors of enrollment in higher education (Heller, 2013; Perna, 2013; Vargas, 2004). Jehangir (2010) describes college knowledge as a "codebook" (p. 30) of both the explicit and implicit expectations that exist at colleges and universities. Students who receive college knowledge from their families, schools, or communities have an advantage. And while there are some programs designed to fill this opportunity gap (e.g., TRIO programs, nonprofit organization programs), college knowledge continues to create challenges for many student populations, including but not limited to first-generation college students.

What Is Jargon?

One distinct aspect of college knowledge is the language and acronyms that institutions use to create their own jargon. Terms as seemingly familiar on campus as *major*, *minor*, and *office hours* can cause confusion and be isolating for first-generation college students. There is an assumption that these words will make sense to everyone; as such, we often shorten these words into acronyms that make even less sense (Jehangir, 2010). The campus activities and involvement center becomes CAIC (pronounced cake); the college of health and human services becomes HHS; and the program of study becomes the POS—yet another acronym that could be confused, as this one often means "piece of shit" in everyday language. As one student offered in my research study:

> Yeah, all the letters can be confusing: A.A., A.S., A.A.S. . . . I know what B.S. means, just not by these terms! *[laughing]* I know a semester is longer than a quarter. I know full-time from part-time because of my [after-school] job. I mean, if you go by common sense—what it [financial aid] has in the name—I mean if you're getting aid financially, you're getting a little bit of money. (Ardoin, 2018, p. 61)

This highlights that students can often use common sense to surmise the meaning of some jargon and acronyms, but that tactic does not always result in clarity or confidence in their navigation of higher education.

As the in-group, we—current students, administrators, and faculty—get so caught up in making our own lives easier that we unintentionally—or intentionally, in some cases—speak or write in ways that block others' comprehension and create more elitist practices in higher education. This leaves those without this assumed knowledge and language as the out-group, including many first-generation college students. Even texts written to assist first-generation college students in the process of getting to and through college (Clark, 2017; Flores, 2014; Lenfestey & Kever, 2016) use jargon without necessarily explaining it, and when definitions are offered, only a few choice terms (e.g., *in-state*, *private*, *public*, *HBCU*; see Clark, 2017) are explained while many others still remain a mystery.

To further complicate higher education jargon and acronyms, there are layers of this kind of language that exist in our work. First, we have the broad U.S. higher education jargon and acronyms—things like *FAFSA*, *Pell Grants*, *major*, *minor*, and *prerequisite*—then we have the institutional-based jargon that is specific to each campus, followed by the discipline-based jargon for each academic area of study or within the student affairs/student life areas on campus. Figure CC6.1 highlights how this layering can work. Learning this

Figure CC6.1. Jargon.

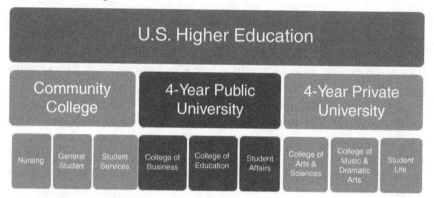

new, multifaceted language of higher education is just one of many transitional elements for first-generation college students and can generate feelings of marginalization and isolation (Ardoin, 2018; Jehangir, 2010).

Decoding the Jumble of Jargon

As educators, we should know that it is our role to introduce people to concepts and assist people along their learning journey. Yet, when it comes to higher education jargon and acronyms we often neglect our role as educators, assuming, rather, that it is the student's job to acclimate themselves to this new language. However, if we truly want to create more equitable systems and retain the first-generation college students we admit, we must realize that it is our job to be student ready and not just students' job to be college ready (Brown McNair et al., 2016). Simple changes, like explaining what jargon means or using more universal language, can help first-generation college students decode the jumble of jargon we have created in higher education. (Yes, we created this mess and often knowingly perpetuate it.) It can also be helpful to introduce students to peers, as well as faculty and staff members, who can identify with their experience of learning this new language.

Research Findings

In my own research on how jargon influences college access (Ardoin, 2018), I found three steps that can help decode university jargon; from the individual frame, these include (a) becoming aware, (b) recognizing and defining terms, and (c) finding processes of seeking and understanding information. Shifting these to office, departmental, or institution-wide frames, the first two remain: (a) becoming aware and (b) recognizing and defining terms, while the third shifts to (c) finding processes to share information. First, offices, departments, or institutions should engage in practices that allow them to reflect on how much jargon and how many acronyms are being used in their conversations and presentations, on their websites, and throughout their promotional materials. Second, once terms are identified, administrators and faculty members should discuss what they mean by these terms and collectively decide on which definition they will use in describing those terms. Finally, offices, departments, or institutions should identify processes by which jargon and acronym use will be reduced or how definitions will be shared. This should involve revamping presentation content, websites, and marketing materials while also creating new documents such as "campus dictionaries" or "course codebooks" that offer the most common jargons or acronyms that students might encounter.

Institutional Example

Some colleges and universities have already taken on the task of decoding the jumble of jargon in their environment. A few years ago, my undergraduate alma mater—Louisiana State University (LSU)—created "LSU Terminology" posters featuring our mascot, Mike the Tiger. The posters focused on campus-specific jargon and acronyms, such as building codes to help people find locations and names for campus traditions—such as the campus yearbook, called *The Gumbo*, which could easily be confused with the popular Louisiana food item. Posters were given out at new student orientation, and a version was also posted on the university website. Efforts such as this are helpful, and they fall short of offering the layered jargon that first-generation college students may need to learn. Campuses need to brainstorm ways they can break down language barriers at all levels within higher education (see Figure CC6.1), define and reduce jargon and acronyms, and create less elitist and more equitable environments.

Discussion Questions

1. Why might you be using jargon in your conversations with students, administrators, or faculty members? What relationships could be fostered by shifting your language?
2. How much jargon appears on your office or department website or other promotional materials to campus and external constituents? How might this be influencing people's understanding of what you do or why they should engage with you?

3. What jargon is used in your policy documents? How might that be influencing people's understanding of the policy and ability to adhere to it?
4. How might you reduce the use of jargon in your sphere of influence or provide explanations of it? How should you consider this in orientation and onboarding processes?

References

Ardoin, S. (2018). *College aspirations and access in working-class rural communities: The mixed signals, challenges, and new language first-generation students encounter.* Lexington.

Brown McNair, T., Albertine, S., Cooper, M. A., McDonald, N., & Major Jr., T. (2016). *Becoming a student-ready college: A new culture of leadership for student success.* Jossey-Bass.

Clark, K. (2017). *Decoding college: Stories, strategies, and struggles of first-generation college students.* Rowe.

Flores, A. D. (2014). *50 things I wish someone would have told me about college: Straight talk for first-generation students from first-generation graduates.* Serolf.

Heller, D. (2013). The role of finances in postsecondary access and success. In L. Perna & A. P. Jones (Eds.), *The state of college access and completion: Improving college success for students from underrepresented groups* (pp. 96–114). Routledge.

Jehangir. R. R. (2010). *Higher education and first-generation students: Cultivating community, voice, and place for the new majority.* Palgrave Macmillan.

Lenfestey, K. & Kever, S. (2016). *Every student has a story: Personal narratives from first-generation college students.* TRIO Support Services at IPFW.

Perna, L. (2013). Conclusions: Improving college access, persistence, and completion: Lessons learned. In L. Perna & A. P. Jones (Eds.), *The state of college access and completion: Improving college success for students from underrepresented groups* (pp. 208–224). Routledge.

Vargas, J. (2004). *College knowledge: Addressing information barriers to college.* Education Resources Institute.

14

SUPPORTING TRANSFER FOR FIRST-GENERATION COMMUNITY COLLEGE STUDENTS

Gloria Crisp, Rebecca Robertson, and Elizabeth Cox Brand

Today, community colleges are the first and often the only point of college access for nearly 40% of the approximately 17.1 million undergraduate students in higher education (Shapiro et al., 2020). Although research shows that more than 80% of students enroll in community colleges with the intent to transfer and earn a bachelor's degree, only about 25% transfer within 5 years, and fewer successfully complete a bachelor's degree (Horn & Skomsvold, 2011; Jenkins & Fink, 2015). The National Student Clearinghouse Research Center reports that the 6-year bachelor's completion rate for students who enrolled in community college in 2011 was under 15% (Shapiro et al., 2020). Further, transfer inequities exist between groups, including but not limited to a "racial transfer gap" between White and racially minoritized students (Crisp & Nuñez, 2014).

Inequities in transfer can be studied through the broader lens of historically underserved students who attend accessible institutions—namely our nation's community colleges. The large majority of students who enroll in community colleges identify with one or more groups that continue to be marginalized and understudied, including women, African American students, Latinx students, Native American students, low-income students, LGTBQ students, adult students, and/or students with disabilities (Cohen et al., 2014; Engle & Tinto, 2008). Many of these students also identify as *first-generation*. Although the majority of studies define *first generation* as students whose parents did not attend college (Nuñez & Cuccaro-Alamin,

1998), scholars have expanded this definition to include students whose parents attended college but did not graduate or even to involve students whose parents may have graduated college but did not earn a bachelor's degree (e.g., Engle & Tinto, 2008; Radunzel, 2018). The diverse group of students identified as *first-generation* are a critical population to study, as they represent the majority of community college students and at the same time transfer and/or complete degrees at inequitable rates when compared to students whose parents attended and/or graduated college (hereafter referred to as *continuing-generation students*) (Nuñez & Cuccaro-Alamin, 1998; Radunzel, 2018). Unfortunately, with a few notable exceptions, little attention to date has been granted to studying transfer or degree completion among first-generation students who begin postsecondary education at a community college.

In this chapter we help fill this gap by critically examining transfer among first-generation students who begin college at a community college. We begin by describing community college students, giving attention to those who are identified as first-generation, and provide an overview of the community colleges' role in promoting transfer to colleges and universities that offer bachelor's degrees. Next, we offer a synthesis of the limited empirical findings to date regarding the experiences, practices, and/or policies related to transfer for community college students. Within this, we highlight the limited amount of research that has been done specific to first-generation students, including preliminary findings from research evaluating new transfer policy in the state of Oregon. Implications for institutional practice and policy related to promoting transfer are provided. We conclude with recommendations for research focused on supporting transfer for first-generation students.

First-Generation Community College Students

To address transfer inequities it is crucial to consider the diversity of the community college student body and the complex circumstances that frame students' pursuit of postsecondary education, as these contribute to complicated enrollment and transfer patterns. The turn of the 21st century saw an acceleration of growth in community college enrollment, up from 4 million in 1980 to 7.5 million in 2010, representing a growth rate of 23% from 2000–2010 (Cohen et al., 2014). This growth can be attributed to the development of new community college programs, the expansion of recruiting efforts, and the impact of the 2008 recession, which drove many unemployed adults to pursue higher education. The result is a community college student body that is more diverse than ever. Demographically, the majority of community college students identify as female (56%), 24% as Latinx, 13% as African American, and 6% as Asian/Pacific Islander (American Association of Community Colleges, 2018). The 2012 U.S. Department of Education National Community Engagement Survey report showed that a quarter of community college students had dependents. More than three quarters (78%) of students enrolled in community college worked and a third worked full-time. Additionally, nearly half of the students enrolled at community college who were classified as dependents were from low-income households (Cohen et al., 2013).Unfortunately, the large majority of institutions, including community colleges, were and are still designed to serve White, middle- to upper-class males who attend college full-time (Thelin, 2019). As such, it should come as no surprise that many colleges are struggling to support and graduate today's diverse student population.

As an added layer to diversity, data show that first-generation students are overrepresented at community colleges (American Association of Community Colleges, 2012). Unfortunately, very little is known about the characteristics of first-generation students who begin college at a community college. However, similar to the broader population of community college students, first-generation students have often been described as being more likely than continuing-generation students to be adult students, female, or students with disabilities; come from low-income backgrounds; and identify as students of color (e.g., Inman & Mayes, 1999). Once enrolled, it is notable that first-generation students have also been shown to be more likely to work off campus, attend college part-time, and have access to fewer resources when compared to continuing-generation students (Radunzel, 2018). Moreover, this group of students is more likely to delay enrollment in college after high school and is disproportionately required to enroll in and complete developmental courses, delaying timely progress toward a certificate or degree (Inman & Mayes, 1999; Nuñez & Cuccaro-Alamin, 1998).

Although the data only include students from two states, recent research by Radunzel (2018) provides the most detailed descriptive comparison to date of first-generation and continuing-generation students enrolled at community colleges. The most salient descriptive differences between the two groups of students are summarized in Table 14.1. Importantly, data from the community college sample revealed that first-generation students were more likely than continuing-generation students to identify as female, African American or Latinx, and low income; work more than 21 hours per week; and/or enroll part-time during the first year of college. At the same time, both first-generation and continuing-generation students attending community colleges were shown to have equally high degree aspirations, with 82%

TABLE 14.1
**Comparison of Characteristics of First-Generation and
Continuing-Education Community College Students**

Characteristic	First-Generation Community College Students (%)	Continuing-Education Community College Students (%)
Female	61	47
African American or Latinx	32	15
Income less than $36,000	58	19
Worked 21 hours or more	34	18
Enrolled part-time	44	32
Intended to earn a bachelor's degree or higher	82	92

Source: Radunzel (2018).

of first-generation and 92% of continuing-generation students desiring to earn a bachelor's degree or higher. Although Radunzel's work contributes by distinguishing salient demographic characteristics of first and continuing education students, we recognize that these data are extremely limited in that they lack nuance, do not represent students' college experiences, and do not show the heterogeneity within either group of students. Moreover, blunt quantitative comparisons can unintentionally harm students by leading researchers or administrators to label first-generation students as "at risk" and/or to make assumptions about who first-generation students are or why they are less likely to transfer and complete a degree.

The Transfer Function

Community colleges are primarily thought of as serving a vertical transfer function in higher education, namely, providing students with the general education and major preparation courses needed to transfer to a baccalaureate-granting institution (Taylor & Jain, 2017). Between 1910 and 1960 the percentage of 18-year-old students who enrolled in community college rose from 5% to 45% (Cohen et al., 2014). The exponential increase in college enrollment could have been accommodated by increasing the capacity of existing baccalaureate-granting institutions; instead, the idea took hold that universities in the United States should follow the European model and concentrate on research and specialized scholarship (Cohen et al., 2014). In the late 19th century, leading voices called for higher education in the United States to consign general education to a separate institution, called the junior college, giving birth to what today we think of as the community college (Cohen et al., 2014).

Brint and Karabel (1989) contend that community colleges were founded as part of an existing hierarchy of colleges and universities in response to demand for educational opportunities as a means to upward mobility. The researchers argue that the management of ambition was tacitly embedded into the community college mission; from their inception, junior colleges functioned to sort students into different positions in a stratified capitalist economy. The transfer function allowed exceptional students from nonaffluent classes the opportunity for advancement through the baccalaureate degree, while simultaneously providing education and training for those whose ability or ambition would not take them as far (Brint & Karabel, 1989; Cohen et al., 2014). Against this historical backdrop, the contemporary community college serves multiple and often contradictory missions. Pertinent to examining community colleges in terms of transfer are the tensions between providing open-access educational opportunities and the simultaneous need to improve student success and transfer rates.

Although vertical transfer does comprise one of the core missions of the community college, the transfer landscape is complex, with students engaging in a variety of transfer patterns. Research on transfer patterns has shown that about one third of first-time students transfer institutions at least once during their postsecondary experience (Hossler et al., 2012; Shapiro et al., 2020; Wang et al., 2016). Transfer behavior has become increasingly complex in recent years, with students transferring both to and from community colleges and bachelor's degree–granting institutions (Hossler et al., 2012; Taylor & Jain, 2017). Additionally, there are students who enroll concurrently, attending more than one institution at the same time (Crisp, 2013). Research findings have shown that students transfer for many reasons including nonacademic purposes such as personal reasons, dissatisfaction, scheduling issues, family responsibilities, and financial problems (Crosta, 2014; Taylor & Jain, 2017).

First-generation community college students can face unique challenges that may impact their enrollment and transfer patterns. Potential challenges faced by first-generation students include attending underfunded and under-resourced secondary schools, having dependents, and working full-time while enrolled. Further, it is possible to see relationships between first-generation students' enrollment patterns and low persistence and transfer rates. For instance, first-generation students are highly likely to attend community college part-time, which research has shown to be correlated with a lower probability of persistence and degree attainment (Nuñez & Cuccaro-Alamin, 1998). Likely due in some measure to part-time enrollment status, as well as experiences and inequitable policies and practices that will be discussed in the next section, first-generation students may face challenges with navigating the college context, making friends or getting to know faculty, which can also impact persistence. Additionally, first-generation community college students disproportionately enroll in certificate or vocational programs, which may not readily lend themselves to vertical transfer (Nuñez & Cuccaro-Alamin, 1998). At the same time, first-generation students have been shown to be more likely to borrow money and take out larger loans, resulting in large amounts of debt without the benefit of a degree (Radunzel, 2018). The interactions between the aforementioned challenges faced by first-generation students can negatively impact their transfer and degree completion rates. It should therefore not be surprising that on the whole, first-generation students have been found to be less likely than their continuing-generation peers to persist, transfer, and/or complete a degree (Radunzel, 2018).

Transfer and Articulation Policies

In response to low transfer and graduation rates, states and institutions have spent considerable resources to replace fragmented transfer efforts with mandatory statewide policies and transfer partnerships in hopes of facilitating transfer and timely degree completion (LaSota & Zumeta, 2016; Millard, 2014; Wellman, 2002). These efforts vary across states but may be generally categorized into four types of policy, including (a) transferable core courses, (b) common course numbering systems, (c) guarantee of transfer of an associate degree to the bachelor's-granting institution, and most recently (d) statewide reverse transfer. Currently, at least 30 states have implemented one or more transfer/articulation policies (Education Commission of the States, 2018). Although a full discussion of transfer policies is beyond the scope of this chapter, a summary of these policies with state-specific examples is found in Table 14.2.

Factors Influencing Student Transfer

Unfortunately, researchers and policymakers know extremely little about the college experiences and institutional policies and practices that facilitate or serve as barriers to transfer and success for first-generation community college students. In the following section, we provide an overview of transfer research, giving focus to the dearth of scholarship specifically centered on first-generation students.

Students' Characteristics and Experiences

The majority of transfer scholarship to date has focused on student characteristics and precollege experiences that are in some way related to predicting

TABLE 14.2
Sample of State Transfer Policies

Policy	Description	Example
Transferable core of lower-level division courses	General education courses agreed on across public colleges and universities in the state. Courses must be transferable at all public institutions.	California: Public institutions must work together to develop, maintain, and disseminate a common core curriculum for students who intend to transfer. Any student who completes the transfer core curriculum has completed the lower-division general education requirements (ref: Cal Educ. Code § 66720).
Statewide common-course numbering	A uniform numbering or course naming system used across all public colleges and universities for core, lower-level courses	Tennessee: The Higher Education Commission maintains a common course number system that ensures course equivalency and helps facilitate student transfer (ref: Tenn. Code Ann. § 49-7-202(f)).
Statewide guaranteed transfer of an associate degree	Guarantee that students can transfer all credits earned as part of an associate degree and begin at the university as a junior. In most cases, students may not be required to complete additional general education courses.	Florida: The State articulation agreement provides that all associate in arts graduates will have met all general education requirements and will be granted admission to the upper division of a state university or Florida College System institution (ref: Fla. Stat. § 1007.23).
Statewide reverse transfer	Requires public colleges and universities to retroactively grant students an associate degree who did not complete the requirements prior to transferring.	West Virginia: There is a process whereby students are awarded an associate degree that was begun at a public institution offering an associate degree but was completed at a public university (ref: Procedural Rule 133-60).

Source: Education Commission of the States (2020).

transfer (Wang et al., 2016). In sum, findings suggest that a combination of student-demographic characteristics and academic experiences prior to and while enrolled at a community college are significantly related to persistence and/or transfer. To begin with, being a student whose parents attended or graduated from college has been consistently shown to increase the odds that a student will successfully transfer and earn a degree (e.g., Crisp & Nuñez, 2014; Dougherty & Kienzl, 2006; Porchea et al., 2010). In addition, students who identify as male, White or Asian American, and have middle to high socioeconomic status have been shown to be more likely to transfer (e.g., Andrews et al., 2014; Dougherty & Kienzl, 2006; Jenkins & Fink, 2015; Wang, 2012). Not surprisingly, scholars have found that students who are more academically successful prior to and during college and who perform particularly well in mathematics coursework have an increased odds of transferring to a bachelor's degree–granting institution (e.g., Crisp & Nuñez, 2014; Hagedorn et al., 2008; Porchea et al., 2010; Wang, 2012). Additionally, community college students have been shown to be more likely to transfer who do not have substantial work or family commitments and/or who enroll in college immediately after high school and attend college full-time (Anderson et al., 2006; Crisp & Nuñez, 2014; Dougherty & Kienzl, 2006; LaSota & Zumeta, 2016). It is important to mention here that the large majority of transfer scholarship has given focus to students' characteristics and experiences prior to college and has failed to control or properly account for the role of community college experiences in shaping transfer decisions and outcomes.

Although a disproportionate number of community college students are classified as first-generation, our review identified relatively few studies that have given explicit attention to studying transfer among first-generation community college students. Existing work focused on first-generation students, and community college students in particular, has tended to frame identified risk factors as deficits, further marginalizing students who desire to transfer by not giving space to provide context and recognize the strengths and assets students bring to college (Laanan & Jain, 2016). For example, early research explained low transfer rates among first-generation students by describing students as lacking necessary transfer information and being poorly prepared and therefore not able to meet the academic and social demands of college (e.g., London, 1996; Mitchell, 1997). Similarly, Engle and Tinto (2008) suggest that first-generation students may have difficulty navigating the transfer process due in part to a lack of cultural capital—such as familial support, role models, and guidance regarding the college system. Exceptions include early work by Rendon (1995), who brought attention to challenges that first-generation students may face in being perceived as different, leaving old friends, changing identities, breaking family codes of unity and loyalty, and living between two worlds. Also, Garrison and Gardner (2012) assert that first-generation students possess notable psychological capital (assets), including proactivity, goal direction, optimism, and reflexivity. The strengths and assets that first-generation and historically marginalized students bring to college are valuable and contribute to a rich educational environment for all students.

Radunzel's (2018) analysis of academic and nonacademic factors predicting student persistence, transfer, and graduation rates is one of the only studies to date to specifically predict transfer among first-generation students attending community colleges. Data were pulled from a sample of first-time entering freshmen attending 44 community colleges and 23 bachelor's degree–granting institutions in two states. In addition to the previously mentioned characteristics and experiences that have been empirically linked to outcomes for first-generation students (e.g., gender, race/ethnicity, working, enrolling full time), Radunzel's hierarchical modeling accounted for students' educational goals, financial resources, intentions to live on campus, and the distance between home and the college. Findings revealed that first-generation college students were at a greater risk of not being retained to the second year of college at both community colleges and bachelor's degree–granting institutions even after controlling for variables and characteristics shown to be related to student success. A model was run predicting transfer type (i.e., transfer to a bachelor's degree–granting institution versus another community college) among the sample of community college students. As one might expect, first-generation college status was shown to decrease students' odds of transferring to a bachelor's degree–granting institution. Working fewer than 30 hours per week, high educational aspirations, and first-year grade point average were found to increase students' odds of transfer. Additionally, being female, low income, and living far from campus were variables that were shown to decrease the odds that students would transfer to a bachelor's degree–granting institution (Radunzel, 2018).

Institutional Practices

Many community colleges make efforts to design programs, services, and college/university partnerships with the understanding that the large majority of students desire to transfer to a bachelor's degree–granting institution. Unfortunately, holes and inconsistencies in college/university partnerships and articulation agreements and a lack of advising resources and/or related support services have been shown to impede transfer and/or lead to credit loss (e.g., Dowd et al., 2013; Hodara et al., 2016; Taylor & Jain, 2017). Importantly, Turk and Chen (2017) found that participation in a number of cocurricular and extracurricular activities significantly increased students' odds of transferring to a bachelor's degree–granting institution. In particular, participation in activities was found to double students' odds of transferring. However, as previously noted, first-generation students attending community colleges often need to work off campus and/or may have family commitments making it difficult to engage in out-of-class activities. Findings also suggest that institutional agents (i.e., faculty, advisers, and leaders dedicated to supporting students) can play a key role in supporting first-generation and other minoritized groups. Dowd et al. (2013) found that "the intervention of institutional agents is particularly important for low-status students, whose home and social environments often do not include adults with first-hand experiences or status in postsecondary education" (p. 4).

Smith and Miller (2009) sought to identify promising practices for first-generation and other student groups to transfer from community colleges to bachelor's degree–granting institutions. The researchers used mixed methods to examine institutional policies and practices at six Texas community colleges that had higher than expected transfer rates. Findings identify three common themes or characteristics that contributed to the institutions' transfer rates, including (a) a structured academic pathway, (b) a student-centered culture, and (c) culturally sensitive leadership. Similar to Jain et al.'s (2011) concept of promoting a transfer-receptive culture, all six colleges were shown to cultivate a transfer culture where students were well supported both academically and socially and provided resources designed with the needs of transfer students in mind.

Findings by Smith and Miller (2009) revealed that high-transfer institutions maintain high expectations about students' ability to transfer. One way that this commitment was demonstrated was through the development of bachelor's degree plans with students regardless of whether the student had intentions to transfer. Other successful elements of the academic pathway included articulation agreements, a dual enrollment program, developmental coursework initiatives, and active learning methods built into the curriculum. Second, colleges were found to develop a student-centered culture that was demonstrated by efforts such as flexible tutoring and advising services and administrative support for innovative programming, including volunteer faculty tutoring, mentoring, and summer bridge programs. Third and finally, Smith and Miller's work revealed that high-transfer colleges had executive leaders and faculty who had personal experiences that allowed them to understand students' lived experiences. Culturally sensitive leaders and faculty came from similar backgrounds as the students (e.g., first generation). Both leaders and faculty served as role models and mentors for students. Building on this idea, Jain et al. (2011) found that providing space for students of color to connect with and learn from transfer students with similar backgrounds was an effective means of promoting transfer and reducing the racial transfer gap.

Transfer Policies and Initiatives

Although there is a good amount of research focused on predicting transfer, there has been surprisingly little research studying the impacts of transfer policy, both within or between states (Taylor & Jain, 2017). This is particularly concerning given the large amount of time and resources being dedicated to policy development and implementation in states such as Oregon. Existing evidence has shown mixed findings, with some work finding a positive relationship between transfer policy and transfer rates. For example, LaSota and Zumeta (2016) used a national data set to study transfer among different groups of students. State transfer policy contexts were included in the modeling. Results indicated that a statewide transfer guide significantly increased the odds that students would transfer within 6 years. However, the model did not account for variation in the accessibility or utilization of the guides. Moreover, among first-generation students, the presence of common course numbering systems was related to a substantial increase in the odds that students would transfer. However, common course numbering was only shown in four states.

Other research findings, however, suggest that state transfer policy may have little effect on improving transfer rates (e.g., Anderson et al., 2006). One of the most rigorous evaluations to data was conducted by Baker (2016), who studied transfer legislation in California designed to provide programmatic structure and transfer information to students. A difference-in-differences framework was used to estimate the effects of the legislation. Results indicated that the introduction of associate degrees for transfer (ADTs) led to increases in the number of students earning associate degrees. However, a significant effect was not shown for the policy in increasing the number of students who successfully transferred to the state's universities. Taylor and Jain (2017) note that state transfer policies are uneven and diverse and operate differently across states.

It is important to examine transfer in context (Hossler et al., 2012). Hodara et al. (2017) studied credit mobility in 10 states. The researchers sought to understand the different policy approaches that states are using related to credit mobility as well as how and why community college students may lose credit when transferring. Findings indicated that although students were able to transfer credits, these credits didn't always apply toward their major or degree program at the bachelor's degree–granting institution. Rather, transfer credits were often counted as electives. The researchers also found that existing transfer policies across the 10 states may not be addressing the common reasons students lose credit, such as student uncertainty regarding their major and institutional resource constraints with advising.

Studying First-Generation Transfer in Oregon

At the time this chapter was written, we were conducting transfer research focused on first-generation students in the state of Oregon, where half of students enrolled at public bachelor's-granting colleges and universities are transfer students (Higher Education Coordinating Commission [HECC], 2017). In the late 1980s, Oregon implemented the associate of arts Oregon transfer (AAOT) degree in order to facilitate the transfer process for students. In 2008, Oregon community colleges standardized their AAOT degree requirements to further reduce bureaucratic obstacles to transfer. Despite these changes, just 62% of Oregon community college transfer students complete a degree within 6 years, compared to 82% of native university students. Additionally, many transfer students complete more credits than those who start at a bachelor's-granting institution (HECC, 2017).

In 2017 the HECC identified unclear transfer pathways and credit loss as the two biggest issues impacting transfer success and graduation rates. The HECC subsequently worked with community colleges, public universities, and Oregon lawmakers to pass state legislation designed to streamline transfer between Oregon's community colleges and public universities (Oregon State Legislature, 2017). This legislation, House Bill (HB) 2998, requires Oregon's community colleges and public universities to establish common 30-credit foundational curricula and major-specific, unified, statewide transfer agreements (USTAs). Additionally, the legislation requires community colleges to "provide specified information to student when student attending community college informs community college that student intends to transfer to public university" (HB 2998). Drawing on Oregon as an illustration provides insight into the types and evolution of statewide policies instituted in response to fragmented and complex transfer pathways, all with the aim of increasing student educational attainment and decreasing students' time to degree.

Prior research focused on transfer knowledge and experiences among community college students in Oregon has been extremely limited. The exception is a 2016 study conducted by graduate students at the University of Oregon. Findings uncovered several challenges with the community college advising process in Oregon related to transfer, including but not limited to adviser availability, advisers lacking transfer information, and advisers being misinformed about transfer options (Austin et al., 2016). Our project extends

Austin et al.'s work by documenting first-generation community college students' knowledge of the transfer process in Oregon. Our project aimed to evaluate the impacts of HB 2998 on improving vertical transfer and timely graduation rates in Oregon. The first stage provided critical baseline data by documenting first-generation community college students' knowledge and understanding of the transfer process prior to the full implementation of the legislation. To collect these data, we undertook focus group interviews with first-generation students at four Oregon community colleges purposefully chosen to represent different types (e.g., small rural, medium, and large urban community colleges) that have transfer as an important part of their mission. Participants included groups of six to 12 students at each college who intended to transfer to a public institution in Oregon and who identified as first-generation. Interview questions explored students' awareness of available transfer resources, knowledge of the steps in the transfer process, perceptions regarding the role of advisers in providing guidance, as well as their perceived obstacles to transfer.

Based on the limited nature of this initial study, we offer our preliminary insights into first-generation Oregon community college students' knowledge of the transfer process. Overall, focus group data revealed that the first-generation community college students had clear intent to earn a bachelor's degree but very little knowledge of the transfer process. Participants' knowledge was limited to vague and incorrect notions that they must complete 2 years at a community college before applying to a bachelor's-granting institution. Students who participated in the study were all, to varying degrees, unfamiliar with the specifics of the transfer process, such as unit requirements, necessary courses, timing, the transfer application, and transferring credits. In general, students expressed a desire for their college to cultivate their interest in, and knowledge of, the transfer process. Participants shared that they would have liked, and in some cases expected, the community college to reach out to them with information and guidance regarding transfer. With few exceptions, participants did not tend to seek out transfer information from websites, pamphlets/fliers, or posters around campus. When students did seek information, for instance regarding schedule planning and course registration, they sought assistance and help from institutional agents they knew and trusted (e.g., faculty, academic adviser). Findings also show that high school teachers and counselors play an important role in first-generation student perceptions of transfer and introduction to the process.

Reflecting on the assets that these first-generation students bring to college and the transfer process, participants overwhelmingly expressed optimism about their future and confidence in their ability to navigate the transfer process and succeed in college. It was revealed through the focus group interviews that a number of the participants were reverse transfers from bachelor's degree–granting institutions. These participants expressed that they felt that community college faculty and advisers were invested in their success, something they had not felt at the institutions they transferred from. In terms of barriers, our data show that students are facing several notable barriers to transfer, including a lack of financial resources and/or familiarity with financial aid, notable holes in specific knowledge regarding the transfer process, and questions and uncertainty regarding students' major/career track.

Implications for Policy and Practice

It is imperative for institutions and policymakers to continue to work to identify effective and equity-conscious strategies for supporting student transfer and degree completion for first-generation students. In the modern college environment, improving the transfer pipeline is more critical than ever (Millard, 2014). The large numbers of transfer students, the decreasing number of high school graduates, and the increase of community college promise programs (e.g., Perna & Leigh, 2019) combine to make transfer too vital to remain an afterthought on campuses. Although transfer is important for all students, it is particularly critical for first-generation students and others who continue to be underserved in higher education (Bragg, 2017). Bachelor's degree aspirations for too many first-generation students are going unfulfilled (Radunzel, 2018). Community colleges cannot lose sight of the college's mission and role as the entry point to postsecondary education for first-generation students and those who continue to be marginalized and underserved. Fortunately, research findings provide several implications for how community colleges, universities, and policymakers can make transfer more equitable by giving focus to and better supporting the needs of first-generation community college students.

To begin with, it is crucial that college and university leaders promote a transfer-receptive culture to encourage students who are interested in transferring (Jain et al., 2011). The development of a transfer culture should include frequent communication with their feeder university's advising staff, designation of a staff member as a transfer specialist, and development of transfer-centric events (e.g., hosting first-generation alumni who have successfully transferred to talk with current students). Ideally, all members of the campus should send a clear message to first-generation students that the campus believes in their potential to transfer and succeed (Smith & Miller, 2009). By designating individuals as transfer specialists, the campus raises the profile and importance of transfer students to the university. Moreover, transfer-receiving institutions should create a campus-wide transfer advising committee to facilitate access to accurate and timely information for faculty and staff and to establish a consistent, institution-wide definition of *transfer student* (to ensure all departments are identifying and reporting consistently).

It is important not to lose sight of the "human aspects of the transfer process" (Dowd et al., 2013, p. 13). This applies to both community colleges and universities that can get wrapped up in policies, events, and practices and forget the powerful influence individuals within institutions may have with students. Equity-minded leaders should dedicate resources to hire and professionally develop institutional agents who have firsthand knowledge that allows them to understand students' lived experiences, can serve as mentors and role models, and are dedicated to building relationships with first-generation students and supporting transfer (Smith & Miller, 2009). Faculty and staff who serve as transfer agents can also play an important role in having high expectations of students and lifting up and validating students as capable of transferring and earning a bachelor's degree. We also recommend that first-generation college students be provided with transfer strategies to help them navigate the transfer process (Radunzel, 2018). For instance, community college programs such as orientation and student success courses should include "transfer college knowledge" (Hodara et al., 2017, p. 35). Hodara et al. recommend that advisers assist students in selecting a path early in their academic journey and developing a smaller number of pathways that may map to several bachelor's degree programs. Transfer-receiving institutions can be important partners in these efforts, for example by connecting students with opportunities on their campus before or shortly after students arrive. It is important that both the community college and transfer-receiving institution be held responsible for facilitating transfers and supporting students after transfer. Colleges and universities can utilize the framework provided by Xu et al. (2017) to help identify and measure the effectiveness of transfer partnerships. Rigorous evaluations of transfer initiatives are critical to providing policymakers and institutional leaders with formative and summative data that can provide real-time implementation of evaluation findings (Poisel & Joseph, 2018).

States that do better in the realm of transfer policy have a more integrated, comprehensive approach to transfer—they do not focus only on transfer as an academic matter. Transfer policies need to be refined so they can better meet the needs of community college students who have not decided on a major. State policy, to be truly impactful, needs to go beyond articulation agreements. States should consider providing transfer student aid and incentivizing institutional transfer completion (rewarding transfer student outcomes in institutional funding). For example, a statewide articulation agreement could include financial aid packages at both the community college and bachelor's-granting institution (Wellman, 2002). Additionally, states should prioritize data systems that can help identify and track transfer student outcomes and perform statewide transfer policy audits to determine how current policies relate to transfer performance and measurement. But as we have outlined, we cannot forget the human factor in transfer policy. States should create and fund policy initiatives so both community colleges and universities may provide better counseling and advising for students.

Recommendations for Future Research

We conclude by offering our ideas for scholarship we feel is most needed to move knowledge forward in the coming years specific to serving and supporting first-generation students in transferring from community colleges to bachelor's degree–granting institutions. Following the recommendation of Taylor and Jain (2017), we argue that future research should not only document inequities in transfer (although that is important) but also consider how and why inequities in transfer are perpetuated by policies and institutions. An important first step is to better understand the unique needs of first-generation college students (Radunzel, 2018). The majority of transfer scholarship to date has been quantitative and has failed to give adequate focus to documenting the voices of marginalized transfer student communities, including first-generation students, racially minoritized students, low-income students, lesbian, gay, bisexual, trans*, and queer students, and students with disabilities. As such, we recommend qualitative research that gives space to students' experiences with the transfer process and that considers the needs of community college students with different identities and lived experiences (e.g., first-generation and continuing-generation students). Within this, it is critical that transfer research (as well as the broader student success literature) move away from scholarship that intentionally or unintentionally frames first-generation students in a deficit way or that blames students' failures on what they lack or have not yet experienced.

We believe that scholarship is needed that studies systems and structures to hold institutions and policymakers accountable for their role in perpetuating transfer inequities. Taylor and Jain (2017) note that students' access to and experiences with transfer are currently not equal. Research is therefore needed to explore the ways in which existing institutional practices and policies may unintentionally serve as hindrances or obstacles to transfer. For example, our preliminary findings suggest that first-generation community college students in Oregon may not be receiving basic information regarding the steps to transferring to a bachelor's-granting institution. Additionally, we recommend that research is warranted to better understand the role of institutional (transfer) agents in supporting transfer for first-generation and other minoritized groups. Very little research to date has studied transfer from the perspective of transfer agents, advisers, or faculty (Taylor & Jain, 2017).

Finally, we strongly recommend rigorous research and evaluation work that studies transfer policy in context. Despite decades of statewide transfer legislation, relatively little is known regarding the efficacy of policies in supporting transfer and degree completion (Taylor & Jain, 2017). Continued evaluation of state systems is needed to understand the degree to which policies are continuing to meet intended outcomes (Hodara et al., 2018) as well as which policies may be unintentionally perpetuating transfer inequities. It is not enough to understand whether a policy is effective. Scholars must push to understand who policy and practices work for and under which conditions the policies and practices can be most effective for different groups—including but not limited to first-generation students. Moreover, building on recent work by Hodara et al. (2017), we recommend that transfer scholars study the implementation of new/expanded policy as well as focus on particular aspects and outcomes of transfer policy (e.g., credit mobility). Further, the role that state legislators, institutional leaders, and systems play in adopting and implementing policy warrants empirical attention (Bragg, 2017).

References

American Association of Community Colleges. (2012). *Reclaiming the American dream: A report from the 21st-century commission on the future of community colleges.*

Anderson, G. M., Sun, J. C., & Alfonso, M. (2006). Effectiveness of statewide articulation agreements on the probability of transfer: A preliminary policy analysis. *Review of Higher Education, 29*, 261–291. https://doi.org/10.1353/rhe.2006.0001

Andrews, R., Li, J., & Lovenheim, M. F. (2014). *Heterogeneous paths through college: Detailed patterns and relationships with graduation and earnings* http://www.aacc21stcenturycenter.org/wp-content/uploads/2014/03/21stCenturyReport.pdf (Working Paper 19935). National Bureau of Economic Research. http://www.nber.org/papers/w19935

Austin, E., Henson, A., & Wiroll, C. (2016). *Demystifying higher education transfer: Identifying common barriers facing transfer students in Oregon.* Department of Planning, Public Policy, and Management, University of Oregon.

Baker, R. (2016). The effects of structured transfer pathways in community colleges. *Educational Evaluation and Policy Analysis, 38*(4), 626–646. https://doi.org/10.3102/0162373716651491

Bragg, D. D. (2017). Transfer matters: Forward to the special issue on transfer. *Community College Review, 45*(4), 267–272. https://doi.org/10.1177/0091552117728572

Brint, S., & Karabel, J. (1989). *The diverted dream: Community colleges and the promise of educational opportunity in America, 1900–1985.* Oxford University Press.

Cohen, A. M., Brawer, F. B., & Kisker, C. B. (2013). *The American community college* (6th ed.). Jossey-Bass. https://www.wiley.com/en-us/The+American+Community+College%2C+6th+Edition-p-9781118449813

Crisp, G. (2013). The influence of co-enrollment on the success of traditional age community college students. *Teachers College Record, 115*(10), 1–25. https://www.tcrecord.org/Content.asp?ContentId=17156

Crisp, G., & Nuñez, A. (2014). Understanding the racial transfer gap: Modeling underrepresented minority and nonminority students' pathways from two- to four-year institutions. *The Review of Higher Education, 37*(3), 291–320. https://doi.org/10.1353/rhe.2014.0017

Crosta, P. M. (2014). Intensity and attachment: How the chaotic enrollment patterns of community college students relate to educational outcomes. *Community College Review, 42*(2), 118–142. https://doi.org/10.1177/0091552113518233

Dougherty, K. J., & Kienzl, G. S. (2006). It's not enough to get through the open door: Inequalities by social background in transfer from community colleges to four-year colleges. *Teachers College Record, 108*(3), 452–487. https://www.tcrecord.org/content.asp?contentid=12332

Dowd, A. C., Pak, J. H., & Bensimon, E. M. (2013). The role of institutional agents in promoting transfer access. *Education Policy Analysis Archives, 21*(15). https://doi.org/10.14507/epaa.v21n15.2013

Education Commission of the States. (2020, February 24). *50-state comparison: Transfer and articulation policies.* https://www.ecs.org/transfer-and-articulation-policies-db

Engle, J., & Tinto, V. (2008). *Moving beyond access: College success for low-income, first generation students.* The Pell Institute.

Garrison, N. J., & Gardner, D. S. (2012). *Assets first generation college students bring to the higher education setting* (ED539775). https://files.eric.ed.gov/fulltext/ED539775.pdf

Hagedorn, L. S., Cypers, S., & Lester, J. (2008). Looking in the review mirror: Factors affecting transfer for urban community college students. *Community College Journal of Research and Practice, 32*(9), 643–664. https://doi.org/10.1080/10668920802026113

Higher Education Coordinating Commission. (2017). *State of Oregon: Research—university student data.* https://www.oregon.gov/highered/research/Pages/student-data-univ.aspx

Hodara, M., Martinez-Wenzl, M., Stevens, D., & Mazzeo, C. (2016). *Improving credit mobility for community college transfer students: Findings and recommendations from a 10-state study.* Education Northwest. https://educationnorthwest.org/sites/default/files/resources/improving-credit-mobility-508.pdf

Horn, L., & Skomsvold, P. (2011). Web tables: Community college student outcomes: 1994–2009 (NCES 2012-253). National Center for Education Statistics. https://nces.ed.gov/pubsearch/pubsinfo.asp?pubid=2012253

Hossler, D., Shapiro, D., Dundar, A., Ziskin, M., Chen, J., Zerquera, D., & Torres, V. (2012). *Transfer & mobility: A national view of pre-degree student movement in postsecondary institutions.* National Student Clearinghouse Research Center. https://nscresearchcenter.org/wp-content/uploads/NSC_Signature_Report_2.pdf

Inman, W. E., & Mayes, L. (1999). The importance of being first: Unique characteristics of first-generation community college students. *Community College Review*, *26*(4), 3–22. https://doi.org/10.1177/009155219902600402

Jain, D., Herrera, A., Bernal, S., & Solórzano, D. (2011). Critical race theory and the transfer function: Introducing a transfer receptive culture. *Community College Journal of Research and Practice, 35*(3), 252–255. https://doi.org/10.1080/10668926.2011.526525

Jenkins, D., & Fink, J. (2015). *What we know about transfer.* Community College Research Center, Teachers College, Columbia University. https://ccrc.tc.columbia.edu/publications/what-we-know-about-transfer.html

Laanan, F. S., & Jain, D. (2016). Advancing a new critical framework for transfer student research: Implications for institutional research. In X. Wang (Ed.), *The evolving landscape of transfer research* (New Directions for Institutional Research, no. 170, pp. 9–21). Jossey-Bass. https://doi.org/10.1002/ir.20181

LaSota, R. R., & Zumeta, W. (2016). What matters in increasing community college students' upward transfer to the baccalaureate degree: Findings from the Beginning Postsecondary Study 2003–2009. *Research in Higher Education, 57,* 152–189. https://doi.org/10.1007/s11162-015-9381-z

London, H. B. (1996, November/December). How college affects first-generation students. *About Campus, 1*(5), 9–13, 23. https://doi.org/10.1002/abc.6190010503

Millard, M. (2014). *Students on the move: How states are responding to increasing mobility among postsecondary students.* Education Commission on the States. https://www.ecs.org/clearinghouse/01/12/29/11229.pdf

Mitchell, K. (1997). Making the grade: Help and hope for the first-generation college student (ED413886). *ERIC Review, 5*(3), 13–15.

Nuñez, A., & Cuccaro-Alamin, S. (1998). *First generation students: Undergraduates whose parents never enrolled in postsecondary education* (NCES 98-082). National Center for Education Statistics. https://nces.ed.gov/pubsearch/pubsinfo.asp?pubid=98082

Oregon State Legislature. (2017, August). *HB 2998 enrolled.* https://olis.leg.state.or.us/liz/2017R1/Measures/Overview/HB2998

Perna, L. W., & Leigh, E. W. (2017). Understanding the promise: A typology of state and local college promise programs. *Educational Researcher, 47,* 155–180. https://doi.org/10.3102/0013189X17742653

Poisel, M. A., & Joseph, S. (Ed). (2018). *Building transfer student pathways for college and career success.* University of South Carolina, National Resource Center for The First-Year Experience & Students in Transition and the National Institute for the Study of Transfer Students.

Porchea, S. F., Allen, J., Robbins, S., & Phelps, R. P. (2010). Predictors of long-term enrollment and degree outcomes for community college students: Integrating academic, psychosocial, socio-demographic and situational factors. *Journal of Higher Education, 81*(6), 750–778. https://doi.org/10.1080/00221546.2010.11 779077

Radunzel, J. (2018). *They may be first but will they last?: Retention and transfer behavior of first-generation students* (ACT Working Paper 2018-5). http://www.act.org/ content/dam/act/unsecured/documents/R1708-retention-firstgen-2018-04.pdf

Rendon, L. I. (1995). *Facilitating retention and transfer for first generation students in community colleges* (Paper presentation). New Mexico Institute, Rural Community College Initiative, Espanola, NM.

Shapiro, D., Dundar, A., Huie, F., Wakhungu, P. K., Yuan, X., Nathan, A. & Hwang, Y. (2020, September). *Tracking transfer: Measures of effectiveness in helping community college students to complete bachelor's degrees* (Signature Report no. 13). National Student Clearinghouse Research Center. https://nscresearchcenter.org/ tracking-transfer/

Smith, C. T., & Miller, A. (2009). *Promising practices for promoting transfer among low-income and first-generation students: An in-depth study of six exemplary community colleges in Texas* (ED508915). https://files.eric.ed.gov/fulltext/ ED508915.pdf

Taylor, J. L., & Jain, D. (2017). The multiple dimensions of transfer: Examining the transfer function in American higher education. *Community College Review, 45*(4), 273–293. https://doi.org/10.1177/0091552117725177

Thelin, J. R. (2019). *A history of American higher education* (3rd ed.). Johns Hopkins University Press.

Turk, J. M., & Chen, W. (2017). *Improving the odds: An empirical look at the factors that influence upward transfer.* American Council on Education. https://www .acenet.edu/news-room/Pages/Improving-the-Odds-An-Empirical-Look-at-the- Factors-That-Influence-Upward-Transfer.aspx

Wang, X. (2012). Factors contributing to the upward transfer of baccalaureate aspirants beginning at community colleges. *The Journal of Higher Education, 83*(6), 851–875. https://doi.org/10.1080/00221546.2012.11777272

Wang, X., Wickersham, K., & Sun, N. (2016). The evolving landscape of transfer research: Reconciling what we know in preparation for a new era of heightened promise and complexity. In X. Wang (Ed.), *The evolving landscape of transfer research* (New Directions for Institutional Research, no. 170, pp. 115–121). Jossey-Bass. https://doi.org/10.1002/ir.20189

Wellman, J. V. (2002). *State policy and community college—Baccalaureate transfer.* National Center for Public Policy and Higher Education and the Institute for Higher Education Policy. http://www.ihep.org/sites/default/files/uploads/docs/ pubs/statepolicycommunitycollege.pdf

Xu, D., Ran, F. X., Fink, J., Jenkins, D., & Dundar, A. (2017). *Strengthening transfer paths to a bachelor's degree: Identifying effective two-year to four-year college partnerships.* Community College Research Center. https://ccrc.tc.columbia.edu/ publications/strengthening-transfer-paths-bachelors-degree.html

MOVING ON IN MILWAUKEE

Easing the College Transition Process
for 2-Year College Students

Pablo Muirhead

S trong advising, support, and the reduction of unnecessary barriers are keys to helping first-generation college students transfer from 2- to 4-year institutions. In Wisconsin, the Milwaukee Area Technical College's (MATC) Teacher Education Program (TEP) helps students interested in earning their teaching license transfer and earn their teaching license at nearby colleges. A major goal of the program is to recruit students who reflect the diverse backgrounds of K–12 students into the teaching profession. This chapter describes the program and provides some ideas on how to help transfer students succeed.

First-generation college students offer much to the educational institutions they inhabit. Their life experiences, perspectives, and motivations enhance the learning experience for their peers as well as their instructors. These strengths are often coupled with challenges that hamper their potential for success. Over half of MATC's enrollment comprises first-generation students. In addition to being predominantly lower income and students of color, a significant number of our students are older, with responsibilities beyond pursuing a college degree. Additionally, many of our first-generation students come from inadequately funded "sending schools," which can place them behind their peers, a phenomenon common among first-generation college students (Ishitani, 2006).

In this reflection, I share the work I do in supporting students seeking to earn a teaching license by starting at a 2-year college, MATC in Wisconsin, before transferring to a 4-year partner. I will begin by describing some of the demographics of our students in the TEP at MATC. I will then share how our program aims to help students complete the transition to a 4-year degree. I will also share recommendations for the 2- and 4-year partners to increase student success.

221

Future Teachers

There is an imbalance between teachers set to retire in the next decade and the pipeline to replace those teachers. Additionally, there exists a pronounced division between the racial/ethnic makeup of students and that of their teachers. The Associate of Arts–TEP at MATC was born out of the necessity to address these two issues. Entering its 31st year, this program has worked with hundreds of students in helping them pursue their teacher licensure.

The students in our program are 65% students of color, are 35% male, and have a mean age of 27. This is exactly the type of diversity that most schools of education are looking for and school districts are looking to hire. The challenge for our students, however, is successfully navigating the higher education process in order to transfer to a 4-year university and ultimately complete their degree and earn their teacher certification. Students work to succeed in school while balancing their complex lives. The hurdles many of our students face are daunting. Whether it's dealing with childcare needs, homelessness, an unplanned pregnancy, an eviction, a deported family member, or simply figuring out how to pay for books, our students share a common denominator, and that is their dedication and commitment. However, there is only so much an individual can handle before needing to take a break from school to bring balance to other aspects of their life. That prolongs the path that many need to stay on to achieve their degrees. In many ways, the idea of a 2- or 4-year university pertains only to those who can go to school full-time without other interruptions.

The TEP at MATC

Our challenge becomes helping students, many of whom are first-generation college students (and who truly understand what many K–12 public school kids go through), achieve their goal of completing a 4-year degree and earning their teaching certification. What has proved successful (as shown in our transfer numbers) has been strong advising, meaningful support mechanisms, and the reduction of unnecessary obstacles.

Strong Advising With 2-Year Degree Completion in Mind

One of the delicate aspects of our course of study for students is the reality that our students transfer to a variety of institutions to pursue different licenses. This requires a constant understanding of the requirements at our transfer partners' institutions. Licensure changes at the state level continually impact program requirements as well. The requirements of our partner schools and the state requirements for teacher certification do not always align with the requirements for the TEP at MATC. Accordingly, every student requires individualized advising. It is important to help students establish early on where they plan on earning their 4-year degree to provide better advising. Pivotal to student success is opening the lines of communication with the transfer institutions. Our program brings in transfer advisers from our various partners every semester to work with our students in course selection. In some cases, our students are better off transferring before completing their associate's degree. However, this presents a unique problem for the 2-year institution as our funding hinges in part on the graduates that we produce.

Support Mechanisms

Support mechanisms are critical to student success, and they are inextricably linked to strong advising. By understanding each student's story, it becomes clear what supports they need. A strong connection to a faculty member or an adviser at each institution is essential in supporting students. Additionally, the existence of a network, or informal cohort, helps to keep students on track to completion. In many cases, the identification of financial support is also necessary.

Reduction of Obstacles

Continual dialogue with our 4-year partner institutions helps reduce unnecessary obstacles for our students. For instance, we have lobbied for policy changes at the state level to reduce the standardized tests that students need to take. We have also identified courses that do not transfer easily and have created replacement courses that transfer more seamlessly.

Recommendations

Based on my experiences chairing the TEP at MATC and working extensively with our 4-year partners, I recommend the following to both 2- and 4-year institutions:

- Consider the impact that each teacher education student will have on thousands of students throughout their teaching career and ensure that they get the support they need.
- Develop and maintain strong relationships between, and among, institutions that educate teacher candidates.

- Identify and either remove or circumnavigate barriers to student success.
- Consider how you can increase student success by developing strong partnerships.

Discussion Questions

1. What are some policies that impede the success of transfer students from or to your school?
2. How are transfer students supported at your 2-year college or at your university?
3. What structures need to exist so that students can transition from 2- to 4-year institutions smoothly?
4. Who are the key players at both 2- and 4-year institutions that need to come together to strengthen partnerships and ensure that the transfer process is seamless for students?

References

Ishitani, T. F. (2006). Studying attrition and degree completion behavior among first-generation college students in the United States. *Journal of Higher Education, 77*, 861–885. https://doi.org/10.1353/jhe.2006.0042

15

LEARNING WHERE
THEY LIVE

First-Generation College Students
in the Residence Halls

Paul Gallagher

R esidential halls (RHs) foster an environment that integrates college
students' personal and social development with their academic
learning. There have been several studies involving a variety of U.S.
colleges that show that living in an RH for even 1 year contributes to students' broad learning, psychosocial development, and overall satisfaction
with their college education (Inkelas et al., 2007; Pascarella & Terenzini,
2005; Pike, 1999). Among the many benefits that students gain from their
RH are the ease of creating social networks with peers, the support of RH
staff, academic advising from RH deans or associated faculty, and a range of
leadership opportunities within the RH community.

Students who are the first in their families to go to college are a demographic that can especially gain from the social, cocurricular, and academic
opportunities available to students living in residence, for the advantages
of living in RH communities that researchers have identified correspond
directly to several of the disadvantages and risk factors of first-generation
students. The data show that, compared to continuing-generation students,
first-generation students have more difficulty integrating socially on campus,
the academic transition from secondary school to college is more challenging, the sense of belonging to the institution is much lower, there is lower
participation in cocurricular activities, and they are at greater risk of not
completing a degree (Engle & Tinto, 2008; Longwell-Grice et al., 2016;
Pascarella et al., 2004; Terenzini et al., 1996).

Despite a growing literature on first-generation students, significantly less attention has been given to first-generation students living in RHs. The studies that have been done were limited to one or a small number of college campuses (Adsitt, 2017; Bradbury & Mather, 2009; Hall & O'Neal, 2016; Setari, 2017). One possible reason for the scarcity of studies on first-generation students in RHs is that the majority of first-generation students in the United States attend 2-year colleges, most of which do not offer housing, while those studying at 4-year colleges often do not live on campus. Many first-generation students are part-time students and/or not of traditional college age (17–22) and have dependents, statuses that would exclude them from most on-campus housing arrangements. However, one may be optimistic that research on first-generation students in RHs will grow as higher education specialists continue to take interest in measuring the impact of residential learning communities (RLCs) and living learning communities (LLCs) on at-risk students (Hall & O'Neal, 2016; Setari, 2017; Zhao & Kuh, 2004).

Since nearly all students in conventional RHs are of traditional college age and study full-time, this chapter is necessarily limited to this subgroup of first-generation students who are living in an RH or very similar student accommodation, that is, where there is some formal programing and engagement with residential life staff, even if these are minimal. I draw on research of first-generation students, findings in student development in RHs, and my own experience in diverse RH communities to highlight the advantages of residential living for first-generation students. I also identify strategies that student affairs professionals and RH administrators can apply to their institutional settings to support the development and learning of first-generation students living in their campus accommodation.

The Intersections of First-Generation Disadvantage

First-generation students face significant challenges across several intersections when they arrive at college. They are mostly from low-income or working-class backgrounds (Engle & Tinto, 2008; Pascarella et al., 2004; Terenzini et al., 1996), are employed during the semester at higher rates than their continuing-generation peers (Engle & Tinto, 2008), and report finances as a primary concern while at college (Bui, 2002). Indeed, finances are often a factor in first-generation students' decisions to leave postsecondary education before completing a degree. As 49% of first-generation students in the United States in 2012 were White (Redford & Hoyer, 2012), half of this population is also navigating the intersection of race on their college campus.

Most first-generation students of all races attended secondary schools with less academic rigor than those students who have a parent with a college education, and thus they are arriving on campus without adequate academic preparation. The financial and educational disadvantages of first-generation students can be compensated with special programs such as targeted financial aid, preenrollment "bridging" classes, academic writing centers, and peer tutoring. These cannot eliminate all financial and academic disadvantages, but they are invaluable services for many students. First-generation students also benefit from schemes like the inclusion of a local bus pass in an enrollment package and the flexibility that evening sections of courses offer to those who are required to hold employment while studying.

What has proven to be more difficult to measure, and especially to mitigate, is first-generation students' deficit in what Bourdieu (1986) called *cultural capital*, that degree of familiarity and ease of navigation one has within the dominant culture. A scholarship can pay for books or a laptop, but it does not remove the feelings of inadequacy, the sense that one does not belong in this place of articulate, well-informed peers and learned professors. If student affairs professionals only needed to say, "Go to your professors' office hours," first-generation students would already be enjoying the same frequency and quality of interaction with faculty as their continuing-generation peers. Yet first-generation students do not interact with faculty as much. They may even feel that faculty are uncaring, which is as understandable as it is untrue because there can be quite a cultural distance between these students and their professors (Bradbury & Mather, 2009; Padgett et al., 2012). It takes more than financial aid and writing workshops to help students overcome the feeling that the college campus is an alien, even intimidating, place.

How, then, do first-generation students learn to approach faculty, to gain confidence in their peer interactions, and to feel that the college campus is where they too belong? They learn how to do these things through immersion in the culture of the academy, a culture that shares many of the same values as the American middle-class culture in which their continuing-generation peers have been immersed since childhood. By simply living in an RH, where one is exposed to the social behavior of these peers, first-generation students are learning how college "works," something that is much harder to pick up when one is commuting to rather than living on campus.

Cultural Capital

The deficit in cultural capital is the most pernicious disadvantage that first-generation students face. As mentioned, college is a cultural space in which first-generation students struggle to discern the unwritten rules and norms of academic life. They are less likely than their peers whose parents are college educated to approach professors for help outside the lecture hall and to access student services (Engle & Tinto, 2008; Padgett et al., 2012). First-generation students do not know how to advocate for themselves because they do not know the culture of higher education.

One of the more detailed studies of cultural capital at work in educational settings is Lareau's (2011) influential work, *Unequal Childhoods: Class, Race, and Family Life*, in which she distinguishes two fundamental parenting styles. First, there is "concerted cultivation" (p. 2), practiced by middle- and upper-class parents, in which children have organized activities, their hobbies are encouraged, and their opinions solicited, the aim of which is to foster children's talents to prepare them for entry into the social world of adults. In many ways, the children of middle-class parents are already behaving like adults when they use their powers of reason to articulate their preferences and to negotiate for them. Parents who practice concerted cultivation intervene with teachers or health care professionals on behalf of their children. Such interventions lead to more personalized attention and a healthy sense of entitlement in the child, who is learning how to engage authority and to advance their individual needs. Second, there is the "accomplishment of natural growth" (Laraeu, 2011, p. 3) parenting style, which is practiced by low-income and working-class parents. For these parents, there is a clear separation between children and adults. Hence, they tend to give directives to children, telling them what to do rather than soliciting their cooperation or agreement. "Natural growth" children have more control over their leisure time, much of which is spent "hanging out" with friends rather than engaged in organized activities. They inhabit a social world that is more childlike and includes fewer nonkin adults than middle-class children. Low-income and working-class parents intervene less with authorities like teachers than middle-class parents, and they are generally accepting of authority figures. When they do disagree with authority, they disengage in frustration rather than argue for their point of view as do middle-class parents.

When meeting new arrivals on the college campus in late summer, often one can readily recognize which students were raised by which of these parenting styles. For example, first-generation students, most of whom would have had a natural growth upbringing, are more likely to leave an administrative office without the special accommodation they need or before they get clear answers to their questions. In his bestseller *Outliers: The Story of Success*, Malcolm Gladwell (2008) illustrated the importance of cultural capital on college campuses through the sad story of Chris Langan, one of the statistics of first-generation attrition. A prodigy from a poor and fractured family, Langan enjoyed a minor celebrity in the 1990s and early 2000s for having one of the highest IQs in the United States. Digging into Langan's background, Gladwell learned that he earned a perfect score on his SAT and was offered full scholarships to Reed College and the University of Chicago. He chose Reed, where he earned straight A's in his first semester. Then, he did not complete the second semester, which he blames on an uncaring college bureaucracy after his mother did not complete a parents' financial statement for the renewal of his scholarship. Langan later enrolled in Montana State University, where he soon dropped out when he was denied permission to transfer from a morning to an afternoon class, which became a necessity when his car broke down for the last time. Langan's "explanations," wrote Gladwell (2008),

> as heartbreaking as they are, are also a little strange. His mother forgets to sign his financial aid form and—just like that—no scholarship. He tries to move from a morning to an afternoon class, something students do every day, and gets stopped cold. (p. 96)

Despite a perfect score on his SAT, Langan could not have been more unprepared for college, because he was lacking the cultural skill set of the middle class.

Building Cultural Capital in the RH

The RH is a place where first-generation students can begin to adjust to the culture of the academy and to learn the ins and outs of interpersonal as well as institutional engagement that their middle-class peers already absorbed from their family and secondary-school environments. When living in an RH for months at a time, first-generation students begin to discern the ways in which their peers navigate institutional spaces for their own advantage—for example, how to get a larger room in the RH next year, or negotiate deadline extensions with faculty, or find the campus jobs that are not advertised. By observing their peers, first-generation students will also come to appreciate how one voluntary role in a student club or college office can open new doors of advantage and expand one's network of useful acquaintances.

Astin (1993) discovered that peer groups are the most important source for college student growth and development. This should not be surprising, because late adolescence is the stage in life where parents are exerting less influence than they did during childhood and early adolescence. The college years are also a time when students spend less time in the social world of high school friends, as they may not be attending the same institution or, for many first-generation students, their friends are not going to college at all. Many college students have moved out of their parents' home for the first time, which transfers further influence to the new peer group on campus. The RH is an environment in which students bond closely to one another given the frequency of their contact, their common purpose in pursuing a college degree, and the common experiences that come from these. As every residential life staff member has observed, students whose rooms are close together can especially form very strong bonds with one another, which are a critical source of emotional support that lasts throughout a student's college journey.

For first-generation students, who are more likely to report that they do not feel that they belong to their college community because of their academic ability or class background (Garriott et al., 2011), the support of college friends in the RH are especially important. Even if one perceives the faculty to be distant and classroom peers unfriendly, the RH is still a home on campus where one has friendships and residential staff who represent a more personalized side of the institution. Students thereby gain a sense of belonging to their college, even if that is mostly due to their experiences in the RH. This is an important function of the RH, as social integration and institutional commitment are critical to the retention and graduation of all students (Tinto, 1993) and especially those who are the first in their family to go to college (Woosley & Miller, 2009). A circle of friends in the home-like environment of the RH provides first-generation students with a source of emotional support and practical guidance as they make their way through the cultural labyrinth of college.

The support of friends on campus can be very important to first-generation students as their families back home may not understand their struggles on campus, or they may not be supportive of their educational goals. The journey to college is often a solo one for first-generation students, as they are normally searching for colleges and submitting applications without the guidance of their parents. Parents of first-generation students can also be unsupportive when they make demands that conflict with time allotted for study or college social activities.

The lack of family support that first-generation students face is a matter of culture, not personality. One speaks of first-generation students as living in two cultures: the academic culture of the campus and the culture at home, quite often a low-income or working-class home. A number of researchers have observed the challenge of personal identity that first-generation students face as they continually go in and out of these two cultural spheres (Bradbury & Mather, 2009; Lehmann, 2013; Longwell-Grice et al., 2016). For these students, the university years are not a straightforward immersion in student life and the adventure of personal discovery but a more limited space of new freedoms that are subordinate to familial responsibilities. Even as family

LEARNING WHERE THEY LIVE   *231*

members take pride in their first member going to college, they can also assume, falsely, that they have taken on an air of self-importance on account of their new educational status (Bradbury & Mather, 2009; Longwell-Grice et al., 2016).

Students who commute from home and those who make frequent visits home while living away at college will alternate between these two cultures more frequently, which may impact how quickly and to what degree they integrate into the college community. There is yet to be any comparative study of the adjustments and experiences of commuting and residential first-generation students. My speculation, based on the experiences of students in RHs cited in the referenced literature, is that students would acclimatize to college life more quickly and learn to manage their bicultural status more effectively if they were to live in RHs, that is, spend most of their time in the college cultural sphere.

The RH itself is a cultural space in which first-generation students lack capital. As Adsitt (2017) found in her research, the shared living spaces of the RH can at times have a negative impact by magnifying cultural and class differences for first-generation students. The RH can also be detrimental to first-generation students on campuses where the RHs tend to be social and not necessarily academic environments. This had been my experience as a dean and head of college in RHs at the Universities of Melbourne and Sydney in Australia, where the university is seen as a place of study and the RH as a place of socialization and recreation. In that environment, the RH can negatively affect first-generation students' academic performance as they often come from secondary schools with less rigorous academics, and they therefore do not have the experience of their continuing-generation peers in balancing a social life with a demanding curriculum.

Identifying First-Generation Student Needs Early

Research shows that the first-semester and first-year experiences have been critical to students' retention and persistence (Levitz & Noel, 1993; Tinto, 1993; Upcraft & Gardner, 1989). Woosley and Shepler's (2011) work has added to this scholarship as they give specific attention to first-generation students' early integration experiences. In another study, Woosley and Miller (2003) zoom in on the first 3 weeks of college for all students and their impact on academic performance, retention, and degree completion. The results show that, even at 3 weeks, "retention and academic performance are predicted by the early transition experiences of academic integration, social integration, and institutional commitment, even when gender, ethnicity, and entrance exam scores are included in the analysis" (p. 1266).

These studies highlight the need for college administrators and residential life staff to get to know their new students early, especially at-risk subgroups like first-generation students, and to connect with them individually and through intentional programs in the first weeks of the new academic year. As Kuh et al. (2010) point out, students who arrive on campus with less academic preparation and knowledge of college "need explicit directions to use institutional resources and support services profitably" (p. 110). Peer support programs, like resident adviser (RA) circles and buddy systems, can be enlisted to ensure that students are passing through administrative offices effectively and gaining knowledge of support services across the campus.

It is important for RH administrators themselves to gain an early rapport with their first-generation students to facilitate their adjustment to college life through personalized engagement. Information that is relevant to understanding each student's needs and potential challenges includes their educational and family backgrounds. What was their secondary education like? Are there siblings? Do they come from a single-parent household? How frequently will they travel home on weekends? An RH administrator is also interested in knowing about employment commitments and financial circumstances (e.g., full financial aid or multiple sources for loans) that may prevent them from participating in residential life programs due to time commitments or a lack of disposable income. An early one-on-one session with first-generation students allows RH administrators to identify each student's particular academic or social adjustment challenges. In my experience, students who are disappointed with or even offended by the social environment of the RH tend not to share this with peers or RAs but with RH administrators instead. When I learn of these integration problems early, I am able to guide students in their integration at the same time that I am working with my RA team to enact a strategy to increase the peer effort to make this student feel at home in our RH community.

First-Generation–First Semester At Yale-NUS College

An intentional program that I deliver in the first weeks of semester 1 at Yale-NUS College in Singapore, where I closely advise approximately 300 students in the Saga College residence, is First-Gen–First Sem. Still in its early trials, the program is both a social occasion and an academic advising evening in which I share with students my own experience as a first-generation university student in Canada. Simply telling students about my misunderstandings and wrong turns through university elicits their own tales of present travails with incomplete forms, important email from various campus departments misplaced, and so on. Students appreciate hearing each other's backgrounds as well as my own, as they are unaware of their peers' first-generation status prior to the program. They also take an interest in each other's family life as we talk about living in the two cultures of campus and working-class homes.

In First-Gen–First Sem, I relate to students what researchers are saying about them as a demographic. I address the negative findings, such as retention rates and less academic preparation compared to their continuing-generation peers, but I focus on the positive ones, which I frame as practical advice for my students' own steps toward a successful integration into academic culture. For example, while first-generation students have lower levels of participation in extracurricular activities, those who do get involved with campus societies demonstrate growth in their personal development and even in higher-order cognitive skills by their second and third year of university (Pascarella et al., 2004). Such students have adapted to the culture of higher education, and they are noticeably closing the sociocultural and grade gaps between themselves and their continuing-generation peers. They are closing these gaps because students with more educated parents show much smaller outcomes in comparison to the social and academic gains that first-generation students are enjoying through their extracurricular activities. The research also shows that first-generation students who put in more study hours are getting more benefit from those extra hours than their peers. Again, the gains from extra study hours are much smaller for continuing-generation students.

The message to my first-generation students is clear and positive: While you may be "behind" your peers in some ways, you can make up for that by getting involved in clubs and activities outside of the classroom and by putting in just a few more study hours. It is noteworthy that participation in sports, part-time work, and many kinds of volunteer work do not help first-generation students; indeed, these frequently show negative impacts (Pascarella et al., 2004). That is to say, being the executive of one student society and playing one sport will be more beneficial to a student's development than playing two sports. Further, I point out to my students that leadership opportunities in RHs are more fitting for inexperienced leaders as these are often smaller in scale than many organizations that are campus wide and since the reach of the office is limited to the close-knit RH community.

It should be noted that, while it is beneficial to connect first-generation students to each other through an occasional program like First-Gen–First Sem, the research indicates that clustering first-generation students together in one RH or a nonresidential LLC may inhibit their development. As they are all unfamiliar with middle-class and academic culture, their proximity to each other could inhibit their acquisition of cultural capital (Lohfink & Paulsen, 2005; Pascarella et al., 2004). Among other habits, first-generation students pass over extracurricular life and thereby miss its developmental and networking opportunities, as they focus narrowly on maintaining their academic standing (Lohfink & Paulsen, 2005).

The Importance of Mentors

One of the implicit aims of First-Gen–First Sem is to open a space in which I can become a mentor to my first-generation students, as mentors can play a crucial role in their adjustment to college (Kirkner & Levinson, 2017; Longwell-Grice et al., 2016). As a live-in dean of the RH, I am able to mentor students very intentionally, because I interact with them at least weekly as a member of the same residential community at the same time that I represent the wider campus as a senior college administrator. At colleges where students are assigned academic advisers from the faculty, they too can be mentors. Meeting with their advisees periodically each semester, the professors are able to support their students in so many small ways as well as advise them on larger decisions like major selection. The social identities of advising faculty could further establish a foundation of trust and empowerment. However, contact with advisees can be as infrequent as once per semester, which is not conducive to building relationships. Yet a mentor need not be a faculty or staff member. Under the Oxbridge RH model in Australia, for example, I drew on the postgraduate students on my tutoring team and members of the Senior Common Room to mentor various first-year students at risk. The alumni networks of particular RHs are another source of mentors who can help first-generation students adapt to the academy and begin to accumulate some cultural capital of their own outside of college.

Given first-generation students' reticence, these relationships need to be intentional and potential mentors need to appreciate this. If it is to be effective, the mentor relationship will need to be structured to ensure that sufficient contact and some minimal outcomes are met. To borrow a phrase from Longwell-Grice et al. (2016), the mentors of first-generation students need to practice "intrusive advising" (p. 42).

Conclusion

The RH provides students with an environment in which to meet peers who have similar interests and yet who are different in other ways, such as background, race, or career goals. Students living together in an RH often form close bonds with each other and become a source of support for one another, emotionally as well as academically, through informal study sessions. They help each other to survive and to thrive in their college life. This peer support is crucial to first-generation students who come to college from an intersection of identities, both conspicuous—economic, academic, racial—and less visible, namely, social class upbringing. The full immersion in college life and exposure to the study and interpersonal styles of continuing-generation peers allows first-generation students to tune in to the frequencies of college culture. In other words, they are acquiring valuable cultural capital through their residential experience. The friendships forged in the RH thus facilitate first-generation students' entry to the wider college community. As Blimling (2015) writes, "It is through the peer environment that new students come to understand the university and engage in campus life outside the classroom" (p. 201).

First-generation students need more than a network of informal peer support, however. They also need to build relationships—cultural capital—with faculty and administrators, who are the representatives of the institution. Unlike friends, administrators know the operations of the college from the inside. Moreover, they provide the institutional support and advising that friends naturally cannot. RH administrators and residential life staff are uniquely placed to create intentional programs for first-generation students in the residence halls and to connect them with mentors from the academy as well as professional life. Given the success of RH communities in transitioning first-year students into college life, effort should be placed on drawing more first-year students into on-campus accommodation and finding the means to make that move affordable for them.

References

Adsitt, N. Z. (2017). *Stretching the circle: First-generation college students navigate their educational journey* (UMI no. 10617890) [Doctoral dissertation, Syracuse University]. ProQuest Dissertations & Theses Global database.

Astin, A.W. (1993). *What matters in college: Four critical years revised.* Jossey-Bass.

Blimling, G. S. (2015). *Student learning in residential colleges: What works, what doesn't, and why.* Jossey-Bass.

Bourdieu, P. (1986). The forms of capital. In J. Richardson (Ed.), *Handbook of theory and research for the sociology of education* (pp. 241–257). Greenwood.

Bradbury, B. L. & Mather, P. C. (2009). The integration of first-year, first-generation college students from Ohio Appalachia. *NASPA Journal, 46*(2), 258–281.

Bui, K. V. T. (2002). First-generation college students at a four-year university: Background characteristics, reasons for pursuing higher education, and first-year experiences. *College Student Journal, 36*(1), 3–11.

Engle, J., & Tinto, V. (2008). *Moving beyond access: College success for low-income, first-generation students.* The Pell Institute for the Study of Opportunity in Higher Education.

Garriott, P., Hudyma, A., Keene, C., & Santiago, D. (2011). Social cognitive predictors of first- and non-first-generation college students' academic and life satisfaction. *Journal of Counseling Psychology, 62*(2), 253–263.

Gladwell, M. (2008). *Outliers: The story of success.* Little, Brown and Company.

Hall, B., & O'Neal, T. (2016). The residential learning community as a platform for high-impact educational practices aimed at at-risk student success. *Journal of the Scholarship of Teaching and Learning, 16*(6), 42–55.

Inkelas, K. K., Daver, Z. E., Vogt, K. E., & Leonard, J. B. (2007). Living-learning programs and first-generation college students' academic and social transition to college. *Research in Higher Education, 77*(5), 861–885.

Kirkner, T., & Levinson, J. (2017). Ubiquitous transitions at two-year colleges. In J. R. Fox & H. E. Martin (Eds.), *Academic advising and the first college year* (pp. 63–83). University of South Carolina, National Resource Center for The First-Year Experience & Students in Transition and NACADA: The Global Community for Advising.

Kuh, G. D., Schuh, J. H., Whitt, E. J., & Associates (2010). *Student success in college: Creating conditions that matter.* Jossey-Bass.

Lareau, A. (2011). *Unequal childhoods: Class, race, and family life* (2nd ed.). University of California Press.

Lehmann, W. (2014). Habitus transformation and hidden injuries: Successful working-class students. *Sociology of Education, 87*(1), 1–15.

Levitz, R., & Noel, L. (1989). Connecting students to institutions: Keys to retention and success. In M. L Upcraft, J. N. Gardner (Eds.), *The freshman year experience* (pp. 65–81). Jossey-Bass.

Lohfink, M. M., & Paulsen, M. B. (2005). Comparing the determinants of persistence for first-generation and continuing-generation students. *Journal of College Student Development, 46*(4), 409–428.

Longwell-Grice, R., Zervas Adsitt, N., Mullins, K., & Serrata, W. (2016). The first ones: Three studies on first-generation college students. *NACADA Journal, 36*(2), 34–46.

Padgett, R. D., Johnson, M. P., & Pascarella, E. T. (2012). First-generation undergraduate students and the impacts of the first year of college: Additional evidence. *Journal of College Student Development, 53*(2), 243–266.

Pascarella E. T., Pierson, C. T., Wolniak, G. C., & Terenzini, P. T. (2004). First-generation college students: Additional evidence on college experiences and outcomes. *The Journal of Higher Education, 75*(3), 249–284.

Pascarella E. T., & Terenzini, P. T. (2005). *How college affects students: A third decade of research* (Vol. 2). Jossey-Bass.

Pike, G. R. (1999). The effects of residential learning communities and traditional residential living arrangements on educational gains during the first year of college. *Journal of College Student Development, 40*(3), 269–284.

Redford, J., & Hoyer, K. (2017). *First-generation and continuing-generation college students: A comparison of high school and postsecondary experiences* (NCES 2018-009). National Center for Education Statistics. https://nces.ed.gov/pubs2018/2018009.pdf

Setari, R. R. (2017). *Support networks of "educational pioneers": A methodological approach for examining the impact of a residential learning community on first-generation students* (UMI no. 10628873) [Doctoral dissertation, University of Kentucky]. ProQuest Dissertations & Theses Global database.

Terenzini, P. T., Springer, L., Yaeger, P. M., Pascarella, E. T., & Nora, A. (1996). First-generation college students: Characteristics, experiences, and cognitive development. *Research in Higher Education, 37*(1), 1–22.

Tinto, V. (1993). *Leaving college: Rethinking the causes and cures of student attrition* (2nd ed.). University of Chicago Press.

Upcraft, M. L., & Gardner, J. N. (1989). A comprehensive approach to enhancing freshman success. In M. L. Upcraft, J. N. Gardner (Eds.), *The freshman year experience* (pp. 1–12). Jossey-Bass.

Woosley, S. A., & Miller, A. L. (2009). Integration and institutional commitment as predictors of college student transition: Are third week indicators significant? *College Student Journal, 43*(4), 1260–1271.

Woosely, S. A., & Shepler, D. K. (2011). Understanding the early integration experiences of first-generation college students. *College Student Journal, 45*(4), 700–714.

Zhao, C. M., & Kuh, G. D. (2004). Adding value: Learning communities and student engagement. *Research in Higher Education, 45*(2), 115–138.

ADVICE FOR ADVISERS

Hadyn K. Swecker and Matthew Fifolt

The first year of college is critical for the persistence of first-generation college students. Moreover, research consistently reports academic advising as an effective retention strategy among first-generation college students. Researchers have suggested that first-generation, low-income students commonly lack both economic resources to succeed at the postsecondary level as well as social capital or the knowledge to understand the world of higher education (i.e., college knowledge) (Almeida, 2015; Petty, 2014). Since first-generation college students frequently do not have a strong college-going culture, they may not know what educational options are available to them. Academic advisers can be instrumental in the success of first-generation college students.

Academic Advising

Academic advising is an interaction that occurs between a student and an academic adviser. Academic advising can be done one on one, online or in person, or in a group setting with professional staff or faculty members. This critical conversation focuses on academic advising between professional staff members and first-generation students.

First-generation students are multifaceted and experience college differently because of their background; therefore, academic advisers should be intentional with their communication and support. There are different styles of academic advising in the research literature; the prevailing models include prescriptive, developmental, proactive (also known as intrusive), and appreciative advising. Drake et al. (2013) also identified advising as teaching, learning-centered advising, motivational interviewing, strength-based advising, self-authorship theory, advising as coaching, constructivism and systems theory, Socratic advising, and a hermeneutic approach to advising.

Prescriptive Advising

In *prescriptive advising*, the academic adviser tells the college student what they should do. The adviser has the knowledge and tells the student what classes to take, what to major in, and what to do regarding policies and deadlines. Within the prescriptive advising model, the academic adviser provides the information and the student complies (Crookston, 1972; Frost, 1991; Gordan, 1992). As its name suggests, advisers "prescribe" actions for students to take with little to no input from the student.

Developmental Advising

Developmental advising differs from prescriptive advising in that the relationship between the academic adviser and student is collaborative. The academic adviser encourages and provides resources for the student, and the student is engaged in the process, empowered, and takes responsibility for their own decisions (Crookston, 1972, 1994; Frost, 1991; Gordan, 1992). It is a holistic approach to advising that involves engagement between adviser and student. Developmental advising promotes skills such as decision-making, problem-solving, and evaluation, skills that students can use in both present and future situations (Crookston, 1972, 1994). Within the developmental advising model, an adviser leads a student through steps to select a major. An adviser might also provide course options that match the student's interests and major. Additionally, advisers encourage students to bring their ideas for classes to take. Discussions with students include academic interests as well as personal and professional goals.

Proactive Advising

Proactive advising, also known as *intrusive advising*, is just that: an adviser being proactive in approaching and working with college students. It is a combination of developmental and prescriptive advising (Earl, 1988). In order to establish and maintain a relationship, academic advisers initiate communication with students (Varney, 2007). If a student is experiencing academic difficulty, an adviser would contact the student and encourage them to identify and use academic resources (Earl, 1987; Frost, 1991). If a student has not decided on a major, the adviser would reach out to the student to discuss resources and ideas for selecting a major. The adviser may also encourage students to come prepared to discuss course options for registration and remind the student about upcoming registration deadlines. Some benefits of proactive (intrusive) advising include increased rates of retention and completion, maximized student contact, relationships built on trust, higher grade point averages, and increased number of hours attempted

(Glennen, 1975; Glennen & Baxley, 1985; Schwebel et al., 2008; Vander Schee, 2007).

Appreciative Advising

In *appreciate advising*, advisers use positive, open-ended questions to help students discover and achieve their goals, dreams, and future (Bloom, 2008). The six phases of appreciative advising are "disarm, discover, dream, design, deliver and don't settle" (Bloom et al., 2008, p. 11). Advisers establish a rapport with students, embolden students to dream about their future selves, consult with students as they are creating their plans, and challenge them to continue to thrive. Something as simple as walking out to greet a student and leaning forward while listening to a student are details that are important in appreciative advising. Examples of questions that may prompt future thinking include the following: Where do you see yourself in 10 years? What is your dream job? What do you enjoy doing for fun? What is an accomplishment you are proud of?

Academic Advising Strategies

Academic advisers can play a key role in connecting students with critical information and resources. By recognizing that first-generation college students often have few social supports to guide them (e.g., family members with college degrees), these students may not know how to ask the right questions or even what the right questions are. Therefore, academic advisers cannot assume that students come from a place of knowledge regarding academic coursework, student support services, and other aspects of college life. Advisers must be deliberate about helping students transition to this new and unfamiliar setting. One easy step to take is to simply articulate the acronyms used to describe aspects of college, like names of buildings and academic majors. Almeida (2015) also recommended intentionally connecting first-generation, low-income students with individuals who have more familiarity with the college-going culture (e.g., continuing-generation peers, TRIO academic services, student affairs).

Lash and Thomson (2015) identified specific strategies that academic advisers can use to support first-year, first-generation college students:

- Educate the campus community about first-generation college students (FGS)
  - Educate staff/faculty about needs of FGS at departmental meetings
  - Share FGS reports and statistics with the campus community
  - Build a FGS web presence

- Communication
  - Send weekly email communication to students and parents
  - Include information in communications regarding resources, deadlines, and strategies for success and engagement
- At-risk monitoring
  - Identify academically at-risk FGS through student information system
  - Reach out proactively via text messaging to at-risk students
  - Follow up with FGS about academic, social, and emotional concerns
  - Make appropriate referrals
- Midterm grade collection and intervention
  - Celebrate grades of B or higher via email
  - Intervene via email, text, and phone regarding grades of C– or lower

Kalinsowski Ohrt (2016) articulated two additional strategies for working with first-generation college students including (a) extending office hours to be available to students when they need assistance and (b) demonstrating subject-matter knowledge. Kalinsowski Ohrt (2016) stated:

> If advisers are only available 9:00 a.m.–5:00 p.m., and students are only on campus 4:00–10:00 p.m., the students will not discern any kind of support system around them. If advisers are unavailable, it implies they do not care or, minimally, they do not want to consider students' needs in the decision-making process. (para. 20)

With regard to subject-matter expertise, Kalinsowski Ohrt (2016) suggested that knowledge of courses and schedules allows advisers to build trust and rapport with students. The author stated, "Advisers can explain the curriculum and why it is set up in the way it is, point out classes that may be challenging and offer ideas on how to balance course loads with their (students') lives outside of academics" (para. 19). This level of adviser competence, observed the author, lays the foundation for working with first-generation students in future advising appointments.

Academic advising has long been considered one of the leading resources for retaining first-generation students in higher education (Baldridge et al., 1982). As noted by Swecker et al. (2013), colleges and universities can capitalize on their retention efforts by intentionally connecting first-generation students with the resources necessary to persist to graduation. However, if mainstream institutions of higher education are going to meet the needs of an increasingly diverse student population, including first-generation college students, they will have to modify existing services and schedules to accommodate students' needs first (Conrad & Gasman, 2015).

Discussion Questions

1. Why do you think that academic advising is an effective retention strategy among first-generation college students?
2. What academic advising style and strategies would you use in advising first-generation college students?
3. What do you see as similarities and differences between advising first-generation college students and continuing-generation college students?
4. What information and resources would be helpful to include in training you to advise first-generation college students more effectively?

References

Almeida, D. J. (2015). College readiness and low-income youth. In W. G. Tierney & J. C. Duncheon (Eds.), *The problem of college readiness* (pp. 89–113). State University of New York Press.

Baldridge, J. V., Kremerer, F. R., & Green, K. C. (1982). *Enrollments in the eighties: Factors, actors and impacts* (ASHE-ERIC/Higher Education Research Report No. 3). American Association for Higher Education.

Bloom, J. (2008). Moving on from college. In V. N. Gordon, W. R. Habley, T. J. Grites & Associates (Eds.), *Academic advising: A comprehensive handbook* (2nd ed.) (pp. 178–188). Jossey-Bass.

Bloom, J. L., Hutson, B. L., & He, Y. (2008). *The appreciative advising revolution*. Stipes.

Conrad, C., & Gasman, M. (2015). *Educating a diverse nation: Lessons from minority-serving institutions*. Harvard University Press. https://doi.org/10.4159/9780674425477

Crookston, B. B. (1972). A developmental view of academic advising as teaching. *Journal of College Student Personnel, 13*, 12–17.

Crookston, B. B. (1994). A developmental view of academic advising as teaching. *NACADA Journal, 14*(2), 5–9, http://dx.doi.org/10.12930/0271-9517-14.2.5

Drake, J. K., Jordan, P., & Miller, M. A. (Eds.) (2013). *Academic advising approaches: Strategies that teach students to make the most of college*. Jossey-Bass.

Earl, W. R. (1987). Intrusive advising for freshmen. *Academic Advising News, 9*(3). http://www.nacada.ksu.edu/Resources/Clearinghouse/View-Articles/Intrusive-Advising-for-Freshmen.aspx

Earl, W. R. (1988). Intrusive advising of freshmen in academic difficulty. *NACADA Journal. 8*(2), 27–33. http://dx.doi.org/10.12930/0271-9517-8.2.27

Frost, S. H. (1991). *Academic advising for student success: A system of shared responsibility* (ASHE-ERIC Higher Education Report no. 3). The George Washington University, School of Education and Human Development.

Glennen, R. E. (1975). Intrusive college counseling. *College Student Journal, 9*(1), 2–4.

Glennen, R. E., & Baxley, D. M. (1985). Reduction of attrition through intrusive advising. *NASPA Journal, 22*(3), 10–14.

Gordan, V. N. (1992). *Handbook of academic advising.* Greenwood.

Kalinsowski Ohrt, E. (2016). Proactive advising with first-generation students: Suggestions for practice. *The Mentor: An Academic Advising Journal, 18.* https://doi.org/10.26209/mj1861250

Lash, A., & Thomson, K. (2015). *Proactively meeting the needs of first-year, first-generation college students.* Proceedings of the 34th Annual Conference on the First-Year Experience, Dallas, TX. https://sc.edu/nrc/presentation/annual/2015/handouts/CT-270%20Proactively%20Meeting%20the%20Needs%20of%20First-Year%20First-Generation%20Students.pdf

Petty, T. (2014). Motivating first-generation college students to academic success and college completion. *College Student Journal, 2,* 257–264.

Schwebel, D. C., Walburn, N. C., Jacobsen, S. H., Jerrolds, K. L., & Klyce, K. (2008). Efficacy of intrusively advising first-year students via frequent reminders for advising appointments. *NACADA Journal, 28*(2), 28–32. http://dx.doi.org/10.12930/0271-9517-28.2.28

Swecker, H., Fifolt, M., & Searby, L. (2013). Academic advising and first-generation college students: A quantitative study on student retention. *NACADA Journal, 33*(1), 46–53. http://dx.doi.org/10.12930/NACADA-13-192

Vander Schee, B. A. (2007). Adding insight to intrusive advising and its effectiveness with students on probation. *NACADA Journal, 27*(2), 50–59. http://dx.doi.org/10.12930/0271-9517-27.2.50

Varney, J. (2007, September 1). Intrusive advising. *Academic Advising Today, 30*(3). https://nacada.ksu.edu/Resources/Academic-Advising-Today/View-Articles/Intrusive-Advising.aspx

16

CAREER DEVELOPMENT NEEDS OF FIRST-GENERATION COLLEGE STUDENTS

Heather Maietta

The growth in enrollment of first-generation students entering higher education over the past 20 years is truly remarkable. In 2007, just over 15% of incoming students were first-generation, while today that number (depending on how you define the population) has doubled or even tripled (Redford & Hoyer, 2017). A wealth of research on first-generation students reveals obtaining a degree is an avenue of upward social mobility and increased economic advantage for this population and their greater community (Woolcock & Narayan, 2000). Because of the opportunities for social mobility, first-generation students are attending college in greater numbers than ever before. Yet the excitement that those numbers generate for first-generation advocates is tempered by the realization that a mere 30% of them will graduate in 4 years, and less than half will receive a degree after 6 years of study (DeAngelo et al., 2011). The good news is that there are strategies that work and resources that can help the first-generation student population persevere toward completion (Davis, 2010; Roksa & Silver, 2019; Tierney & Auerbach, 2004). Many of these strategies have already been touched on in other chapters, but here I would like to focus on a relatively neglected campus asset available that—if utilized—has a remarkable impact on retention: career services (Maietta, 2014). This chapter will analyze the myriad obstacles first-generation students face in making informed career decisions and the particular challenges they encounter as they move from the academy to the workforce. The chapter will also examine supports that can be provided to first-generation students in assisting them in making a successful college-to-career transition.

Career Services Barriers for First-Generation College Students

There are a number of barriers that impact the career development and postgraduate trajectory of first-generation students: social capital and residential status, cultural capital and the academy, parental education and involvement, employment and finances, and challenges forming career goals. In the forthcoming sections I will describe each barrier as well as touch on the challenges first-generation students face at the point of transition from college to the workforce.

Social Capital and Residential Status

Social capital is shaped by income, work, domicile, and family history—a culmination of life experiences, expectations, and family aspirations (Jehangir, 2010). The extent to which one's existing network of people and community can work to create pathways or entry points to particular spaces and contexts in one's academic and professional life is linked to one's *social capital*. This intangible, invisible barrier is one which students whose parents have not gone to college often face. Low or nonexistent social capital related to career support is problematic for college students and new graduates who are first-generation. Increasing one's social capital is said to be a benefit of attending college, and residential status can be a contributing factor in social capital development. Yet, many first-generation students are unable to benefit from the social capital gains residential status offers as they are more likely to commute. Being a commuter student impacts their ability to seamlessly integrate into the social environment of their chosen institution or readily take advantage of the resources or services available (Moschetti & Hudley, 2016). Research shows that re-acculturation, or the switching of membership from one culture to another, is critically important to early career development (Bruffee, 1999). The more exposure students have to the campus environment, the higher their social capital gains, and in turn, the more opportunities available both during college and postgraduation. Because first-generation students are more likely to live off campus, they experience more difficulty navigating campus services from the onset and continue to struggle with this throughout the college experience. Commuting, in fact, creates a social capital deficit, often prohibiting students from attending campus events (e.g., career workshops) they might otherwise attend because of residential proximity

(Kasworm, 2010). Residential status also plays a role in a student's participation in extracurricular activities, such as service-learning, study abroad,
and leadership organizations. First-generation students have difficulty
seeing how the value of such activities connect to and prepare them for
the wider world of work (Maietta, 2014). Lastly, social integration is also
impacted by living arrangements: Those living in Greek housing or in the
residence halls have the greatest opportunity for social integration, while
first-generation students commuting from home or longer distances lack
the opportunities provided by living on campus (Armstrong & Hamilton,
2013). All these missed opportunities negatively impact the career decision-making prospects of first-generation students, as being absorbed into
the large and dense networking structure of the institution has both immediate and long-term professional benefits often not realized until many
years postgraduation.

Cultural Capital and the Academy

Closely related to social capital is *cultural capital*—the often unstated knowledge base and skills used to demonstrate cultural competence (e.g., the ability
to use and understand academic or industry-specific language) and navigate
institutions like college (Bourdieu, 1977, 1984, 1986) or the corporate world.
Although cultural capital promotes academic success through different pathways, parents of first-generation students typically lack knowledgeable internal compasses and external support systems. Parents are often oblivious to
the plethora of campus services available and are unaware that their first-
generation student would benefit from access to these pertinent resources.
Armstrong and Hamilton (2013) describe cultural capital deficits as a "black
hole" that continues to exert its gravitational pull on first-generation students
even as they transition to college, and "as much as [students] want to escape
. . . identities are tightly linked to home" (p. 44). Consequently, for students
not raised with or exposed to the language of the academy or students not
accustomed to discussing and fostering early career choices, simple terms like
industry or *networking* or *career fair* can be foreign. The idea of cultivating
one's professional network from the moment college begins is rarely a data
point offered to first-generation students at orientation, and because many
first-generation students aren't naturally absorbed into the social fabric of the
institution, these networks do not grow as organically as they do for many
non-first-generation students. As first-generation students have positive,
meaningful interactions with faculty and staff, cultural capital can increase
over time; however, first-generation students are to some extent unaware of
their professional needs and less likely to readily pursue interactions to gain

these necessary experiences (Ward et al., 2012). Add to this the social integration challenges these students face and the cultural capital deficits multiply. Depending on the career path first-generation students choose, many will enter the workplace with low work-related cultural capital as well, with the result that this shortfall follows them after college.

Parental Education and Involvement

Parental education and level of involvement in their student's college-going experience and postcollege transition play a significant role in the career success of first-generation college students. What defines and distinguishes first-generation students is that neither of their parents graduated from college; therefore, when a first-generation student graduates with a college credential, they will be the first member of the family to do so. Educational resilience as described by Wang et al. (1993) is "the heightened likelihood of success in school and other life accomplishments despite environmental adversities brought about by early traits, conditions, and experiences" (p. 19). Many first-generation students report feeling motivated to complete college because doing so would make their parents proud and enable them to serve as role models for others in their family and community (Byrd & Macdonald, 2005; Wang, 2014). Yet, the responsibility to act as a role model or create parental pride may hinder first-generation college students' career decision-making capabilities, leading the student to make academic and career decisions not for personal fit but under the influence of their family.

In terms of involvement, scholars have dedicated much attention to understanding how parental involvement contributes to educational outcomes (Coleman, 1988; Bourdieu & Passeron, 1977). College students perceive family to be a significant influence in their career decision-making (Bright et al., 2005), yet in terms of tangible career support it is difficult for first-generation parents to leverage their often insufficient resources and knowledge (Hamilton, 2016; Hamilton et al., 2018; Lareau, 2011). Career-related supports such as networking connections, crucial financial compensation needed to pursue unpaid internships, or the necessary resources available for study abroad opportunities are inaccessible. Absence of these supports continue to hinder the upward career mobility of first-generation college students postgraduation.

Employment and Finances

The Pell Institute's 2018 *Indicators Report* shows that higher education prospects and results remain highly inequitable across family income groups—and for many indicators the disparities are greater now than in the past (Cahalan et al., 2018). Approximately half of today's working learners are low-income students holding a job that is not an option but an economic necessity (Carnavale & Smith, 2018). First-generation students are more likely to hold full-time employment to pay for personal and family expenses (Jehangir, 2010; Stebleton & Soria, 2013), which may be an additional benefit in that they are gaining work experience, but the multiple responsibilities can also cause further stress (Moschetti & Hudley, 2015). Working also decreases the likelihood that first-generation students have the time to participate in internships/co-ops unless they are paid. This is an important gap in the work experience of first-generation students because interning or working at a job that aligns with their field of study improves both academic and career performance and solidifies the value of academic effort as economic gain. On the flip side, not participating in an internship/co-op excludes first-generation students from many internship/co-op talent pools from which companies directly and naturally select full-time employees. Unfortunately for low-income students, in today's labor market there are fewer and fewer high-quality job opportunities with career-building work experience available to students while they are in school, and higher-income students tend to have more access to these opportunities (not to mention the fact that many can afford unpaid internships/co-ops) (Carnevale & Smith, 2018). Students who come from lower socioeconomic backgrounds are more apt to work in less lucrative industries, such as food services, sales, and administration, which do "not provide the deeper technical and general skills that foreshadow good entry-level career jobs" (Carnevale & Smith, 2018, p. 3). The impact of finances and employment has far-reaching ramifications in other areas of student life as well. First-generation students who have a job out of necessity are more vulnerable to declining grades resulting from the number of hours worked per week in order to maintain a living (which typically equals or exceeds 40 working hours). The effects of needing to work while going to college follow first-generation students after graduation as well. Although approximately 70% of college students today work in some capacity (Carnevale & Smith, 2018), it is highly unlikely that the actual earnings of those who need to work to earn a living or gain valuable work experience would cover the cost of college. The long-term ramifications of this dynamic are that first-generation students are more likely to rely on student loans to pay tuition and fees and graduate with seemingly insurmountable debt, leaving them at a greater disadvantage when entering the workplace of long-term earning and investing than their non-first-generation counterparts.

Challenges Forming Career Goals

First-generation students feel the weight of importance that decisions take on during college, yet often set uninformed or misinformed career goals without understanding the longer-term liabilities associated with these decisions. The U.S. labor market has experienced a steady decline in work opportunities for teenagers since the 1970s, when over half of teenagers gained work experience, to today, when only a quarter do so (Morisi, 2017). This not only causes financial strain for first-generation students who need to pay for college but also limits their work experience and exposure to the workplace itself going into college—both of which provide a host of benefits to future career decision-making. Although research indicates first-generation students have a stronger desire to attend college and deeper aspirations to accomplish set career goals than non-first-generation students (Inman & Mayers, 1999), many reach college with an unclear picture of exactly what these career goals are and have limited information on how to actually achieve their goals through the college experience. For example, an empirical analysis by Trejo (2016) found first-generation students were more likely to prefer majors with strong labor market rewards and a clear postgraduate path. And it is true that students with career-oriented majors tend to secure jobs earlier and—at least in the short term—track higher earnings than many liberal arts—focused pathways. What is surprising are the results from Eismann (2016), who reported that a high percentage of first-generation students tended to favor non-career-oriented majors. This suggests that these students may lack important resources and support, leading them to make less knowledgeable academic decisions than their non-first-generation counterparts with respect to fulfilling their career goals.

College-to-Workforce Transition Challenges

If the barriers noted previously were not enough, first-generation students also are subject to a unique set of challenges as they transition from college to the workplace. A helpful way of understanding transitions as "turning points" can be found in Schlossberg's (1984) adult transition theory. Specifically, transitions occur between periods of stasis that promote self-evaluation and urge one to redefine goals and strategies (Brown & Lent, 2000; Levinson, 1986). In 2010, Overton-Healy (2010) conducted groundbreaking research to call attention to the unique transitional issues first-generation students face during their senior year as they complete formalized education. Between 2012 and 2014 a follow-up study was conducted at two small, private colleges in the Northeast. Both studies revealed the following crucial insights into how first-generation students approached the transition as they left college:

- First-generation students harbor feelings of isolation and resentment from friends and family, but also guilt for "leaving" their family behind to pursue something unfamiliar to them. At the same time first-generation students feel a strong sense of family loyalty and an acute need to meet their expectations.
- First-generation students acknowledged attending college not for deeper learning or love of a topic of study but rather as a path to upward mobility. They expressed frustration at the excessive roadblocks they experienced en route to obtaining their degree.
- Lastly, the study revealed that first-generation students have a strong desire to ensure maximum use of their degree, starting by conducting a successful job search. They expressed a sense of being underprepared due to nonparticipation in career-related activities (i.e., career fairs) because of family or work obligations and not having a professional support system (social capital) to draw on for the job search (Maietta, 2014).

How first-generation students grapple with these issues as they transition out of college is a large determinant in how successful they will be postgraduation. Senior year is a time when the university can build strong positive affinity with first-generation students, and it might be the last occasion to help them develop important life success skills. This presents tremendous opportunity for career services to make a meaningful, lasting impact; however, that impact should not begin in the senior year and cannot end at graduation. If first-generation students do not receive the support they need to address the barriers previously noted before entering the workforce full-time, it will be much more difficult for them to identify and achieve their career goals in addition to enjoying long-term success in the workplace.

Career Development Support Systems for First-Generation College Students

After considering the numerous obstacles that affect the career development of first-generation students, one might think that their postgraduate trajectory is necessarily bleak. Yet, nothing could be further from the truth. In fact, there are several systems of support for first-generation students that, if provided by the institution, markedly improve the college-to-career transition. A closer look reveals just how influential career professionals can be with respect to first-generation retention and postgraduate success, while at the same time serving as strategic thought leaders and cross-campus collaborators in reducing obstacles for the first-generation population. Successful interventions that are supported by existing literature include family support, engagement, readiness programs, mentoring, community building, and increased financial support (Deloitte, 2017). Considering these interventions, the following are just a few of the many areas career services could focus their efforts to support first-generation students.

Enrollment Management

A comprehensive approach that integrates career services fully into the campus-wide retention efforts is an excellent strategy for supporting first-generation students (Maietta, 2016). First-generation students and their families want and need clarity on financing college, academic expectations, and navigating year-to-year enrollment decisions. Given the attitudes and values with which first-generation students approach the college experience, it makes perfect sense to highlight career services as a focal point in helping them assimilate to college as well as prepare to enter the workforce full-time. This also speaks to a greater need for career services to partner with transition advisers and other first-generation support specialists.

Advising

Traditionally, in terms of college to career, academic advising has had little connection to students' career decision-making, career instruction, or even something as specific as integrating labor market research into an informed major declaration. Identifying and implementing effective advising structures for first-generations (and low-income students, which many first-generation students also are) is essential. Academic services staff, faculty, coaches, and others who advise and guide first-generation students would benefit from conversations with career services regarding the details of why first-generation students have difficulty assimilating to campus, their deficits in cultural capital, their struggles with finances and employment, and the challenges they face in forming career goals. At the same time, integrating career services into the advising conversation as early as possible helps first-generation students understand the important links between academic decisions and workforce connections. It would provide first-generation students a direct link to a ready supply of professionals who can assist with social and cultural capital integration, and it offers first-generation students another lifeline to the institution overall, improving retention odds and loosening the gravitational pull away from campus so prevalent in the first-generation population.

Faculty

The faculty–student relationship is arguably the single most influential connection first-generation students have in college. First-generation students have a strong desire to communicate and interact with faculty early and often, in and out of the classroom, and if prompted will take advantage of these encouraged interactions. However, these interactions do not happen organically. Many students have a surface-level understanding, if any, of the course registration process and how majors influence career choice. Faculty can increase their knowledge of first-generation student needs and implement strategies through the advising process, as well as create referral programs enlisting the expertise of career services as partners. First-generation students are typically unaware there are experts on campus who can help them plan for course registration, and instead tend to think and make decisions in purely transactional, present-focused terms. If we want first-generation students to benefit completely from the faculty experience, it is important for our educators to focus their pedagogy to accommodate the needs of these students as well as know what university resources are available and encourage their use. Faculty should consider participating in or even spearheading academic-to-career discussions with all students, but specifically with those who are first-generation. Career services can partner closely with faculty to create cross-campus advising teams and ensure that first-generation students have equal access to academic awards and prestigious experiential learning opportunities. They can be instrumental in the classroom environment by orchestrating meet-and-greets with faculty and select employers and coach first-generation attendees beforehand so they feel less intimidated.

Parents

Engaging parents is another area where career services can make strides in supporting first-generation college students. Research shows that students have higher GPAs and are more likely to persist if emotional support is received by families (Roksa, 2017), yet families are often unaware of how to provide relevant career information, industry-related guidance, or emotional support (Moschetti & Hudley, 2016). Despite the wealth of career resources and services available, most first-generation students do not take advantage of these supports, often because they are unaware that they exist. Enlisting the parents of first-generation college students as advocates in a

career services engagement campaign not only educates parents on the benefits of such supports but also increases the likelihood that parents will, in
turn, promote these valuable campus resources more frequently.

Mentoring

According to Cerezo (2020) having someone to connect with from a similar
background may provide first-generation students with the opportunity to
see what is possible, whether it be networking support, career advice, a job
referral, or simply someone to talk with about the college-to-career transition.
Overall, first-generation students who engage in mentoring are positively
impacted by the experience. Whether it be faculty members, student affairs
professionals, peer-to-peer relationships, or college staff, mentor opportunities exist across campus. Mentor relationships between students and alumni
are especially helpful to students interested in learning more about a specific career path or how a course of study translates to occupational choice.
Students interested in connecting with high-profile professionals might also
enlist a business mentor who sits on the school's board of trustees or alumni
board. Regardless of the type of connection, for career-related purposes,
mentors share current and relevant industry and organizational knowledge,
expertise, and/or skills, which create invaluable learning opportunities for
first-generation students.

Institution-Wide Collaborations

Large-scale sustainable change is best guided by involvement from experts
in the field. If the unique needs of first-generation students are to be met by
integrating career services more fully into the first-generation student experience, career services will need representation at the senior cabinet level in
some capacity. It is no secret that there is a disconnect between education
and workforce need, and first-generation students are greatly impacted by a
broken system of unclear pathways and limited information regarding how
to make critical career decisions that have lifelong economic consequences.
Carnevale et al. (2017) gave five recommendations for large-scale overhaul of
academic and workforce integration using data and technology:

1. Integrate projections of educational demand in the workforce with
   college administrative data and state wage records to attract and retain
   employers and industries.
2. Link earnings data for industries and occupations with student enrollment
   data to aid program design, planning, and assessment.

3. Combine developed competencies and learning outcomes with occupational data and employer/industry expert feedback to ensure a more fit-based match between academia and industry.
4. Inform the college major and career selection process by comparing the skills, values, and interest data gathered from first-generation students with occupational and labor market data as well as employment and wage projections.
5. Connect job seekers to jobs and postsecondary education and training programs using data on competencies, résumés, online job ads, and occupational demand.

Closing the gap between education and workforce need is a start, but what is also needed is an increase in the flow of communication between higher education and industry. By improving language use between the academy and the workplace, the education students receive can be more easily translated to workforce need.

Transitions and the First-Generation College Student

Schlossberg (1984) emphasized that change resolution can only occur if there is a widespread understanding of what the change is, how it is occurring, and the effect of the change on other aspects of life. Career services can not only support first-generation students with their transition to college as well as to the workforce by helping demystify academic and career uncertainties but also educate faculty and administrators on how to systemically weave career education into the fabric of the campus and the educational life cycle of first-generation students. For example, if first-generation students feel resistance from family for having to spend too much time on school-related activities that cut into what was once designated family time, they are more likely to pull away from the institutional culture. Career services can help mitigate this pull by creating group sessions, workshops, seminars, and career-related educational materials geared specifically for first-generation students and their families. Career services can also be instrumental with respect to the transition from college to career for first-generation students. Actively seeking employment may be one of the most confusing and anxiety-ridden closure experiences for first-generation students. Wood (2004) looked at the semester prior to graduation, finding that some seniors experience a "crisis of imagination" (p. 73) exemplified by strong uncertainty leading to analysis paralysis. Unable to resolve their changing identities, many seniors enter a mode of mental stagnation. While many non-first-generation seniors can turn to their family and friends to help them weather the stresses of the senior year, the final year is an "unknown" for first-generation students—there are no previous family experiences to compare to or draw advice from, so the first-generation student is often alone in the journey. At the same time, because of their deficits in social integration and cultural capital, the self-efficacy of first-generation students is low, making them particularly vulnerable to the stagnation described by Wood (2004). Here is a pivotal opportunity for career services to help fill the transitional void. Schlossberg et al. (1995) found that, despite lack of knowledge or experience, if students feel supported during a transition it will be easier for them to weather the stresses that accompany it. By emphasizing the eventual payoff of working and studying hard, career services can help their first-generation advisees build a positive outlook, increasing their self-efficacy during this critical period. Unmasking the hidden yet frequent challenges first-generation students face early, partnering with campus constituents, and spearheading intervention strategies that work is a service that career centers can and should provide (Maietta, 2016).

These are just a few of the many areas of campus that career services can proactively partner with to support first-generation students while at the same time creating an ecosystem that encompasses career development as a core mission of the institution. Such partnerships could result in connecting first-generation students with both targeted career interventions and work-integrated learning opportunities early in their undergraduate career, for example. This would not only bestow the retention benefits discussed in previous chapters but also ensure first-generation students are making informed academic decisions grounded in work realities. Other areas for partnerships include alumni/advancement, student affairs, international programs/study abroad, service-learning, multicultural affairs/diversity services, athletics, tutoring services, and clubs/organizations.

Conclusion

Although awareness is increasing, many institutions are still slow to acknowledge first-generation students as a vulnerable population, while those that do recognize first-generation students as needing support have insufficient knowledge of their needs and how to implement effective strategies to support them. Career services can help address that knowledge gap, and the transitions that the first-generation student population experiences during their time in college provide an opportunity for career services to collaborate with all areas of campus to ensure the retention and postgraduate success of this critical population. Institutions can enact changes to the support structure for first-generation students identified in this chapter with the assistance of career services if they

- identify, understand, and acknowledge their first-generation population;
- recognize a need and desire to support this critical population;
- allocate appropriate resources where resources are needed most;
- act intentionally with intervention strategies and continued financial allocation; and
- continuously assess and improve support services for first-generation students.

Positioning themselves as experts in first-generation college student best practices, career services can partner with offices across campus to educate faculty and staff while helping guide these changes and showcasing the benefits to the postgraduate success of first-generation students. Although impossible to offer a comprehensive account of the career needs and support possibilities for first-generation college students, I hope this chapter provided a starting point for continued growth in this area.

References

Armstrong, E. A., & Hamilton, L. T. (2013). *Paying for the party: How college maintains inequality*. Harvard University Press. https://doi.org/10.1080/21568 235.2018.1554272

Bourdieu, P. (1977). Cultural reproduction and social reproduction. In J. Karabel & A. H. Halsey (Eds.), *Power and ideology in education* (pp. 487–581). Oxford University Press. https://doi.org/10.1177/003231877803000219

Bourdieu, P. (1984). *Distinction: A social critique of the judgement of taste*. Harvard University Press. https://monoskop.org/images/e/e0/Pierre_Bourdieu_Distinction_A_Social_Critique_of_the_Judgement_of_Taste_1984.pdf

Bourdieu, P. (1986). The forms of capital. In J. G. Richardson (Ed.), *Handbook of theory and research for the sociology of education* (pp. 241–258). Greenwood.

Bourdieu, P., & Passeron, J. C. (1977). *Reproduction in education, society, and culture*. SAGE.

Bright, J. H., Pryor, R. L., Wilkenfeld, S., & Earl, J. (2005). Influence of social context on career decision making. *International Journal for Educational and Vocational Counseling, 5*, 19–36. https://link.springer.com/article/10.1007%2Fs10775-005-2123-6

Brown S., & Lent, R. (2000). *Handbook of counseling psychology*. Wiley. https://doi.org/10.1177/1069072707305769

Bruffee, K. A. (1999). *Collaborative learning: Higher education, interdependence, and the authority of knowledge* (2nd ed.). John Hopkins University Press.

Byrd, K. L., & MacDonald, G. (2005). Defining college readiness from the inside out: First-generation college student perspectives. *Community College Review, 33*, 22–37. http://dx.doi.org/10.1177/009155210503300102

Carnevale, A. P., Garcia, T. I., & Gulish, A. (2017). *Career pathways: Five ways to connect college and career.* Georgetown University Center on Education and the Workforce. https://cew.georgetown.edu/

Carnevale, A. P., & Smith, N. (2018). *Balancing work and learning: Implications for low-income students.* Georgetown University Center on Education and the Workforce. https://1gyhoq479ufd3yna29x7ubjn-wpengine.netdna-ssl.com/wp-content/uploads/Low-Income-Working-Learners-FR.pdf

Cahalan, M., Perna, L. W., Yamashita, M., Wright, J., & Santillan, S. (2018). *2018 indicators of higher education equity in the United States: Historical trend report.* The Pell Institute for the Study of Opportunity in Higher Education, Council for Opportunity in Education (COE), and Alliance for Higher Education and Democracy of the University of Pennsylvania (PennAHEAD). http://pellinstitute.org/downloads/publications-Indicators_of_Higher_Education_Equity_in_the_US_2018_Historical_Trend_Report.pdf

Cerezo, T. L (2020). *Factors attributing to success: Perceptions of first-generation, community college alumni's journey to degree attainment* [Unpublished doctoral dissertation]. Regis College.

Coleman, J. (1988). Social capital in the creation of human capital. *American Journal of Sociology, 94*, 95–120. https://www.jstor.org/stable/2780243

Davis, J. (2010). *The first-generation student experience: Implications for campus practice, and strategies for improving persistence and success.* Stylus. https://doi.org/10.1111/teth.12092

DeAngelo, L., Franke, R., Hurtado, S., Pryor, J. H., & Tran, S. (2011). *Completing college: Assessing graduation rates at four-year institution.* Higher Education Research Institute, University of California, Los Angeles. https://heri.ucla.edu/DARCU/CompletingCollege2011.pdf

Deloitte Insight. (2017, March 16). *Success by design.* https://www2.deloitte.com/us/en/insights/industry/public-sector/improving-student-success-in-higher-education.html

Eismann, L. (2016, November 1). First-generation students and job success. *NACE Journal*, 11–16.

Hamilton, L., Roksa, J., & Nielsen, K. (2018). Providing a "leg up": Parental involvement and opportunity hoarding in college. *Sociology of Education, 91*(2), 111–131. https://doi.org/10.1177/0038040718759557

Hamilton, L. T. (2016). *Parenting to a degree: How family matters for college women's success.* University of Chicago Press.

Inman, W. E., & Mayers, L. (1999). The importance of being first: Unique characteristics of first generation community college students. *Community College Review, 26*(4), 3–22. https://doi.org/10.1177%2F009155219902600402

Jehangir, R. R. (2010). *Higher education and first-generation students. Cultivating community, voice, and place for the new majority.* Palgrave Macmillan. https://doi.org/10.1111/teth.12031

Kasworm, C. E. (2010). Adult learners in a research university: Negotiating undergraduate student identity. *Adult Education Quarterly, 60*(2), 143–160. http://dx.doi.org/10.1177/0741713609336110

Lareau, A. (2011). *Unequal childhoods: Class, race, and family life, with an update a decade later* (2nd ed.). University of California Press.

Levinson, D. J. (1986). A conception of adult development. *American Psychologist, 41*, 3–13. https://psycnet.apa.org/doi/10.1037/0003-066X.41.1.3

Maietta, H. M. (2014). *First-generation college seniors: Challenges and support.* [Unpublished research].

Maietta, H. M. (2016, November 1). Career development needs of first-generation students. *NACE Journal, 19*–25.

Morisi, T. L. (2017, February). Teen labor force participation before and after the great recession and beyond. *Monthly Labor Review*, 1–17. https://www.bls.gov/opub/mlr/2017/article/teen-labor-force-participation-before-and-after-the-great-recession.htm

Moschetti, R. V., & Hudley, C. (2016, August 15). Social capital and academic motivation among first-generation community college students. *Community College Journal of Research and Practice Online) Journal, 39*(3), 1066–8926. https://doi.org/10.1080/10668926.2013.819304

Overton-Healy, J. (2010). *First-generation college seniors: A phenomenological exploration of the transitional issues of the final college year* [Doctoral dissertation, Indiana University of Pennsylvania]. https://www.proquest.com/docview/365715906

Padgett, R. D., Johnson, M. P., & Pascarella, E. T. (2012). First-generation undergraduate students and the impacts of the first year of college: Additional evidence. *Journal of College Student Development, 53*(2), 243–266. https://doi.org/10.1353/csd.2012.0032

Redford, J., & Hoyer, K. M. (2017). First-generation and continuing-generation college students: A comparison of high school and postsecondary experiences (NCES 2018-009). U.S. Department of Education, National Center for Educational Statistics. https://nces.ed.gov/pubs2018/2018009.pdf

Roksa, J. (2017, August). *Family resources, siblings, and exchange of support between low-income young adults pursuing higher education and their families* (Paper presentation). RC28 Conference, New York. https://www.researchgate.net/publication/318888854_Family_Resources_Siblings_and_Exchange_of_Support_Between_Low-Income_Young_Adults_Pursuing_Higher_Education_and_Their_Families

Roksa, J., & Silver, B. R. (2019). "Do-it-yourself" university: Institutional and family support in the transition out of college. *The Review of Higher Education, 42*(3), 1051–1071. Johns Hopkins University Press. https://doi.org/10.1353/rhe.2019.0029

Schlossberg, N. K. (1984*). Counseling adults in transition: Linking theory to practice.* Springer.

Schlossberg, N. K., Waters, E. B., & Goodman, J. (1995). *Counseling adults in transition: Linking practice with theory* (2nd ed.). Springer.

Stebleton, M. J., & Soria, K. M. (2013). Immigrant college students' academic obstacles. *The Learning Assistance Review, 18,* 17–24. https://www.immigration-research.org/system/files/Immigrant_College_Students_Academic_Obstacles.pdf

Tierney, W. G., & Auerbach, S. (2004). Toward developing an untapped resource: The role of families in college preparation. In W. G. Tierney (Ed.), *Nine propositions relating to the effectiveness of college preparation programs* (pp. 29–48). State University of New York Press.

Trejo, S. (2016). An econometric analysis of the major choice of first-generation college students. *The Developing Economist, 3*(1), 1–2. http://www.inquiriesjournal.com/a?id=1407

Wang, M. C., Haertel, G. D., & Walberg, H. J. (1993). *Educational resilience in the inner cities* (Report no. 93-5d). National Center on Education in the Inner Cities. https://files.eric.ed.gov/fulltext/ED399312.pdf

Wang, T. (2014). I'm the only person from where I'm from to go to college: Understanding the memorable messages first-generation college students receive from parents. *Journal of Family Communication, 14*(3), 270–290. https://doi.org/10.1080/15267431.2016.1264401

Ward, L., Siegel, M., & Davenport, Z. (2012). *First-generation college students: Understanding and improving the college experience from recruitment to commencement.* Jossey-Bass.

Wood, F. B. (2004). Preventing postparchment depression: A model of career counseling for college seniors. *Journal of Employment Counseling, 41,* 71–79. https://psycnet.apa.org/doi/10.1002/j.2161-1920.2004.tb00880.x

Woolcock, M., & Narayan, D. (2000). Social capital: Implications for development theory, research, and policy. *The World Bank Research Observer, 15*(2), 225–249. https://doi.org/10.1093/wbro/15.2.225

THEY'RE HERE. NOW, WHAT CAN WE DO TO KEEP THEM?

Katharine Moffat

Faculty on the college campus are in an ideal position to serve the important role of mentoring students, and research has shown that students who are mentored by faculty are more likely to thrive (Tinto, 1993). This is true for students in general, and it is especially true for first-generation students. Like faculty, higher education professionals working in academic advising and student affairs should have consistent contact with students on campus, which allows them ample opportunity to provide first-generation students with the support and mentoring they need. This critical conversation will explore a few of the ways in which faculty and staff across campuses can identify and target first-generation students to establish and sustain mentoring initiatives. I am mindful of the fact that faculty and staff usually have limited time and resources to implement new initiatives. The programming recommendations discussed identify cost and time barriers or constraints campuses should consider before embarking on any new initiatives to assist first-generation college students on their campus.

Faculty and staff mentoring is a proven high-impact educational practice that is especially impactful for first-generation students. As Astin (1993) has shown, consistent and high-quality interactions (i.e., mentoring) between faculty and/or staff and students have positive impacts on student retention. These interactions are especially important for first-generation students, who are at higher risk of attrition than their continuing-generation peers (Dennis et al., 2005; Thayer, 2000). Such mentoring can be implemented in a number of ways, with mentors providing first-generation students with essential information, emotional support, guidance, and shared experiences. Hahs-Vaughn (2004) argues that mentoring within the college environment is essential for the success of first-generation students. If campuses are serious about combatting the low retention rates of their first-generation students, they should give serious consideration to implementing a mentoring program that partners first-generation college students with faculty and/or staff, especially staff working within student affairs and academic advising.

One issue campuses face in implementing such a mentoring program, however, is that not all institutions, departments, or programs assess and track students' first-generation status. While virtually all students could benefit from mentoring, it is difficult to pinpoint which students to target in a first generation–focused initiative when first-generation students are not identified on applications, orientation intake forms, or other information requests. Once it is established that collecting these data is important, then making the argument that such a program is necessary is easy. As has been demonstrated in earlier chapters, there are multiple definitions a campus could use in defining their first-generation student population, and it is important for each campus to consider what definition of *first-generation college student* will work best for them.

Once the population of students is identified, what is the next step? Higher education professionals should determine what programs or services already exist on campus that support first-generation students. Faculty and staff who are interested in building or expanding mentoring programs could partner with existing supports (e.g., TRIO) to connect with students, piggyback off existing initiatives, and utilize spaces and resources already dedicated to first-generation college students. If first generation–focused programming does not exist on campus, a formal mentoring program can be built from the ground up. Campuses can also choose to encourage the incorporation of mentoring initiatives into the day-to-day work of their faculty and staff more informally if they feel this would be more effective. There are a variety of ways to incorporate and strengthen faculty mentoring initiatives for virtually every budget and situation. In the pages that follow, I give examples of different mentoring formats that have been implemented at colleges and universities that are focused on supporting and retaining first-generation college students.

Faculty mentoring within academic departments is one example of a formal mentoring program that could be implemented on campus. With this type of program, students are assigned an instructional faculty mentor when declaring their major. Mentors are responsible for meeting with mentees at least once per semester to provide primarily academic guidance but also point students toward career advice and resources. This can be entirely or mostly cost-free but does require a time commitment from faculty mentors outside of teaching and research. Academic advisers and support staff within these departments could assist in organizing the mentor/mentee matches and evaluating satisfaction with the program from both ends of the relationship. In departments with high enrollment but fewer faculty members, this format may be difficult to implement on a large scale but may be manageable given the number of first-generation enrollees. Within academic unit mentoring is the format utilized by the Texas A&M First-Generation Engineering (FGEn) Student Mentoring Program, a component of the campus-wide Aggie Mentoring Network. FGEn students in the program are paired with a faculty or staff members in the engineering department. Many of the faculty and staff in this program are first-generation college graduates themselves. Faculty mentors commit themselves to spending extra time with the students that are assigned to them.

Academic adviser mentoring within academic or student support units is another option that has been implemented on campuses across the country. With this model, advisers are assigned a case load of first-generation mentees who they meet with in extra advising sessions each semester. Advisers within their respective units divide up the pool of first-generation students and connect with mentees individually. The trusting and close nature of the adviser-advisee relationship encourages students to air any concerns they may have and talk openly about their experiences. Academic advisers are well equipped to work with diverse populations of students (including first-generation students). Advisers are also knowledgeable about campus, and they can direct students to on- and off-campus resources as appropriate to assist them in navigating collegiate life. Many academic advisers, first-generation and not, likely already engage in this mentoring relationship with their students in an informal manner. Although not likely to be cost intensive, this format certainly requires advisers to commit the time necessary to build a relationship beyond their advising sessions.

Less formal programs are also an option for campuses to consider. These could be informal coffee hours with faculty and staff, group outings, or organized social events. With these types of events, faculty and staff can socialize in a relaxed, informal setting with first-generation college students to discuss issues that first-generation students face. Faculty and staff are also able to establish relationships with first-generation college students outside of the more formal classroom and office settings. This format has costs associated with it (e.g., refreshments, transportation, space costs, etc.). It can also be time intensive to plan an event, although an event could be as simple as meeting at a school athletics event or gathering to attend an existing on-campus function. The event needs to be publicized to attract the projected number of students. The ODU F1RST faculty program at Old Dominion University (ODU) coordinates events for faculty and first-generation students, such as seminars on networking and interviewing, and distributes a newsletter to subscribers with important information and resources. Social events and faculty profiles are kept up to date on the ODU F1RST website for students to access at their convenience. Students decide on their desired level of involvement in the program; they can fully commit to meeting with a faculty mentor and/or attend the social and networking events they find interesting.

Related to individual department mentoring programs, some schools have embarked on campus-wide faculty mentoring programs for their first-generation students. These ambitious programs target first-generation students specifically and match them with faculty for the purpose of developing one-on-one mentoring relationships. Organizers create group events at which the faculty and students are partnered for the purpose of meeting and socializing. These types of campus-wide initiatives require a great deal of faculty interest and usually require one key person on campus who can create and maintain the mentor/mentee matches and plan group events or outings during the year. There may or may not be costs associated with events, but the mentoring relationship itself need not have any cost associated with it. The Legacy Scholars program at the University of Alabama is an example of a campus-wide faculty mentoring initiative open to all first-year, first-generation students. Students are matched with a faculty or staff member who was also a first-generation student. All participants are encouraged to attend social and community service events with other Legacy Scholars.

The final type of mentoring program I want to highlight involves programming and initiatives within departments in student affairs. With this type of initiative, student affairs professionals working within their individual units identify their first-generation students and then develop mentoring initiatives for them. Many such units already engage in mentoring but could further focus their efforts on matching first-generation mentors and mentees. The We CU! mentoring program at Chapman University utilizes this approach. We CU! operates within the Promising Futures Program and is a designated support program for first-generation college students. Led by the Promising Futures Program staff, We CU! solicits participation from students, faculty, and staff across campus from all academic backgrounds.

Regardless of the format and budget available, quality and consistent interactions are key elements in improving first-generation student retention. Students engaged in positive mentoring relationships with faculty and staff are more likely to persist to graduation if they are able to develop a sense of belonging on the campus. Having mentors who assist them in navigating the system is a key component of developing this sense of belonging among first-generation college students (Astin, 1993; Hahs-Vaughn, 2004).

Retention of first-generation college students is ethically and financially an issue for all professionals in higher education. Campuses can (and should) commit to the success of first-generation college students through intentional mentoring programs despite time limitations and ever-increasing work expectations. The extra effort and willingness to provide advice, perspective, and reassurance can be instrumental for a student who is on the fence about returning. As mentioned previously, faculty and staff working in higher education are in an ideal position to serve the important role of mentoring students, and research has shown that students who develop relationships with faculty and staff are more likely to stay on through graduation (Longwell-Grice & Longwell-Grice, 2008). This is true for students in general, and it is especially true for first-generation students.

Resources and Additional Readings

- "How to Help First-Generation Students Succeed" by Mikhail Zinshteyn (2016, March 13). *The Atlantic.* https://www.theatlantic.com/education/archive/2016/03/how-to-help-first-generation-students-succeed/473502/
- Selected examples of first-generation faculty and staff mentoring programs:
  - Legacy Scholars at the University of Alabama: https://fye.sa.ua.edu/programs/legacy-scholars/
  - Texas A&M First-Generation Engineering Student Mentoring Program: https://mentoring.tamu.edu/p/p3/about
  - We CU! Mentoring Program at Chapman University: https://www.chapman.edu/students/academic-resources/first-generation/mentoring.aspx
  - ODU F1RST Faculty at Old Dominion University: https://www.odu.edu/success/programs/first-faculty

Discussion Questions

1. Does your campus and/or department have any mentoring programs or initiatives? If so, what do these programs look like? How well do these programs address the needs of first-generation college students?
2. Given limited resources, how could advising or student affairs offices develop mentoring initiatives for first-generation students?

3. What benefits would there be to faculty and staff members who participated in a mentorship program for first-generation students?
4. What are the benefits of having first-generation faculty and staff serve as
   mentors for first-generation college students?

References

Astin, A. W. (1993). *What matters in college: Four critical years revisited.* Jossey-Bass.

Dennis, J. M., Phinney, J. S., & Chuateco, L. I. (2005). The role of motivation, parental support, and peer support in the academic success of ethnic minority first-generation college students. *Journal of College Student Development, 46*(3), 223–236. https://doi.org/10.1353/csd.2005.0023

Hahs-Vaughn, D. (2004). The impact of parents' education level on college students: An analysis using the beginning postsecondary students longitudinal study 1990–92/94. *Journal of College Student Development, 45*(5), 483–500. https://doi.org/10.1353/csd.2004.0057

Longwell-Grice, H., & Longwell-Grice, R. (2008). Testing Tinto: How do retention theories work for first-generation college students? *Journal of College Student Retention, 9*(4), 407–420. https://doi.org/10.2190/CS.9.4.a

Thayer, P. B. (2000). *Retention of students from first-generation and low income backgrounds.* [Short paper]. Department of Education, National TRIO Clearinghouse, 1–9.

Tinto, V. (1993*). Leaving college: Rethinking the causes and cures of student attrition* (2nd ed.). University of Chicago Press.

17

ADMISSIONS ISN'T ACCESS

First-Generation College Graduates in Medical Schools

Hyacinth Mason, Jeffrey Winseman, and Erin Ayala

First-generation (FG) medical students often possess a track record of highly desirable traits for a physician, such as grit, self-determination, and innovative thinking, as well as important insights into the complex health disparities facing the U.S health-care system today. However, *cultural capital* (what one knows about the culture they are in) and *social capital* (who one has as their guide) (Bourdieu, 1986) may be in short supply for FG students, leaving them encumbered by what researchers have shown to be invisible yet very real barriers that do not affect their continuing-generation (CG) counterparts (Gardner, 2011).

Programming for FG students has received increasing focus at the undergraduate level over the past several years (e.g., Inkelas et al., 2007). However, there are a limited number of models for programming in medical school that support FG medical students. Education and training prototypes that will prepare medical educators to receive and successfully serve this student population have similarly not been developed.

Data from 2008 show that 20% of U.S. medical school matriculants (USM) identified as FG (Grbic et al., 2010). Of African American and Hispanic USM, 34% and 37%, respectively, self-reported as FG. In 2018 the American Medical College Application Service (AMCAS), the centralized medical school application-processing service of the American Association of Medical Colleges (AAMC, 2017), created the First-Generation College Student Indicator to allow medical schools to more accurately identify FG applicants.

This chapter discusses findings from a national wellness study of U.S. medical students that investigated whether stress, self-care, and quality of life differed by generation status (i.e., FG versus CG). We hypothesized that differences would exist such that FG medical students would report higher stress, lower self-care, and lower quality-of-life scores. The findings inform practical suggestions for retaining, supporting, and maximizing positive academic and wellness outcomes for FG students.

Methods

For the purpose of this study, FG medical students were defined as those who self-reported that their parent(s) or legal guardian(s) had not earned a 4-year college degree or higher. CG medical students were defined as those who self-reported that at least one parent or legal guardian had earned a 4-year college degree or higher.

Participants and Procedures

This study was conducted by the contributors of this chapter: an assistant dean for student support and inclusion at Albany Medical College (Hyacinth Mason), the director of medical student mental health at Albany Medical Center (Jeffrey Winseman), and a former postdoctoral fellow at Albany Medical Center who now serves as an assistant professor at Saint Mary's University of Minnesota (Erin Ayala). All have worked to promote health and wellness for medical students and other graduate-level students through their varying roles.

The data set included responses from 871 U.S. medical students who participated in a national wellness survey conducted between December 2015 and March 2016 (Ayala et al., 2017). A respondent-driven sampling method was used to recruit medical students throughout the United States (Babbie, 2004). The research team contacted administrators from all Liaison Committee on Medical Education (LCME)–accredited medical institutions in the United States and asked them to invite medical students to participate in a voluntary and confidential survey on wellness. Study participants were also recruited via professional listservs, student organizations, and institutional administrations. Qualtrics was used to distribute the survey and record responses. The current study was approved by the Albany Medical College (AMC) Institutional Review Board. The authors also obtained a certificate of confidentiality from the U.S. National Institutes of Health.

Study Measures

Stress, self-care, and quality of life were measured in this study. Demographic information was also collected. The perceived stress scale, a 14-item instrument, was used to measure how often participants experienced feelings associated with stress in the past month (Cohen et al., 1983). Self-care was measured using the health–promoting lifestyle profile II (HPLPII), a 52-item measure that operationalizes self-care as a multifactorial construct with the following six domains: nutrition, physical activity, interpersonal relations, spiritual growth, stress management, and health responsibility (Walker et al., 1995). We used the World Health Organization's 26-item quality-of-life scale to measure quality of life. This measure includes four subscales that examine an individual's physical, psychological, social, and environmental well-being (Skevington et al., 2004). In addition, participants were asked to record their age, gender, sexual orientation, racial background, FG student status, marital status, and year in medical school.

Data Analysis Plan

This was a cross-sectional observational study that looked at the wellness measures for students during the 2015–2016 academic school year. Student responses were exported from Qualtrics to IBM SPSS Statistics Version 22.0 for analysis. Descriptive statistics and means were calculated as the first step in the analysis. We used bivariate analyses to examine differences in wellness indicators by generational status. Independent t-tests were used to determine whether there was a difference in each wellness measure by generational status. The piecewise alpha level for this study was set at $p = .05$.

Results

Eight hundred and sixty medical students provided complete information on the variables of interest. Participants represented 49 LCME–accredited U.S. medical institutions and all 4 years of training. One hundred and twenty-three (14.3%) participants self-identified as FG college students, while 723 (84.1%) identified as CG college students. Participants ranged in age from 20 to 45 ($M = 25.64$, $SD = 3.29$). Our total medical student sample was 62.9% female and 74.3% Caucasian. See Table 17.1 for complete demographic and generational status data (gender, racial, year in medical school, marital status).

The bivariate analysis showed that FG students had lower levels of wellness than CG students. See Table 17.2 for complete results of the study. FG students reported lower levels of self-care and environmental quality of life compared with CG students. In comparison to CG students, FG students felt the need for faculty to role–model self-care and felt the need to more strongly support their family and personal obligations. FG students were also more likely to report higher engagement in self-care and lower stress levels if they thought that their medical school was interested in and supportive of their unique life situations.

TABLE 17.1

Demographic Characteristics of the Sample by Generational Status

Variable	FG medical students		CG medical students	
	n	%	n	%
Gender				
Female	74	61	465	64
Male	47	39	260	36
Year in medical school				
MS1	45	37	219	30
MS2	24	19	199	27
MS3	29	24	159	22
MS4	25	20	148	20
Racial/ethnic background				
Caucasian	74	60	525	72
Asian	10	8	89	12
African American	10	8	38	5
Hispanic	20	16	40	6
Native American	5	4	6	<1
More than one race	4	4	27	4
Sexual orientation				
Heterosexual	109	88	656	91
Homosexual	4	3	18	2
Bisexual	7	6	34	5
Pansexual	2	2	8	1
Queer/gender fluid	1	1	5	<1
Asexual	0	0	4	<1
Marital status				
Single	64	52	476	66
Living with partner	13	11	67	9
Married	33	27	118	16
Engaged	8	6	60	8
Separated/divorced	5	4	4	1

TABLE 17.2

Descriptive Statistics, Correlations, and Paired Sample t-Tests by FG and CG Status

	Status	n	M	SD	M	t	df	P	Effect size	
									d	P
To what extent do you engage in self-care?	FG	123	4.53	1.40	-.243	-1.870	846	.062	.176	.062
	CG	725	4.77	1.32						
To what extent does your medical school explicitly encourage self-care?	FG	123	4.08	1.43	-.251	-1.735	846	.083	.171	.083
	CG	725	4.33	1.49						
To what extent do your faculty model self-care?	FG	121	3.69	1.44	-.367	-2.827	843	.005	.270	.005
	CG	714	4.06	1.30						
To what extent does your medical school support family and personal responsibilities?	FG	123	3.72	1.55	-.385	-2.552	846	.011	.252	.011
	CG	725	4.11	1.55						
Stress	FG	121	28.26	8.07	.979	1.277	833	.202	.123	.202
	CG	714	27.29	7.75						
Self-care	FG	116	2.45	0.44	-.095	-2.221	778	.027	.232	.027
	CG	664	2.55	0.42						
Physical quality of life	FG	121	73.76	18.08	-2.80	-1.822	841	.069	.168	.069
	CG	722	76.56	15.22						
Psychological quality of life	FG	120	58.26	21.26	-3.58	-1.880	836	.060	.178	.060
	CG	718	61.84	18.97						
Social quality of life	FG	123	62.74	27.08	-4.44	-1.716	153.29	.088	.178	.054
	CG	719	67.18	22.90						
Environmental quality of life	FG	122	66.11	16.27	-6.17	-4.453	834	<.001	.410	<.001
	CG	714	72.28	13.74						

Note: M = Mean, SD = Standard deviation, CI = Confidence interval.

Discussion

Recent research indicates that FG students may struggle along the pathway to becoming a physician (Brewer & Grbic, 2010; Grbic et al., 2010). Anecdotes gathered through the course of our work with medical students who self-identify as FG students support this finding. These challenges include (a) financial stress—getting to and through medical school is expensive; (b) difficulty with the cultural transitions (e.g., medical hierarchies, customs and norms of medical culture, repeated exposure to different family values and mores); (c) difficulty explaining the stress of medical school and the new opportunities they have found in medical school to family, friends, and other social supports; (d) answering the question "What do your parents do?"; and (e) navigating "imposter syndrome" (Russell, 2017) and "stereotype threat" (Steele & Aronson, 1995).

While the challenges FG students sometimes face may at times seem daunting, FG students can thrive with the support of faculty and staff who can provide tools to help them confront and manage those challenges. At AMC, we have begun work to address these challenges. To help students adapt to the new academic environment, we conduct assessments and promote dynamic and integrative study methods for our students. Each student is assigned an academic dean, but FG students also have access to additional faculty dedicated to providing supplemental support, advice, and advocacy.

Financial-related issues have been found to be a major reason for student withdrawal (Habley et al., 2010). To help address financial stress, our financial aid office sees financial guidance as a powerful tool in helping students, particularly those without a financial safety net, stay in school even when there are particularly challenging times. AMC's financial aid staff work one on one with students to clarify the financial aid process, provide explicit guidance and financial literacy education, help navigate emergency funding needs, and assist in developing financial plans tailored to students' specific financial circumstances.

FG medical students bring unique strengths with them into medical training. Perseverance, empathy, cultural sensitivity, first-person insight into health disparities, strong connections to community and family, and experience defying the odds are qualities observed among these students during their undergraduate years (Checkoway, 2018). Given the resilience, persistence, cultural humility, and tenacity required to successfully pursue a medical degree, these qualities are what make FG students superb physician prospects.

In 2017, students formed 1GMed, an organization dedicated to supporting and advocating for medical students who are the first in their families to graduate from college. In 2020, this AMC organization formally became a chapter of the National First-Generation and Low-Income in Medicine Association (FGLIMed), a multi-institutional, national organization dedicated to promoting visibility and community among premedical students, medical students, physicians, faculty, and administrators who identify as FG or who are from low-income family backgrounds. Since 2018, FG students and their mentors have participated in targeted discussion groups over dinners and lunches that address the cultural transition to medical school life and culture.

AMC has also committed to providing mental health services to all students at no cost. The clinic is staffed by Department of Psychiatry staff, and services include psychotherapy and psychiatric medication management. Common concerns for medical students in general include adjustment to the stress of training, anxiety, depression, work-life balance, substance use and abuse, and career concerns. In contrast to CG students, FG students frequently face additional pressures associated with the tasks of individuation (Liversage et al., 2018). This process can precipitate new symptoms as FG students work to maintain a strong central family role made more prominent with their entry into medical school while at the same time exploring new and separate identities as emerging physicians in a vibrant academic community. As counseling for FG students will often revolve around these themes, it is crucial for counseling center staff to be aware of the unique challenges FG students experience and to prioritize opportunities for students to connect with other important social and academic resources within the medical school.

To affirm and celebrate the unique path of FG students in medicine, FG members of the class of 2018 at Albany Medical College were, for the first time, recognized during commencement. Students wanted a subtle form of recognition. Prior to graduation, each self-identified FG medical student was given a black and gold cord (in recognition of their presence as leaders and scholars) and a pin to wear on their white coat as they continue along their career path. During our school's 180th commencement ceremony in 2018, our vice dean at the time, a FG college graduate himself, wore a cord and gave a short explanation of its significance before degrees were awarded. This tradition has continued. Each year a passage explaining the significance of the cords is also included in the graduation program. The passage reads:

Albany Medical College formally recognizes the achievements of our first-generation graduates. First-generation students represent any student are the first in their family to go to college. These first-generation students wear a simple black and gold honor cord in addition to their gowns and hoods, representing their presence as leaders and scholars in the medical community. Albany Medical College acknowledges and honors each of them and their unique paths that led to this important day.

AMC's FGLIMed chapter also cosponsored a Building the Next Generation of Academic Physicians Conference (BNGAP) (Sánchez et al., 2011) in September 2018. BNGAP aims to provide medical students, residents, fellows, and junior faculty—particularly those from diverse socioracial and ethnic groups—with tools, knowledge, skills, and experiences that help learners thrive in medical school as they explore and potentially embark on a career in academic medicine. Future plans are for FGLIMed to partner with AMC's BNGAP chapter to develop a mentorship program that matches FG faculty with medical students, residents, and/or fellows.

Our data illuminate the need for educators to understand and demonstrate greater awareness of the experiences of FG students. This approach often requires a shift from deficit mindsets to asset-based approaches that are strategic, inclusive, and proactive and acknowledge the social determinants of medical education. As we tailor support for FG students, it is important to recognize how intersectionality and the intersecting identities (e.g., gender, race/ethnicity, ability status, sexual orientation) of this diverse group of learners may impact their experiences along the physician pathway (Castro, 2014; Checkoway, 2018; Liversage et al., 2018). Our aim must be for students to connect and thrive in their new home, to help them move beyond individual statuses and toward opportunities for leadership, advocacy and academic achievement. When students, in partnership with faculty and staff, move toward full ethnic, racial, and socioeconomic equity, options for what is possible in health care delivery grow and are strengthened. As Youngclaus and Roskovensky (2018) stated, "Diversity of U.S. medical school matriculants remains a persistent challenge but one worth addressing because increasing diversity improves the quality of medical education and health for all" (p. 1). We agree.

References

Association of American Medical Colleges. (2017). *American medical college application service 2018 application: New questions.* https://aamc-orange.global.ssl. fastly.net/production/media/filer_public/7d/4c/7d4c5b3c-be52-4c93-b382-8dcc9ea7ffd3/2018_amcas_new_questions-_fact_sheet.pdf

Ayala E. E., Omorodion A. M., Nmecha D., Winseman J. S., & Mason, H. R. C. (2107). What do medical students do for self-care? A student-centered approach to well-being. *Teaching and Learning in Medicine, 29*(3), 237–246. https://doi.org/10.1080/10401334.2016.1271334

Babbie, E. R. (2004). The logic of sampling. In A. Rubin and E. Babbie (Eds.), *The practice of social research* (10th ed.) (pp. 178–217). Thomson/Wadsworth.

Bourdieu, P. (1986). The forms of capital. In J. G. Richardson (Ed.), *Handbook of theory and research for the sociology of education* (pp. 241–258). Greenwood.

Brewer, L., & Grbic, D. (2010, December). Medical students' socioeconomic background and their completion of the first two years of medical school. *Association of American Medical Colleges Analysis in Brief, 9*(11). https://www.aamc.org/download/165418/data/aibvol9_no11.pdf

Castro, E. L. (2014). Underprepared and at risk: Disrupting deficit discourses in undergraduate STEM recruitment and retention programming. *Journal of Student Affairs Research and Practice, 51*(4), 407–419. https://doi.org/10.1515/jsarp-2014-0041

Checkoway B. (2018). Inside the gates: First-generation students finding their way. *Higher Education Studies, 8*(3), 72–84. https://doi.org/10.5539/hes.v8n3p72

Cohen S., Kamarck T., & Mermelstein, R. (1983). A global measure of perceived stress. *Journal of Health and Social Behavior, 24*, 386–396.

Gardner, S. K., & Holley, K. A. (2011). "Those invisible barriers are real": The progression of first-generation students through doctoral education. *Equity and Excellence in Education, 44*, 77–92. https://doi.org/10.1080/10665684.2011.529791

Grbic D., Garrison G., & Jolly P. (2010, August). Diversity of U.S. medical students by parental education. *Association of American Medical Colleges Analysis in Brief, 9*(10). https://www.aamc.org/download/142770/data/aibvol9_no10.pdf

Habley, W., Valiga, M., McClanahan, R., & Burkum, K. (2010). *What works in student retention? Public four-year colleges and universities.* American College Testing.

Inkelas, K. K., Daver, Z. E., Vogt, K. E., & Leonard, J. (2007). Living-learning programs and first-generation college students' academic and social transition to college. *Research in Higher Education, 48*, 403–434. https://doi.org/10.1007/s11162-006-9031-6

Liversage, L., Naudé, L., & Botha, A. (2018, January) Vectors of identity development during the first year: Black first-generation students' reflections. *Teaching in Higher Education, 23*(1), 63–83.

Russell, R. (2017). On overcoming imposter syndrome. *Academic Medicine, 92*(8), 1070. https://doi.org/10.1097/ACM.0000000000001801

Sánchez J. P., Castillo-Page L., Spencer D. J, Yehia B., Peters L., Freeman B. K., & Lee-Rey E. (2011). Commentary: The building of the next generation of academic physicians initiative: Engaging medical students and residents. *Academic Medicine, 86*, 928–31. https://doi.org/10.1097/ACM.0b013e31822220df

Skevington, S. M., Lotfy, M., & O'Connell, K. A. (2004). The World Health Organization's WHOQOL-BREF quality of life assessment: Psychometric properties and results of the international field trial. A report from the WHOQOL

Group. *Quality of Life Research, 13,* 299–310. https://doi.org/10.1023/B:QURE. 0000018486.91360.00

Steele, C. M., & Aronson, J. (1995). Stereotype threat and the intellectual test performance of African-Americans. *Journal of Personality and Social Psychology, 69*(5), 797–811. https://doi.org/10.1037/0022-3514.69.5.797

Walker, S. N., Sechrist, K. R., & Pender, N. J. (1995). *The health promoting lifestyle profile II.* University of Nebraska Medical Center, College of Nursing.

Youngclaus, J., & Roskovensky, L. (2018, October). An updated look at the economic diversity of medical students. *Association of American Medical Colleges, Analysis in Brief, 18*(5). https://www.aamc.org/download/493046/data/october2 018anupdatedlookattheeconomicdiversityofu.s.medicalstud.pdf

BECOMING THE ARCHITECT

First-Gen Graduate Students Claiming the Label

Adj Marshall

C urrent graduate students often respond with confusion when asked how their first-generation (first-gen) identity affects their experience as a graduate student. This is not surprising given that many of today's grad students were enrolled in their undergraduate studies at a time when *first-gen* as an identity marker existed solely as a research term. I find that the inability of graduate students to articulate this intersectional space fosters an environment where needs go unrecognized and as a result fail to be supported. These types of environments breed a lack of understanding that can hinder grad student success by limiting students' ability to discuss strengths and challenges as first-gens and advocate for support mechanisms that meet student needs. The first-gen identity has only recently gained recognition by students and institutions, meaning the intricacies of the identity are still not fully understood and continue to evolve rapidly. While a number of first-gen undergraduate needs have been identified and support mechanisms put into practice, little research or programming has been directed toward first-gen graduate students. As we come to understand the first-gen identity more fully, it is essential that we look at its impacts on students at all levels of postsecondary education, not just the undergraduate level. I believe we are at a turning point in the history of the first-gen identity, one where first-gen graduate students (FGGSs) can be on the ground floor of collaboratively defining this unique intersectional space according to our own voices and self-identified needs.

Defining First-Gen

As an undergraduate, I could tell you all the ways in which I was different from my peers, but if you asked me what a first-gen student was, I would have told you it was a student whose parents had immigrated to America. The first-gen identity was nonexistent when I was an undergraduate, a little over a decade ago. While Billson and Terry first defined the term *first-gen college student* in 1982 as someone whose parents did not attend college, it would take almost 25 years before the first-gen terminology would begin to make headway outside of the academic lexicon. It was Engle and Tinto's pivotal 2008 report on college success for first-gen college students that made the term leap from academia to common usage. The year this report came out I was serving as a college success adviser for low-income first-gen students. My experience as a recent first-gen college graduate served as a "success story" for my students to aspire to. I had broken the cycle of poverty to become one of the pioneering 11% of low-income first-gen students to gain access to higher education and walk out the gates with a diploma. I left behind almost 90% of my peers who never made it through. First-gen college students make up a small minority of the total graduating population each year. This greatly restricts the number of first-gen undergraduates even eligible to continue on to graduate studies at either the MA or PhD level. While first-gen students may aspire to graduate education, they are less likely than their non-first-gen peers to earn graduate degrees (Engle & Tinto, 2008). Additionally, data collected by the National Science Foundation's Higher Education Research and Development Survey (2014) indicates that first-generation graduate student numbers have been declining for decades and continue to do so today.

Moving From Deficit to Asset Models

Historically, the lack of clarity surrounding the first-gen college student label may have served to disguise the fact that first-gen students were being viewed through an educational deficit lens. Rendón et al. (2000) posit that educational deficit thinking suggests "cultural patterns of marginalized groups are essentially inferior and essentially predispose students within those groups to poor academic performance" (p. 141). Many initial policies and programs created were structured to assimilate first-gen students toward more conventional educational norms rather than adjusting institutional norms to meet student needs. Deficit thinking models often encourage students to conform to dominant practices or risk becoming academic failures.

In recent years researchers and academic institutions have shifted toward models grounded in a strength or asset-based approaches. Torres et al. (2009) note that newer student support models draw on critical race theory (CRT), queer theory, and postmodern feminism while applying an intersectional framework. This allows for the incorporation of individual students' personal strengths, skills, interests, and cultural backgrounds into student support practices. Asset-informed models approach student challenges from a strengths perspective positioning institutions to change to meet student needs rather than forcing students to change to meet institutional norms. Within these student-centered models, first-gen college students are able to bring more of their whole self to their educational experience than was previously possible within the deficit-informed approach.

Claiming Ownership

As institutional practices have shifted away from deficit-thinking models, more of today's first-gen undergraduates have embraced the first-gen identity in ways that fit their needs. They may have joined a first-gen affinity group before arriving on campus, enrolled in a for-credit class on being first-gen while attending, or joined a first-gen alumni group upon graduation. Despite this orientation shift, institutions and researchers continue to retain ownership of the first-gen label by serving as the authors of its meaning. This represents what Yasso (2005) acknowledges as the "contradictory nature of education, wherein schools most often oppress and marginalize while they maintain the potential to emancipate and empower" (p. 76). Institutional ownership over the first-gen definition at some level ensures that institutions will continue to control the terms on which support is available to first-gen students. Altering this power dynamic will require that students be an integral part of the authorship process by defining new iterations of the first-gen identity like that of the FGGS identity.

What's Missing

Since 2008 the volume of research on first-gen undergraduates has expanded exponentially as institutional and student awareness around the first-gen identity has grown. While considerable research has been conducted about the experience of first-gen undergraduates in the past decade, little has focused on FGGS experiences (Gardner, 2013). The dearth of research looking at FGGSs may be viewed as a call to action for academic researchers to explore the FGGS experience. I, however, see this void slightly differently: I view it as an opportunity for FGGSs to become the architects of their own identity. The current research vacuum, combined with an entering class of FGGSs who are informed and empowered by their first-gen undergraduate experience, creates the potential for a shift in paradigm, one where FGGSs define the framework from which the FGGS identity is constructed. I believe this shift has the potential to profoundly alter the future of the first-gen identity label and its surrounding power structures as well as ensure FGGS supports originate from an assets-based approach rather than a deficit one.

The New Phase in First-Gen Identity Development

While completing my first master's degree I struggled to understand my place within the institution and sought out fellow FGGSs I knew existed but who seemed invisible to me. It was my experience as a college adviser for low-income first-gen students that had taught me the importance of first-gen affinity groups. There was no recognition of FGGSs on my campus, and most of the MA, PhD, and MD candidates who gathered together had never engaged with "first-gen" as part of their student identity before we met. Together we discussed personal passions, family responsibility, institutional values, cultural capital, social networks, and academic structures. It was through these self-organized gatherings that I was first able to construct for myself and then articulate what it meant to be a FGGS. This self-authored understanding of identity was pivotal in helping me navigate both internal and external struggles I faced as an FGGS.

I believe we are now entering a new phase of first-gen identity development, one where FGGSs will be instrumental in developing the understanding of the first-gen identity itself. The newest iteration of self-aware first-gen undergraduates recently turned FGGSs are uniquely poised to disrupt the power dynamic inherent in the first-gen label by joining together in solidarity to define the framework from which FGGS identities are constructed.

Today's graduate students have the same opportunity I did for self-authorship and have the potential take it to the next level by demanding these self-authored understandings be honored as the foundation of institutional definitions and wider support practices. Centering the development of the graduate student first-gen identity around students' own narratives ensures that the FGGS identity marker will be constructed in ways that best serve grad student needs first rather than institutional needs. Additionally, having FGGS voices serve as the driving force of the framework development ensures the FGGS identity is grounded in an assets-based approach from the onset rather than a deficit approach. The hope is that by disrupting the traditional approaches to identity marker development FGGSs will be able to bring more of their whole selves to their grad school experience, articulate their FGGS identity and have developed the tools to advocate for their needs both individually and collectively as a community.

Conclusion

The first-gen identity continues to build momentum as we speak. Institutions are listening and actively engaged in working toward bettering the first-gen experience. Researchers continue to find new frontiers with the first-gen experience to explore and more first-gen students are standing proudly to be counted among the ranks of those who have succeeded despite odds being stacked against them. As we move toward a better future for first-gen students it is important to remember this is an ongoing struggle, one that is still in its earliest stages. First-gen students, but particularly low-income first-gen students, need support at all stages of their education from preschool through graduate school.

As Gardner (2011) notes there are many elements of the first-gen undergraduate identity that persist into graduate school. New research studies of FGGSs are beginning to showcase the ways in which FGGS identity is distinct from the first-gen undergraduate experience (Miles, 2017; Warnock and Appel, 2012). As we explore these distinctions and work to construct an intersectional definition of the FGGS identity it is essential that graduate students themselves be an integral part of the defining process. Despite the fact that many institutions have shifted away from the deficit model, it still frames many educational practices targeted at marginalized groups, including first-gen students. Ensuring grad students take this opportunity to define the FGGS identity marker will be essential to their ability to articulate their identity through a positive lens and move toward self-advocacy.

Discussion Questions

1. What new challenges does graduate school present to first-gen college students?
2. What responsibilities do institutions have to ensure that FGGSs are fully integrated into the campus culture?
3. What expectations should FGGSs have of their programs to ensure their success?
4. How should first-gen undergraduate and graduate inclusion practices differ?

References

Billson, J. M., & Terry, M. B. (1982). In search of the silken purse: Factors in attrition among first-generation students. *College and University, 58*(1), 57–75.

Engle, J., & Tinto, V. (2008). *Moving beyond access: College success for low-income, first-generation students*. The Pell Institute for the Study of Opportunity in Higher Education. https://files.eric.ed.gov/fulltext/ED504448.pdf

Gardner, S. K. (2013). The challenges of first-generation doctoral students. In K. A. Holley & J. Joseph (Eds.), *Increasing diversity in doctoral education: Implications for theory and practice* (New Directions for Higher Education, no. 163, pp. 43–54). Jossey-Bass. https://doi.org/10.1002/he.20064

Miles, J. M. (2017). *Aspirations and interlopers: First-generation, underrepresented, low income masters students*. https://digitalcommons.humboldt.edu/cgi/viewcontent.cgi?/&httpsredir=1&article=1084&context=etd

National Science Foundation. (2014). *Higher education research and development survey* (HERDS). https://www.nsf.gov/statistics/srvyherd/

Rendón, L. I., Jalomo, R. E., & Nora, A. (2000). Theoretical considerations in the study of minority student retention in higher education. In J. M. Braxton (Ed.), *Reworking the student departure puzzle* (pp. 127–156). Vanderbilt University Press.

Torres, V., Jones, S. R., & Renn, K. A. (2009) Identity development theories in student affairs: Origins, current status and new approaches. *Journal of College Student Development, 50*(6), 577–596. https://doi.org/10.1353/csd.0.0102

Warnock, D. M., & Appel, S. (2012). Learning the unwritten rules: Working class students in graduate school. *Innovative Higher Education, 37*(4), 307–321. https://doi.org/10.1007/s10755-011-9204-x

Yosso, T. J. (2005) Whose culture has capital? A critical race theory discussion of community cultural wealth. *Race, Ethnicity and Education, 8*(1), 69–91.-https://doi.org/10.1080/1361332052000341006

WHEN FIRST-GENERATION COLLEGE STUDENTS BECOME DOCTORAL CANDIDATES

Heather Maietta

W hy is the topic of first-generation doctoral student success important? You cannot work in, study, or follow higher education as an industry without having frequent conversations on retention needs and efforts for this population of undergraduate students. Yet at the doctorate level, first-generation retention is rarely discussed, let alone managed.

Doctoral student attrition in higher education is a hidden crisis that must be addressed. We have too few underrepresented students successfully graduating from doctoral programs to meet our overall educational objectives—one of which is a diverse workplace. If we cannot retain first-generation doctoral students, they cannot graduate to the classroom to teach future generations of diverse students in postsecondary education. If we in the academy truly value and are committed to equal workplace representation, this hidden crisis needs to be discussed, researched, and managed.

A review of the literature on first-generation college students reveals a central focus on the undergraduate experience. Although strides have been made over the past 10 years to increase support for this population, there is still much work left to be done—particularly as first-generation students continue their education by pursuing graduate degrees. While the U.S. Census Bureau (2013, 2019) reported doctoral and professional degree earners are among a select group in the United States (with barely 3% of the country holding this distinction—a percentage that has remained stagnant since 2013), it might be surprising to learn that approximately 30%

of all doctoral students are first-generation (National Science Foundation [NSF], 2018).

At the start of the new millenium, the poignant lack of research on the lived experiences of first-generation doctoral students painted a picture that after receiving their bachelor's degree, the need for support ends (Adams, 2011; Gardner & Holley, 2011). Contemporary research on this population reveals this is not true. In fact, first-generation doctoral students continue to face the same hurdles as undergraduates—along with new challenges as they pursue an advanced degree (Cunningham & Brown, 2014; Gardner, 2013). For example, factors that influence academic self-regulation are shaped in early life by parents' education level through social learning in the home more than through social support while the student is in school. These behaviors persist into midlife (Williams et al., 2019). To further complicate matters, given that many adult doctoral students are balancing multiple responsibilities, relying on friends and classmates for academic self-regulation can be problematic as these relationships may not have time or space to develop naturally.

The research that does exist shows that first-generation doctoral students demonstrate remarkable resiliency in the pursuit of a degree, yet institutions could do more to help first-generation doctoral students persevere (Vasil & McCall, 2018). Before we examine how graduate programs could effectively design their degree offerings to better meet the needs of this population, it is important to further consider the complexities of the first-generation doctoral student experience.

Issues Confronting First-Generation Doctoral Students

First-generation doctoral students enter graduate school with different social, cultural, and academic backgrounds than their continuing-generation peers. This can impact their ability to navigate the complicated, unspoken bureaucracy of graduate school. From program choice (prestige versus convenience) and research design rigor to forming a doctoral committee and working informational networks, first-generation doctoral students are less aware of the complexities of doctoral study.

Social Capital

Undergraduate research on the first-generation college student often focuses on the idea of the *imposter syndrome*, where an individual feels like an intellectual counterfeit (Clance & Imes, 1978; Topping & Kimmel, 1985). Individuals who suffer from imposter syndrome experience it as a real and pervasive obstacle when trying to acclimate to the campus environment, which feels foreign to them. Research on first-generation doctoral students reports similar feelings of not belonging and that these feelings are often linked to their struggles with socializing into the doctoral experience (Helm et al., 2012; Ramirez, 2017). In other words, first-generation doctoral students struggle with "internalizing the expectations, standards, and norms of a given society, which includes learning the relevant skills, knowledge, habits, attitudes, and values of the group that one is joining" (Austin & McDaniels, 2006, p. 400). Research has yet to reveal whether feelings of being an imposter ease or disappear as first-generation college students acclimate into graduate school. The ability to socialize positively and productively into a doctoral program has a significant impact on the doctoral experience, degree completion, and successful postdoctoral career trajectory, so it is crucial that students overcome whatever fears they have of being "found out" as an imposter.

Much of the socialization research centers around doctoral students in general understanding the norms and expectations of "the faculty role" to prepare future graduates for the professoriate (Gardner, 2009), and feedback from students on the value of preparation received has been mixed (Ramirez, 2017). Yet the content and trajectory of first-generation socialization into a doctoral program might be seen in a much different light if it was recognized that their postgraduate destination is more likely than not outside of the academy. According to the NSF's 2017 Survey of Earned Doctorates, less than half (46%) of all doctoral graduates pursue employment in higher education (including tenure, nontenure, adjunct, and administrative roles), while 35% choose business/industry, and the remaining opt for government/ nonprofit or entrepreneurship. Based on other data, one would expect the percentage of graduating first-generation doctoral students going into the academy to be even lower, and therefore generally benefitting from socialization of a different kind altogether.

Cultural Capital

We know from the research on first-generation undergraduates that simply going to college is half the battle, and there is strong evidence to similarly suggest that a student's journey toward a doctorate is equally influenced by the formal education of their parents. The same holds true when we look at the end of the journey for graduate students. In terms of degree completion, the percentage of first-generation doctoral students who persist is lower than their continuing-generation counterparts. According to the NSF's 2017 Survey of Earned Doctorates, numbers of graduates from families in which neither parent holds more than a high school diploma declined in the past

20 years, while the graduation rate for those students whose parents received more than a secondary education rose during the same interval. Just over 17% of doctorates went to graduates with parents whose highest education level is a high school diploma, compared to 13% with some college, 26% with a bachelor's degree, and nearly 43% with advanced education (NSF, 2018).

Cultural capital linked to an educational setting has been defined as skills, knowledge, or abilities that might reward a particular social setting (Bourdieu, 1984). As a result of having a cultural capital deficit, many first-generation doctoral students struggle to understand the unspoken bureaucracy and rules of graduate education (Gopaul, 2015). Historically underrepresented populations, such as low socioeconomic or first-generation students, report challenges with dual existence or "living in two worlds" (Holley & Gardner, 2012) in which they toggle between their college world and their personal or "cultural" world. While trying to socialize into the rigorous and demanding doctoral culture, first-generation doctoral students are often challenged to leave behind previous identities or communities. At the same time, first-generation doctoral students struggle with graduate school socialization because of their cultural capital deficits. These issues are only compounded further as a growing percentage of first-generation doctoral degree recipients choose to enter the white-collar workforce with training that has provided little in the way of preparation for the world of work outside of the academy. Golde and Dore (2001) note doctoral students "are not well prepared to assume the faculty positions that are available, nor do they have a clear concept of their suitability for work outside of research" (p. 5). In short, low cultural capital has implications for overall educational and occupational success.

Academic Capital

Another challenge that plagues many first-generation doctoral students is their early educational choices. While socialization into the college experience might not have begun in one's culture, choosing undergraduate and graduate programs strategically and thoughtfully can boost first-generation students' academic capital advantage, acculturating them to the "life of the academy" well before they pursue doctoral education. Yet many first-generation students lack the family input to aid them in negotiating undergraduate and graduate school decisions and therefore are left to traverse the doctoral landscape independently. Furthermore, first-generation doctoral students characteristically hold undergraduate degrees from schools without doctoral programs and are more likely to have attended community college for part of their undergraduate experience (Hoffer et al., 2002). Attending community college provides less exposure to advanced degree structures, which (even indirectly) can have an impact on graduate decision-making (McCall, 2007). Their academic capital deficits also limit the exposure they receive for opportunities like early field experiences, internships, and lab work, where introduction to research faculty is more prevalent.

Financial Capital

First-generation doctoral students are more likely than their non-first-generation peers to make educational choices based on financial considerations. This in turn influences factors related to their choice of school, the prestige of the institution, and the research foci available (Arnold et al., 2012). Some first-generation students remain at the institution where they complete their undergraduate degree, deciding for reasons of comfort and cost to decline or defer pursuing programs that may be a better fit. In general, first-generation students are more likely to choose an educational institution based on its proximity to their home, typically staying within 50 miles geographically (Higher Education Research Institute, 2007). First-generation students are also more likely than their continuing-education peers to be older and therefore have dependents. The tug of war in balancing graduate school responsibilities with the financial responsibilities of children, aging parents, and extended family obligations are negatively correlated to doctoral degree completion.

It's worth taking a closer look at the question of degree completion, as the lower socioeconomic status of first-generation doctoral students in comparison to their continuing-generation peers has discernable repercussions. First-generation doctoral students have a slightly higher time to degree completion (NSF, 2018) which leads to higher debt acquisition. Tellingly, there is clear research demonstrating that the more financial support a doctoral student has, the less time they take to achieve a degree (Abedi & Benkin, 1987; Bowen & Rudenstin, 1992; DesJardins et al., 2002). Researchers on first-generation doctoral students attribute this phenomenon to finances and what Lovitts (2001) maintains is difficulty with cognitive mapping. In Lovitts's view, some first-generation doctoral students may not understand that fellowships or assistantships exist to support their graduate education, instead believing they must pay out of pocket or through loans or grants as they did for their undergraduate degree. This circles back to the impact of earlier educational decisions by first-generation college students and the lack of exposure to graduate assistants as instructors, leaving these now doctoral students unaware of mainstream funding options.

Throughout this section, the challenges and barriers faced by first-generation doctoral students reveals a steep uphill climb to doctoral completion. In terms of entering the higher education pipeline, it is worth noting at the outset that the number of doctoral recipients (and the faculty who teach them) are fewer, and the application process for doctoral candidates is more stringent and criteria are more selective. Even more challenging, first-generation doctoral candidates come to the process with misaligned academic backgrounds, significant financial challenges, and low social and cultural capital to draw on. Yet despite these liabilities, institutions and the community at large can make specific and measurable strides in supporting the growth and forward movement of first-generation doctoral students. The next section will present some of the strategies available to assist first-generation doctoral candidates in surmounting these barriers.

Supporting the Self-Efficacy in First-Generation Doctoral Students

Self-efficacy is a dynamic and responsive set of self-beliefs that serve as the foundation for operating within performance domains (Lent et al., 2005). Doctoral pursuits are a gateway to a specialized career path, and therefore self-efficacy has a large impact on said pursuits. Williams (2005) proposed three domains that impact a graduate student's self-efficacy—academic, research, and social. Doctoral programs and institutions can address each of these domains to increase the successful completion of first-generation doctoral students through changes to program operations, investigative support, and emotional socialization (Maietta, 2019).

Program Operations

A student's belief in their ability to successfully execute course-based activities and assignments is their *academic self-efficacy* (Jackson, 2002; Zimmerman, 1995). Positive academic self-efficacy depends in part on whether the operational needs of the first-generation doctoral student are met by a department or program. These operational needs include

- strong programmatic communication and support through transmission outlets such as open houses, candidate interviews, new student orientation, course sequencing, dissertation process advising, and so on;
- being taught goal-setting and time management techniques to ensure not only semester-to-semester success and time to degree completion but also reaching doctoral study goals and achieving balanced work-life responsibilities;

- dissertation chapter–specific courses that not only provide instruction on only how to craft each chapter of the dissertation but also allow for structured, organized time to do so throughout the semester in a classroom setting where accountability is at a maximum (Maietta, 2019); and
- financial coaching around the monetary complexities of doctoral program costs, including the dissertation process.

Operational support is key in communicating to the first-generation doctoral student that they are being offered a level academic playing field relative to their second-generation peers. If all operational questions are anticipated and addressed, fewer first-generation doctoral students will have to rely on navigating the hidden bureaucracy of the higher education system in isolation.

It is important for doctoral advisers to tailor the adviser–student relationship in such a way as to generate a sense of personal commitment in each student (Wallace, 2000). This individual advising technique also allows faculty to set program expectations early and clearly, so the first-generation student understands the rules of the doctoral program and recognizes how to use their strengths to navigate it. Faculty advisers who also happen to be first-generation can share their own first-generation status and the struggles they went through. If first-generation faculty aren't available, enlisting successful first-generation doctoral graduates to provide mentoring advice is also an option.

Investigative Support

A student's belief about their competence in completing research-related activities is *research self-efficacy*. It includes activities such as data collection and analysis, research integration, and technical writing (Betz, 1989; Forester et al., 2004). These are activities first-generation doctoral students may not have become familiarized with in their earlier undergraduate and graduate programs. Doctoral programs routinely require students to be proficient in and perform complex statistical analyses and/or advanced literature searches. First-generation students might be less familiar with the research-heavy and independent elements of the doctoral experience, and thus may need additional supports. Of course, no faculty adviser can be an expert in all statistical qualitative and quantitative methodologies, any more than they can be expected to be acquainted with the entire literature field, and students should be encouraged to conduct sophisticated research studies for their dissertations. Yet deficits in statistical and research support are real and prevalent, and for first-generation doctoral students and faculty advisers to maintain open, proactive communication and a strong working relationship, they must be honest with each other about research limitations and agree to seek outside expertise as the situation warrants. Additionally, departments must be responsible and held accountable for offering research support for both first-generation students and faculty advisers to bridge the gap and ensure complex and original research is being produced by all students, including those who are first-generation.

In addition, departments can provide investigative support to first-generation doctoral students to ensure strong research self-efficacy by

- creating dedicated research-related and statistical methodology tutorials and workshops that supplement the classroom learning experience;
- offering faculty-supported or student-led collegiate writing networks where doctoral students can connect with like-minded scholars across campus for writing support and process understanding (Wilson, 2019);
- employing research support specialists (e.g., statisticians, research librarians) who work directly and specifically with doctoral students to help them perform research design and execution;
- partnering with the campus information technology department or the math department to offer additional and supplemental statistical support courses/workshops/tutorials for students;
- creating methodological-specific research groups within doctoral cohorts or between doctoral programs across campus so first-generation doctoral and continuing-generation doctoral students can work together; and
- being purposeful on how the dissertation committee is designed to ensure balance and expertise are represented.

The dissertation research process helps transform the student to an independent scholar and creator of knowledge on the path to subject-level mastery. An institution that offers investigative support to enhance the research self-efficacy of first-generation doctoral students will help them demonstrate the in-depth knowledge and expertise needed to advance to degree completion.

Emotional Socialization

Feelings of belonging are one of the most reported challenges faced by first-generation college students at all levels of education. This *social self-efficacy*, or a student's belief in their ability to build meaningful, beneficial shared relationships with faculty, advisers, and peers, is the cornerstone of successful doctoral completion for first-generation students (Wallace, 2000; Williams,

2005). Feeling emotionally supported through encouragement, motivation, accountability, and a strong and consistent sounding board, helps foster a sense of belonging and can combat feelings of isolation experienced by many first-generation doctoral students.

The overall climate of the doctoral program also has an impact on socialization, for first-generation students' socialization within the academic community is imperative and is a strong predictor of retention. A feeling of belonging can be facilitated by

- creating a welcoming atmosphere for all students;
- nurturing peer-to-peer connections early in the recruiting process;
- introducing cohort-based support services; and
- having faculty members and advisers be present in the lives of their first-generation students.

Providing first-generation students with teaching and research-related professional development opportunities can also serve as an incentive for these students to increase their emotional connection to the institution and their doctoral program, thus strengthening their self-efficacy. Given longer time-to-degree, first-generation students will greatly benefit from emotional, candid mentoring and guidance, further benefiting their self-efficacy needs.

Final Thoughts

If instituted, the operational, investigative, and emotional changes argued for here will significantly benefit first-generation doctoral students. First-generation students frequently evoke their status with a sense of pride and feel their accomplishments are not despite but rather because of their background (Maietta, 2014). Any dissertation adviser will attest that a student's personal commitment to completing a doctoral degree cannot be understated. Knowing that first-generation doctoral students believe in themselves and see their status not as a deficit but an asset ought to spur all parties involved, to redouble their efforts at supporting this critically important population of graduate students.

References

Abedi, J., & Benkin, E. (1987). The effects of students' academic, financial, and demographic variables on time to the doctorate. *Research in Higher Education*, *27*(1), 3–14. https://www.jstor.org/stable/40195800

Adams, S. G. (2011). *Exploring first-generation African American graduate students: Motivating factors for pursuing a doctoral degree* (Publication No. 3486899) [Doctoral dissertation, University of Arkansas]. ProQuest Dissertations and Theses.

Ardoin, S., Clayton, A., Nguyen, D., & martinez, b. (2019). How first-generation college students live with social class differences on campus. In J. C. Garvey, J. C. Harris, D. R. Means, R. J. Perez, & C. J. Porter (Eds.), *Case studies for student development theory: Advancing social justice & inclusion in higher education* (pp. 105–107). Routledge.

Arnold, K. D., Lu, E. C., & Armstrong, K. J. (2012). The ecological view of college readiness. *ASHE Higher Education Report, 38*(5), 91–107. https://onlinelibrary.wiley.com/doi/abs/10.1002/aehe.20005

Austin, A. E., & McDaniels, M. (2006). Preparing the professoriate of the future: Graduate student socialization for faculty roles. In J. C. Smart (Ed.), *Higher education: Handbook of theory and research* (Vol. 21) (pp. 397–456). Springer.

Betz, N. E. (1989). Implications of the null environment hypothesis for women's career development and for counseling psychology. *The Counseling Psychologist, 17*(1), 136–144. https://doi.org/10.1177/0011000089171008

Bourdieu, P. (1984). *Distinction: A social critique of the judgement of taste* (R. Nice, Trans.). Harvard University Press.

Bowen, W. G., & Rudenstin, N. L. (1992). *In pursuit of the PhD.* Princeton University Press.

Clance, P. R., & Imes, S. A. (1978). The impostor phenomenon in high achieving women: Dynamics and therapeutic intervention. *Psychotherapy: Theory, Research, and Practice, 15*(3), 241–247. https://doi.org/10.1037/h0086006

Cunningham, A. T., & Brown, W. A. (2014). The role of psychological well-being in first-generation graduate students. *National Association of Students Affairs Professional Journal, 14*(1), 51–77. https://www.nasap.net/wp-content/uploads/2014/02/Spring-2014-NASAP-Journal.pdf#page=51

DesJardins, S. L., Ahlburg, D. A., & McCall, B. P. (2002). A temporal investigation of factors related to timely degree completion. *Journal of Higher Education, 73*(5), 555–581. https://doi.org/10.1353/jhe.2002.0042

Forester, M., Kahn, J. H., & Hesson-McInnis, M. S. (2004). Factor structures of three measures of research self-efficacy. *Journal of Career Assessment, 12*(1), 3–16. https://doi.org/10.1177/1069072703257719

Gardner, S. K. (2009). Student and faculty attributions of attrition in high and low-completing doctoral programs in the United States. *Journal of Higher Education, 58*(1), 97–112. https://doi.org/10.1007/s10734-008-9184-7

Gardner, S. K. (2013). The challenge of first-generation doctoral students. In K. A. Holley & J. Joseph (Eds.), *Increasing diversity in doctoral education: Implications for theory and practice* (New Directions for Higher Education, no. 163, pp. 43–54). Jossey-Bass. https://doi.org/10.1002/he.20064

Gardner, S. K., & Holley, K. A. (2011). "Those invisible barriers are real": The progression of first-generation students through doctoral education. *Equity & Excellence in Education, 44*(1), 77–92. https://doi.org/10.1080/10665684.2011.529791

Golde, C. M., & Dore, T. M. (2001). *At cross purposes: What the experiences of today's doctoral students reveal about doctoral education.* Pew Charitable Trusts. http://www.phd-survey.org/report%20final.pdf

Gopaul, B. (2015) Inequality and doctoral education: Exploring the "rules" of doctoral study through Bourdieu's notion of field. *Higher Education, 70*(1), 73–88. https://www.doi.org/10.1007/s10734-014-9824-z

Helm, M., Campa, H., III, & Moretto, K. (2012). Professional socialization for the PhD: An exploration of career and professional development preparedness and readiness for PhD candidates. *Journal of Faculty Development, 26,* 5–23.

Higher Education Research Institute. (2007). *First in my family.* University of California, Los Angeles.

Hoffer, T. B., Welch, V., Webber, K., Williams, K., Lisek, B., Hess, M., & Guzman-Barron, I. (2002). *Doctorate recipients from United States universities: Summary report 2002* (Vol. 2004). National Opinion Research Center. https://www.norc.org/PDFs/publications/SED_Sum_Rpt_2002.pdf

Holley, K. A., & Gardner, S. (2012). Navigating the pipeline: How socio-cultural influences impact first-generation doctoral students. *Journal of Diversity in Higher Education, 5*(2), 112–121. https://doi.org/10.1037/a0026840

Jackson, J. (2002). Enhancing self-efficacy and learning performance. *The Journal of Experimental Education, 70*(3), 243–254. https://doi.org/10.1080/00220970209599508

Lent, R. W., Brown, S. D., Sheu, H., Schmidt, J., Brenner, B. R., & Treistman, D. (2005). Social cognitive predictors of academic interests and goals in engineering: Utility for women and students at historically Black universities. *Journal of Counseling Psychology, 52*(1), 84–92. https://www.doi.org/10.1037/0022-0167.52.1.84

Lovitts, B. E. (2001). *Leaving the ivory tower: The causes and consequences of departure from doctoral study.* Rowman and Littlefield.

Maietta, H. M. (2014). First-generation college seniors: Challenges and support. [Unpublished research].

Maietta, H. N. (2019). *Faculty advising as a progression strategy for first-generation doctoral students* (Paper presentation). NACADA Conference on Academic Advising, Burlington, VT.

McCall, T. (2007). *Beyond the undergraduate: Factors influencing first-generation student enrollment in and completion of graduate education* [Unpublished doctoral dissertation]. Ohio University, Athens.

National Science Foundation. (2018). *Doctorate recipients from U.S. universities: 2017* (Special Report NSF 19-301). https://ncses.nsf.gov/pubs/nsf19301/

Ramirez, E. (2017). Unequal socialization: Interrogating the Chicano/Latino(a) doctoral education experience. *Journal of Diversity in Higher Education, 10*(1), 25–38. https://doi.org/10.1037/dhe0000028

Roksa, J., Feldon, D. F., & Maher, M. (2018). First-generation student in pursuit of the PhD: Comparing socialization experiences and outcomes to continuing-generation peers. *The Journal of Higher Education, 89*(5), 728–752. https://doi .org/10.1080/00221546.2018.1435134

Topping, M. E., & Kimmel, E. B. (1985). The imposter phenomenon: Feeling phony. *Academic Psychology Bulletin, 7*(1), 213–226.

U.S. Census Bureau. (2013). *Educational attainment of the population 18 years and over, by age, sex, race, and Hispanic origins: 2013.* https://www.census.gov/data/ tables/2013/demo/educational-attainment/cps-detailed-tables.html

U.S. Census Bureau. (2019). *Educational attainment in the United States: 2019. U.S.* https://www.census.gov/data/tables/2019/demo/educational-attainment/cps-detailed-tables.html

Vasil, M., & McCall, J. M. (2018). The perspectives of two first-generation college students pursuing doctoral degrees in music education. *Journal of Music Teacher Education, 27*(2), 67–81. https://doi.org/10.1177/1057083717717464

Wallace, D. D. (2000). *Critical connections: Meaningful mentoring relationships between women doctoral students and their dissertation chairpersons.* [Doctoral dissertation] LSU Historical Dissertations and Theses. 7395. https://digitalcommons.lsu.edu/ gradschool_disstheses/7395

Williams, E. G. (2005). *Academic, research, and social self-efficacy among African American pre-McNair scholar participants and African American post-McNair scholar participants* [Doctoral dissertation]. VTech Works. https://vtechworks.lib. vt.edu/handle/10919/11286

Williams, P. E., Wall, N., & Wade, W. (2019). Mid-career adult learners in an online doctoral program and the drivers of their academic self-regulation: The importance of social support and parent education level. *International Review of Research in Open and Distributed Learning, 20*(1), 63–78. https://files.eric.ed.gov/ fulltext/EJ1207475.pdf

Wilson, S. (2019). Negating isolation and imposter syndrome through writing as product and as process: the impact of collegiate writing networks during a doctoral programme. In L. Pretorius, L. Macaulay, & B. Cahusac de Caux (Eds.), *Wellbeing in doctoral education: Insights and guidance from the student wxperience* (1st ed.) (pp. 59–76). Springer. https://doi.org/10.1007/978-981-13-9302-0_7

Zimmerman, B. J. (1995). Self-efficacy and educational development. In A. Bandura (Ed.), *Self-efficacy in changing societies* (pp. 202–231). Cambridge University Press.

HOW A COLLEGE REBUILT ITSELF BY CENTERING FIRST-GENERATION COLLEGE STUDENTS

Staci Weber

In 1911, Helen Temple Cooke founded Pine Manor College (PMC) to serve traditionally underserved students, women. About 100 years later, the college became coeducational and recommitted to serving students who did not have equal access to higher education. Indeed, over 80% of students are from low-income families, are the first in their families to attend college, and are students of color.

I joined the PMC team in 2015 as the chief student affairs officer. I identify as a White, upper-middle-class woman whose parents both hold advanced degrees. While this case study is written from my perspective, the outcomes reflect an accumulation of ideas, diversity, and experiences of PMC employees and campus partners.

Mission and Vision

When I came to PMC, employees' commitment to student success was palpable, despite low employee morale and a lack of college spirit. From my perspective, the college needed to be strengthened and mission aligned; outsourced services needed oversight and review; and all campus departments needed better systems, communication, and accountability.

In summer 2016, a new president took the helm and began to strengthen the college's leadership. He led the college through a strategic planning process and by May 2017, the college adopted "Educating With Purpose: Pine Manor College Strategic Plan Framework, 2017–2022"

(Pine Manor College, 2017). The plan included an updated mission statement that read:

> The mission of Pine Manor College is to make certain that all graduates are prepared to take meaningful steps in their lives: engaging in new jobs and careers, continuing to learn, and positively contributing to their communities. Students, including those who are the first in their families to attend college, who are looking for a purposeful education in a personalized and inclusive learning community will find a home at Pine Manor College. (Pine Manor College, 2017, p. 2)

The plan also focused on five key areas including "increase student success and graduation rates" and "further a culture of social justice and responsibility" (Pine Manor College, 2017, p. 3). After the board approved the strategic plan, student affairs and community members came together to address the question: What should student affairs do to lead the campus in becoming a school centered on first-generation college students' success?

One Strategy: A Focus on First-Generation College Students

To prepare for our meetings, student affairs and community members read work on communities of cultural wealth (Yosso, 2005, 2006), validation theory (Rendón & Muñoz, 2011), critical race theory (CRT) (Ladson-Billings, 1998; Solórzano & Yosso, 2001), and sense of belonging (O'Keeffe, 2013) before the first meeting. The intention in choosing those articles was to

> center the students we serve . . . [and] create a program and a structure that fits their needs, rather than the needs of historically traditional college students. To do this work thoughtfully and purposefully, [we] will ground our work in Critical Race Theory and Cultural Wealth. (S. Weber, personal communication, May 15, 2017

At our first meeting, we reflected on our strengths, weaknesses, opportunities, and threats (SWOT analysis) and gave people space to share. Through this process and additional conversations, the team concluded that we should prioritize formalized mentorship to increase student persistence.

We proposed, and later executed, that every PMC student would receive a student success coach ("coach") and a faculty adviser. The coaches would utilize holistic advising to offer academic, sociopsychological, cocurricular, financial, and career support and intrusive advising (Earl, 1988; Muraskin, 1997) to take a proactive approach and asked questions based on predetermined topic areas. The topics came from a review of relevant literature, conversations with students, and coaches' experiences in the field. To best integrate faculty, we took advantage of an already existent program where First Year Seminar professors serve as first-year students' advisers. A coach would then work with two to three First Year Seminar professors and their respective classes. Once student affairs committed to this model, we focused on restructuring, budgets, professional development, and policies.

Restructuring: Buy-In, Personnel, and Physical Space

The student affairs team included myself (who oversaw housekeeping, food services, and campus safety, along with the departments in student affairs), an associate dean of student life and community engagement (who focused on residential life and oversaw a director of student engagement), an associate dean of student services (who oversaw a director of student services), a director of community development and standards, a college counselor, a director of athletics, and three athletic coaches. In the restructure, the associate dean of student life and community engagement transitioned into the associate dean of student affairs to bring leadership to the new Initiative for Student Success ("Initiative") and supervise three coaches. The director of student engagement became one of the three coaches, and we hired two additional coaches (one who focused on international students). In addition, I hired a director of residential life. The president also hired a director of operations to oversee student services, housekeeping, food services, campus safety, information technology, and facilities. Due to an inclusive planning process, acceptance of the Initiative came rather easily.

Since our restructure, we have shifted from community standards to restorative justice and outsourced our counseling services through establishing a partnership with a local mental health community center. A change in counseling services has doubled the number of therapists on campus, eliminated the need to triage students to off-campus services, given us year-round access to care, and decreased our costs. We have also transitioned most of our part-time athletic coaches into full-time positions.

With a priority on the Initiative, we put the student success team on the first floor of the student center and created a global community center and a communal space for students to study, nap, meet with professors, and find free school supplies and toiletries.

Budget

We moved monies around to create a budget for the Initiative, which included emergency monies for small loans, school supplies, and snacks. We allotted monies for student affairs staff to eat one meal a week in the dining hall to enhance student affairs' presence in high-traffic areas, and we set aside more monies for professional development.

Professional Development

We have focused our professional development on three key areas:

- *Racial and social equity* to allow the PMC community to delve into complex topics such as institutional racism, microaggressions, and privilege, so employees can appropriately challenge themselves, their colleagues, and our college's policies and practices
- *Trauma-informed approach* to provide employees with a better understanding of students' behaviors and actions rather than be dismissive or use those behaviors to reinforce stereotypes or stigmas
- *Restorative justice* (Karp, 2014) to provide employees with tools for facilitation and community building and restoring, which are rooted in indigenous beliefs and work to dismantle the school to prison pipeline

Policies and Practices

Student affairs worked to enhance our policies and practices by rewriting the student handbook and divisional letters from a restorative, trauma-informed lens. We doubled our paid leadership opportunities on campus to improve student engagement and sponsored a Free Application for Federal Student Aid (FAFSA) Day to increase timely financial aid applications. We continued to offer year-round housing, free laundry services, and food vouchers to our students.

Conclusion

Our work to better serve first-generation college students extends to all realms of campus, not just student affairs. Our admissions team builds relationships with prospective students to assist them through their application process. Team members have rewritten the financial aid award letter for clarity and worked closely with families to ensure they understood their financial aid packages. Faculty adopted more experiential learning pedagogies, and the Learning Resource Center and librarians have offered more mobile (and always free) services to meet students' needs. While PMC is still working to better itself, we have made great strides in focusing on first-generation college students and have seen increases in student persistence from year to year and celebrate a graduation rate that is four times the national average for first-generation, low-income students.

Addendum

I wrote this case study in March 2019, when the team at PMC had diversified our revenue streams and secured financially solvency after 20 years of losses. Our financial model made the institution less tuition dependent than most private colleges and allowed us to financially support over 80% of our first-generation college students who were from low-income backgrounds. As a result of our redesign, completed applications in admissions, admitted students, and matriculated students increased by 68%, 59%, and 7%, respectively by fall 2019. The persistence of all degree-seeking students has gone from 66% in 2017 to 71% in 2019, and persistence of students in the new student cohort increased from 58% in 2017 to 67% in 2019. From 2016 to 2018, persistence of all Boston Public School students increased from 69% to 92%, and persistence of first-time, first-year Boston Public School students increased from 47% to 87%.

By March 2020, one year after submitting this case study to the editors, the COVID-19 pandemic caused colleges and universities across the country to abruptly move into remote education and close residential programs. PMC's revenue streams dried up as we could no longer run our English language programs, childcare services, and special events. As the senior leadership team and the board of trustees realized that we would become existential, the presidents of PMC and Boston College crafted an amazing opportunity.

PMC has integrated with Boston College to form the Pine Manor Institute for Student Success at Boston College. Through a $50 million endowment and Boston College's current programming for students of color and FG college students, PMC's Initiative will have the opportunity to become a national model to restructure and rethink higher education for FG college students. The agreement between institutions also provided PMC's staff and faculty the opportunity to conduct a 2-year "teach out" to matriculated students to ensure all community members a soft landing. Through this agreement, PMC's mission and values should continue through the Pine Manor Institute for Student Success as Boston College committed to "educating immigrant and first-generation students, in an educational partnership of mutual benefit that will accelerate and expand Pine Manor College's mission" (Dunn, 2020, para. 2).

Discussion Questions

1. What are the potential benefits of this merger for both schools?
2. How could a merger such as this work be implemented at public universities?
3. How would first-generation college students benefit from this type of merger?

References

Dunn, J. (2020). *Pine Manor College, Boston College announce institutional agreement.* Boston College. https://www.bc.edu/bc-web/bcnews/campus-community/announcements/pine-manor-institutional-agreement.html

Earl, W. R. (1988). Intrusive advising of freshmen in academic difficulty. *NACADA Journal, 8*(2), 27–33. https://doi.org/10.12930/0271-9517-8.2.27

Karp, D. (2014). *The little book of restorative justice for colleges and universities: Repairing harm and rebuilding trust in response to student misconduct.* Good Books.

Ladson-Billings, G. (1998). Just what is critical race theory and what's it doing in a nice field like education? *International Journal of Qualitative Studies in Education, 11*(1), 7–24. https://doi.org/10.1080/095183998236863

Muraskin, L. (1997). *"Best practices" in student support services: A study of five exemplary sites.* https://eric.ed.gov/?id=ED411739

O'Keeffe, P. (2013). A sense of belonging: Improving student retention. *College Student Journal, 47*(4), 605–613.

Pine Manor College. (2017). *Educating with purpose: Pine Manor College strategic plan framework, 2017–2022.* http://www.pmc.edu/Websites/pmc/images/PMC%20Strategic%20Plan%20Framework.pdf

Rendón, L. I., & Muñoz, S. (2011). Revisiting validation theory: Theoretical foundations, applications, and extensions. *Enrollment Management Journal* (Summer), 22.

Solórzano, D., & Yosso, T. (2001). Critical race and LatCrit theory and method: Counter-storytelling. *International Journal of Qualitative Studies in Education, 14*(4), 471–495. doi:10.1080/09518390110063365

Yosso, T. J. (2005). Whose culture has capital? A critical race theory discussion of community cultural wealth. *Race Ethnicity and Education, 8*(1), 69–91. https://doi.org/10.1080/1361332052000341006

Yosso, T. J. (2006). *Critical race counterstories along the Chicana/ Chicano educational pipeline.* Routledge.

WHAT'S IN A NAME?

Narratives and Counternarratives of the First-Generation Moniker

Rashné Jehangir and Kelly Collins

Language carries culture and culture carries the entire body of values by which we perceive ourselves and our place in the world.

(Ngugi, 1986, p. 16)

S o much of higher education is bound up in words. We have a language all our own, and within that language there are dialects attributed to disciplines, fields of study, arenas of work—each replete with subtext. Language is power—it determines how we think about something or someone and in turn how that naming impacts the recipient's view of themselves. In the last 5 years the term *first-generation* has become hot—it is a buzzword, and everyone is interested.

Many of us in higher education connect to the term personally, as an aspect of our own story, and proudly claim "I'm the first." Others encounter the language of first-generation for the first time as they seek to enter campus communities and wonder if the term applies to them too. As a contingent identity and status, one that is bound up in the lives and experiences of other people, namely our families and home communities, the first-generation moniker is . . . complicated. Nguyen and Nguyen (2018) articulated this complexity in noting how varied the use of the term *first-generation* has been in the literature and institutional practice. They argued that "*Leaving* the term unquestioned limits the capacity to grasp how these students' backgrounds and identities shape their decisions and relationships to others and to institutions, and risks reproducing the very inequality that education researchers wish to mitigate" (p. 146).

To those who have spent decades working in TRIO programs, multi-cultural initiatives, Talent Search, and more, this new embrace of a term we have long used and fought for is both gratifying and maddening all at once. Why? Because as the first-generation movement becomes increasingly popular we need to consider primarily the intersectional identities that embody the first-generation experience, as well as the varying positionalities of those who employ this term in policy, research, and praxis. This requires attention to ways in which our first-generation students' journey to and through higher education is tied up in the old and new narrative of what it means to be the first in your family to go to college.

Who Is a First-Generation?

> The way we imagine discrimination or disempowerment often is more complicated for people who are subjected to multiple forms of exclusion. . . . The good news is that intersectionality provides us a way to see it. (Crenshaw, 2017)

First-generation students are not a monolithic group, even though institutions and literature may seek to portray them this way. It is critical to acknowledge the complex intersectionality inherent to the first-generation identity and how giving attention to these identities can allow students to see themselves more fully and institutions to serve them more effectively (Jehangir 2010; Nguyen & Nguyen, 2018; Orbe 2008). To consider the first-generation experience through an intersectional lens is to see that "race, class, gender, sexuality, ethnicity, nation, ability, and age operate not as unitary, mutually exclusive entities, but as reciprocally constructing phenomena that in turn shape complex social inequalities" (Collins, 2015, p. 2). First-generation college students are a heterogeneous group of students who are traversing a path unknown to their families, encountering a wide variety of institutional and social barriers as they navigate higher education access and persistence (Kezar, 2011). They represent a broad range of students who are new to the academy, including students from low-income backgrounds, students from minority ethnic and racial groups, adult learners, immigrants, nonnative English speakers, and students with disabilities (Engle & Tinto, 2008; Jehangir, 2010; Jehangir et al., 2015; Walpole, 2007).

Socioeconomic (SES) class is a foundational lens with which to explore aspects of the first-generation experience. Walpole (2007) argued that

> while first-generation students, who are defined by their parents' educational levels, clearly face trials similar to low-SES and low-income students, scholars typically do not explicitly describe these students as belonging to a larger group that includes low-SES and low-income students. (p. 9)

First-generation students are more likely than their continuing-generation peers to come from low-income households, with 27% of first-generation students reporting a household income of $20,000 or less, compared to 6% of continuing-generation students (Redford & Mulvaney Hoyer, 2017). The report also found that 54% of first-time students left college without a degree because of financial barriers, compared to 45% of continuing-generation students. The experiences at the intersections of low-income and first-generation identities adds important context to the narratives of how, where, and why students seek higher education.

Given these differences, why group these students together? There are several reasons: First, despite differences and sometimes because of these differences, this seemingly disparate assemblage of students shares an understanding of what it means to be an outsider to the academy. They also live the challenges of intersectionality in that different forms of discrimination coincide to constrain them in multiple ways. Second, these intersectional constraints perpetuated by racism, classism, and more are not new to them—they have often traversed, negotiated, and challenged these structural inequities in other aspects of their lives. This is a strength—and giving them language to name this and negotiate it with others is integral to building a sense of belonging in an alien place. Third, using the term *first-generation* to encompass the experience of diverse students who have experienced multiple forms of exclusion is a form of political and resistance capital. It gives voice to students who come to the academy in search of upward mobility for themselves and their families. The capital of this collective coalition and their allies allows students and institutional agents to demonstrate that constraints are real but also deeply reflective of the opportunity gap that perpetuates situational and generational poverty (Beegle, 2003) as well as access to high-impact educational resources for first-generation students (Kuh et al., 2005).

That being said, it is important to say that clustering students for convenience or as a more palatable proxy label for whatever form of diversity your campus espouses is vastly different from creating communities of belonging with an intentionality that shapes policy, practice, and assessment on different campuses. Here is the rub: Not all first-generation students are low income, or students or color, or immigrants, but there is enough significant overlap in these categories that institutions need to begin developing a richer portrait of the intersectionality of their campus to tailor support around *their* first-generation students. This portrait in turn provides interesting insights on recruiting and admissions plans in higher education and allows us to ask: What does access really mean to your campus? As Nguyen and Nguyen (2018) assert, the multidimensional definitions of first-generation status are not a deficit, but rather an opportunity for institutions to embrace and illustrate the unique intersectional identities that comprise the first-generation community on their campuses. If *first-generation* simply becomes a proxy for "diverse" students without attention to implications of race, social class, and poverty in admissions as well as support following matriculation, then it is being misused.

Tracing the History of First-Generation Language

The federal definition and history of first-generation status demonstrates the complexity of the first-generation identity and also traces the way in which this term cultivates a political coalition to formalize access to higher education. The U.S. Department of Education defines *first-generation status* as

> an individual, neither of whose parents completed a baccalaureate degree; or an individual who, prior to the age of 18, regularly resided with and received support from only one parent and whose supporting parent did not complete a baccalaureate degree; or an individual who, prior to the age of 18, did not regularly reside with or receive support from a natural or adoptive parent. (Higher Education Act Amendments, 1998: Amendment F, para. 1)

As we trace the first-generation moniker in federal and academic lexicons, we find that the term *first-generation student* is relatively new and nebulous.

The first public record of the term *first-generation student* appeared in federal legislation in 1980, as part of Public Law 96, Statute 1408 (Higher Education Act, 1965). This statute authorized funding for "Special Programs for Students From Disadvantaged Backgrounds," including the federal TRIO programs, and defined *first-generation status* thus: "(1) the term 'first-generation college student' means a person neither of whose parents completed a baccalaureate degree" (Higher Education Act Amendment, 1980, p. 42). While this term has evolved over time to include students with a variety of custodial guardianship statuses and household configurations, the inception of the TRIO programs originated the term *first-generation* as we know it today.

Even before the language of first-generation emerged in legislation, TRIO had established its role as the primary college access intervention for students who are historically excluded from higher education. According to the Council for Opportunity in Education (COE, 2016), "The TRIO programs were the first national college access and retention programs to address the serious social and cultural barriers to education in America" (para. 2). The TRIO programs were founded in 1965 as a component of President Lyndon B. Johnson's administration's Great Society program and the war on poverty. The founding of the TRIO programs reflected the popular perspective that college attainment has a powerful ability to increase social and economic mobility.

> The logic behind the first equal opportunity programs was that by bringing higher education within the financial reach of all Americans, lower-income students would enroll in greater numbers. This would result in their finding better jobs, earning higher wages, and moving out of poverty. (Mumper et al., 2016, p. 215)

Alongside the TRIO programs, the war on poverty programs included the federal Head Start, AmeriCorps, Teacher Corps, and Job Corps initiatives, programs that thrust open the doors of educational and employment opportunities to millions of working-class and low-income Americans.

The war on poverty initiatives aimed to alleviate poverty and racial inequities through the expansion of the federal government's role in educational and employment enrichment programs while also stabilizing the U.S. economy. As TRIO expanded to serve students at over 950 U.S. colleges and universities, the Higher Education Act was amended to establish the first-generation status as one component of program eligibility, alongside low-income status (COE, 2016). Over time, TRIO eligibility has continued to expand to encompass students from increasing "disadvantaged" statuses, including students who are veterans or have disabilities, among other eligible identities (COE, 2016).

Beyond the federal definition, the history of the first-generation moniker in academic and cultural lexicons demonstrates the amorphous utility of the term. A recent *New York Times* profile of the first-generation identity noted that the definition has been found to vary across academic institutions and among university agents, citing the research of Robert K. Toutkoushian, who analyzed eight different versions of the term *first-generation* at colleges and universities. The research demonstrated that, across a sample of 7,300 students, the number of students who could be defined as *first-generation* ranged from 22% to 77% (Sharpe, 2017). The challenges of creating a conclusive definition of *first-generation students* is reflected in the academic literature as well, as noted in the research of Nguyen and Nguyen (2018), who found 18 different definitions of *first-generation status* in a comprehensive review of higher education research journals.

Beginning with the GI Bill, the 1944 legislation providing full college tuition to returning World War II veterans that marked the opening of doors to many who were new to the academy, first-generation college students have more often than not included working-class students and students historically impacted by generational and situational poverty. The GI Bill offers a rare historical example of first-generation students exerting choice and agency as they navigated college enrollment. Eligible GIs were able to enroll in their chosen university without encountering structural barriers (Mumper et al., 2016). This was important because "many of these students were first-generation college enrollees who came from families that had little experience of or expectation for a college education" (Thelin, 2004, p. 266). Mumper et al. (2016) assert that

> one important feature of the GI Bill was that it provided benefits to all veterans, regardless of gender, race, ethnic background, or income level. The benefits of the GI Bill allowed many Black and Hispanic veterans to use their education to boost themselves and their families into the middle class. (p. 214)

Despite this increase in inclusion, it is important to note that the vast majority of GI Bill recipients were White men (Thelin, 2004). However, the GI Bill instigated an initial surge in access for many historically excluded groups in higher education who sought higher education as a pathway to social class mobility.

While the appearance of this term in the 1980 Higher Education Act was a victory of policy passages that paved the way for federally funded TRIO programs, the larger literature in higher education has used this term as a proxy of deficiency. Even scholarship that has recognized the inherent challenges that first-generation students face with financial constraints, limited familial knowledge of the educational milieu, and work-life challenges often frames the first-generation experience as lacking in critical skills, capital, and resources to succeed in higher education. As the face of America changes, more and more first-generation students include communities of color as well as refugee and immigrant students, many of whom are also low-income. There is no argument that poverty impacts social mobility and access and success in college (Engle & Tinto, 2008; Goldrick-Rab, 2016). There is also no argument that racism intersects with poverty at disproportionate rates in the United States such that communities of color's efforts at upward mobility are thwarted in every arena ranging from homeownership to health care to access to education. These opportunity gaps have shaped the first-generation experience and yet a significant body of literature frames the first-generation narratives as if the onus for these failures rests in the students and the communities themselves. A search of the literature will reveal that *first-generation* is closely associated with language like *at risk, disadvantaged, lacking in social capital,* and *lacking in familial support.* It is no surprise then, that many first-generation students did not embrace this moniker, except in rare dedicated spaces where they found other students who shared these experiences. From parent weekend to spring break, to references in classroom, first-generation students are often reminded that they do not belong—and when a body of literature characterizes their lived experiences as inherently deficient, this trickles into practice too. Many students describe interactions with advisers and faculty in college and high school that question their ability to access certain colleges, majors, or career paths. To be clear, many first-generation students are low-income, and they do not understand the social mores and customs of higher education the way middle-class students do. But, this gap is not inherent to who they are, nor should it define their presence in higher education. Instead this reveals the tensions within the term *first-generation* and should prompt consideration of the ways to unpack these tensions to consider how the term is used institutionally versus how students may be empowered to claim this identity.

Contingent Identities—Both Visible and Invisible

First-generation identity formation is often an individual process for each student, one that is shaped simultaneously by resonance and dissonance, visibility and invisibility, and aversion and affinity. Many students are unaware of the impact of their first-generation status until someone names it for them and assists them in recognizing the absence of information or familial experience with the norms, mores, and implicit expectations of college. Many do see how vastly their life has differed from their peers, but they don't see it as a lack until they come into places that privilege social mores and ways of knowing that they did not grow up with. Because first-generation identity often accompanies working-class and low-income status, it is challenging and potentially alienating for students to publicly claim intrinsic identities that are associated with shame and exclusion. As higher education professionals seek the language and practices that support first-generation student inclusion and success, it is critical to question whether it is fair and appropriate to ask students to claim an identity that is laden with developmental processes and identification dilemmas.

A common socialization ritual within first-generation communities is sharing the story of when you discovered your first-generation status, often precipitated by the question, "When did you find out you are first-generation?" Many first-generation students learn of their first-generation status for the first time as they apply to college or receive a notification of eligibility to TRIO or other first-generation–specific campus programs. It is common for student affairs professionals to assist students in identifying with the first-generation moniker, as students often express trepidation about the legitimacy of their first-generation status. "But my mom went to community college for two semesters," or "My older sister went to college" are common concerns espoused by students as they make meaning of and attempt to relate to first-generation status. For some students, their initial resistance to this identity is connected to a sense that the institution is classifying them as first-generation and the deficit narrative that they have associated with it. For others, it is an empowering relief to discover an affinity identity that recognizes their experiences being the first in their family. Again, the process of identifying as first-generation is multidimensional, intersectional, and above all, complicated.

Socioeconomic and first-generation status, unlike issues of gender or race, are often invisible identities, which makes it particularly difficult to address overtly as a social issue (Warnock & Hurst, 2016). This invisibility, however, does not negate the barriers that first-generation students face within higher education institutions. The literature about first-generation students tends to address the connections between student individual characteristics and college success, and also the institutional barriers to educational success negatively impacting students. This focus contributes to an overall deficit lens regarding the first-generation student identity and experience, emphasizing the lack inherent to first-generation students' social capital. While there are multiple established definitions of first-generation status, the field continues to seek an understanding of how first-generation students define themselves, and how they make meaning of their own social, cultural, and familial capital while negotiating institutional barriers in higher education.

Role of Institutional Agents

When we seek to define the experiences of first-generation students in higher education, it is important to consider the ways that campuses and institutional agents enact and promote first-generation status within the institutional culture and mission. Higher education access and success for first-generation students is often framed as a strategy of increasing diversity as part of an institutional change agenda. The size and retention of the first-generation student population is often a tracked metric within institutional diversity agendas (Kezar, 2011; Nguyen & Nguyen, 2018). In *On Being Included: Racism and Diversity in Institutional Life*, Ahmed (2012) explores the experiences of university diversity practitioners, institutional agents tasked with enhancing and promoting diversity on campus. The study revealed that diversity professionals consistently report an ambivalent relationship to higher education institutions, often reporting feeling that they are "simultaneously working 'for' and 'against' them" (Ahmed, 2012, p. 15).

The quest to enroll "diverse" students, or students with identities that have been historically excluded or marginalized in higher education, takes on an ethos of welcoming, including, or incorporating students of color, first-generation, and low-income students into the university. This work is often relegated to certain individuals on campus who work to provide advocacy, support, and advising to first-generation students, typically within campus diversity and special population programs. Professionals who work with first-generation students are often cast into this role, assisting students in identifying with this identity, and often calling on them to promote the visibility of the first-generation community. Students in first generation–specific programs are encouraged to represent the community at campus events in order to increase institutional support and awareness of the program. They are invited to advocate for TRIO funding within local and national policy forums (COE, 2016). Both professionals and students are always aware of the tenuous nature of grant-funded support programs, and advocacy and promotion is embedded within the culture of this work.

Ahmed (2012) frames this expectation, common in programs serving historically underrepresented students, within the logic of "conditional hospitality" (Derrida & Dufourmantelle, 2000, p. 73). Universities grant access and services to first-generation students on an implicit condition that they assimilate into the dominant campus culture and become exemplars of the institutional diversity mission. This has been one area of change and growth in the last decades, and many institutions in intentional partnership with their students have created centers, events, programmatic offerings in student affairs, curricular planning, and visibility campaigns. For example, the University of California (UC) system developed the First-Generation Initiative to support the 42% of UC undergraduates who are first-generation (UC, 2019). The program features an array of programs and services on every UC campus and seeks to help first-generation students build networks and social connections; provide academic, housing, and financial services; and connect students with opportunities, from community service to study abroad (UC, 2019). A network of similar initiatives is being developed at colleges and universities across the United States, indicating an increasing recognition and commitment to first-generation success beyond the silos of campus diversity programs.

Claiming the First-Generation Identity

Sometimes when people move forward, they forget to look back, they forget to be there. Being the first in my family to live on campus, I have definitely gathered the momentum to move me and my family forward. It is a push, pull, drag, shove situation, but my recognition of this has helped me be mindful of the things in my peripheral vision and behind me. (Pa, first-generation student)

Despite the complexity of the term *first-generation* and the way in which institutions may use it, there has also been empowerment and agency connected with the way this term has gained positive visibility in higher education over the last 5 years. This effort toward visibility and changing the narrative of who first-generation students are is an effort to claim this identity and to see intersectionality as a strength.

As the student quote at the head of this section suggests, first-generation students come to higher education with forms of capital that are often delegitimized as valuable ways of knowing. First-generation allies, advocates, and scholars have a part in supporting students in claiming their first-generation identities by actively reflecting on their linguistic, navigational, and familial capital (Yosso, 2005). This is a way to capitalize on the strengths of their intersectional identities and to demonstrate that the skills they have already cultivated are significant—we must name them and claim them as such. Speaking multiple languages, code-switching, navigating government offices and rental agreements, translating for their parents, and working two jobs have prepared them to succeed in college. And yes, there are things they are unprepared for too: Like many newcomers they must learn new protocols, but without being forced to give up all they came with. Instead, they should be encouraged to translate these skills into new settings.

Gerstle (2006), when writing about the experience of immigrants, noted how newcomers are not granted the full weight and legitimacy of their citizenship even if they have the right papers. He noted that the formal dimension of access is but one part of citizenship; it is rather in the political-cultural dimension where we grasp the mores of the new world. Most important is the political-institutional dimension where newcomers work together to establish their own place and "seek political influence, p. 28." In naming intersectionality as intrinsic to the first-generation identity and creating space, support and resources for students, staff, and faculty to claim it, we move toward voice, agency, and full citizenship in the academy.

References

Ahmed, S. (2012). *On being included: Racism and diversity in institutional life*. Duke University Press.

Beegle, D. M. (2003). Overcoming the silence of generational poverty. *Talking Points, 15*(1), 11–20.

Bui, K. V. T. (2002). First-generation college students at a four-year university: Background characteristics, reasons for pursuing higher education, and first-year experiences. *College Student Journal, 36*(1), 3–11.

Burdman, P. (2005). *The student debt dilemma: Debt aversion as a barrier to college access*. Center for Studies in Higher Education, 1–26.

Council for Opportunity in Education. (2016). *Resources*. https://coenet.org/trio.shtml

Collins, P. H. (2015). Intersectionality's definitional dilemmas. *Annual Review of Sociology, 41*, 1–20.

Crenshaw, K. (2017). *Panel on intersectional feminism* [Panel]. 2017 Annual Conference of Netroots Nation, Atlanta, GA.

Derrida, J., & Dufourmantelle, A. (2000). *Of hospitality (Cultural memory in the present)*. Stanford University Press.

Engle, J., & Tinto, V. (2008). *Moving beyond access: College for low-income, first-generation students*. The Pell Institute. http://www.pellinstitute.org/downloads/publications-Moving_Beyond_Access_2008.pdf

Gerstle, G. (2006). The political incorporation of immigrant groups: A historical perspective on the American experience. In P. Straum (Ed.), *American Arabs and political participation* (pp. 27–40). Woodrow Wilson International Center for Scholars.

Goldrick-Rab, S. (2016). *Paying the price: College costs, financial aid, and the betrayal of the American dream*. University of Chicago Press.

Higher Education Act of 1965, H.R. 621, 89th Cong., 1st Sess. (1965)

Jehangir, R. R. (2010). *Higher education and first-generation students: Cultivating community, voice, and place for the new majority*. Palgrave Macmillan.

Jehangir, R. R., Stebleton, M. J., & Deenanath, V. (2015). *An exploration of intersecting identities of first-generation, low-income students* (Research Reports on College Transitions no. 5). National Resource Center for the First-Year Experience and Students in Transition.

Kezar, A. (2011). *Recognizing and serving low-income students in higher education: An examination of institutional policies, practices, and culture*. Routledge.

Kuh, G. D., Kinzie, J., Schuh, G., & Whitt, E. J. (2005). *Student success in college: Creating conditions that matter*. Jossey-Bass.

Mumper, M., Gladieux, L. E., King, J. E., & Corrigan, M. E. (2016). The federal government and higher education. In M. N. Bastedo, P. G. Altbach, & P. J. Gumport (Eds.), *American higher education in the 21st century* (pp. 212–237). Johns Hopkins University Press.

Ngũgĩwa T. (1986). *Decolonising the mind: The politics of language in African literature*. J. Currey.

Nguyen, T., & Nguyen, B. M. D. (2018). Is the "first-generation student" term useful for understanding inequality? The role of intersectionality in illuminating the implications of an accepted—yet unchallenged—term. *Review of Research in Higher Education, 42*, 146–176.

Orbe, M. P. (2008). Theorizing multidimensional identity negotiation: Reflections on the lived experiences of first-generation college students. In M. Azmitia, M. Syed, & K. Radmacher (Eds.), *The intersections of personal and social identities* (New Directions for Child and Adolescent Development, no. 120, pp. 81–95). Jossey-Bass. https://doi.org/10.1002/cd.217

National Center for Education Statistics. (2017). *First-generation and continuing-generation college students: A comparison of high school and postsecondary experiences*. https://nces.ed.gov/pubsearch/pubsinfo.asp?pubid=2018009

Redford, J., & Mulvaney Hoyer, K. (2017). *First-generation and continuing-generation college students: A comparison of high school and postsecondary experiences*. National Center for Education Statistics. 1–27. https://nces.ed.gov/pubs2018/2018009.pdf

Sharpe, R. (2017, November 3). Are you first-generation? Depends on who's asking. *New York Times*. https://www.nytimes.com/2017/11/03/education/edlife/first-generation-college-admissions.html

Thelin, J. R. (2004). *A history of American higher education*. Johns Hopkins University Press.

University of California. (2019). *University of California student opportunity: First-generation*. https://www.universityofcalifornia.edu/initiative/student-opportunity/first-generation-students

Walpole, M. (2007). Economically and educationally challenged students in higher education: Access to outcomes. *ASHE-ERIC Higher Education Report, 33*(3), 1–113. https://doi.org/10.1002/aehe.3303

Warnock, D. M., & Hurst, A. L. (2016). "The poor kids' table": Organizing around an invisible and stigmatized identity in flux. *Journal of Diversity in Higher Education, 9*(3), 261–276.

Yosso, T. (2005). Whose culture has capital? A critical race theory discussion of community cultural wealth. *Race Ethnicity and Education, 8*(1), 69–91.

Nicole Zervas Adsitt, PhD, is an associate professor currently serving as director for the Centers for Student Engagement and Academic Advisement at Cayuga Community College in Auburn, New York. Prior to this role, she served as the coordinator for developmental studies. She has over 15 years of experience in higher education, including several years of experience working with access and support programs. She earned her BS from Nazareth College and her MS and PhD from Syracuse University in higher education, where she was a recipient of the School of Education All University Doctoral Prize.

Rodrigo Aguayo, MEd, is the program coordinator for the Project MALES student mentoring program. He earned a bachelor of arts in psychology from Texas State University with a minor in criminal justice. He completed his master's in education in the College & University Student Personnel Administration (CUSPA) program in spring 2018 at The University of Texas at Austin. His research interests focus on Latino, first-generation students in higher education.

Scott Amundsen, PhD, is an associate professor and serves as the director of the professional studies program at Winthrop University in Rock Hill, South Carolina. Before joining the faculty at Winthrop University, he served in a range of administrative roles, including dean and provost. His research areas include underserved populations, military students, enrollment management, distance education, strengths-based/appreciative advising, and student athletes.

Sonja Ardoin, PhD, is a learner, an educator, a facilitator, and an author. Proud of her hometown of Vidrine, Louisiana; her working-class Cajun roots; and her first-generation college student to PhD journey, Ardoin holds degrees from Louisiana State University, Florida State University, and North Carolina State University. A self-described scholar-practitioner, Ardoin made the move from full-time administrator to full-time faculty member in 2015 and currently serves as assistant professor of student affairs administration at Appalachian State University. She studies social class identity, college access, and success for rural and first-generation college students, student and women's leadership, and career preparation and pathways in higher education and student affairs. She stays engaged in the higher education field through presenting, facilitating, and volunteering with national organizations such as the Association for the Study of Higher Education (ASHE), NASPA, American College Personnel Association (ACPA), LeaderShape, Zeta Tau Alpha, Delta Gamma, and Peer Forward and reviewing for several journals. She is also a contributor to the NASPA Center for First-Generation Student Success advocacy group, the NASPA Socioeconomic and Class Issues in Higher Education Knowledge Community, and the Association of Fraternal Leadership and Values (AFLV) Board of Directors.

Erin Ayala, PhD, is a licensed psychologist and core faculty member in the counseling psychology doctoral program at Saint Mary's University of Minnesota. A former postdoctoral fellow at Albany Medical Center, she has authored several peer-reviewed research publications on prevention and health promotion, stress, and self-care for students and early career professionals. Other research interests include health and sport psychology, multiculturalism and diversity, training, and supervision. She is an associate editor for *Psi Chi Journal of Psychological Research*. Through her work at Saint Mary's, she prioritizes the needs of adult learners, many of whom are first-generation college students.

Khanh Bui, PhD, was born and raised in Vietnam until the age of 8. At the end of the Vietnam War, her family fled Vietnam in a fishing boat and were rescued as political refugees and settled in the United States. She is the first person in her family to graduate from high school. She earned a BA, an MA, and a PhD in psychology from the University of California, Los Angeles (UCLA), with funding from a National Science Foundation graduate research fellowship. Since 1997, she has taught introductory statistics, intermediate statistics, research methods, introductory psychology, first-year seminar, and social psychology at Pepperdine University in Malibu, California. Her research interests include ethnic minority adolescent mental health; academic achievement among underprivileged students, especially first-generation college students; and loneliness. She enjoys mentoring students and delights in seeing them pursue their calling.

Emmet Campos, PhD, currently directs Project MALES and the Texas Education Consortium for Male Students of Color. As director, Campos serves as the chief operations officer for all Project MALES and Consortium activities and is responsible for communications and engagement with key partners. He received his PhD in cultural studies in education/curriculum and instruction from The University of Texas at Austin. Previously, he directed grant-funded initiatives focused on men of color and Latina/o student's college transfer and completion at the Center for Community College Student Engagement; served as project director for the Institute for Community, University, and School Partnerships; and has taught at The University of Texas at Austin, St. Edward's University, and Austin Community College.

Kelly Collins is a PhD candidate in the University of Minnesota's organizational leadership, policy, and development track in the higher education program. She currently serves as a course instructor and academic skills coach with the University of Michigan's counseling services. Prior to her graduate work, Collins served as a TRIO professional for 7 years. As a low-income, first-generation, and Indigenous student, she is committed to studying the intersections of academic capitalism, neoliberal public policy, and low-income student access.

Elizabeth Cox Brand, PhD, is the executive director of the Oregon Student Success Center. Originally from Iowa, Brand received her doctorate in educational policy and leadership from Iowa State University in 2007. After graduation, she accepted the position of assistant director of the California Community College Collaborative, a community college research and policy center at the University of California, Riverside. Brand came to Oregon in 2011 as director of communications and research for the Oregon Department of Community Colleges and Workforce Development and moved to the Oregon Community College Association in 2014 to assume the position of director of student success and assessment. Brand has professional experience in K–12, community colleges, and universities, with a particular emphasis on student services and enrollment management.

Gloria Crisp, PhD, is a professor at Oregon State University. She has a diversity of professional experiences working with community colleges and 4-year institutions as an institutional researcher and faculty member. Her survey instrument, the college student mentoring scale (CSMS) is currently being used at institutions around the country and abroad to evaluate the effectiveness of mentoring relationships. Crisp has published over 40 articles and book chapters including a recent issue of *New Directions for Community Colleges* and *ASHE Higher Education Report* focused on mentoring undergraduate students. Currently, Crisp's research is focused toward studying student transfer within and between accessible colleges and universities. She is also engaged in empirical work to describe and better understand bachelor's degree–granting institutions that have accessible admissions policies.

Steven P. Dandaneau, PhD, serves as executive director of the Reinvention Collaborative and associate provost at Colorado State University. In these roles, Dandaneau provides leadership for a national consortium of leading research universities focused on innovation in undergraduate education and works with colleagues to strengthen the undergraduate experience at Colorado State University. Dandaneau previously served as vice provost for undergraduate studies, Kansas State University; associate provost and director, Chancellor's Honors and Haslam Scholars programs, University of Tennessee, Knoxville; visiting professor of sociology, University of Maryland, College Park; and director, University Honors & John W. Berry, Sr. Scholars programs, University of Dayton. Dandaneau is a first-generation student who earned a BA in economics (with honors) from Michigan State University and an MA and a PhD in sociology from Brandeis University. He is the proud recipient of the First Scholars First Generation Champion award (2018), bestowed by The Suder Foundation.

Nate Deans Jr., born and raised in the city of Milwaukee, has dedicated his career to teaching urban students. He graduated from the University of Wisconsin-Milwaukee (UWM) in 2011 with degrees in English education and literary and critical studies. He currently teaches at his alma mater, Riverside University High School, and is highly involved with a number of student organizations and mentoring programs, in addition to his administrative duties. Deans was the recipient of the Milwaukee Public Schools Start, Stay, Succeed Award in 2017 and the UWM Graduate of the Last Decade Award in 2018. He was also nominated for the Wisconsin Teacher of the Year Award in 2016. He and his wife and fellow educator (who also teaches in the Milwaukee Public Schools) raise their three girls, Nyla, Nakayla, and Nora, in their home in Glendale, Wisconsin. Deans aspires to further his impact on urban students by advocating for equitable practices in the City of Milwaukee.

Matthew Fifolt, PhD, is an assistant professor in the Department of Health Care Organization and Policy at the University of Alabama at Birmingham (UAB) School of Public Health. Fifolt received his doctorate in educational leadership from UAB and University of Alabama (2006); a master's degree in higher education administration from the University of South Carolina (1995); and a bachelor's degree in communication from Valparaiso University (1993). Fifolt has published in a variety of peer-reviewed publications in the research areas of evaluation and assessment, systems-building, and underserved populations; he is currently the technical editor of the *MidSouth Literacy Journal.*

Paul Gallagher, PhD, is assistant dean (Saga College) and lecturer of humanities at Yale-NUS College in Singapore. He was educated in Canada, where he earned a BA at Brock University with a double major in German and philosophy and later an MA and a PhD in the Department of Religious Studies at McMaster University. He also holds a graduate diploma in psychotherapy from the Cairnmillar Institute in Australia. Gallagher taught systemic theology from 2007 to 2013 at the University of Divinity and the United Faculty of Theology, both in Melbourne, Australia. He is the author of *Citizens of Heaven, Residents of the Earth: The Politics of the Sermon on the Mount* (VDM Verlag, 2008). Gallagher has devoted much of his career to student well-being and residential life. His previous student life roles have been dean of well-being at Queen's College, University of Melbourne; dean and deputy principal and later acting principal at St Mary's College, University of Melbourne; and vice rector at St John's College, University of Sydney.

Yvonne Garcia is a doctoral student at the Center for the Study of Higher and Postsecondary Education (CSHPE) at the University of Michigan. Previously she worked at California State University, Fullerton in a research center. She is active in student affairs associations and social justice initiatives.

Mike Gutierrez, MEd, earned both a BA in psychology in 2013 and an MEd in college and university student personnel administration (CUSPA) in 2015 from The University of Texas at Austin (UT Austin). Gutierrez worked as the program coordinator for Project MALES (Mentoring to Achieve Latino Educational Success) within the Division of Diversity of Community Engagement at UT Austin for 2 years. As program coordinator, Gutierrez oversaw the expansion of the mentoring program to three school districts in the Austin area and the robust growth of the undergraduate student cohort and supervised graduate assistants serving as mentoring site coordinators. With Project MALES, he worked along with Victor B. Saenz and Emmet Campos in an advisory role for the Texas Education Consortium for Male Students of Color. Currently, Gutierrez works with Student Success as senior program coordinator focusing on first-generation programming, leaver's campaign, and Posse foundation. His research interests include first-generation college students, academic and nonacademic outcomes for men of color, enrollment management, and the role of student success initiatives.

David Hernández, PhD, is associate professor of Latina/o studies at Mount Holyoke College. His research focuses on immigration enforcement and the U.S. detention regime. He is completing a book on this institution titled *Alien Incarcerations: Immigrant Detention and Lesser Citizenship* for the University of California Press. He is also the coeditor of *Critical Ethnic Studies: A Reader* (Duke University Press, 2016). Other work has appeared in journals such as *Border-Lines, Harvard Journal of Hispanic Policy, Journal of Race and Policy, Latina/o Studies*, and *NACLA Report on the Americas*.

Mackenzie Hoffman graduated from the University of Wisconsin–La Crosse in 2015 with a BS in interpersonal communication studies. After her undergraduate studies, she worked as a peer mentor graduate assistant in the Student Success Center at the University of Wisconsin–Milwaukee (UW-Milwaukee). While at UW-Milwaukee she earned an MS in administrative leadership with a concentration in adult, continuing, and higher education administration (ACHEA). She currently works as an academic adviser at Bryant and Stratton College in Wauwatosa, Wisconsin.

Rashné Jehangir, PhD, is an associate professor in the College of Education and Human Development where she teaches in an interdisciplinary first-year experience program and in doctoral and master's programs in multicultural teaching and learning. She began her career as an adviser for first-generation and low-income college students in the federally funded Student Support Services TRIO program. She is the recipient of the Distinguished Horace T. Morse Teacher Award at the University of Minnesota. Her recent books include *Higher Education and First-Generation College Students: Cultivating Community, Voice and Place for the New Majority* (Palgrave McMillan, 2010) and *An Exploration of Intersecting Identities of First-Generation, Low-Income Students* (Stylus, 2015). Her scholarship is featured in several journals, including *Journal of College Student Development, Innovative Higher Education, Urban Education*, and the *Journal of the First-Year Experience and Students in Transition*. She is regularly invited to speak at faculty development institutes around the country and has presented at numerous conferences, including the National Conference on Race and Ethnicity, the Conference of the First-Year Experience and Students in Transition, Association for the Study of Higher Education (ASHE), and NASPA: Student Affairs Professionals in Higher Education. Her research and teaching interests focus on experiences of low-income, first-generation students and underrepresented students, identity development, learning communities and design of undergraduate programs, and participatory action research.

Lucy LePeau, PhD, is associate professor of higher education and student affairs at Indiana University and associate director for the National Institute for Transformation and Equity (NITE). LePeau has produced over 50 publications and presentations on approaches educators take in academic affairs and student affairs partnerships to create more equitable campus environments, organizational change, and improved student affairs teaching and practice. She has published in journals such as *The Review of Higher Education, The Journal of Higher Education*, and *The Journal of College Student Development*. She was a recipient of the 2018 Indiana University Trustees Teaching Award and Emerging Scholar Award from ACPA-College Student Educators International.

Sherry Lee Linkon, PhD, is a professor of English and director of the writing program at Georgetown University. Her teaching and research involve two main areas: teaching and learning in the humanities and the interdisciplinary study of working-class culture. In working-class studies, Linkon's work focuses on social class in higher education, deindustrialization, and contemporary working-class literature. Her edited collection *Teaching Working Class* (University of Massachusetts Press, 1999) was named one of the most important academic books of the 1990s by *Lingua Franca* magazine. With John Russo, she coauthored *Steeltown USA: Work and Memory in Youngstown* (University Press of Kansas, 2002) and coedited *New Working-Class Studies* (ILR Press, 2005). Her forthcoming book, *The Half-Life of Deindustrialization,* examines early 21st-century working-class narratives reflecting the continuing effects of economic restructuring, primarily in Rust Belt cities. She was the founding president of the Working-Class Studies Association, and she edits a weekly blog, *Working-Class Perspectives.*

Hope Longwell-Grice, PhD, is the associate dean of academic affairs in the School of Education at the University of Wisconsin–Milwaukee. Longwell-Grice earned her BA, MA, and PhD degrees in education from the University of Delaware. Since their time at the University of Wisconsin in Milwaukee, husband Robert Longwell-Grice and she have written together on the topic of first-generation student experience. Longwell-Grice's research interests have been in teacher education, social justice education, and the intersection of identity and place. In Milwaukee, she is involved with developing a teacher pipeline to address the teacher shortage in Wisconsin. She happily became a grandparent this spring, which sparks joy in her life.

Robert Longwell-Grice, EdD, is a senior adviser for the School of Education at the University of Wisconsin–Milwaukee (UWM). Previously he served as the director of academic services for the School of Education at UWM and was the associate dean of students for the UWM campus. He has a master's degree in counselor education from Pennsylvania State University and a doctorate in educational and counseling psychology from the University of Louisville.

Prior to UWM, Longwell-Grice worked at the University of Delaware, New England College (in the United Kingdom and New Hampshire), and the University of New Hampshire. In 2019 he was featured in the documentary film *First Gens*. He is a first-generation college student whose dissertation was a case study of working-class, first-generation White males.

Heather N. Maietta, PhD, is an associate professor in the higher education leadership program at Regis College. She is an award-winning educator, author, speaker and coach, and founder of Career In Progress, a consulting firm that helps college career and academic advising centers innovate their service delivery by fully integrating career advising into the larger campus ecosystem. She has coached and educated thousands of career professionals in higher education, workforce development, talent management, K–12, and private practice to rethink career literacy and support. Her research agenda investigates first-generation college students as they matriculate through college and graduate into the workforce, the upward mobility of first-generation families, the career needs of transfer students, and doctoral student completion. Maietta is a National Association of Colleges and Employers Coaching Faculty member, a Facilitating Career Developments national trainer, and a graduate of the National Career Development Association Leadership Academy. She lives in the Greater Boston area.

Adj Marshall was the first person in her family to attend and graduate from college, earning her bachelor of arts while supporting her brothers' pursuits of their associate degrees. Her experience of growing up as a member of a chronically poor, and often homeless, single-parent family contributed immensely to her work as an experiential-learning educator and advocate for educational socioeconomic justice. Marshall has piloted student success initiatives for low-income first-generation students with College Visions, Community Action and Phillips Academy Andover. In 2013, with the support of Class Action, she founded the First-Generation College Student Summit. The summit brings together over 200 faculty staff and students annually to identify problems and discuss grassroots solutions to first-generation college student challenges. Currently, she works with international partnerships and programs at Tufts University. Her research interests, which began with her graduate studies at Brown University and the School for International Training, continue to focus on the role of arts in social-justice change-making movements and education.

Hyacinth Mason, PhD, received her BA from Grinnell College in Iowa, her MPH from the University of Illinois, and a PhD in preventive medicine from the University of Southern California, where she also completed an NIH Cancer Fellowship. Prior to moving to Albany Medical College (AMC), she served as faculty director for the Meharry Medical College–Vanderbilt Ingram Cancer Center Cancer Partnership and AIDS coordinator for the City of Pasadena, California. Mason currently serves as assistant dean for student support and associate professor in the departments of medical education and community and family medicine at AMC. As part of her commitment to diversity and inclusion in the health care workforce, she serves on AMC's admissions committee, and as mentor for student clubs: Student National Medical Association, Latino Medical Student Association, 1GMD (a first-generation medical student club), Public Health and Medicine, Building the Next Generation of Academic Physicians, and LGBTQ Club.

Katharine Moffat is a graduate program coordinator for the Department of Environmental Toxicology at the University of California Davis. She previously served as academic adviser with Student-Athlete Academic Services at the University of Hawai'i at Manoa. She enjoys working with, supporting, and learning from first-generation students at both the undergraduate and graduate levels. Moffat is originally from Rhode Island and attended the University of Rhode Island for undergraduate work. She earned an MA in sociology and an MEd in educational psychology from the University of Hawai'i at Manoa. Her MEd thesis explores how first-generation Division 1 football student athletes make meaning of their first-generation status.

Roxanne Moschetti, PhD, is an associate professor in the department of child and adolescent development at California State University, Northridge. She received her doctoral and master's degrees from the Gevirtz Graduate School of Education at the University of California, Santa Barbara. Moschetti began her education at a community college as a low-income, first-generation college student facing both housing and food insecurity. It was only through various resources geared toward underrepresented students that she was able to successfully transfer to a 4-year university and become the first person in her family to receive a bachelor's degree. Realizing how important the support of these programs was to her educational success, she eventually received her doctorate with the promise to continue focusing her efforts on improving the experiences of economically and educationally disadvantaged students like herself. Building on the idea that access to relevant social networks contributes to college access, entry, and success, her current research focuses on investigating the attitudes, experiences, social support systems, and knowledge among students who are the first in their family to attend college, using the lens of social capital theory.

Pablo Muirhead, PhD, builds bridges between cultures through language education, inspiring him to grow daily. Raised bilingually, he was fortunate to spend his upbringing between the United States and Peru. Later, he went on to live in Indonesia and Germany, where he gained proficiency in both the languages and cultures of his hosts. These experiences helped set him on a career as a language educator and inform what he does. In addition to having taught from middle school to the university levels, he frequently presents at local, state, and national conferences on issues of language education. He is a member of his local school board as well as a member of the board of directors of the American Council on the Teaching of Foreign Languages. Upon earning his PhD in urban education from the University of Wisconsin-Milwaukee, he has taught both Spanish and teacher education at Milwaukee Area Technical College. Since 2013 he has served as the chair of teacher education, where he helps aspiring teachers complete their general education requirements before transferring to a 4-year institution to complete their licensure.

Ryan D. Padgett, PhD, is the assistant vice president for enrollment and student success for the division of academic affairs at Northern Kentucky University. In this position, he provides leadership for career services, new student orientation and parent programs, TRIO Student Support Services, University Connect and Persist (UCAP), and the Veterans Resource Station. Prior to this role, he was the assistant director of research, grants, and assessment at the National Resource Center for The First-Year Experience and Students in Transition, where he facilitated several national surveys and oversaw research collaborations and grant opportunities between the National Resource Center and the higher education community and across the University of South Carolina campus. Padgett received a PhD in educational policy and leadership studies, higher education from The University of Iowa and an MS in higher education from Indiana University. He has published multiple manuscripts on college impact, research methodology, and the first-year experience in national journals and book chapters, including 2009 National Survey of First-Year Seminars: Ongoing Efforts to Support Students in Transition; 2011 National Survey of Senior Capstone Experiences: Institutional-Level Data on the Culminating Experience; *Journal of College Student Development; Journal of Higher Education*; and *New Directions for Institutional Research*. Padgett also serves on the editorial board of the *Journal of the First-Year Experience & Students in Transition* and is a Teagle Assessment scholar.

Les Riding-In, PhD, (Pawnee/Osage) is assistant dean and director of graduate studies for the College of Liberal Arts at The University of Texas at Arlington

(UT Arlington). Riding-In also serves as vice chair for the Board of Trustees for Pawnee Nation College and is the lead adviser for UT Arlington's Native American Student Association. Growing up, he spent his summers on his great-aunt's farm in rural Southeast Oklahoma, a Comanche allotment. His aunt, Julia Mahseet, was a founding officer for the North American Indian Women's Association and presented twice in front of Congress on Indian Soil Conservation. Today, his involvement is in honor of his Aunt Julia.

Rebecca Robertson is a PhD student in the College of Education at Oregon State University. She is an educator and a critical scholar who employs ethnographic research methods to address key issues in higher education and beyond. Her research interests include higher education diversity, communities of practice, student activism. and social media. Robertson's current research examines the dilemmas of higher education diversity work through the lens of student social media activism. Over the course of her 17-year career in higher education she has held posts as associate faculty at College of the Redwoods, lecturer and graduate coordinator of the MA in applied anthropology program at Humboldt State University, and visiting professor for the University Study Abroad Consortium (USAC) at the Universidad de País Basque in San Sebastian, Spain.

Victor B. Sáenz, PhD, is the founder and executive director of Project MALES and the Texas Education Consortium for Male Students of Color. He is currently chair in the Department of Educational Administration at The University of Texas at Austin. He is also a faculty fellow with the Division of Diversity and Community Engagement and a faculty affiliate with the Center for Mexican American Studies. Sáenz has published in numerous peer-reviewed journals and also has three book projects underway, including one on Latino males in higher education (Stylus). His current research on this topic examines their experiences at both 2-year and 4-year institutions as they navigate their college pathways.

Michael J. Smith, PhD, is an associate professor of educational leadership and policy in the Portland State University College of Education whose research explores the college choice process for low-income African Americans. Additionally, he has written about the impact of privatization on the recruitment of international students and domestic underrepresented students. Recently he has explored how economic social capital impacts the first-year adjustment of Chinese students with English as a second language. He holds a PhD from the University of California, Los Angeles, an MA from the University of Michigan, and a BA from Loyola Marymount University.

Ana K. Soltero López, PhD, is an assistant professor in the Department of Literacy, Early, Bilingual and Special Education (LEBSE) at California State University, Fresno. She teaches courses on culturally sustaining pedagogy, teacher inquiry, and the undocumented student experience. Her primary research focus is K–20 Latinx educational access, retention, and persistence. Some topics of interest include the preparation of teachers of color, emergent bilingual students, identity development, and critical race theory. Soltero López's recent scholarship focuses on the identity and social interactions of undocumented Latinx high school, community college, and university students. Her current projects expand her expertise by investigating the impact of the phasing out of DACA, teacher and counselor professional development, and undocumented emergent bilinguals in the Central Valley of California.

Hadyn K. Swecker, PhD, received her BS in business administration-finance from Auburn University, MS in higher education student affairs with a minor in communications from Florida State University, and PhD in educational leadership in a joint program between The University of Alabama and The University of Alabama at Birmingham. Some of Swecker's experiences include being the director of admissions for The University of Alabama at Birmingham School of Medicine, director of academic success, academic adviser, and a first-year experience instructor. She has worked with a variety of students throughout her career in higher education through academic advising, leadership development, student organizations, and volunteer coordination.

Vasti Torres, PhD, is a professor of Educational Leadership and Policy Studies at the Indiana University School of Education. Previously she was a professor in the Center for the Study of Higher and Postsecondary Education (CSHPE) and associate faculty member in Latino studies at the University of Michigan. She has been the principal investigator for several grants, including a multiyear grant investigating the choice to stay in college for Latino students as well as a multiyear grant looking at the experiences of working college students. She has worked on several community college initiatives including Achieving the Dream and Rural Community College Initiative. Her professional service includes being vice president for Division J: Postsecondary Education for the American Educational Research Association (AERA) from 2019 to 2021; in 2007 she became the first Latina president of a national student services association—American College Personnel Association (ACPA)—and in 2020 she began her term as the editor of the *Journal of College Student Development*. Previously she has served as the dean of the College of Education at the University of South Florida and director of the Center for Postsecondary Research (CPR) in the School of Education at Indiana University. Her awards include the Contribution to Knowledge Award from both ACPA and NASPA. She was also honored as a Diamond Honoree, Senior Scholar, Wise Woman, and the Latino Network John Hernandez Leadership Award by the American College Personnel Association. Other honors include the Professional Achievement Alumni Award from the University of Georgia, program associate for the National Center for Policy in Higher Education, Hispanic Scholarship Fund Alumni Hall of Fame in 2014, and in 2008 the Indiana University Trustees Teaching Award. In 2011–2012 she served as a Fulbright Specialist in South Africa. Torres is a graduate of Stetson University and holds a PhD from the University of Georgia.

Staci Weber, PhD, completed her doctorate in postsecondary education administration from Syracuse University (NY), where her dissertation focused on first-generation college students who utilized college access and support programs throughout their college-going journey. Weber received her MEd in student affairs practice in higher education from the University of Delaware, Delaware, and her BA in psychology from Franklin & Marshall College, Pennsylvania. Weber served as dean of student affairs at Pine Manor College before moving into the role as special assistant to the president. Along with experience in student affairs, Weber has worked in academic services and enrollment management. Weber's passion lies in strategic planning and college access and retention.

Jeffrey Winseman, MD, is professor of psychiatry, director of student psychological services, and residency training director in the Department of Psychiatry at Albany Medical College. He received his medical degree from the State University of New York at Buffalo and completed residency training at New York Presbyterian Hospital–Weill Cornell Medical College. Prior to coming to Albany Medical Center, Dr. Winseman was medical director of health and psychological services at Bennington College, where he worked with students individually and served with students on multiple task forces for positive change. In his role at Albany Medical College, he serves students and physicians at all stages of their careers and is a frequent administrative consultant for students at risk. He has published widely on student mental health since 2001 and is president of the New York State Capital District Branch of the American Psychiatric Association in Albany, New York.

Pheng Xiong is a higher education and student affairs professional with 10 years of experience in the field of student affairs. Xiong is currently the university registrar at the University of Hawai'i at Mānoa and is a candidate for degree in the doctoral program in higher education administration at Morgan State University in Baltimore, Maryland. His research interests include first-generation college student retention and persistence, intersectionality, and lesbian, gay, bisexual, trans*, and queer (LGBTQ) student success and development.

role models, 75–79
Roskovensky, L., 273

Sáenz, Victor B., 6, 134, 167
Savage Inequalities (Kozol), 149
Schlossberg, N. K., 249, 254–55
scholarships, 94, 96, 208, 227
Schultz, T. W., 40
Scott-Clayton, Judith, 177
self-efficacy, 287–90
self-promotion, 151
sense of belonging
    for college students, 180, 187–88
    community policies for, 303
    counseling services for, 179
    for FGS, 13, 22, 225
    for first-generation doctoral
        students, 290
    for Latinx students, 132, 135
    leadership and, 186
    low-SES students with, 100–101
    mentoring for, 263
    in RH, 230
    social ties for, 42
    student involvement for, 180, 187
    of White students, 107
SES. *See* socioeconomic status
sexual identity, 121
Shepler, D. K., 180, 231
Slate, J. R., 104
Smith, C. T., 210
Smith, Michael J., 3
social capital, 29, 266
    categories of, 41–42
    in college, 102–3, 109–10
    of college students, 42, 123–24
    connections in, 97
    of FGS, 122–23, 245–46
    of first-generation doctoral
        students, 283–84

function of, 41–42
    relationships in, 101
    of White males, 109
social circles, 187
social class, 90, 94
    capital forms in, 97–98
    components of, 93
    educational attainment in,
        30–32
    FGS identity of, 4, 95
    gender and, 153
    household income and, 15–16
    identities from, 92–93
    networks in, 29–30
    sexual identity and, 121
    upper-middle, 151
    upward mobility of, 25, 30–31
    wealth and, 26–30, 33–35, 92
    well-being and, 106–7
social emotional learning, 168
social equity, 297
social interactions, 22
socialization
    emotional, 289–90
    for FGS, 307–8
    of first-generation doctoral
        students, 284
social self-efficacy, 289–90
social settings, 285
social ties, 42–43
socioeconomic status (SES), 4, 43,
    72, 144. *See also* poverty
    African Americans with low,
        77–81
    Black parents and, 78–79
    Black teenagers and, 77
    college students with low, 103
    community colleges and, 103–5
    of FGS, 47, 100–101, 302–3
    financial aid for low, 79–81

of first-generation doctoral
    students, 286
high school students and, 168–69
income and, 96
race/ethnicity and, 124–25
sense of belonging for low,
    100–101
in transfer function, 208
White males with low, 108–9
White students with low, 107
sociology, 26–27
Soria, K. M., 123, 178–79
standardized testing, 35, 223
Stanton-Salazar, R. D., 101, 110
Staples, R., 79
statistical analyses, 288
Stebleton, M. J., 123, 178–79
Steidel, A. G. L., 130
Stein, W. J., 163
Stevens, R. A., 125
storytelling, 163
strategic planning process, 294–95
strengths, weaknesses, opportunities,
    and threats (SWOT analysis),
    295–96
Stuber, J., 106
student affairs, 297
student background characteristics,
    62–63, 66
student services programs, 55–56
students of color
    capital models and, 148
    economics and male, 169
    as FGS, 306
    as first-generation community
        college students, 203
    first-year programs for, 162
    lived experiences of, 146, 151
    low-income, 141
    in MATC program, 221–22

PMC with, 298
Project MALES benefiting,
    166–71
as study participants, 185
transfer policies and, 210–11
undocumented, 139
study participants, 185
Suder Foundation, 32, 94
support mechanisms, 223
Supreme Court, U.S., 32
Survey of Earned Doctorates, 284
Swail, W. S., 154
Swecker, Hadyn, 8, 241
SWOT analysis. *See* strengths,
    weaknesses, opportunities, and
    threats

TAMU. *See* Texas A&M University
Taylor, J. L., 211, 216
Teacher Education Program (TEP),
    221–24
teaching certification, 221–22
TEP. *See* Teacher Education
    Program
Terenzini, P., 101
Terrance, D., 161
Terry, M. B., 277
Texas A&M University (TAMU),
    166
Thailand, 189–90
Thomson, K., 240
Thunder, A., 163
time-management skills, 187
Tinto, V., 22, 102, 123–24, 208
Titus, M. A., 43
Tom (study participant), 192–93
Torres, Vasti, 5, 129–30, 133–35
Torres, Yvonne Garcia, 5
Toutkoushian, R. K., 45, 90, 305
transfer function

Student Affairs books from Stylus Publishing

Developing Effective Student Peer Mentoring Programs
*A Practitioner's Guide to Program Design, Delivery,
Evaluation, and Training*
Peter J. Collier
Foreword by Nora Domínguez

The First Generation College Experience
*Implications for Campus Practice, and Strategies for
Improving Persistence and Success*
Jeff Davis

**Intersections of Identity and Sexual Violence on
Campus**
Centering Minoritized Students' Experiences
Edited by Jessica C. Harris and Chris Linder
Foreword by Wagatwe Wanjuki

**A Guide to Becoming a Scholarly Practitioner in
Student Affairs**
Lisa J. Hatfield and Vicki L. Wise
Foreword by Kevin Kruger

Making Global Learning Universal
Promoting Inclusion and Success for All Students
Hilary Landorf, Stephanie Doscher, and Jaffus Hardrick
Foreword by Caryn McTighe Musil

**Overcoming Educational Racism in the Community
College**
*Creating Pathways to Success for Minority and Impoverished
Student Populations*
Edited by Angela Long
Foreword by Walter G. Bumphus

Student-Centered Pedagogy and Course Transformation at Scale

Facilitating Faculty Agency to IMPACT Institutional Change
Chantal Levesque-Bristol
Foreword by George D. Kuh

Pursuing Quality, Access, and Affordability

A Field Guide to Improving Higher Education
Stephen C. Ehrmann
Foreword by Jillian Kinzie

The Analytics Revolution in Higher Education

Big Data, Organizational Learning, and Student Success
Edited by Jonathan S. Gagliardi, Amelia Parnell and Julia Carpenter-Hubin
Foreword by Randy L. Swing

Academic Leadership and Governance of Higher Education

A Guide for Trustees, Leaders, and Aspiring Leaders of Two- and Four-Year Institutions
Robert M. Hendrickson, Jason E. Lane, James T. Harris and Richard H. Dorman
Foreword by Stan Ikenberry

Conducting an Institutional Diversity Audit in Higher Education

A Practitioner's Guide to Systematic Diversity Transformation
Edna Chun and Alvin Evans
Foreword by Benjamin D. Reese, Jr.

Contested Issues in Troubled Times

Student Affairs Dialogues on Equity, Civility, and Safety
Edited by Peter M. Magolda, Marcia B. Baxter Magolda and Rozana Carducci
Foreword by Lori Patton Davis

Leadership & Administration books from Stylus

Digital Leadership in Higher Education
Purposeful Social Media in a Connected World
Josie Ahlquist

Enhancing Assessment in Higher Education
Putting Psychometrics to Work
Edited by Tammie Cumming and M. David Miller
Foreword by Michael J. Kolen

Race & Diversity books from Stylus

Multiracial Experiences in Higher Education
Contesting Knowledge, Honoring Voice, and Innovating Practice
Edited by Marc P. Johnston-Guerrero and Charmaine L. Wijeyesinghe
Foreword by G. Reginald Daniel

Social Class Supports
Programs and Practices to Serve and Sustain Poor and Working Class Students through Higher Education
Edited by Georgianna Martin and Sonja Ardoin
Foreword by Russell Lowery-Hart

Becoming a White Antiracist
Stephen D. Brookfield and Mary E. Hess

What Inclusive Instructors Do
Principles and Practices for Excellence in College Teaching
Tracie Marcella Addy, Derek Dube, Khadijah A. Mitchell, and Mallory SoRelle
Foreword by Peter Felten and Buffie Longmire-Avital

Square Pegs and Round Holes
Alternative Approaches to Diverse College Student Development Theory
Edited by Fred A. Bonner II, Rosa M. Banda, Stella L. Smith and aretha f. marbley
Foreword by Jamie Washington
Afterword by Amelia Parnell

Promoting Inclusive Classroom Dynamics in Higher Education
A Research-Based Pedagogical Guide for Faculty
Kathryn C. Oleson
Foreword by Tia Brown McNair

Race & Diversity books from Stylus

Doing Social Justice Education
A Practitioner's Guide for Workshops and Structured Conversations
D. Scott Tharp
With Roger A. Moreano
Foreword by Jamie Washington

Bandwidth Recovery for Schools
Helping Pre-K-12 Students Regain Cognitive Resources Lost to Poverty, Trauma, Racism, and Social Marginalization
Cia Verschelden
Foreword by Kofi Lomotey

Islamophobia in Higher Education
Combating Discrimination and Creating Understanding
Edited by Shafiqa Ahmadi and Darnell Cole
Foreword by Shaun R. Harper

Transformative Practices for Minority Student Success
Accomplishments of Asian American and Native American Pacific Islander–Serving Institutions
Edited by Dina C. Maramba and Timothy P. Fong
Foreword by Robert T. Teranishi

Straddling Class in the Academy
26 Stories of Students, Administrators, and Faculty From Poor and Working-Class Backgrounds and Their Compelling Lessons for Higher Education Policy and Practice
Sonja Ardoin and becky martinez
Foreword by Jamie Washington

The Diversity Consultant Cookbook
Preparing for the Challenge
Written and Edited by Eddie Moore, Jr., Art Munin, and Marguerite W. Penick-Parks
Foreword by Rev. Jamie Washington, PhD
Afterword by Joey Iazzetto

Race & Diversity books from Stylus

Creating the Path to Success in the Classroom
*Teaching to Close the Graduation Gap for Minority, First-
Generation, and Academically Unprepared Students*
Kathleen F. Gabriel
Foreword by Stephen Carroll

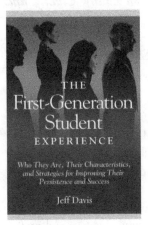

The First-Generation Student Experience

Implications for Campus Practice, and Strategies for Improving Persistence and Success

Jeff Davis

Copublished with ACPA

"Davis should be applauded for his effort to shed light on first-generation students and their experiences in particular. He tasks the field of higher education with better accounting for first-generation students and for working to identify a universal definition for *first-generation students* as coming from families where neither parent holds a college degree. The book is accessible to scholars and student affairs administrators and, most importantly, to the very population I suspect Davis hopes to reach with this book, first-generation students who are navigating the often rough and chilly waters on their way to being the first in their families to earn a college degree."— *Journal of College Student Development*

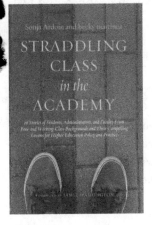

Straddling Class in the Academy

26 Stories of Students, Administrators, and Faculty From Poor and Working-Class Backgrounds and Their Compelling Lessons for Higher Education Policy and Practice

Sonja Ardoin and becky martinez

Foreword by Jamie Washington

"*Straddling Class in the Academy* is a must-read for students and educators. Ardoin, martinez, and their contributors masterfully challenge the myth that class is invisible by sharing their lived experiences navigating class and classism in and outside of the academy. The intersectional nature of contributors' narratives and Ardoin and martinez's analysis highlights the powerful effects of classism and calls for action if we are to create more inclusive and socially just institutions."— *Rosemary J. Perez*, Assistant Professor, School of Education, Iowa State University

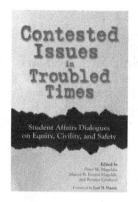

Contested Issues in Troubled Times

Student Affairs Dialogues on Equity, Civility, and Safety

Edited by Peter M. Magolda, Marcia B. Baxter Magolda, and Rozana Carducci

Foreword by Lori Patton Davis

"Just as the first, the second edition of *Contested Issues* will become a go-to book for student affairs graduate courses and professional development opportunities on campus. Magolda, Baxter Magolda, and Carducci have assembled a timely book that engages the most difficult and important issues facing student affairs professionals today—and likely into the future. The array of contributors—representing faculty members and professional staff at all stages of careers—lends to the usefulness of this volume through the presentation of diverse and challenging perspectives."—**Robert D. Reason**, *Professor, Student Affairs and Higher Education, Iowa State University*

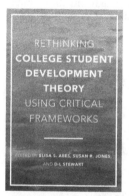

Rethinking College Student Development Theory Using Critical Frameworks

Edited by Elisa S. Abes, Susan R. Jones, and D-L Stewart

"The field has been waiting for this book. It brings together in one place a host of the most thoughtful scholars working in, with, and through critical frameworks in student development theory. On their own, each chapter offers valuable insight; the volume as a whole takes the reader into the latest thinking using critical theory to understand and work with college students."—**Kristen A. Renn**, *Professor of Higher, Adult, & Lifelong Education, and Associate Dean of Undergraduate Studies for Student Success Research, Michigan State University*

22883 Quicksilver Drive
Sterling, VA 20166-2019   Subscribe to our e-mail alerts: www.Styluspub.com